Nights of Dan Curtis

Nights of Dan Curtis

The Television Epics of the *Dark Shadows* Auteur

SECOND EDITION

JEFF THOMPSON

Foreword by Larry Wilcox
Preface by Jim Pierson
Afterword by Ansel Faraj

Ideas into Books®
WESTVIEW
Kingston Springs, Tennessee

© 2020 Jeff Thompson.
All rights reserved, including the right to reproduction
in whole or in part in any form.
No part of this book may be reproduced or transmitted in any form or by any means, electronic or mechanical, including photocopying or recording, or by any information storage and retrieval system, without permission in writing from the author.

Each photograph is courtesy of
Jim Pierson and Dan Curtis Productions.

On the cover: Dan Curtis at his camera.

ISBN 978-1-62880-188-0

Printed in the United States of America on acid free paper.

IDEAS INTO BOOKS ® WESTVIEW
P.O. Box 605
Kingston Springs, Tennessee 37082

To
Sonia and E.D.
Lee Anne
Jonathan
Katy and Bruce
Madelyn
Kate and Kevin
Blakely
Mackenzie
Kameron
Kelly and Jake
Kimberly
and
to Dan Curtis

Table of Contents

Foreword by Larry Wilcox 1

Preface by Jim Pierson 3

Introduction: Dan Curtis as *Auteur* and Influence 5

I. The Career of Dan Curtis: An Overview 13

II. *Dracula* 131

III. *Melvin Purvis, G-Man; The Kansas City Massacre*, and More 153

IV. *The Last Ride of the Dalton Gang* 171

V. *The Winds of War* 189

VI. *War and Remembrance* 207

VII. *Intruders: They Are Among Us* 233

Conclusion: Dan Curtis and Television Horror and Drama 243

Afterword by Ansel Faraj 249

Chapter Notes 251

Bibliography 257

Index 267

Foreword
Larry Wilcox

Dan Curtis was a very passionate director, and you could see it in his excited eyes. Directing is hard labor as you have to be there first in the morning giving directions to the crew who are preparing for the first set-up of cameras and lights and locations. With the sun ever moving, the conditions change rapidly, and you must "match" the previous shots. So the pressure is on from the lighting to the actors' availability. Sometimes, actors fly in for a movie and have only a window of time before they start their next movie. Sometimes, actors or actresses throw tantrums and slow down the movie.

Dan was a good leader, and everyone worked hard to support his hard work and his passion for this piece. We filmed *The Last Ride of the Dalton Gang* up in Placerville, California, and Stockton, California. I took my son Derek, and Derek played me as a little boy—as young Emmett Dalton—and that *made* the picture for me. I also took to Northern California; my horses and I went to roping competitions on the weekend.

Dan became a kind of mentor for me as a director. He loved the low-angle shots (we call them the Hero Shot or the John Wayne Shot), and he was a strong believer in full-frame composition. His shots were staged to have lots of visual clutter in them, both foreground and background, to make a frame more interesting. He was a master of camera placement, and if you know anything about camera direction, it can become very confusing where to place a camera for continuity and to match looks. For example, if you "cross the line," which is a term used for learning to be a film director, you can mix up all of the close-ups and looks. Actors will be looking camera-left to talk to someone who was previously established in a wide shot to be on the *other* side of the camera—so the actor is now looking the wrong direction. This is rather simple stuff in the beginning, but when you have ACTION and you have actors sitting at a round table, it can be confusing. Dan loved to confuse the crew and the script supervisor with his excellence as he would cross the line and change the looks all the time—but you knew that HE knew what he was doing and how he was going to cut it. People would argue, and he would say, "I know how I am going to cut it, so leave me alone." I think Dan also reveled in his photography style. His composition of shots and the grainy feel were a team effort of the gaffers, the art director, and the Director of Photography, but all were directed by Dan Curtis. He loved directing, and he was very efficient.

Directing warrants volumes of skill sets, and one skill set is not enough as you continue the Hollywood Race of "validation of talent." I did not feel Dan was an actor's director, but he was a good artist. He hired good actors, and he seemed to love the process of reading and casting actors. He was proud of "his team," and he enjoyed making his team a family during the shoot.

As a cowboy from Wyoming, this was a great job—being paid to play an old cowboy and a young cowboy in one movie. I got to work with very good actors who always make you look better than you are, and I got to work with a good and very passionate professional director. As he was honing his skills as a director without showing vulnerability, I was doing the same as an actor by crossing multiple decades in one character.

Television was a big deal in those days, with only three major networks, so ratings were off the charts. Today, the markets of distribution are so fragmented that those rating days are memories of the Golden Years of Television.

I know that Dan Curtis put his artistic signature on *The Last Ride of the Dalton Gang*, and that is a differentiation point. I did not agree with his opening titles and his music, which were some of his favorite parts of the movie, and yet his movie won awards. I felt the music and titles were in conflict with the movie and disrupted the thematic equilibrium. However, every time you go to a new barber for a haircut, he will tell you the last barber cut your hair wrong. So…who am I to say? So with humility, now that I have left my mark on the fire hydrant, I must say I still enjoyed this Western movie. An excellent director and an excellent signature of a movie.

Actor, Marine, race-car driver, rodeo rider, and businessman **Larry Wilcox** starred as Officer Jon Baker on NBC-TV's *CHiPs* (1977-1983). He directed two *CHiPs* episodes, produced the 1998 *CHiPs* reunion TV-movie, and executive-produced *The Ray Bradbury Theater* (1985-1992). In 2016, Wilcox executive-produced and starred in the film *94 Feet*. His official Internet website is **www.larrywilcox.net**.

Preface
Jim Pierson

Dan Curtis was a creative chameleon. After growing up as the son a of dentist in Bridgeport, Connecticut, and attending Syracuse University—where he focused on business subjects—Curtis changed his name (from Cherkoss) and headed to Chicago in the early 1950s, becoming a salesman for the National Broadcasting Company's distribution division. This would involve not only peddling old *Hopalong Cassidy* films on television but also placing new programing and specials.

Ultimately, Curtis decided to strike out on his own and in 1963 came up with the idea to attach microphones to professional golf players who would compete in *The CBS Match-Play Golf Classic* (later retitled simply *The CBS Golf Classic*). The show would run for a decade and win Curtis an Emmy. For his advertising executive friend Ed Graham, Curtis next sold Graham's animated series *Linus! The Lion-Hearted* (1964-1966), in which Curtis even voiced a character in one episode, at CBS in a sponsorship deal with Post Cereals. (Curtis also had a talent for drawing, which at one point he considered pursuing professionally.)

With funds from his sales successes, Curtis decided it was time to begin producing television shows. He secured rights from National Periodical Publications to adapt its *Batman* property for weekly television for CBS in 1964 with Don Murray to star as the Caped Crusader/Bruce Wayne and Sammy Davis Jr. to portray the arch-villain Joker. The deal fell apart, however, when CBS programming chief James Aubrey was abruptly terminated by the network following a scandal in the spring of 1965. But the setback for Curtis would prove to be temporary, if not fortuitous, as his attentions would quickly focus on another ambitious project that would lay the groundwork for his future as a producer of television epics.

In his youth, Curtis had been an avid reader of pulp novels and stories devoted to fantasy and mystery. He also enjoyed the classic horror films released by Universal Pictures. After a dream that eerily resembled the story of *Jane Eyre*, Curtis convinced ABC-TV to commit to a daytime drama called *Dark Shadows* that would evoke Gothic tales of romance and intrigue. Dan Curtis Productions was off and running. Debuting on June 27, 1966, and continuing for 1,225 episodes through April 2, 1971, *Dark Shadows* would establish Curtis as the kingpin of genre television and film for decades to come, opening the door for him to create, produce, direct, and occasionally even write a substantial body of work that would make an impact on millions of viewers worldwide, culminating with the monumental miniseries *The Winds of War* and *War and Remembrance* in the 1980s.

During his decades in television and film, Dan Curtis learned and adapted as he went along, using his considerable creative energies, his strength of salesmanship, his empowering charisma, his boundless enthusiasm, and his endless appetite for challenge to accomplish a career that was never ordinary.

Jim Pierson is a Los Angeles-based producer who served as marketing and promotions director for Dan Curtis Productions. He continues to represent the Curtis estate and oversee *Dark Shadows* projects in addition to producing. documentaries and *My Music* specials for public television. Jim is also active in film and television preservation.

"Express to Terror" director Dan Curtis converses on the set of *Supertrain* (NBC, 1979).

INTRODUCTION

Dan Curtis as *Auteur* and Influence

Many devotees of film can recognize an Alfred Hitchcock movie, a Stanley Kubrick film, or a Tim Burton movie just by looking at it. The same can be said for a Dan Curtis production. From his beginnings as one of the chief architects of ABC-TV's *Dark Shadows* (1966-1971), Dan Curtis could be considered an *auteur* (i.e. the predominant author of his productions and the person most responsible for their tone and vision) because of his intense involvement in numerous aspects of his films, from casting, producing, and directing to writing, script-doctoring, and shot-composing. Charles Correll, Curtis's Emmy Award-winning director of photography for *The Long Days of Summer* (1980) and *The Winds of War* (1983), declared, "When you work with Dan, he has the tendency to choose most of the compositions. He is very clear as to how he wants the pictures composed and the size of the lenses. I was always amazed at how much he knew about all of that, and I loved his choices because they were always very bold and challenging."[1]

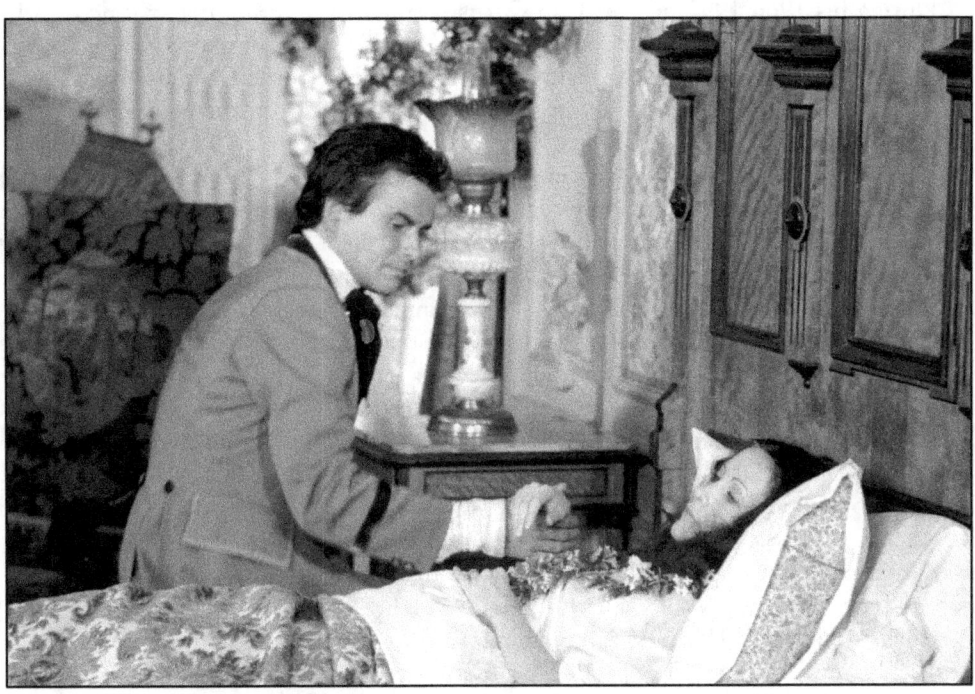

Dead of Night (1977): Horst Bucholz (*The Magnificent Seven*) and Anjanette Comer (*The Loved One*) co-star in "No Such Thing as a Vampire," one of the three segments of the trilogy.

Furthermore, Curtis the *auteur* was able to tap into the mood of a particular cultural movement whether it was the 1970s-era fascination with demonology (as evidenced in his *Norliss Tapes* and *Dead of Night* in 1973 and 1977, respectively) or the late-1980s/early-1990s interest in New Age mysticism (as manifested in his drastic updating of the Maggie Evans character for the 1991 *Dark Shadows*).[2] Curtis had the ability both to follow and to shape trends when his made-for-TV movies in the 1970s perpetuated the subgenre of the occult/suspense movie of the week, when he added his own caper movie (1974's *The Great Ice Rip-Off*) to the then-current wave of heist films (e.g. 1974's *Bank Shot*), and when he and casting director Mary Jo Slater assembled multicultural casts for *Angie the Lieutenant* in 1992 and his *Dark Shadows* remake in 2004.

Curtis further distinguished himself by his attraction to multi-faceted projects. *The Night Stalker* (1972) was equal parts newspaper procedural, *film noir*, and horror. *The Great Ice Rip-Off* (1974) and *Supertrain* (1979) were a blend of comedy, drama, and mystery. *Me and the Kid* (1993) brought together elements of slapstick comedy, crime drama, and kids' adventure. Curtis demonstrated great confidence in choosing the stories that he felt personally suited to tell, e.g. *When Every Day Was the Fourth of July* (1978), *The Long Days of Summer* (1980), *Me and the Kid* (1993), and *The Love Letter* (1998). He engaged in self-reflection before and after making a film, as his forthcoming quoted comments demonstrate, and he was always ready to defend his material if he felt that it was being overlooked or dismissed, as his emphatic 1997 editorial about *War and Remembrance* (1988, 1989) proved to readers of the *Los Angeles Times*.

During his 1966-1992 heyday, Dan Curtis seemed to have the magic touch. All he had to do was talk to ABC executive Brandon Stoddard about making *Dark Shadows*, and Curtis received a 26-week commitment. He pitched something as offbeat as *The Norliss Tapes* (NBC, 1973) or *The Great Ice Rip-Off* (ABC, 1974) to the network brass, and it became a movie of the week.

Years later, Brandon Stoddard implored Curtis to direct the mammoth *War and Remembrance* (1988, 1989). Not only did TV executives such as Stoddard want to work with Curtis time and again, but actors clamored to make a second, third, or even fourth film with the director, thereby establishing Curtis alongside Woody Allen or Robert Altman as an *auteur* with a recognizable stock company of regular performers.

The impact of Dan Curtis's work cannot be denied. *Dark Shadows* mesmerized an entire generation of baby boomers and made a teen idol of Barnabas Collins, the reluctant vampire. J. Gordon Melton, author of *The Vampire Book: The Encyclopedia of the Undead* (1994), noted that the three most significant vampires in all of popular culture are Bram Stoker's Dracula, Dan Curtis's Barnabas, and Anne Rice's Lestat.[3] Curtis filmed his own epic version of *Dracula* (1974), and his Barnabas character has starred in two television series, one TV pilot (never aired), two theatrical films (42 years apart), more than three dozen paperback novels, more than six dozen comic books, and even a modern ballet.

Curtis's made-for-TV movies, including *The Night Strangler* (1973); *Melvin Purvis, G-Man* (1974); and *Trilogy of Terror* (1975), often scored blockbuster ratings—none more so than Curtis and Richard Matheson's production of *The Night Stalker*, the telefilm that introduced Carl Kolchak, another TV character as culturally significant as Barnabas Collins. On Tuesday 11 January 1972, an amazing one-third of all TV households in the United States watched *The Night Stalker*. Stephen King later declared, "*The Night Stalker* was one of the best movies ever made for TV."[4]

One year later, on Tuesday 16 January 1973, ABC presented *two* Dan Curtis productions in one night: Richard Matheson's *Night Strangler* in prime time and Sam Hall's *Frankenstein* in late-night. There were countless nights when viewers of all ages avidly watched Curtis's movies and miniseries and their reruns. It was always exciting to see the words A DAN CURTIS PRODCTION flash across the screen.

This book focuses on Dan Curtis's television epics of the horror, crime, Western, war, and sci-fi genres: *Dracula* (1974), *The Last Ride of the Dalton Gang* (1979), the 1974 Melvin Purvis movie and its 1975 sequel *The Kansas City Massacre*, *The Winds of War* (1983) and *War and Remembrance* (1988, 1989), and *Intruders* (1992). *Nights of Dan Curtis* is an outgrowth of numerous writings that came before it. As a lifelong fan of *Dark Shadows*, *Burnt Offerings* (1976), and all of Dan Curtis's productions, I wrote articles for more than one dozen different *Dark Shadows* fanzines, including *The World of Dark Shadows*, *Collinwood Revisited*, *Lone Star Shadows*, *The Parallel Times*, and *Shadows of the Night*, beginning in 1975 and continuing for more than two decades.

In the mid-1980s, I wrote a book about Gold Key Comics' *Dark Shadows* comic books, and in the mid-1990s, I again wrote about the comic books for *Dark Shadows: The Comic-Strip Book*, edited by Kathryn Leigh Scott and Jim Pierson (Pomegranate Press, 1996). In 2006, webmaster Stuart Manning published one of my articles about the comic books on his website *Dark Shadows Journal*, and in 2009, Warren Buff published two of my comic-book articles in his electronic fanzine *Southern Fandom Update*. Finally, in the early 2010s, Daniel Herman asked me to write about the Gold Key *Dark Shadows* comic books, Gold Key's single *Dark Shadows Story Digest Magazine*, and the *Dark Shadows* newspaper comic strip for eight books of comics reprints published by Hermes Press.

In the 1990s, I served as a photographer for *The Dark Shadows Collector's Guide*, by Craig Hamrick (Clique Publishing, 1991), and as the *Dark Shadows* consultant to both *The Vampire Book: The Encyclopedia of the Undead*, by J. Gordon Melton (Visible Ink Press, 1994; 2nd ed. 1999), and *TV Tie-Ins: A Bibliography of American TV Tie-In Paperbacks*, by Kurt Peer (Neptune Publishing, 1997). My own book-length writing about my love for *Dark Shadows* and its multimedia incarnations continued in 1989-1990 when I wrote my master's thesis about *Dark Shadows* novelist Dan "Marilyn" Ross (1912-1995) and four of his greatest historical novels: *China Shadow*, by "Clarissa Ross" (Avon Books, 1974); *The Raven and the Phantom*, by "Dana Ross" (Pocket Books, 1976); *Moscow Mists*, by "Clarissa Ross" (Avon Books, 1977); and *Only Make-Believe*, by "Clarissa Ross" (Leisure Books, 1980). In May 1991, I received my M.A. degree in English from Tennessee State University, where I have taught English since 1985.

The four direct antecedents to *Nights of Dan Curtis* are writings that originated in 2005-2009. In May 2005, I wrote seven entries for *You're Next! Loss of Identity in the Horror Film*, Midnight Marquee Press's 2008 multi-author book. I chose to focus on loss of identity in five of Dan Curtis's films—*House of Dark Shadows* (1970), *Night of Dark Shadows* (1971), *Trilogy of Terror* (1975), *Burnt Offerings* (1976), and *Trilogy of Terror II* (1996)—as well as in E.W. Swackhamer's *Death at Love House* (1976; very similar to *Night of Dark Shadows*) and Gordon Hessler's *The Strange Possession of Mrs. Oliver* (1977;

another *Trilogy of Terror*-style vehicle for Karen Black). The book was edited by Anthony Ambrogio and published by Susan and Gary Svehla.

One year later (summer/fall 2006), I wrote my doctoral dissertation about the horror films of Dan Curtis, their impact on popular culture, and the "participatory culture" (i.e. fandom) devoted to Curtis's many productions. In May 2007, I received my Ph.D. degree in English from Middle Tennessee State University.

In 2007-2008, I reshaped my dissertation into a book, *The Television Horrors of Dan Curtis:* Dark Shadows, The Night Stalker, *and Other Productions, 1966-2006* (McFarland, 2009). With a new foreword by Jim Pierson, my book focused on 17+ of Curtis's horror productions: *Dark Shadows* (1966-1971, 1991, 2004), *The Strange Case of Dr. Jekyll and Mr. Hyde* (1968), *House of Dark Shadows* (1970), *Night of Dark Shadows* (1971), *The Night Stalker* (1972), *The Night Strangler* (1973), *Frankenstein* (1973), *The Norliss Tapes* (1973), *The Picture of Dorian Gray* (1973), *Scream of the Wolf* (1974), *Dracula* (1974), *The Turn of the Screw* (1974), *Trilogy of Terror* (1975), *Burnt Offerings* (1976), *Dead of Night* (1977), *Curse of the Black Widow* (1977), and *Trilogy of Terror II* (1996). The book was released in late February 2009. In 2010, *The Television Horrors of Dan Curtis* was nominated for the Rondo Award for the best non-fiction book of the year.

In summer/fall 2009, I wrote *House of Dan Curtis: The Television Mysteries of the* Dark Shadows *Auteur* (Westview, 2010) because much more needed to be said about the great producer-director and his body of work. With a foreword by *Dark Shadows* star John Karlen and a preface by Jim Pierson, *House of Dan Curtis* turned the spotlight on 15+ of Curtis's TV mysteries and crime dramas: *Dead of Night: A Darkness at Blaisedon* (1969); *Wide World Mystery: Frankenstein* (1973); *Wide World Mystery: The Picture of Dorian Gray* (1973); *Wide World Mystery: Shadow of Fear* (1974); *Wide World Mystery: The Invasion of Carol Enders* (1974); *Melvin Purvis, G-Man* (1974); *Wide World Mystery: The Turn of the Screw* (1974); *Wide World Mystery: Come Die with Me* (1974); *Wide World Mystery: Nightmare at 43 Hillcrest* (1974); *The Great Ice Rip-Off* (1974); *The Kansas City Massacre* (1975); *The Big Easy* (1982); *Johnny Ryan* (1990); *Angie the Lieutenant* (1992); and *Intruders: They Are Among Us* (1992). *House of Dan Curtis* was released in late June 2010.

Several people, including romance novelist Jamie Jones (*Lesson Plans*) and non-fiction author Jonathan Lampley (*Fan Culture*), told me, "Now that you've written *House of Dan Curtis,* you have to write *Night of Dan Curtis*!" In summer/fall 2015, I wrote the first edition of this book, *Nights of Dan Curtis: The Television Epics of the* Dark Shadows *Auteur* (Ideas, 2016). The book was released in late 2016 and was nominated for the Rondo Award for the best non-fiction book of the year.

In spring/summer 2018, I prepared a revised second edition of *The Television Horrors of Dan Curtis* (McFarland, 2019), and one year later I prepared this revised second edition of *Nights of Dan Curtis.* This new edition combines material from *The Television Horrors of Dan Curtis, House of Dan Curtis,* and *Nights of Dan Curtis* and adds plenty of new information.

This 1968 photograph of Marj Dusay of *Dead of Night: A Darkness at Blaisedon* (1969) appears on the cover of Jeff Thompson's book *House of Dan Curtis: The Television Mysteries of the* Dark Shadows *Auteur* (Westview, 2010).

Chapter I offers an overview of the career of Dan Curtis and information about every Dan Curtis production, from *Challenge Golf* and *The CBS Golf Classic* in 1963 to *Saving Milly* and *Our Fathers* in 2005. *Dracula, The Last Ride of the Dalton Gang*, the two Melvin Purvis movies, the two *War* miniseries, and *Intruders* are mentioned only in passing because they are the subjects of their own chapters. All of Curtis's other productions are showcased in detail. The chapter ends with an assessment of Tim Burton's 2012 film *Dark Shadows,* "dedicated to the memory of Dan Curtis," and a look at David Gregory's 2019 documentary *Master of Dark Shadows: The Gothic World of Dan Curtis.*

Chapter II focuses on *Dracula,* adapted by Richard Matheson (*Duel, Somewhere in Time*) and filmed in Yugoslavia and England. Curtis's director of photography was Academy Award winner Oswald Morris (*Fiddler on the Roof, The Seven-Percent Solution*). The chapter makes comparisons among Bram Stoker's novel, Matheson's screenplay, and Raymond McNally & Radu Florescu's then-current research about Vlad Tepes, the possible real-life Dracula.

Chapter III examines Dan Curtis's two made-for-TV movies about the real-life Bureau of Investigation agent Melvin Purvis (1903-1960)—*Melvin Purvis, G-Man* (1974) and *The Kansas City Massacre* (1975). Also discussed are John Milius's 1973 AIP feature *Dillinger,* which was a precursor to Curtis's pair of gangster movies, and Michael Mann's 2009 Universal blockbuster *Public Enemies,* which resurrected Purvis and Dillinger for contemporary audiences.

Chapter IV chronicles *The Last Ride of the Dalton Gang,* written by Academy Award winner Earl W. Wallace (*Witness, War and Remembrance*), and compares the actual history of the famous outlaws to their sometimes romanticized portrayal in Curtis's one-and-only Western.

Chapter V looks at the epic miniseries that changed the face of television: *The Winds of War,* written by Herman Wouk, who adapted his novel, with some assistance from Curtis and Wallace. According to Robert MacKenzie of *TV Guide,* "'Miniseries' hardly fits an epic television piece like this. 'Maximovie' might be better."[5]

Chapter VI details the even more stupendous follow-up to the *War* miniseries: *War and Remembrance,* written by Wouk, Curtis, and Wallace. *TV Guide* wrote, "First-rate performances, most notably from the supporting players, and unparalleled combat footage make the monumental megabuck miniseries *War and Remembrance* well worth the 18 hours of viewing time required during the next week-and-a-half. Another 12 hours are slated for the spring."[6]

Chapter VII focuses on *Intruders,* the chilling UFO miniseries that Curtis produced and directed. This "mystery with horror aspects"[7] is a blending of Curtis's masteries of the horror genre and the miniseries format, plus the new elements of science fact and science fiction.

The book's conclusion summarizes the legacy of Dan Curtis's productions and the lasting importance of this major but often unsung figure in American television and popular culture. Just as my other Curtis books set out to do, *Nights of Dan Curtis* attempts to assert, assure, and ensure the esteemed place of Dan Curtis and his movies on the canvas of popular culture. Filmmaker Ansel Faraj's afterword re-emphasizes that goal.

Introduction: Dan Curtis as *Auteur* and Influence   11

Once again, I cannot overemphasize the invaluable assistance of Jim Pierson in the preparation of this book. Through his leadership of the Dark Shadows Festival and his vital involvements with Dan Curtis Productions, Big Finish Productions, MPI Home Video, and film/TV preservation, Jim Pierson has been a major force in perpetuating *Dark Shadows* and the entire body of work of his mentor Curtis, whom Pierson has called "the ultimate fearless leader."[8] I extend a very special thank-you to Jim Pierson not only for helping me and encouraging me along the way but also for writing the preface to this book and for supplying me with every single photograph found herein. However, my thanks do not end there.

I also wish to thank Jo Addie, Anthony Ambrogio, Jeffrey Arsenault, Dr. Linda Badley, Dennis Baker, Marc Ballard, Joyce and Bill Barry, Harry Benshoff, Dr. Laura B.F. Beraha, Eileen and Marc Berger, David Bianculli, Michele Blackledge, Robert Bloch, Mark Booher & Bob Fritz, Ken Bramming, Dr. Will Brantley, Stephon Brisco, Norman Brunette, Jon Burlingame, Bill Byrge, Dale Clark, Melody Clark, Robert Cobert, Joe Collins, David Colton, Julie and Gary Conn, Dick Cowl, Dan Curtis Holdings, Jenny and Mike Darrell, Dr. Jane Davis, Mark Dawidziak, David Del Valle, Bruce Dettman, Stacey and Ben Dixon, Eileen and Keith Dunmire, Charles Ellis, Ansel H. Faraj, Eileen Farrar, Scott Farris, Robert Finocchio, Lynn and Jim Fitzwater, Jonathan Gales, Danielle S.O. Gelehrter, Chris Geny, Scott Gibson, Ed Graham, Greg Greene, Elva and John Griffin, Dr. Johnanna Grimes, Darren Gross & Phil Hansen, Dr. Karen Gupton, Guy Haines, Bruce Hallenbeck, Richard Halpern, Laraine Harford, Jonathan Harrison, Arlena Hayden, Joan Higgins, Douglas Howard, Joe Integlia, Rochelle and Scott Isaacs, Dr. Coreen Jackson, Dr. Laurel Jenkins-Crowe, Dr. Gloria Johnson, Jamie Jones, Katy and Bruce Jumper, Barbara Kannard, John Karlen, Rhonda and Brad Kavan, Mary and Gaines Kergosien, Nancy Kersey, Rod Labbe, Renae and Dave Lackey, Angelia and Curt Ladnier, Kimberly and Jonathan Lampley, Randall D. Larson, Amy and Jay Lipper, Wendy and Ira Lipper, Derek Martin, Richard Matheson, Wallace McBride, Dan McEachern, Cindy and Martin McGeachy, Dr. J. Gordon Melton, Robby Midgett, Jeremy Miller, Dr. Samantha Morgan-Curtis, Gary Mosher, Brigid and Patrick Murphy, Phyllis Muzeroll, Phil Myers, Isaac Neel, Kelly and Jake Neel, Mary Catharine Nelson, Julie and Jerry Nidiffer, Lois and John Nixon, Jacque Nodell, Michelle and John Noel, William F. Nolan, Mary Overstreet, Kameron Parsley, Kate and Kevin Parsley, Kimberly Parsley, Jim Pierson, Cheryl and Jeff Podolsky, Dr. Luke Powers, Judy Price, Dr. Tim Quain, Dr. Jo Helen Railsback, Kathy Resch, Keith Richardson, Scott Richardson, Daryl Allan Ritchie, Marcy Robin, Marilyn and Dan Ross, Nikki and Chad Rush, Helen Samaras, Chris Schlueter, Kathryn Leigh Scott, Dan Silvio, Cindy and Brian Smith, Dr. Connie Smith, Leah and Stephen Soule, Barbara Steele, Joseph Stern, Brinke Stevens, Harriet Stich, Valerie and James Storm, Alex Sutton, Susan and Gary Svehla, Gary Swafford, Donna and Jack Thomas, Wayne Thomas, Harriet and Charlie Thompson, Lee Anne Thompson, Lisa and Boyd Thompson, Sonia and E.D. Thompson, Bob Tinnell, Sy Tomashoff, Ashley Traughber, Mike Turner, Larry Underwood, Joshua Vance, Jeff Vaughn, Steve Vertlieb, Athena Victory & Hercules Invictus, Shirley and David Wadell, Marie Wallace, Dariel and Shawn Washington, Sherry Watson, Dr. Warren Westcott, Cyndi and Robert White,

Larry Wilcox, Tim Wiley, Ann Wilson, Paula Underwood Winters, Emma Wisdom, Tyler Wisniewski, Ken Wright, and Reed Young.

I also thank the stars of *Dark Shadows* (whom I always enjoy seeing at the Dark Shadows Festivals); my colleagues and students at Tennessee State University (where I often show Dan Curtis's "Graveyard Rats"); my former colleagues and students at Watkins College of Art, Design, & Film (where I showed Richard Matheson's *Incredible Shrinking Man* and "Amelia" in 2009-2010); my former colleagues and students at Nashville State Community College (where I showed Curtis's *Dark Shadows* revival series in 1997-1999); my former co-workers and listeners at WAMB-AM 1200 (where I often played Robert Cobert's "Quentin's Theme" and *Winds of War* theme many times between 1981, when I began at WAMB, and 2013, when the station ended); my fellow members of Nashville's Suspense, Sci-Fi, Horror, and Fantasy Meet-Up (where I have signed books and spoken about Dan Curtis); and *you*. Finally, I thank the people to whom this book is dedicated: my parents, my sister, my son, my nieces, my nephews, my great nieces, and, of course, Dan Curtis.

CHAPTER I

The Career of Dan Curtis: An Overview

Dan Curtis turns his love of golf into *The CBS Golf Classic* (CBS, 1963-1973), which he produces at the same time as *Dark Shadows* (ABC, 1966-1971). The 1965-1966 Emmy Award for Outstanding Sports Program is a three-way tie among *ABC's Wide World of Sports*, Curtis's *CBS Golf Classic*, and *Shell's Wonderful World of Golf* on NBC.

Not by coincidence, Dan Curtis translated his lifelong loves of golf, Gothic horror, Westerns, and World War II into his life's work. In his television career, he created golf series (1963, 1963-1973), *Dark Shadows* (1966-1971, 1991), memorable horror films (1972-1977, 1996), the award-winning *Last Ride of the Dalton Gang* (1979), the epic miniseries *The Winds of War* (1983) and *War and Remembrance* (1988, 1989), and more. Curtis's associates remember the fearless director practicing his golf swing in his office, constantly searching for great horror properties to film, and executing the mammoth shooting schedules of the two *War* miniseries with the zeal of an army general. "Even when he directed *Dark Shadows*," actor Jonathan Frid recalled in his talk at the 1993 Dark Shadows Festival, "he approached it as if we were doing *The Winds of War*!"

Curtis was born Daniel Mayer Cherkoss, the only child of Mildred and Edward Cherkoss, on Friday 12 August 1927 in Bridgeport, Connecticut. He gained a half-brother from his dentist-father's second marriage after his mother's death. When Curtis dramatized his childhood in 1930s Bridgeport in two award-winning made-for-TV movies, *When Every Day Was the Fourth of July* (1978) and *The Long Days of Summer* (1980), he added a fictitious younger sister Sarah to his TV family—just as he had given Barnabas Collins of *Dark Shadows* a little sister Sarah.

After serving in the Naval Reserve in 1945, Curtis attended Syracuse University and graduated with a bachelor's degree in sociology in 1950.[1] Two years later, he married Norma Mae Klein, his wife until her death in March 2006 (just 20 days before Curtis's own). Cathy and Tracy, two of the Curtises' three daughters, survived their parents; Linda Curtis died tragically in 1975.

Beginning a career in television in the 1950s, Curtis worked in film sales (TV syndication) for NBC for eight years. "I sold *Douglas Fairbanks Presents* and *Hopalong Cassidy* reruns," Curtis explained, as well as *Victory at Sea* and *Dragnet* reruns.[2] Between 1952 and 1960, Curtis advanced from the position of Eastern field salesman to central sales manager to Eastern sales manager to regional/national sales manager and finally to director of sales. Then, he spent two years in the show-packaging department at MCA, where he sold *Union Pacific* episodes and the Grace Kelly TV special *A Look at Monaco* to local television stations. Later, Curtis sold Ed Graham's cartoon series *Linus! the Lion-Hearted* to CBS for General Foods (1964-1966) and resold *Linus!* to ABC for Post Cereals (1966-1969). Curtis made a cameo voice appearance in one *Linus!* episode as Big-Time Talent Agent, who kidnaps a singing group led by Billie Bird (voiced by Carl Reiner). His experience in selling syndicated reruns prompted him to save all 1225 episodes of *Dark Shadows* for future sales. All but one of the episodes still exist and are available on VHS, DVD, and other media.

By 1962, the 35-year-old Curtis had formed his own company, Dan Curtis Associates (soon renamed Dan Curtis Productions), and created **Challenge Golf** for ABC-TV. The 13-episode series, premiering on Saturday 12 January 1963, featured Arnold Palmer and Gary Player in a best-ball competition against a pair of challengers. In the 12th episode (Saturday 30 March), Palmer and Player's opponents were Byron Nelson and Ken Venturi at the Pebble Beach golf course in California. The 13th and final episode aired on Sunday 7 April 1963.

In mid-1963, CBS, wanting to cultivate its own golf audience, asked Curtis to create and executive-produce *The CBS Match-Play Golf Classic* (later called **The CBS Golf Classic**). "CBS and I owned the show 50-50," Curtis revealed.[3] On these two golf series, it was Curtis who devised the practice of wiring golfers with throat microphones so that the TV audience could hear the players' immediate reactions to their shots (including occasional obscenities when they missed).

The CBS Golf Classic aired for a decade, from Saturday 28 December 1963 to Saturday 21 April 1973, and brought Curtis his first Emmy Award (for Achievement in

Sports) in the 1965-1966 season. Curtis executive-produced the show until 1967; Frank Chirkinian was his producer-director. The series eventually went from one hour to 90 minutes (and from black-and-white to color), and the prize money rose from $166,000 to $225,000. Most of the tournaments took place on golf courses in California, New Jersey, or Ohio. The Emmy Award-winning Curtis, now earning $100,000 per year, was well on his way to becoming a noted television producer.

Dan Curtis's friend Ed Graham (*Linus! the Lion-Hearted*) remembered that Curtis asked him for an idea for a live-action TV series that they could produce together. Graham suggested Batman. In a 2010 e-mail to me, Ed Graham recalled,

> We decided on Don Murray (*The Hoodlum Priest*) to play Batman. We also decided to go with the Rat Pack for villains, starting with Sammy Davis Jr. to play the Joker. Dan took the project to Jim Aubrey, who was head of programming for CBS, and Aubrey decided to go with *Batman* in the fall of 1964—no pilot necessary. We told an excited National Periodical Publications just as Aubrey was *fired* from CBS. We could not go elsewhere without a release from CBS because [attorney Dick] Barovic had granted them first refusal on any of my other projects after *Linus! The Lion-Hearted*. National Periodicals, now eager to go, made their own deal with ABC. [. . .] I think my Batman show would have been a success, but I told Jim Pierson that I'm pretty sure Dan would have bought me out somewhere along the way and done an even better job, himself.[4]

No Ed Graham/Dan Curtis *Batman* series materialized, but James Aubrey and Dan Curtis notably crossed paths again when Aubrey was head of MGM. Meanwhile, Curtis still yearned to try his hand at dramatic television. One night in the summer of 1965, he went to sleep and had a dream that changed the course of television popular culture and the fortunes of third-place ABC. In his dream, Curtis saw a dark-haired young woman riding a train toward a house of dark shadows by the sea—and her destiny. She was a present-day Jane Eyre, soon to be caught up in the intrigues and deceptions of a wealthy, eccentric family and its secrets.

Curtis remembered that he awoke suddenly after the strange dream. "The bedroom was pitch-black, but I could see the figure in my dream clearly—as though I were watching a movie. I saw a girl with long dark hair. She was about 19, and she was reading a letter aboard a train and occasionally staring wistfully out the window." Curtis perceived that the dream girl had been hired as a governess at an old house somewhere on the New England seacoast.

"Then, the train stopped in this dark, isolated town. The girl got off the train and started walking. Finally, she came to a huge, forbidding house. At the door, she lifted a huge brass knocker and gently tapped it three times. I heard a dog howl, and then—just as the door creaked open—I woke up!"[5] Apparently, Curtis, who later mastered the daily cliffhanger on his **Dark Shadows** soap opera, *dreamed* in cliffhangers himself.

"The next morning," he continued, "I wasn't so sure. At breakfast, I told my wife about the dream. When I finished, sure enough, Norma looked at me with wide-eyed enthusiasm and said, 'Dan, that's a great idea for a TV show!' She pointed out that the dream had a Gothic flavor, something eerie and threatening."[6]

Curtis pitched his Gothic idea to ABC executives Brandon Stoddard and Leonard Goldberg. He was supposed to meet with them to discuss a different idea for a series, but his dream of the girl on the train would not leave his mind. Curtis gave ABC that idea instead, to which Goldberg replied, "Dan, haven't you just rewritten *Jane Eyre*?" Curtis's comeback was, "Is anybody doing it on TV right now?"[7]

After briefly considering it as a nighttime program, Curtis and ABC decided to present *Dark Shadows* as a daytime soap opera. It would be videotaped on designer Sy Tomashoff's sets at ABC studios in Manhattan, with Seaview Terrace in Newport, Rhode Island, serving as the exterior of the Collinwood mansion. The show's stars would be Hollywood film actress Joan Bennett, New York stage actor Louis Edmonds, and (as the governess on the train) newcomer Alexandra Moltke. In the wake of the Monday 8 November 1965 premiere of NBC-TV's *Days of Our Lives*, with classic Hollywood star MacDonald Carey heading the cast, Curtis decided to seek Bennett, an even more celebrated movie star, for the anchor role of Elizabeth Collins Stoddard. *Dark Shadows* debuted on Monday 27 June 1966. Also appearing in the early episodes of the show were Conrad Bain, Nancy Barrett, Joel Crothers, Thayer David, Conard Fowkes, Hugh Franklin, David Henesy, Frank Schofield, and Kathryn Leigh Scott. Mitchell Ryan co-starred as Burke Devlin, an adversary of the Collins family.

Dark Shadows (1966-1971): **Kathryn Leigh Scott (left, in a blonde wig, as Maggie Evans) and Alexandra Moltke (as future governess Victoria Winters) play the "You're a jerk!" scene in the debut episode (tape date 13 June 1966; airdate 27 June 1966).**

In its first ten months, *Dark Shadows* was a mysterious but tame soap opera with the flavor of the woman-in-jeopardy Gothic novels that were popular in the 1960s and 1970s. Novelists such as Dorothy Daniels, Dan "Marilyn" Ross, Phyllis A. Whitney, and Daoma Winston were filling bookstore shelves with their stories of young women working as governesses in (seemingly haunted) old, dark houses where their lives were in danger from some unseen threat. Dan Ross went on to write 32 Paperback Library novels based on *Dark Shadows* itself and a half-dozen other vampire novels. However, what made for enthralling reading was *not* generating high-spirited (or highly-rated) television. By early 1967, *Dark Shadows* was facing a danger far worse than creaking doors: cancellation.[8]

"When the show went on the air," Curtis observed, "it was the best-kept secret since Oak Ridge. Nobody was watching it."[9] In 1966 and 1967, only nine to ten million viewers (a paltry number, ratings-wise) were following the stories of the neurotic Collins family of Collinsport, Maine—a far cry from the record 16 to 18 million fans who watched the show in 1968, 1969, and early 1970.[10] What turned the show around was another Curtis innovation: a vampire.

Curtis's own daughters suggested that their father make *Dark Shadows* scarier. As a result, what had begun as an extra-mysterious soap opera only several steps beyond *The Edge of Night* or *The Secret Storm* soon became overtly supernatural. Curtis decided to have fun with *Dark Shadows* and push the envelope since (he thought) the show was going off the air anyway. Curtis had the writers add ghosts, and the ratings increased. Next came a phoenix (Diana Millay) who rose from her ashes and lived again every 100 years. Finally, in April 1967, Curtis and the writers added the character of Barnabas Collins, an 18th-century vampire freed from his chained coffin to terrorize 20th-century Collinsport.

Curtis intended the Barnabas character to be a short-term villain who would kill a few characters and then himself be killed by a stake through the heart. However, Curtis soon realized that Barnabas's portrayer, Shakespearean actor Jonathan Frid, "brought a very Gothic, romantic quality to this role that I guess will live forever."[11] Audiences reacted passionately to the vampire Barnabas, as well as to the witch Angelique (Lara Parker), the werewolf Quentin (David Selby), and the endless stream of ghosts, sorcerers, gypsies, zombies, and mad doctors. Time travel added to the romantic exoticism of *Dark Shadows,* and in mid-1969, as the show was telling a complex tale set in the year 1897, *Dark Shadows* was the highest-rated network program on daytime television.[12] Curtis credited his show with allowing ABC to compete with NBC (*Another World, Concentration*) and CBS (*As the World Turns, Search for Tomorrow*) during the day. Watching *Dark Shadows* led viewers to ABC's other daytime offerings, including *The Dating Game, The Newlywed Game, One Life to Live,* and *Let's Make a Deal,* all of which began runs on ABC between 1965 and 1968.

"The idea was to bring a vampire on as a marauding, evil presence: a Dracula," Curtis reiterated. "There was no other intention. I went off to England to do *Dr. Jekyll and Mr. Hyde* [in 1967], and I said to cast a vampire. And they cast a vampire: they cast Jonathan Frid." Curtis continued,

Frid was a wonderful actor to work with. He had a particular quality; he had a haunting quality about him. He was very "period" to me; he wasn't contemporary. He somehow probably encompassed the kinds of shadings that made a Heathcliff or a Rochester or people like that attractive to women. Here's a guy who's supposed to be a vampire and supposed to terrorize people, but he started getting all this fan mail, and I realized there was something really wild going on here. We had to find a way to perpetuate a vampire—I couldn't kill him off now—and this is the way the love story started.[13]

Curtis's "love story" was Barnabas's doomed love for Josette DuPres (Kathryn Leigh Scott), the 18th-century woman who kills herself when she learns that her beloved Barnabas is a vampire. Curtis realized that this somber love story had become central to the appeal and success of his show.

"The audience really cared about Barnabas," Curtis admitted, "and he became the reluctant vampire. Now, I know a lot of people have tried that since then, but you really cared about him. So we had to take him from the mode of being this horrifying terror to this guy you feel sorry for."[14]

Barnabas Collins reflected the ambivalent social consciousness and pop psychology of the 1960s in that he was not all bad or all good. The vampire was tragic and guilt-ridden, an idea previously implied in the Universal classics *Dracula's Daughter* (1936), *House of Frankenstein* (1944), and *House of Dracula* (1945). A decade before Anne Rice's *Interview with the Vampire* (1976), the complex, multi-faceted, Byronic vampire/anti-hero came of age in Barnabas Collins as the turbulent times posed the questions: should wrongdoers be seen as evil and punished or be considered as victims and rehabilitated? Should Barnabas Collins be despised and staked or pitied and cured? Is vampirism curable like other social diseases? Jonathan Frid often remarked, "I played Barnabas as an alcoholic. I didn't play 'the bite.' I played his problems. He was a guy with a hang-up."[15] As a result, millions of housewives, college students, and school children sympathized with Barnabas and followed his daily exploits. Dr. Julia Hoffman (Grayson Hall) sought to find a cure for him while suffering herself—from unrequited love for the vampire.

Curtis and his writers had hit pay dirt. The ratings skyrocketed for the next several years (until 1970).

One of the many elements that made *Dark Shadows* so memorable was its distinctive music, composed by the Emmy Award-nominated composer Robert Cobert. "I met Dan Curtis in 1966," Cobert recalled, "and there was an immediate rapport, so I was hired and wrote all of the music for *Dark Shadows*"—20 hours of music cues in all.[16] As for the unforgettable theme song, Cobert said, "I whistled the whole theme to Dan as he was putting golf balls on his office floor. His face lit up, and he said, 'I love it!' We then recorded it with a five-piece orchestra"—alto flute, double bass, vibes, harp, and Yamaha synthesizer.[17]

Julliard-educated Cobert had broken into television in the early 1960s by writing music for dramatic specials (*The Scarlet Pimpernel*, *The Heiress*), game shows (*To Tell the Truth*, *The Price Is Right*), and soap operas (*The Young Marrieds*, *The Doctors*). After *Dark Shadows*, Cobert went on to compose the music for almost every Dan Curtis production. Only *When Every Day Was the Fourth of July, The Long Days of Summer, Saving Milly*, three unsold pilots, and a public-service announcement feature music scores by composers other than Cobert. In terms of their long creative partnership, Curtis and Cobert were the Alfred Hitchcock and Bernard Herrmann, or the Tim Burton and Danny Elfman, of television.

Cobert recalled, "As the rapport not only held, but grew, I did for Dan, due to his incredible versatility, an unbelievable variety of projects. The best thing about working with 'Big D' is that he'll let me try anything I want to do musically—even when he is violently opposed to my idea—and then make a truly open-minded decision."[18] Dan Curtis called Robert Cobert "the most brilliant composer around, and he's never let me down. The guy just writes dead-perfect scores."[19] A best-selling soundtrack LP of Cobert's *Dark Shadows* music was released in July 1969 and stayed on the *Billboard* music chart for 19 weeks.

"I have absolutely fond memories of *Dark Shadows*," Curtis declared. "We had a great time, and I loved all of those people; we were like a big family. We were trailblazers in those days. We gave ABC a daytime schedule. It was great fun."[20]

The convoluted storyline of *Dark Shadows* can be easily divided into segments that fans refer to as "pre-Barnabas," "1795," "1897," etc. Henry Jenkins, author of *Textual Poachers: Television Fans and Participatory Culture* (Routledge, 1992), points out that each segment "is reduced to a brief phrase, evoked for an audience which has already absorbed its local significance and fit it into the larger sense of the series's development."[21]

The 1966-1967 **pre-Barnabas** episodes concern governess Victoria Winters (Alexandra Moltke) and her exploration of the secrets of her past and their possible link to the Collins family. Burke Devlin (Mitchell Ryan) returns to Collinsport, Maine, in order to settle a score with Roger Collins (Louis Edmonds). Collins Cannery manager Bill Malloy (Frank Schofield) is murdered, and the ensuing investigation involves Roger Collins, Sam Evans (David Ford), Sam's daughter Maggie Evans (Kathryn Leigh Scott), Maggie's boyfriend Joe Haskell (Joel Crothers), Collinwood caretaker Matthew Morgan (Thayer David), and Victoria, who sees Malloy's ghost. Roger's presumed-dead wife Laura Collins (Diana Millay) returns to Collinwood and seeks custody of her and Roger's troubled son David Collins (David Henesy). Laura is a phoenix who almost succeeds in drawing David into the fire that gives her rebirth every century. Elizabeth Collins Stoddard (Joan Bennett) never wants her daughter Carolyn Stoddard (Nancy Barrett) to know what happened to Elizabeth's long-absent husband. Jason McGuire (Dennis Patrick) blackmails Liz about her husband's presumed fate.

In April **1967**, Jason's friend Willie Loomis (John Karlen) releases the vampire Barnabas Collins (Jonathan Frid) from his chained coffin. Barnabas introduces himself to Elizabeth, Roger, and Carolyn as their "cousin from England." The vampire kidnaps Maggie Evans and tries to make her over as his lost love Josette. The experience causes Maggie to suffer a mental breakdown, and she is committed to Windcliff Sanitarium. The ghost of Sarah Collins (Sharon Smyth) visits her there. Maggie's psychiatrist Dr. Julia Hoffman (Grayson Hall) discovers Barnabas's secret and offers to cure him of his vampirism. Barnabas switches his romantic attentions to Victoria. Julia, feeling rejected, intentionally ruins the experimental cure and causes Barnabas to age drastically until he bites Carolyn and rejuvenates. Elizabeth, Roger, Carolyn, Barnabas, Julia, and Victoria hold a séance that sends Vicki back in time.

The **1795** time period (late 1967-early 1968), one of the greatest stories ever told on television, reveals Barnabas's life as a mortal and dramatizes the witch Angelique's curse that caused his vampirism. Victoria finds herself living in 1795 among Barnabas, his little sister Sarah (S. Smyth), and their parents Joshua (L. Edmonds) and Naomi (J. Bennett). Josette DuPres (K.L. Scott) and her family (D. Ford, G. Hall) arrive from Martinique to prepare for Josette's wedding to Barnabas. Josette's maid Angelique (Lara Parker), who wants Barnabas for herself, bewitches Josette and Jeremiah Collins (Anthony George) into marriage and causes countless other supernatural calamities that Abigail Collins (Clarice Blackburn) and the Reverend Trask (Jerry Lacy) blame on Victoria. Angelique marries Barnabas, who still loves Josette and only Josette. Vicki stands trial for witchcraft, and she is defended by Peter Bradford (Roger Davis), who falls in love with her. Barnabas shoots Angelique, who turns him into one of the living dead—a vampire. Before Barnabas can make Josette his vampire bride, Josette jumps to her death from Widow's Hill. When fortune-hunter Lt. Nathan Forbes (Joel Crothers) tells Naomi that her son is a vampire, she takes poison and dies. Barnabas kills Forbes for his treachery and walls up Trask for tormenting Vicki. Joshua chains his son in a coffin. Victoria, convicted of witchcraft, is about to be hanged when she suddenly returns to 1968.

The **1968** time period brings Cassandra Collins (actually, Angelique) to Collinwood as Roger's new wife. Dr. Eric Lang (Addison Powell) succeeds where Julia failed: he seemingly cures Barnabas of vampirism. Cassandra begins a Dream Curse that works its way through the Collinses and their friends before it reaches Barnabas and (she hopes) reinstates his vampire curse. The Dream Curse fails because of Barnabas's involvement in Dr. Lang's experiment that brings about the *Frankenstein*-like creation Adam (Robert Rodan). Nicholas Blair (Humbert Allen Astredo), a warlock, takes Adam under his wing. Peter's lookalike Jeff Clark appears in town, and Victoria is certain that he is really Peter Bradford. Nicholas falls for Maggie Evans. Adam kidnaps Carolyn. Cassandra kills Dr. Lang. Julia and Barnabas create Eve (Marie Wallace), a mate for Adam, but she is more interested in Nicholas and Jeff/Peter. Nicholas turns Angelique into a vampire, who bites handyman Tom Jennings (Don Briscoe), Tom's cousin Joe Haskell, and Barnabas. Tom, now a vampire, bites Julia before Barnabas vanquishes him. Vicki (now played, briefly, by Betsy Durkin) and Jeff/Peter vanish together into the past. (Alexandra Moltke Isles has left the TV series to have a baby.) Adam kills Eve and then leaves Collinsport with the help of Professor Stokes (T. David). Tom's brother Chris Jennings (D. Briscoe) comes to town to see his disturbed little sister Amy (Denise Nickerson). Chris has a terrible secret: he is a werewolf. David Collins and Amy Jennings become possessed by the ghosts of Quentin Collins (David Selby) and Beth Chavez (Terry Crawford). Learning that Chris and Quentin's fates are connected, Barnabas uses the I Ching wands to go back in time.

Dark Shadows **(1966-1971): Jonathan Frid (as Barnabas Collins) and Grayson Hall (as Dr. Julia Hoffman) pose for a 1968 photo session.**

The extremely popular **1897** time period (March-November 1969) takes Barnabas (a vampire again) back to *fin-de-siècle* Collinwood to try to save the life of the werewolf Quentin Collins. Quentin and his friend Evan Hanley (H.A. Astredo), who are demonology enthusiasts, summon a demon and get Angelique, who is attracted to both Barnabas and Quentin. Quentin and his siblings Judith (J. Bennett), Edward (L. Edmonds), and Carl Collins (J. Karlen) quarrel over their inheritance. Reverend Gregory Trask (J. Lacy) establishes a school in town, but his real goal is marrying Judith and taking her share of the Collins fortune. Edward's missing wife Laura Collins (D. Millay) returns for their children Jamison (D. Henesy) and Nora (D. Nickerson). Quentin realizes that Laura is a phoenix. Angelique stops Laura from staking Barnabas. Magda (G. Hall) puts a curse on Quentin for his mistreatment of her sister Jenny (M. Wallace). Quentin becomes a werewolf. Barnabas defeats Laura and vows to help Quentin and his descendants, including Chris. Gregory's daughter Charity Trask (N. Barrett) becomes possessed by the spirit of Pansy Faye, Carl's former fiancée. Magda regrets cursing Quentin and seeks to help him by giving him a magical, severed hand. The hand's owner, Count Andreas Petofi (T. David), comes to Collinwood to take back his hand. Petofi, a powerful warlock, gives painter Charles Delaware Tate (R. Davis) the ability to bring to life whatever he paints. Quentin meets and falls in love with Amanda Harris (Donna McKechnie), a woman brought to life by Tate. Quentin's werewolf curse ends when Tate paints a *Dorian Gray*-like portrait of him. Barnabas meets Lady Kitty Hampshire (K.L. Scott), who is the reincarnation of Josette. After being tormented by Gregory, Judith turns the tables on her avaricious husband. Barnabas makes plans to go away with Kitty/Josette, but he loses his way in the woods.

Dark Shadows (1966-1971): Jonathan Frid (left, as Barnabas Collins), David Selby (as Quentin Collins), and David Henesy (as Jamison Collins) interact in a scene from the popular 1897 storyline, seen in mid-1969.

Dark Shadows takes a sci-fi turn with the **Leviathan** storyline (late 1969-early 1970), in which shapeless, prehistoric entities possess Barnabas (now human again), Elizabeth, David, and Amy in order to regain their dominion over the earth. The ancient Leviathan creatures waylaid Barnabas in the woods and sent him back to 1969 with an ornate box housing the essence of the Leviathan leader who will be born into the present-day world and pave the way for the new Leviathan age. Antique-shop owners Megan and Philip Todd (M. Wallace and Christopher Bernau) become the caretakers of the essence, which grows from baby to boy to teenager to man, Jebez Hawkes (Christopher Pennock), in record time. Jeb falls for Carolyn and wants her to be his Leviathan bride. Elizabeth's husband Paul Stoddard (D. Patrick) returns to Collinwood. Paul is indebted to the Leviathans. Nicholas Blair returns to aid the Leviathan cause. Chris Jennings still suffers from the werewolf curse despite an attempt by his fiancée Sabrina Stuart (Lisa Richards) to free him through the use of a magical moon poppy.

Quentin's lookalike Grant Douglas surfaces, and Barnabas and Julia realize that he is indeed Quentin Collins. When Barnabas betrays Jeb, he turns Barnabas back into a vampire. Julia seeks to cure Barnabas, whose bloodlust is becoming uncontrollable. Barnabas turns Megan into a vampire. Searching for Quentin's portrait, Julia finds Angelique, living as a mortal woman, married to millionaire Sky Rumson (Geoffrey Scott), who follows the Leviathan cause. Quentin meets Amanda's lookalike Olivia Corey and realizes that she is his lost love Amanda. However, Quentin loses her to Mr. Best (Emory Bass), the personification of death. Angelique is the keeper of Quentin's portrait, whose image has aged monstrously while Quentin has remained young. Jeb fears the werewolf (stuntman Alex Stevens), the only supernatural being that he cannot control. Carolyn marries Jeb. In the East Wing of Collinwood, Barnabas finds a room that is a portal to another world—Parallel Time. Megan bites Roger before Willie and Julia drive a stake through her heart. Jeb and Barnabas cause the Leviathans to lose their foothold on earth. Barnabas fears that he will lose control and vampirize Maggie Evans, but he feels that his cure may lie in Parallel Time. Despite Julia's warnings of the possible dangers, Barnabas enters the parallel world.

The next *Dark Shadows* storyline (April-July 1970) deals with **1970 Parallel Time**, an alternate universe in which the people of Collinsport, Maine, look the same but lead vastly different lives "because they have made different choices." In this world, Quentin is the master of Collinwood, and Elizabeth and Roger are the poor relations. Quentin, whose wife Angelique has died, returns to Collinwood with a new bride, Maggie Evans Collins. Before Barnabas can introduce himself at Collinwood, he is captured by the frustrated writer William H. Loomis and chained in a coffin while Loomis forces Barnabas to tell him his life story. (Jonathan Frid is away filming *House of Dark Shadows* during Barnabas's off-camera captivity.) Collinwood's housekeeper Miss Hoffman is fiercely loyal to Angelique Collins, even months after Angelique's death, and she despises Maggie. Suddenly, Angelique's twin sister Alexis Stokes shows up, and Hoffman and others are convinced that "Alexis" is really Angelique, returned from the dead. Quentin's friend Dr. Cyrus Longworth (C. Pennock) develops a *Jekyll & Hyde*-type serum that allows him to transform from the meek Cyrus into the cruel, lecherous John Yaeger. John abuses Buffie Harrington (Elizabeth Eis) and kills his blackmailer (John Harkins). Barnabas finally frees himself and introduces himself to Quentin, Elizabeth, and Roger as their "cousin from South America." Alexis truly is Alexis, not Angelique—but then, Angelique herself rises from the dead, kills Alexis, and takes her sister's place at Collinwood. John Yaeger kidnaps Maggie Collins. Dr. Julia Hoffman follows Barnabas to 1970 Parallel Time and kills Miss Hoffman before Hoffman can stake Barnabas. Julia takes Hoffman's place at Collinwood. Barnabas finds the kidnapped Maggie, frees her, and kills John Yaeger. Angelique discovers that "Miss Hoffman" is really Julia and imprisons her in the sub-basement of Collinwood. Barnabas finds Julia with the help of Roxanne Drew (Donna Wandrey), a psychic who is being victimized by Angelique and her father Timothy Stokes. Barnabas vanquishes the Angelique of this world, and in retaliation, Stokes sets fire to Collinwood. Barnabas and Julia become separated from Roxanne, who perishes in the flames.

Dark Shadows (1966-1971): Jonathan Frid (as Barnabas Collins) and Donna Wandrey (as Roxanne Drew) pose for a 1970 photo session.

Through the uncanny powers of the parallel-time portal, Barnabas and Julia instantly find themselves back in their own time band but in the future year of **1995** when Collinwood is in ruins and the Collins family is dead except for Quentin and Carolyn, who are insane. This thrilling two-week-long story arc (20-31 July 1970) is practically a two-person show as Barnabas and Julia explore the shocking ruins of Collinwood and try in vain to get answers from Carolyn and Quentin. Meanwhile, Julia becomes possessed by the ghost of Gerard Stiles (James Storm), who is haunting the ruined mansion. Barnabas and Julia also encounter the spirits of Daphne Harridge (Kate Jackson), Tad Collins (D. Henesy), and Carrie Stokes (Kathy Cody). Julia begs Barnabas to leave 1995 without her before Gerard forces her to harm him. Barnabas replies, "Not without you, Julia—*never* without you."

As suddenly as they appeared in 1995, Barnabas and Julia return to the summer of **1970** and attempt to prevent the prophesied destruction of Collinwood. The ghosts of Gerard and the others are already present in the house, and Gerard and Daphne are controlling David Collins and Hallie Stokes (K. Cody). Meanwhile, Barnabas meets a woman named Roxanne—but the Roxanne of this time band has a terrible secret that her friend Sebastian Shaw (C. Pennock) helps her hide. After Maggie Evans suffers an ordeal similar to her 1967 victimization, Sebastian drives her out of town and to Windcliff Sanitarium. (Kathryn Leigh Scott leaves the show to marry Ben Martin and move to Paris.) Through their investigations, Barnabas and Julia realize that the imminent destruction of Collinwood is linked to the events of the year 1840. The prophesied events come to pass, and Collinwood is doomed.

Now, in the autumn of 1970, Barnabas and Julia's quest leads them, and later Professor Stokes, through time, back to **1840**, when the present-day threat to Collinwood originated with the powerful warlock Judah Zachery (Michael McGuire) and his possession of Gerard Stiles. Barnabas and Julia introduce themselves as brother and sister. Quentin Collins, having been presumed lost at sea, suddenly returns to Collinwood and his wife Samantha Collins (Virginia Vestoff), who has already married Gerard. Samantha is torn between Quentin and Gerard, both of whom are attracted to Tad's new governess, Daphne Harridge. Angelique, who is passing through town with her servant Laszlo (Michael Stroka), is shocked to find Barnabas out of the coffin, back at Collinwood, and very different from the Barnabas of 1795. Barnabas meets and falls for Roxanne Drew, but Angelique ruins the match by introducing herself at Collinwood as "Valerie Collins," Barnabas's *wife*. Desmond Collins (J. Karlen) returns from his world travels with the magical, disembodied head of Judah Zachery. The head possesses Gerard, who frames Quentin and Desmond for witchcraft. Once again, a room in the East Wing of Collinwood is discovered to be a portal to a very different 1841—a time when Barnabas lived and died a mortal man, married Josette, and had a son, Bramwell. Quentin and Desmond stand trial for witchcraft. Angelique remembers her life in 1692 as a disciple of Judah Zachery. She helps Barnabas, Julia, and Stokes defeat Judah Zachery and exonerate Quentin and Desmond, but she loses her life in the process. Barnabas realizes too late that he has felt love for Angelique all along. Barnabas chases Angelique's killer Lamar Trask (J. Lacy) into the East Wing, where he dies. Barnabas, Julia, and Stokes return to the present time and find a peaceful, happy Collinwood. The stories of the original 1966-1971 characters come to an end.

Beginning in January 1971, the final three months of *Dark Shadows* divorce themselves completely from the regular characters' time band and tell a *Wuthering Heights*-inspired story that recasts Jonathan Frid and Lara Parker. No longer the vampire and the witch, they become Bramwell and Catherine, star-crossed lovers at the Collinwood of **1841 Parallel Time**. (By this time, Frid no longer wishes to play Barnabas, and Parker finally gets her wish to portray the ingénue instead of the villainess. In 1966, she had auditioned for the role of Victoria Winters.) Bramwell is a poor Collins relation who is ambitious and driven. Catherine Harridge loves Bramwell yet marries his cousin Morgan Collins (Keith Prentice). Although the 1841 Parallel Time storyline involves a vicious ghost and a family lottery (inspired by Shirley Jackson's 1959 novel *The Lottery*), the plot complements the pre-Barnabas episodes in its return to family dynamics, interpersonal relationships, and soap-operatic devices, such as Melanie's secret parentage, Catherine's pregnancy, and Daphne's terminal illness. As *Dark Shadows* draws to a close, Melanie (N. Barrett) learns that her birth mother is Josette Collins (Mary Cooper), and she makes plans to marry Kendrick Young (J. Karlen). Morgan Collins goes mad and dies in a fall. Bramwell and his beloved Catherine defeat the ghost of Brutus Collins (L. Edmonds), and the story ends happily for this alternate Collins family when *Dark Shadows* airs its final episode on Friday 2 April 1971.

Even in its tamer 1966 and 1841 PT days—and certainly in its heyday of vampirism, witchcraft, time travel, lycanthropy, and Leviathans—*Dark Shadows* profited from emotional, convincing, and enthralling writing. Art Wallace, who had written for *Armstrong Circle Theatre* between 1956 and 1960, plotted and scripted most of the first four months of the series (65 episodes). He based some of the characters (e.g. Elizabeth, Jason, Carolyn, Joe) on those in "The House," a television play performed on CBS-TV's *The Web* in 1954 and again on NBC-TV's *Goodyear TV Playhouse* in 1957. Wallace went on to write the made-for-TV movies *A Tattered Web* (1971) and *She Waits* (1972). Next, screenwriter Francis Swann (*Shine on Harvest Moon*) wrote three dozen *Dark Shadows* episodes, and Ron Sproat (*Love of Life*), one of the show's major writers, turned out 214 scripts. Malcolm Marmorstein (*Peyton Place*) wrote 80 episodes, and Joe Caldwell (*Strange Paradise*) wrote 63. Sproat, Marmorstein, and Dan Curtis co-created the Barnabas Collins character.

Beginning in the fall of 1968, Gordon Russell (*A Flame in the Wind*) and Sam Hall (*Adventures in Paradise*) became the head writers of *Dark Shadows*. Russell and Hall wrote 366 and 316 episodes, respectively. They later co-wrote *One Life to Live*. Ralph Ellis (*A Flame in the Wind*) scripted two DS episodes in February 1969. In March 1969, theatrical press agent Violet Welles began writing for *Dark Shadows* and eventually wrote 84 shows. The writers took many of their story ideas from Dan Curtis himself and his love of things that go bump in the night.

Lela Swift, a director of *Studio One in Hollywood* between 1950 and 1952, directed more episodes of *Dark Shadows* than anyone else—580. They included the first and last episodes plus Curtis's one-shot nighttime *Dark Shadows*-style experiment *Dead of Night: A Darkness at Blaisedon* (1969). Swift went on to direct five episodes of *Wide World*

Mystery and more than 825 episodes of *Ryan's Hope*. She passed away on Tuesday 4 August 2015.

Five hundred sixty-eight of the rest of the 1225 episodes of *Dark Shadows* were directed by either Henry Kaplan (*All My Children*), John Sedwick (*The Edge of Night*), or Dan Curtis. Seeing others direct his spooky brainchild inspired Dan Curtis the producer to become Dan Curtis the director. He remembered, "I was producing all the time, and then I finally got to the point where I said, 'This is crazy. I develop the projects; then, I bring in directors, and I tell them what to do.' And I said, 'Why don't I just cut out the middle-man, the director?'"[22]

After spending some time in England and Canada in 1967 to produce the Emmy Award-nominated *Strange Case of Dr. Jekyll and Mr. Hyde* (1968), Curtis returned to the New York studios of *Dark Shadows* and directed a total of 21 daily episodes in 1968 and 1969. "The first time I ever directed was the greatest nightmare that ever happened," Curtis insisted. "I took about two weeks on *Dark Shadows* where I taught myself how to direct—I almost sank ABC while I was doing that—but I've produced *and* directed almost everything I've done since."[23]

His first experience as a director was on episodes #457-461 in March 1968. These episodes delivered the climax of the popular storyline set in 1795-1796, revealing how and why Barnabas Collins became a vampire. Later, Curtis occupied the director's chair for another 1796 interlude, then for three 1969 episodes of the *Turn of the Screw*-like storyline introducing Quentin Collins as a ghost, and finally for six episodes in the 1897 storyline. That saga revealed how and why Quentin became a werewolf. It also changed history by preventing both Quentin's death in 1897 and his existence as a ghost in 1969. Quentin had overcome the werewolf curse and become immortal through a *Dorian Gray*-like portrait, and Dan Curtis had added *director* to his producing and writing credits. His accomplishments throughout the 1970s built on his *Dark Shadows* success and caused the *Los Angeles Times*, in 1978, to crown Curtis "the master of the macabre."[24]

In 1967, around the time of the casting of Jonathan Frid as Barnabas Collins, Curtis took a break from *Dark Shadows* and began preparing a prestigious TV adaptation of Robert Louis Stevenson's 1886 novel, **The Strange Case of Dr. Jekyll and Mr. Hyde**. (Curtis and Stevenson share the curious trait that both *Dark Shadows* and *Jekyll and Hyde* came to their creators in vivid dreams.) The plan was for Rod Serling to write the script, Jason Robards to play Jekyll and Hyde, and Curtis to produce the drama in London. Suddenly, both Serling's script and Robards's services became unavailable, and Curtis had to rethink the production. He hired Jack Palance to star and moved the taping back to New York near the *Dark Shadows* studio. Then, a technicians' strike forced Curtis to move once again, this time to Toronto. Sets for the production had already been built in New York, but Curtis had to start all over with new sets in Canada.

Curtis had hired an accomplished director when he had been in London. Since 1960, Charles Jarrott had directed episodes of the BBC-TV series *Armchair Theatre*, *The Wednesday Play*, and *Haunted*. Jarrott agreed to follow Curtis's production to New York and finally to Toronto. Curtis's script writer was Ian McLellan Hunter, who had written some *Dr. Christian* and *Mr. District Attorney* movies and more recently had scripted the TV series *The Adventures of Robin Hood* (1955-1958) and *The Defenders* (1961-1965).

Hunter's script is one of the more nearly faithful adaptations of Stevenson's story, which has been filmed for movies and television six dozen times, beginning in 1908. Of course, a *completely* faithful filming has never materialized, for it would be devoid of women and probably of heterosexuality. According to critic Elaine Showalter, "While there have been over 70 films and television versions of *Dr. Jekyll and Mr. Hyde*, not one tells the story as Stevenson wrote it—that is, as a story about men."[25]

The dance-hall girls and female prostitutes who populate almost all of the screen adaptations of *The Strange Case of Dr. Jekyll and Mr. Hyde* are not found in Stevenson's novel. It is the story of the London solicitor Gabriel John Utterson, his cousin and dear friend Richard Enfield, and his secretary and confidant Mr. Guest. It is also the story of the prominent physician Dr. Henry Jekyll, his formerly close (now estranged) friend Dr. Hastie Lanyon, and his devoted butler Poole. This is a world of powerful men—doctors, lawyers, educators, even a member of Parliament—and women play little or no part in this world except as servants. Utterson and Enfield take a much-anticipated walk together every Sunday afternoon, and Dr. Jekyll often holds jovial dinner parties for the male intelligentsia of London. None of the men seem to have, need, or want women in their lives; instead, they find fulfillment in their important work and in each other's company.

Ian Hunter's script hints at this circumstance when Drs. Lanyon and Jekyll goad each other by pointing out that neither has a woman in his life, but both men quickly agree that their work makes their lives complete. What Stevenson's novel hints at more concretely (but still nebulously enough for polite reading society) is that these men make up London's hidden but quite organized homosexual community of the late 19th century and that Jekyll's alter-ego Mr. Edward Hyde represents the unbridled, socially taboo homosexual nature that these Victorian men must *hide*. In "Henry Jekyll's Full Statement of the Case," the tenth and final chapter of the novel, Jekyll never reveals the exact nature of his "irregularities" and his "profound duplicity of life," but he confesses that he "hid them with an almost morbid sense of shame."[26] In chapter nine, "Doctor Lanyon's Narrative," Jekyll's estranged friend is equally cryptic. "What he [Jekyll] told me in the next hour I cannot bring my mind to set on paper. I saw what I saw, I heard what I heard, and my soul sickened at it," Lanyon admits. "As for the moral turpitude that the man unveiled to me, even with tears of penitence, I cannot, even in memory, dwell on it without a start of horror."[27] Stevenson allows the reader to decide the exact nature of Henry Jekyll's questionable acts, which began in his youth and continued to the time of this confession and his death.

The Strange Case of Dr. Jekyll and Mr. Hyde (1968): Jack Palance, in Dick Smith's frightening makeup, portrays Mr. Hyde. Smith goes on to create makeup for two *Godfather* movies and two *Exorcist* movies and to win an Academy Award for *Amadeus* (1984).

Almost all screen adaptations of *The Strange Case of Dr. Jekyll and Mr. Hyde* are based most heavily on these final two chapters, in which Jekyll's experiments and Hyde's misdeeds are revealed. The first eight chapters detail Utterson's investigation of the mystery surrounding Jekyll. Readers in 1886 did not realize that Jekyll and Hyde were the same man until the last two chapters, which provided the fantastical explanation. Only the 2004 Australian short film *The Strange Game of Hyde and Seek*, directed by Nathan Hill, approaches the story as Utterson's investigation and not chiefly as Jekyll's story. Paolo Barzman's 2008 *Jekyll and Hyde* TV-movie, set in present-day Boston, divides its time between Jekyll's activities and a female attorney's thorough investigation of Hyde's string of murders.

Of course, a straightforward presentation of the events as Dr. Jekyll experiences them first-hand is a richer cinematic construction than Utterson's mere study of the events. Therefore, the Dr. Jekyll character always is the protagonist, and Utterson, Lanyon, and especially Enfield are often not even included in the film.

Ian McLellan Hunter's Edgar Award-winning script for Curtis does include Enfield (Geoffrey Alexander), Lanyon (Leo Genn), and Utterson although the latter's name is changed to George Devlin (Denholm Elliott). While shifting the focus to Jekyll (Jack Palance), the script, set in London in 1888, remains faithful to the tone of Stevenson's novel. Devlin looks into the matter of Hyde (as Utterson does in the novel), quizzes Jekyll about him, and asks if Hyde is blackmailing Jekyll. Jekyll and Lanyon's strained friendship plays a part as does the faithfulness of Jekyll's butler Poole (Gillie Fenwick). The script also recreates the scene in which Poole summons Jekyll's solicitor to investigate Hyde's pathetic howling in Jekyll's laboratory while, in Stevenson's words in chapter eight, "the whole of the servants, men and women, stood huddled together like a flock of sheep" in their fright.[28] Although in the novel Hyde beats Sir Danvers Carew to death, in this version Hyde beats but does not kill Dr. Lanyon, and although in the novel Hyde changes back to Jekyll before Lanyon's eyes, here Hyde transforms in front of Devlin. The adaptation forgoes Jekyll's suicide for a more sensational climax, a deadly confrontation between Devlin and Hyde in the very room (the hospital amphitheatre) where the movie opens.

In the same vein as Gabriel Utterson's investigation of Edward Hyde's actions, this Henry Jekyll must investigate Mr. Hyde's actions of the night before because Jekyll, at first, has no knowledge of what Hyde has done. This search leads Jekyll to Tessie O'Toole's Windmill music hall, a necessary invention of scriptwriter Hunter's in order to inject heterosexuality and women's roles into the teleplay. Tessie (played by Tessie O'Shea) is a chanteuse and madam who warmly welcomes Dr. Jekyll and informs him that Mr. Hyde "took a real shine to" her employee Gwyneth Thomas, a "dancer" who also privately entertains men in the upstairs "dining rooms." As Gwyneth, Billie Whitelaw (*The Flesh and the Fiends*) provides Mr. Hyde with a female object of desire. However, Hunter offers another subtle hint at Jekyll's "irregularities" when on two different occasions Gwyn offers Jekyll a "cure" for his (in her word) "shyness," which could connote sexual repression, impotence, or homosexuality.

The Strange Case of Dr. Jekyll and Mr. Hyde debuted on the Canadian Broadcasting Corporation network (CBC) on Wednesday 3 January 1968, and it first aired on the American Broadcasting Company network (ABC) on Sunday 7 January. The production received overwhelmingly positive reviews. "It was incredibly gratifying," Dan Curtis remembered. "The reviews on that thing were absolutely incredible."[29] The *Baltimore Sun* raved,

> Dan Curtis, producer of *The Strange Case of Dr. Jekyll and Mr. Hyde*, introduced on ABC last Sunday, made good on all his promises. It was indeed a version of the Robert Louis Stevenson story never before seen in photoplay or television form; it adhered closely to the book; and the artistry of Dick Smith, master of makeup, did surpass anything seen in earlier transformations. What's more, the production, co-produced by the Canadian Broadcasting Corporation, surpassed the best version hitherto offered—the one in which Fredric March played the title role [and won an Oscar for it]. Jack Palance is the new champion in this difficult assignment, and he may hold the title for a long time.[30]

The *Boston Globe* concurred: "Jack Palance, a rugged villain from way back, for my money was the best Jekyll-and-Hyde yet to come along."[31] The *Sacramento Union* added,

> With its overpowering sense of time and place, the production proved immensely effective, all very dark and shadowy and Gothic—and scary. I bow to Dan Curtis and Charles Jarrott, producer and director, for framing the yarn so adeptly. Robert Cobert's music was properly spooky, too, alive with jabs of tense foreboding.[32]

The Strange Case of Dr. Jekyll and Mr. Hyde is scored with *Dark Shadows* music—in a way. Although *Dark Shadows* fans who watch the program today recognize almost every note of music as coming from the 1968-1971 years of the TV series, these music cues actually originated in this 1968 production. Cobert later re-recorded them for use on *Dark Shadows*, and these actual cues were used as the music score of *House of Dark Shadows* two years later. The heartbreaking, operatic music heard at Jekyll and Hyde's death is the same used at the staking of Barnabas Collins at the end of the 1970 film. (The cue was used yet again at the climaxes of Curtis's 1973 adaptations of *Frankenstein* and *The Picture of Dorian Gray*.) Most remarkably, the bouncy music-hall ditties that Cobert composed for the scenes at Tessie O'Toole's music hall took on new life on the *Dark Shadows* TV series as "I'm Gonna Dance for You," associated with Nancy Barrett's Pansy Faye character, and "Quentin's Theme," the hit record and Grammy Award nominee forever associated with David Selby's several Quentin Collins characters on TV and in *Night of Dark Shadows* (1971). "When Dan told me there was a new spook [Quentin] coming on *Dark Shadows* and he needed a theme song," Cobert laughed, "I said, 'You remember what I wrote for Billie Whitelaw? You loved that! Use that!'"[33]

The Strange Case of Dr. Jekyll and Mr. Hyde, which ABC reran on Wednesday 25 June 1969, was a prestigious entry into prime-time television producing for Dan Curtis. He, Charles Jarrott, Ian Hunter, and Jack Palance had created a quality production that enjoyed several TV airings and later life on VHS and DVD. According to *Cleveland Plain Dealer* film and television critic Mark Dawidziak,

> Although often overlooked because it was done for the so-called "small screen" and shot on videotape, this Curtis gem is cherished by a fiercely devoted group of horror fans, Stevenson devotees, and TV scholars. The

sheer brilliance of this *Dr. Jekyll and Mr. Hyde* demands special attention in any discussion of the Curtis career and accomplishments.[34]

The television academy took notice and bestowed four technical and two major Emmy Award nominations on *Dr. Jekyll and Mr. Hyde.* Tony Award-winning Welsh music-hall entertainer Tessie O'Shea was nominated for Outstanding Supporting Actress in a Drama Series or Special but lost to Barbara Anderson for *Ironside. Jekyll and Hyde* was nominated for Outstanding Dramatic Program of 1967-1968 but lost to *Elizabeth the Queen*, a *Hallmark Hall of Fame* drama co-starring Judith Anderson and Charlton Heston. Despite losing all six awards, the Dan Curtis production took its place in television history as an early example of Curtis's brand of "ornately atmospheric horror," in the words of *The Hollywood Reporter*.[35]

Back in New York in 1969, Curtis unveiled **Dead of Night: A Darkness at Blaisedon**, an unsold pilot about ghost hunters (ABC, Tuesday 26 August). This hour-long videotaped drama essentially was an attempt to duplicate *Dark Shadows* in prime time, complete with *Dark Shadows* personnel in front of the camera (Thayer David, Louis Edmonds) and behind it (Robert Cobert, Sam Hall, Lela Swift, Trevor Williams).

The director of *Dead of Night* was Curtis's *Dark Shadows* director Lela Swift. *Dark Shadows* star Kathryn Leigh Scott called Swift (1919-2015) "a remarkable, seasoned, award-winning woman director, who was a pioneer in the era of live television [*Suspense, The Web*]. She was present for all initial casting and directed the premiere episode of *Dark Shadows.* Dan became her protégé. She stood by, mentoring Dan when he directed his first episodes of the show, and advised him on his first feature, *House of Dark Shadows*."[36] Naturally, Curtis entrusted his nighttime pilot to Lela Swift.

In the autumn of 1968, Swift directed *A Darkness at Blaisedon* at NBC Studios in Brooklyn, New York. Dan Curtis produced the pilot, and Robert Cobert scored it with his tried-and-true *Dark Shadows* music cues, as well as some new compositions. According to film-music expert Jon Burlingame, "Cobert believed that his penchant for using vibraphone and percussion as suspense-generating devices originated with this project; the *Dead of Night* music cues resurfaced on *Dark Shadows*."[37] Indeed, the pilot's main-title theme later became the *Dark Shadows* cue associated with the disembodied head of Judah Zachery in the 1840 storyline in 1970.

Kerwin Mathews (*The Seventh Voyage of Sinbad*) stars as psychic investigator Jonathan Fletcher, and Sajeed Rau plays his assistant Cal Bellini. The split-level set of Fletcher's Greenwich Village apartment would have appeared every week if *Dead of Night* had become a series. Art director Trevor Williams also created the foyer, library, staircase, and other areas of Blaisedon, a Victorian mansion somewhere on the Hudson River, as well as the cottage of its caretaker Seth Blakely. As played by Thayer David, Seth was a close approximation of David's initial *Dark Shadows* role as the surly caretaker Matthew Morgan.

Dark Shadows fans have often remarked that their favorite show featured almost every type of monster except a mummy. A mummy does appear in Paperback Library's *Barnabas, Quentin, and the Mummy's Curse* (April 1970), by Dan "Marilyn" Ross, and in Gold Key Comics' *Dark Shadows* #6 (August 1970), by Don Arneson, as well as in *Dead of Night* (not to mention *Ryan's Hope*, the serial that Lela Swift directed after *Dark Shadows*). As *Dead of Night* begins, Jonathan Fletcher and Cal Bellini are studying an

Egyptian mummy "from the sixth century B.C."—Sam Hall's indication that these characters have had adventures before this "first episode." Jonathan later reveals that he dropped out of law school and became a psychic investigator when his father's ghost appeared to him.

Dead of Night: A Darkness at Blaisedon (1969): Cal Bellini (as Sajeed Rau) and Kerwin Mathews (as Jonathan Fletcher) confront the supernatural in this unsold pilot, shot in the Brooklyn, New York, television studio where *Another World* and later *As the World Turns* are produced.

A Darkness at Blaisedon serves as the "origin episode" of the character who would have co-starred with the two men if *Dead of Night* had become a series. Angela Martin (Marj Dusay) starts out as the men's client, but by the end of the hour, she has decided to quit her secretarial job in San Francisco and go ghost-hunting with her new friends.

Angela has inherited the great house of Blaisedon and wants to sell it but cannot because it is haunted by the vengeful ghost of Commodore Nicholas Blaise (*Dark Shadows* star Louis Edmonds) and his younger wife. Melinda Blaise died, apparently of influenza, in 1916 at age 28. Her husband, the Commodore, followed her in death one year later at age 64. Now, their ghosts haunt Blaisedon, and Lela Swift uses several high-angle shots to suggest that a presence is hovering over the house and watching Jonathan, Angela, and Cal.

In a reprise of the seminal *Dark Shadows* storyline—later reused in Curtis's *House of Dark Shadows* (1970) and *Dracula* (1974)—a living woman resembles another character's long-dead beloved. Angela Martin looks exactly like Melinda Blaise (as seen in a painting), and the Commodore's ghost covets her. At one point, Angela slips Melinda's ring on to her finger and becomes possessed by Melinda—a plot device that coincidentally was central to the initial months of the syndicated Canadian television serial *Strange Paradise* (1969-1970), written by Ian Martin.

In *A Darkness at Blaisedon,* Sam Hall tries out a couple of ideas that would later shape his and Dan Curtis's script of *Night of Dark Shadows* (1971). Caretaker Seth Blakely, like *NODS* housekeeper Carlotta Drake, is aware of the presence of the ghost in the house and seeks to assist its mission of controlling the living. Melinda Blaise, like Angelique Collins, is wrongfully accused of something. Just as Angelique is accused of being a witch but is not, Melinda is accused of infidelity when she actually has been faithful to the insanely jealous Commodore. Evidence that Jonathan Fletcher finds in a secret room and an opened grave bears this out.

Dead of Night echoes *Dark Shadows* not only in music, sets, and cast but also in the aforementioned grave-digging and secret-room plot points, as well as in a séance conducted by Jonathan, Angela, Cal, and the caretaker. Lela Swift shoots the actors, at their séance table, from above to show how their fingers are "touching at all times."

Viewers who happened to catch *Dead of Night: A Darkness at Blaisedon* in its one-and-only showing on Tuesday 26 August 1969 were treated to an atmospheric and viable (if slow-moving) nighttime reincarnation of *Dark Shadows*. However, ABC passed on the pilot, and it did not become a series.

According to Dark Shadows Festival chairman Jim Pierson, "Dan wanted to transfer *Dark Shadows*-style success to prime-time, but ABC decided *Blaisedon* wouldn't work in prime-time with a *Dark Shadows* videotape format. It should have been half an hour, too."[38] Long after its one network airing, *Dead of Night: A Darkness at Blaisedon* came to VHS in 1992 and to DVD in 2008.

The 1970s began with Curtis's direction of the aforementioned 1970 MGM theatrical feature **House of Dark Shadows** at the Lyndhurst estate in Tarrytown, New York, while the *Dark Shadows* TV series continued. The film, written by Sam Hall and Gordon Russell, was shot between Monday 23 March and Friday 1 May 1970. Half of the television cast (including Jonathan Frid and Grayson Hall) filmed the movie in Tarrytown while the other half (including David Selby and Lara Parker) carried the TV show in Manhattan.

MGM rented Lyndhurst for Curtis and his 55 actors and crew members for $35,000. Curtis filmed in most of the mansion's rooms and bedrooms, all laden with antiques and paintings, and he also utilized the estate's huge coach house (glimpsed in one 1966 episode of *Dark Shadows* itself), the barren greenhouse (for a scene cut from the film), and the empty, crumbling indoor swimming pool (for one of the most frightening scenes of the movie—"If I catch this one, Carolyn isn't dead"). Curtis and his cast and crew also filmed scenes at the Sleepy Hollow Cemetery, down the street from Lyndhurst; in Scarborough, New York; and in Westport and Norwalk, Connecticut.

Curtis and the cast and crew commuted to and from Lyndhurst, only an hour's drive from Manhattan, for the nine-hour work days. Curtis filmed only during the day; he used the day-for-night lensing technique for nighttime scenes. The cast used the basement of Lyndhurst for wardrobe and screening rooms, the souvenir shop for the makeup room, and the stable for a cafeteria. Kathryn Leigh Scott remarked, "We'd worked together so long as a close-knit group, isolated in our TV studio on West 53rd Street. Filming on location at Lyndhurst seemed like a natural extension—we'd just taken our show on the road."[39]

House of Dark Shadows (1970): Jonathan Frid stars as the vampire Barnabas Collins in the MGM feature.

House of Dark Shadows is a bloodier, more violent retelling of the TV show's 1967 storyline, in which Willie Loomis (John Karlen) releases the 18th-century vampire Barnabas Collins (Jonathan Frid) from his chained coffin in the Collins mausoleum. Barnabas violently preys on the residents of Collinsport, Maine, and he mesmerizes Maggie Evans (Kathryn Leigh Scott), who bears an uncanny resemblance to his lost 1790s love Josette DuPres. During the course of the film, Barnabas strangles several characters to death, he cruelly beats Willie, and he vampirizes his cousin Carolyn

Stoddard (Nancy Barrett), her uncle Roger Collins (Louis Edmonds), and the Collinses' friend, Professor Stokes (Thayer David).

The *Dark Shadows* TV series spotlighted Gothic mystery and doomed romance over violence and body counts, so the gory mayhem of *House of Dark Shadows* was a jarring shift in tone. Frid, who had patented the reluctant, conflicted vampire on *Dark Shadows*, now found himself playing a monster in *House of Dark Shadows*. Barnabas makes Willie his Renfield and Carolyn his slave. Lovesick Dr. Julia Hoffman attempts to cure him of his vampirism and give him a normal life, but she intentionally gives him an overdose of her serum when she realizes that he has chosen Maggie instead of her. Barnabas ages rapidly and displays Dick Smith's horrifying old-age makeup design. Smith recalled, "We decided to make Barnabas bald with a veined, mottled, liver-spotted head, which we basically improvised, on the set."[40] Smith reworked the Old Barnabas design for Dustin Hoffman in Arthur Penn's *Little Big Man* (1970). Later, *The Texas Chainsaw Massacre* (1974) imitated Smith's makeup.

In return for her betrayal of him, Barnabas strangles Julia to death. Although in 1967 the TV Barnabas threatened Julia's life several times, he never would have gone through with such an atrocity. *House of Dark Shadows* demonstrates the diabolical trajectory that the Barnabas character would have followed if Dan Curtis had stuck to his original plan of "letting him bite and kill people for a cycle [13 weeks of soap-opera episodes] and then driving a stake through his heart."[41] Indeed, the film concludes (in a lurid scene shot on Friday 1 May 1970 at the Lockwood-Mathews Mansion in Norwalk, Connecticut) with the bloody running-through of Barnabas by the arrow from a crossbow. Barnabas's death occurs after Carolyn has been staked (in another of the film's most stunning sequences), Stokes has been shot through the heart, and Roger has been impaled on a spear. Although most of the cast has been killed, *House of Dark Shadows* manages a traditional happy ending as Jeff Clark (Roger Davis) rescues his love interest Maggie from the bloodsucker. However, it is not Jeff who is the true hero of the film but poor, hapless Willie, who gives his life to destroy his master. This shattering sequence is scored to Robert Cobert's emotional "Death of Hyde" music cue from *The Strange Case of Dr. Jekyll and Mr. Hyde* (1968).

Cobert wanted to write original music for the film, but Curtis wanted to reuse the TV show music. "I fought Dan tooth and nail on that decision but ultimately lost. While the budget was part of Dan's concern, I sincerely feel that he wanted to use the existing music because the fans liked it and Dan thought they would enjoy hearing it in the film."[42]

Cobert was correct in his observation—the legions of *Dark Shadows* fans certainly did like the familiar music cues—and Curtis was correct in his decision to re-use those cues (actually Cobert's *Jekyll and Hyde* score which had been re-recorded and re-used on *Dark Shadows*). The music of *Dark Shadows* was just as much a character on the show as Barnabas or Elizabeth, and Curtis wanted the fans to have that familiar musical touchstone as a consolation to their forced adjustments to a new Collinwood (Lyndhurst), a new level of violence (gory bitings and stakings), and a somewhat new Barnabas (an out-and-out villain).

House of Dark Shadows **(1970): Thayer David (as Prof. Stokes) accuses Grayson Hall (as Dr. Hoffman) of being in love with a vampire.**

Frederick S. Clarke's *Cinefantastique* magazine—the *Time* or *Newsweek* of all things horror—declared, "The seventies have begun with an inordinate number of vampire films, [and] *House of Dark Shadows* is the superior film of the crop—a fast-paced, harrowing thriller." Clarke continued,

> The screenplay by Sam Hall and Gordon Russell is highly inventive; however, credit for the film's unqualified success must go to director Dan Curtis, who previously had exhibited his skill in the genre by producing, incomparably, the finest version of Robert Louis Stevenson's *Dr. Jekyll and Mr. Hyde* on television several seasons ago. Curtis provides *House of Dark Shadows* with a stylistic flair indelibly his own, a restless, roving visual sense, never content in projecting a static image. Curtis directs Arthur Ornitz's excellent camerawork not at a scene but into it, through it, and around it with an hypnotically fluid ebb and flow of nightmarish montage.[43]

Donald F. Glut, author of *The Dracula Book* (Scarecrow, 1975), added, "Barnabas dies in one of the most vivid stakings ever recorded on film. The fast-paced, atmospheric, and graphic film proved that Curtis was capable of transforming a television soap opera into one of the finest horror films of the year."[44] In the early 1970s, *House of Dark Shadows* was released or re-released on double bills with such diverse films as *The Brotherhood of Satan, Dusty and Sweets McGee, Every Little Crook and Nanny,* and *The Traveling Executioner*.[45]

Meanwhile, on ABC-TV, just as *Dark Shadows,* after the introduction of Barnabas, had gone up like a rocket, it eventually came down just as abruptly. In late 1970, some of the audience—as well as Curtis himself—"became disenchanted" with the TV show, in Curtis's words.[46] Indeed, the viewership had fallen from 18 million to 12 million. Curtis admitted that he lost interest in *Dark Shadows* during the last six months of the show.[47] The final episode, set in the alternate universe of 1841 Parallel Time, was taped on Wednesday 24 March and aired on Friday 2 April 1971.

Five days after the 1225th and final episode had been taped, Curtis began directing **Night of Dark Shadows** (MGM, 1971) on the Lyndhurst estate. Shooting stretched through April and ended on Friday 7 May 1971.

After Jonathan Frid refused to play a risen Barnabas, Curtis abandoned his idea of another vampire movie and, with Sam Hall, crafted a psychological ghost story similar to the TV show's 1970 Parallel Time storyline, which itself was an homage to Daphne Du Maurier's 1938 novel *Rebecca*.[48] *Night of Dark Shadows* also bears a strong resemblance to Charles Beaumont and Roger Corman's 1963 film *The Haunted Palace,* based on H.P. Lovecraft's 1927 story "The Case of Charles Dexter Ward." Both *The Haunted Palace* and *Night of Dark Shadows* involve the public execution of a witch, significant ancestral portraits, an attempted marital rape, a husband (Vincent Price, David Selby) influenced by a ghost, his anguished wife (Debra Paget, Kate Jackson) whom he endangers, and a sinister housekeeper (Lon Chaney Jr., Grayson Hall) who exacerbates the problems.

Under the best of circumstances, *Night of Dark Shadows* faced an uphill battle. It was released four months after *Dark Shadows* had been cancelled, and it lacked the vampire angle that had defined the TV series. Furthermore, *Night of Dark Shadows* lost its soul on the cutting-room floor. As written and filmed, Curtis's follow-up to *House of Dark Shadows* would have been superior to that film and could have been at least a minor masterpiece of early-1970s horror cinema because of its numerous timely qualities (*déjà vu,* reincarnation, witchcraft, ghosts, and a downbeat ending). Instead, Curtis was forced, under a tight deadline, to cut his 129-minute film to 97 minutes. At the behest of the MPAA, the studio subsequently cut it even further, to 93.5 minutes. What is left is a confusing, often unsatisfying narrative which nevertheless delivers enough atmosphere and impact for the *Boston Globe* to call the movie "a cut above the average" and "a horror film for people who don't really like horror films."[49]

Artist Quentin Collins (David Selby) and his wife Tracy (Kate Jackson) move in to Quentin's inheritance, the Collinwood estate, sternly run by Carlotta Drake (Grayson Hall) and handyman Gerard Stiles (James Storm). Soon, Quentin begins having dreams and visions of his lookalike ancestor, Charles Collins, also a painter, who lived at Collinwood in 1810. Quentin is especially drawn to Collinwood's mysterious tower room, where Charles had an affair with Angelique (Lara Parker), his brother's wife, before her public hanging for witchcraft. Angelique's spirit still haunts Collinwood, and Carlotta tells Quentin that he is the reincarnation of Charles Collins and the vessel through which Angelique and Charles's love will live again. Carlotta declares that she herself is the reincarnation of Sarah Castle (Monica Rich), a young girl who lived at Collinwood in 1810 and who witnessed Angelique's unjust hanging.

Night of Dark Shadows (1971): Grayson Hall (as Carlotta Drake) and David Selby (as Quentin Collins) pose outside the Lyndhurst mansion in Tarrytown, New York.

As Quentin falls under the spell of the house and its beautiful ghost, he takes on the identity of his ancestor. He attempts to rape and later drown Tracy, whom he and Carlotta see as a threat to Angelique's plan for Quentin and Collinwood. Quentin, with the help of Tracy and their Gothic-novelist friends Claire and Alex Jenkins (Nancy Barrett and John Karlen), attempts to resist his possession. The deaths of Gerard and Carlotta seem to vanquish the ghost, and the Collinses and the Jenkinses prepare to leave Collinwood forever. Then, Quentin must go back into the house one last time to retrieve his canvases.

When Dan Curtis delivered his 129-minute opus to MGM chief James Aubrey, Aubrey demanded drastic cuts—and gave Curtis as little time as 11 hours to submit them! Aubrey, the so-called Smiling Cobra who at different times tyrannized MGM and CBS, was the basis for the ruthless television executive Robin Stone in Jacqueline Susann's 1969 novel *The Love Machine*. In his film career, Aubrey was accused of tampering with movies by Blake Edwards, Ken Russell, and Sam Peckinpah, as well as this one by Dan Curtis. Therefore, on a moment's notice, Curtis and an MGM staff editor were forced to eviscerate *Night of Dark Shadows* in order to please Aubrey.

As a result, several of Quentin's dream sequences are consolidated, thereby causing his pajamas to change from yellow to blue in the course of one night's sleep. The Jenkinses are edited out of some scenes, and much of Angelique's part is cut. As the film now stands, the audience does not know how Gerard and Carlotta are related (he is her nephew), why Tracy goes to the pool house (she had a dream about it), why Quentin/Charles tries to drown her there (Charles drowned his wife Laura in 1810), why Quentin/Charles limps (off-camera, he fell off his horse), or why Laura Collins (Diana Millay) laughs during Angelique's funeral (Angelique's body is not really in the coffin but is entombed with a still-living Charles in a secret room beneath Collinwood). The viewers also do not understand the reverend's line about Angelique's "threats" (her spoken curse on her executioners is deleted, thereby making the original title *Curse of Dark Shadows* meaningless), and they see Carlotta re-hang Angelique's portrait when they never saw it removed in the first place. Most significantly, what would have been the film's most important and powerful scene—a séance conducted by Quentin, Tracy, Alex, and Claire and the revelation that Angelique was *not* a witch—does not appear in the movie and shortchanges the effect of the ending. Nevertheless, the final moments—when the audience learns the fates of the characters—still have the power to stun. According to *Video Watchdog* editor Tim Lucas, "The material may be derivative, but it is consistently well-handled by writer-director Curtis, and the downbeat finale [. . .] is stimulating."[50]

When Aubrey viewed Curtis's hastily shortened film, he announced, "It's a tight little thriller." Curtis insisted, "But the film doesn't make sense any more!" Aubrey retorted, "With *your* audience, it doesn't matter!"[51]

Understandably, some reviews of the truncated *Night of Dark Shadows* were lackluster. A.H. Weiler, in the *New York Times*, pronounced the movie "a bore" but complimented the many atmospheric shots of Lyndhurst. Weiler wrote, "The attraction of this dour adventure is Lyndhurst, the Gothic Revival mansion, where the film was shot. Its many period rooms, paintings, and objects d'art are richly eye-filling. The somber story shot there, however, is strictly for the low-rent district."[52] Indeed, the titles of the two *Dark Shadows* films could be switched. The Barnabas movie is all about what happens at *night*, while the Quentin film lovingly shows off the bedrooms, stairways, second-floor gallery, and tower room of this Gothic *house* of dark shadows. The *Boston Globe* also noted the film's "visual beauty."[53]

Night of Dark Shadows (1971): Christopher Pennock (as Gabriel Collins), Diana Millay (as Laura Collins), and Thayer David (as Rev. Strack) play a scene set in 1810.

The *San Francisco Examiner* observed, "Dan Curtis, who created the TV series, directed the film in a slow, languid style that contributes to the evocation of a menacing climate."[54] Sensing that important elements were missing from the film, Roger Ebert, in the *Chicago Sun-Times,* added, "Toward the end of the movie, not a lot goes on except for double takes, screams, and lots of bleeding."[55] Granted, the film effectively builds, but the re-edited payoff is hasty and minimal.

Even Robert Cobert's eerie music score suffers in the forced edit. Some of his cues end abruptly, and the scene that explains the film's frequent use of "Quentin's Theme" does not appear in the 93.5-minute cut. In a missing 1810 flashback, Angelique plays the unnamed melody on the piano and tells Charles that the music reminds her of him. The lovers are interrupted by the appearance of Laura, Quentin's wife. The film uses several new recordings of "Quentin's Theme," as well as weird echo effects and some unnerving chase music played on strings and bongo drums.

The love theme from *Night of Dark Shadows* is one of Cobert's most haunting melodies. The tune originated as a piano solo in the final months of the TV series. For the film, Cobert follows a piano rendition of the love theme with a refrain played on harmonica and guitar, a novel combination for Cobert but appropriate to the film's early-1970s origins. Cobert re-used the love theme in *The Invasion of Carol Enders,* a late-night ABC *Wide World Mystery* drama (Friday 8 March 1974) produced by Dan Curtis and directed by Burt Brinkerhoff (*Come Die with Me*).

Laura's intrusion upon Quentin and Angelique at the piano is one of many scenes—approximately 25 percent of the finished film—which Aubrey forced Curtis to eliminate. Other missing scenes, as evidenced in Hall and Curtis's complete shooting script, are Quentin and Tracy's picnic, Quentin's removal of Angelique's portrait, several clarifying discussions, and the all-important séance. In 1989, I wrote and directed *The Night Before,* a play that reinstated many of the missing scenes and afforded the audience at that year's Dark Shadows Festival a seriocomic feel for what the complete *Night of Dark Shadows* might have been like. In 1997, film historian Darren Gross definitively reconstructed the film in the pages of Donna and Tim Lucas's *Video Watchdog* magazine.

Then, in August 1999, Gross found the long-lost, one-and-only 129-minute color separations (footage) of *Night of Dark Shadows* in a film-storage vault in a Kansas City salt mine. Gross recalled, "Being able to finally see all the shots from this legendary [séance] sequence was such a thrilling revelation that I had to stifle any yelps of joy."[56]

Darren Gross and Jim Pierson launched an effort to reconstruct the film for a definitive DVD release. Because only 100 minutes of the soundtrack survive, all of the film's living stars re-recorded their missing dialogue. "That was the hardest I've ever worked!" David Selby told me at the 2008 Dark Shadows Festival. "We had the script, but we didn't know the *exact* words we'd said, so they brought in lip-reading specialists to help us match our dialogue to the picture."[57] Sadly, even with so much of the work toward reconstruction completed, Warner Brothers released a DVD and Blu-Ray of the familiar *cut* version of *Night of Dark Shadows* on 30 October 2012 when it also released *House of Dark Shadows* on DVD and Blu-Ray. (No extra footage of *HODS* still exists.) Perhaps, some day, Warner Brothers will add the missing scenes, either at their correct points within the movie or as DVD extras, in a new, definitive re-release.

Later in 1971, with *Dark Shadows* seemingly behind them, Norma and Dan Curtis and their three daughters spent time on the West Coast before they permanently relocated from New York to California in 1972. For the next eight years (and in the following three decades), Curtis produced and/or directed a string of highly successful made-for-TV movies that captivated an entire generation of baby boomers and their parents. The nights of Dan Curtis productions—horror and Western in the 1970s, war in the 1980s, et al.—were about to begin.

First came **The Night Stalker** (ABC, Tuesday 11 January 1972), the *ABC Movie of the Week* that introduced the character of Carl Kolchak (Darren McGavin), a rumpled, seedy reporter on the trail of a vampire (Barry Atwater) in modern-day Las Vegas. Based on a novel by Jeff Rice (1944-2015), scripted by the great fantasy author Richard Matheson (*I Am Legend, The Shrinking Man, Somewhere in Time*), produced by Curtis, and directed (in August-September 1971) by John Llewellyn Moxey (*The House That Would Not Die, The Last Child, Genesis II*), *The Night Stalker* scored an enormous viewership (a 33.2 rating and a 54 share, representing 75 million viewers) and remains (as of 2019) in the top 20 highest-rated made-for-TV movies. Matheson won the Edgar Award for his script. Stephen King remarked that Matheson "has written for TV with better pace and more dramatic flair than anyone since Reginald Rose" (*Playhouse 90, Studio One, The Twilight Zone*).[58]

Curtis, Matheson, and Moxey give The Night Stalker a *film-noir* feel as the movie opens on a lone man (McGavin), down on his luck and inhabiting a seedy rented room. Like many *film-noir* anti-heroes before him, Carl Kolchak narrates the film. The reporter begins,

> Chapter One. This is the story behind one of the greatest manhunts in history. Maybe you read about it, or rather what they *let* you read about it, probably in some minor item buried somewhere in a back page. However, what happened in that city between May 16 and May 28 of this year was so incredible that to this day the facts have been suppressed in a massive effort to save certain political careers from disaster and law-enforcement officials from embarrassment. This will be the last time I will ever discuss these events with anyone, so when you have finished this bizarre account, judge for yourself its believability and then try to tell yourself, wherever you may be, "It couldn't happen here."

Kolchak concludes the film with those same final four words. Curtis, Matheson, and Moxey were struck by the traditional yet modern nature of Jeff Rice's story, and they successfully imbued the TV-movie with that double-edged sensibility. *The Night Stalker* has the feel of docudrama or, as Matheson characterized it, *cinema verite*. The film details an entire city government's investigation, along with one determined reporter's investigation, of the crimes of a real vampire. The movie showcases the inner workings of the Las Vegas Police Department, the district attorney's office, and the *Las Vegas Daily News* as all of those agencies face this outlandish threat. Even the Las Vegas coroner's office becomes involved via an autopsy scene—from the unsettling point of view of the corpse. At Matheson and Curtis's suggestion, Moxey's camera looks *up* at the medical examiners as they point their scalpels downward. Also, what could be more modern and *real* than the sight of a vampire driving a rented car?

Kolchak humanizes the vampire's victims—Las Vegas showgirls and cocktail waitresses walking alone at night—by listing, in his narration, the dead women's names, ages, occupations, weights, dates and times of the attacks, and other vital statistics. These cold, hard facts add to the modern, clinical feel of the proceedings, as does the press conference that Kolchak attends (and disrupts). Back in the newsroom, Kolchak's altercations with his volatile editor Tony Vincenzo (Simon Oakland) set a seriocomic tone that lasts through all 22 original adventures of Carl Kolchak (*The Night Stalker*, *The Night Strangler*, and 20 episodes of producer Cy Chermak's *Kolchak: The Night Stalker*).

Darren McGavin (left) and Simon Oakland co-star in *The Night Stalker* (1972) and *The Night Strangler* (1973)—both Dan Curtis productions—as well as on the 1974-1975 television series *Kolchak: The Night Stalker* (not a Dan Curtis production).

Another innovative technique is that *The Night Stalker* is not the story of a vampire, per se, as is the case in such films as *Nosferatu* (1922), *Dracula* (1931), *Horror of Dracula* (1958), and *House of Dark Shadows* (1970). *The Night Stalker* (1972) is the story of a reporter—a regular type of guy—and the vampire is a secondary character. Plus, the all-too-real notions of cover-ups and corruption are just as much the monsters of the story as is the vampire Janos Skorzeny. Kolchak defeats Skorzeny (Barry Atwater), but he cannot vanquish censorship or suppression of the facts.

At the same time that *The Night Stalker* demonstrates what would happen if a vampire showed up in a real city like Las Vegas, the film has a traditional side that ties it to classic horror. The story, after all, is a vampire melodrama that climaxes in that most classic of vampires' lairs—an old, dark house—in this case, a dilapidated home that Skorzeny has rented on an otherwise ordinary street on the outskirts of Las Vegas. The house, actually located near Echo Park in Los Angeles, was seen again in Curtis's *When Every Day Was the Fourth of July* (1978).

All of the classic vampire trappings are present: Skorzeny's coffin (even with the added detail of the bloodsucker's native soil inside the casket); Kolchak's explanation of the rules of vampirism; Carl's crucifix, hammer, and mallet; the sunlight that stuns Skorzeny; and the obligatory staking scene. However, another reality check is that after Kolchak stakes the vampire, he faces *murder* charges and must flee Las Vegas! The city officials, deciding that a vampire is "bad for business," have closed ranks, covered up the truth, and either paid off or run off everyone involved. Again, this is what probably would happen if a vampire invaded Las Vegas and threatened the status quo.

John Llewelyn Moxey (1925-2019) remembered that Dan Curtis was very much a presence on the set but did not interfere. "He was very full of helpful hints. [*The Night Stalker*] had a very good script and an innovative and clever storyline with well-drawn characters and a great cast. [Curtis] was the prime mover in bringing these first-rate people together, and everybody fit his particular role perfectly." Moxey remembered the stunt team as "wonderful" and the fight scenes as "still exciting today."[59]

Moxey continued, "*The Night Stalker* was very well publicized by ABC, and the promotion was well handled. There was a certain titillation about there being a vampire in Las Vegas. It tickled the imagination to read about it, and when people started watching, they stuck with it"[60]—to the tune of a record-high TV-movie viewership.

The success of *The Night Stalker* is due not to critics, who barely previewed or reviewed it outside of Los Angeles, but to the tantalizing ABC promos telecast in early January 1972 and to the viewers who made it such a huge hit. *The New York Times* did not review *The Night Stalker* although it described the film in its TV listings as, "Newsman fights censorship, from his editor and the police, trying to prove that Las Vegas is being terrorized by a vampire."[61] In just those few words, the *Times* at least had hit upon what a multi-faceted movie *The Night Stalker* is. The refreshing mixture of humor, horror, newspapers, and *film noir* can be viewed as a reporter-fights-vampire thriller movie or as a reporter-fights-censorship message film.

Another innovative touch is Robert Cobert's double-edged music—"detective jazz," as Cobert himself called it.[62] A detective show set to jazz music is nothing new—it dates back at least to Henry Mancini and his music for *Peter Gunn* (1958-1961)—but scoring a horror movie with "detective jazz" *is* something innovative. Cobert's theme for Carl Kolchak is a modern mixture of jazz and early-1970s funk while his background music accompanying the vampire's attacks on women and battles with police evokes a classic scary-movie sound, full of shimmering strings, shocking brass, and unnerving vibraphone.

"It was spooky stuff," Cobert explained, "but it wasn't a *Dark Shadows* type of spooky. I mean, it was Las Vegas in 1971. That's the whole point. You need something that is spooky but contemporary—something with an edge to it."[63] This dichotomy of modern jazziness versus classic frightfulness perfectly captures the hybrid nature of *The Night Stalker*: realistic, scary; funny, shocking; irreverent, morbid; clinical, supernatural. At some points in *The Night Stalker*, Cobert overlays his horror chords onto his jazz beat for the ultimate effect.

Around the time of *The Night Stalker* in 1972, *Logan's Run* novelist William F. Nolan adapted "Slaughter House," a 1953 story by Richard Matheson, for a possible *ABC Movie of the Week* to be directed by Dan Curtis. A TV-movie never materialized. Also in 1972, Dan Curtis signed Jack Palance to host a syndicated Viacom TV series tentatively titled *Classic Mystery Ghost Stories with Jack Palance*. According to Jim Pierson, "Unfortunately, no tape seems to exist, but wraparound intros were taped with Jack Palance for a pilot presentation."[64]

After the amazing success of *The Night Stalker*, ABC clamored for a sequel, and this time, Dan Curtis produced *and* directed Matheson's script of **The Night Strangler** (ABC, Tuesday 16 January 1973), again starring Darren McGavin as reporter Carl Kolchak and Simon Oakland as editor Tony Vincenzo.

In the sequel, Kolchak and Vincenzo have moved from Las Vegas to Seattle, and the Seattle Underground is the lair of this film's killer, a Civil War-era surgeon who has prolonged his life by concocting an elixir of longevity. Lest he revert to his actual age (as Barnabas Collins does in *House of Dark Shadows*), Dr. Richard Malcolm (Richard Anderson) must replenish his elixir—with the fresh blood of young women—every 21 years. Therefore, Seattle has suffered a spate of unsolved murders for 18-day periods in 1889, 1910, 1931, 1952, and now the present day of 1973. Thus, Carl Kolchak is back on the trail of a supernatural menace.

Matheson's original title for the sequel to *The Night Stalker* was *The Time Killer*, but ABC preferred the more familiar *The Night Strangler*. Dan Curtis filmed the movie over 12 days in Seattle and Los Angeles. The producer-director captured the local flavor of Seattle by showcasing Pioneer Square, the Seattle Underground, the Space Needle, and the city's monorail system. For decades afterwards, Seattle Underground tour guides still pointed out a loveseat prop used in *The Night Strangler* and discarded there. I saw it when I toured the Underground in May 2000.

The Night Strangler opens with more of Carl Kolchak's wry narration: "This is the story behind the most incredible series of murders ever to occur in the city of Seattle, Washington. You never read about them in your local newspapers or heard about them on your local radio or television station. Why? Because the facts were watered down, torn apart, and reassembled—in a word, falsified." Once again, an underlying theme is the people's right to know, and Kolchak is a noble crusader for that privilege.

Kolchak enlists the aid of belly dancer Louise Harper, who helps him locate Dr. Richard Malcolm in his underground laboratory. Jo Ann Pflug plays Louise with a mixture of intelligence and wackiness. Adding to the seriocomic feel of the film is the supporting cast of fondly remembered character actors: Wally Cox as an archivist, Al Lewis as a vagrant, Margaret Hamilton as a professor, and John Carradine as the *Daily Chronicle* publisher who orders Kolchak and Vincenzo out of town after he suppresses Kolchak's exclusive story of the 144-year-old murderer Malcolm. Instead, the noncommittal headline reads, KILLER FOUND—IDENTITY UNKNOWN.

Robert Cobert's "detective jazz" for *The Night Strangler* is even more aggressive in its use of saxophones and percussion for the upbeat theme, strings and vibraphone for scary interludes, and trumpets and muted trombone for weird effects. Cobert called his score "a combination of jazz and longhair music, with really wild harmonies."[65]

This time, many more critics sat up and took notice of *The Night Strangler* (viewed by 35 million TV households) and recognized a good movie when they saw one. Also, the critics noticed and commended the traditional/modern, scary/funny duality of *The Night Strangler*, a hallmark carried over from *The Night Stalker*. Kevin Thomas of the *Los Angeles Times* congratulated the sequel's "well-developed, amusing premise that places an old-style monster in a modern-day world coupled with genuine scariness, colorful characters, and sharp dialogue." Thomas continued,

> Dan Curtis, creator of the long-running horror serial *Dark Shadows*, has directed zestfully as well as produced, and once again Richard Matheson, working from characters created by Jeff Rice, has come through with a lively script. McGavin is terrific, and so is Simon Oakland, [both] well supported by delectable Jo Ann Pflug.[66]

Howard Thompson of the *New York Times* wrote, "This made-for-TV thriller is a yeasty surprise, blending laughs, local color, and real chills."[67] *The Hollywood Reporter* concurred that *The Night Strangler* "achieves its purpose: it is flat-out scary as hell."[68] Indeed, the newsroom high jinks, the Seattle scenery, and the horrific climax (in Malcolm's underground lair, full of cobwebs, test tubes, and rotting corpses) combine to deliver a realistic horror adventure equal to its groundbreaking predecessor.

Director Joe Dante (*Gremlins, Matinee, Small Soldiers*) observed, "I was a big fan of *The Night Stalker*, particularly the first two movies, and the second one, *The Night Strangler*, was surprisingly strong—much better than any sequel has a right to be. There were a lot of neat things going on in that."[69] A possible third Kolchak telefilm, *The Night Killers*, never materialized, and Curtis was not involved with ABC-TV's 20-episode series *Kolchak: The Night Stalker* (1974-1975), produced by Cy Chermak (*The Virginian, Ironside, The Bold Ones*).

Premiering on *Wide World Mystery* on the same night as *The Night Strangler* was **Frankenstein** (ABC, Tuesday 16 & Wednesday 17 January 1973), a largely faithful adaptation of Mary Shelley's 1818 novel, produced and co-written by Curtis (with Sam Hall and Richard Landau) and directed by Glenn Jordan (*Les Miserables, Dress Gray, Barbarians at the Gate*). *Frankenstein* was the first of seven late-night *Wide World Mystery* programs from Dan Curtis Productions in 1973 and 1974.

Curtis's *Frankenstein* takes place mostly in Ingolstadt, Germany, in 1856, more than a half-century after the novel's time setting. The movie's primary focus is on Dr. Victor Frankenstein (Robert Foxworth), the Creature (Bo Svenson), and Agatha DeLacey (Heidi Vaughn). Secondary focus is on Alphonse Frankenstein (Philip Bourneuf), Elizabeth Lavenza (Susan Strasberg), and Dr. Henri Clerval (Robert Gentry), all of whom frequently question Frankenstein about his erratic, obsessive behavior.

Darren McGavin (left) and Richard Anderson play antagonists in *The Night Strangler* (1973).

In this adaptation, Dr. Frankenstein has two lab assistants, Hugo (George Morgan) and Otto (*Dark Shadows* star John Karlen). Frankenstein uses the mortally wounded Hugo's heart as the creature's heart, and the creature later accidentally kills Otto by hugging him much too strongly after Otto has thrown a ball with him and taught him the words "Otto" and "play." Dr. Frankenstein finds the puzzled creature standing over the dead man and begging him, "Otto, play?" This is the first of many instances of poignancy and sympathy for the monster. An important trait of many of Dan Curtis's productions is a degree of sympathy for the evildoer, e.g. Barnabas Collins, Dr. Jekyll, the Night Strangler, Count Dracula, and the crook Harry Banner in *Me and the Kid* (1993). Curtis reflected, "I try to find an additional dimension to the monster. Sometimes, you actually end up feeling sorry for him. We certainly did that with Barnabas Collins and Dr. Jekyll."[70] Writers Curtis, Hall, and Landau and director Glenn Jordan achieve the same effect with the Giant (as Bo Svenson's character is called).

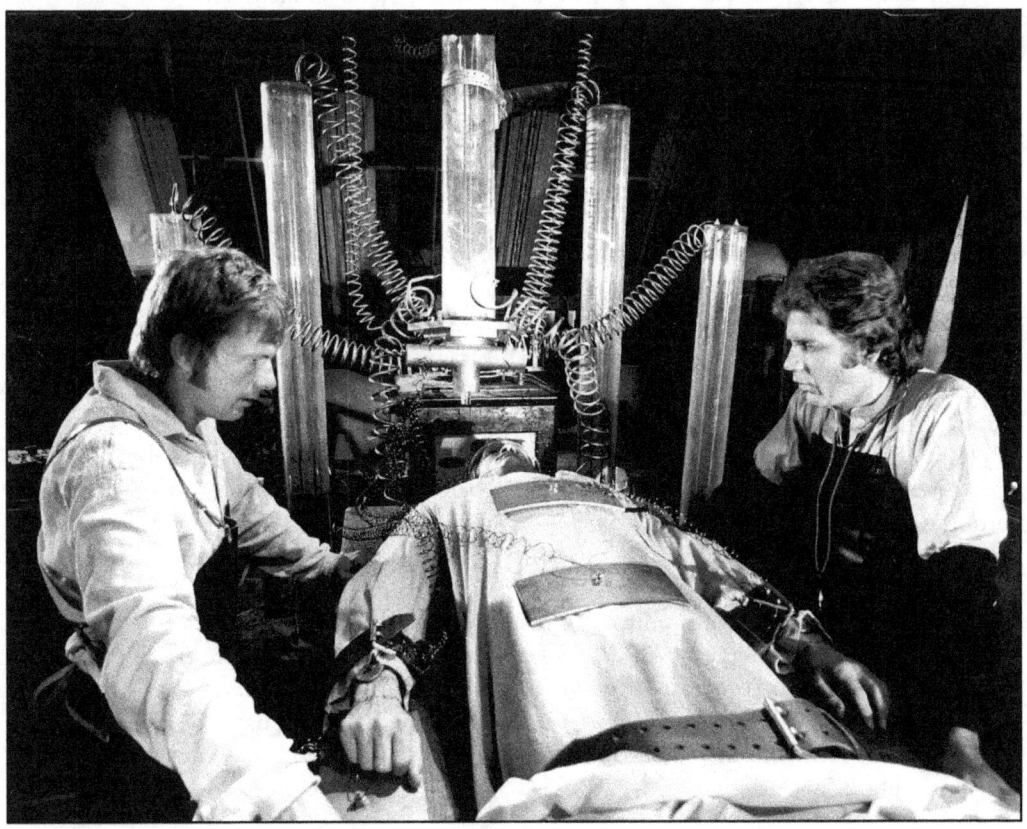

Frankenstein (1973): John Karlen (left), Bo Svenson (on table), and Robert Foxworth co-star in the two-night adaptation produced by Dan Curtis for ABC-TV's *Wide World Mystery*. The *Journal of Frankenstein* calls *Frankenstein* "quite good" and "an admirable adaptation" of Mary Shelley's 1818 novel.

Frankenstein garnered stellar reviews for Dan Curtis Productions. Cecil Smith of the *Los Angeles Times* wrote, "*Frankenstein* is the best shot yet in ABC's ongoing war to woo the midnight audience. Despite a miniscule budget, [*Frankenstein*] is quite a handsome show, with huge, foreboding sets and a splendid array of special effects."[71] *Variety* called the production "extraordinary entertainment" and declared, "*Frankenstein* marks a decided step forward in late-night entertainment. It's really too good to relegate to the insomniacs."[72]

Two years later, in his 1975 book *In Search of Frankenstein*, Radu Florescu paid Curtis the ultimate compliment when he wrote, "This 180-minute television film was probably the most faithful rendering the screen has yet seen." Florescu observed of this "really first-class" adaptation of Mary Shelley's 1818 novel that "for the very first time, an attempt was made to try and stay reasonably close to Mary Shelley's original conception of the monster." Florescu continued,

> With Robert Foxworth as Victor Frankenstein and Susan Strasberg as Elizabeth, Bo Svenson emerged as a literate, well-spoken, and sensitive monster. Although the plot once again had the creature created electrically rather than biologically, director Glenn Jordan adhered to Shelley's desire to have her monster seek a mate in order to pacify his destructive impulses. Admittedly, the intricate flashback mechanism of the novel was again shunted aside, but at least a sincerely admirable linkage between printed page and movie (or TV, in this case) screen was attempted.[73]

Next, attempting to recreate the reporter-versus-the-supernatural magic of the Kolchak films, Curtis directed **The Norliss Tapes** (NBC, Wednesday 21 February 1973) from a script by William F. Nolan (*Space for Hire*). Nolan adapted *The Norliss Tapes* from a story idea by novelist Fred Mustard Stewart (*The Mephisto Waltz*). "It had something to do with a walking dead man," Nolan recalled. "Beyond that, everything in the teleplay is mine. I wrote it without any references whatever to the Stewart story."[74] Robert Cobert composed the atmospheric music.

Roy Thinnes, already a cult favorite for his starring roles in the TV series *The Long Hot Summer* (1965-1966) and *The Invaders* (1967-1968), portrays David Norliss, a brooding author who writes books debunking the occult—"fake mediums, phony astrologers," and the like. However, Norliss is in crisis because his latest investigations have brought him face to face with supernatural forces all too real. He demands a meeting at his home with his editor Sanford Evans (Don Porter), but before the editor arrives, Norliss has vanished. All that is left is a stack of audiocassette tapes containing Norliss's narrations of the paranormal events that he has witnessed. If *The Norliss Tapes* had become a weekly series, the lost protagonist might never have been seen in the present time—only in flashbacks dramatizing the events of each new cassette tape that Evans auditions.

The Norliss Tapes (1973): Roy Thinnes (*The Invaders*) stars as the missing journalist David Norliss.

In the pilot adventure, Evans listens as Norliss's taped voice reveals how he aids Ellen Cort (Angie Dickinson), who is convinced that her recently deceased sculptor-husband James has returned from the dead and is terrorizing Monterey, California. At one point, Norliss narrates a *Night Stalker*-esque scene in which a young woman, walking alone at night, is murdered. Claude Akins, who played Kolchak's adversary Sheriff Butcher in *The Night Stalker*, returns to portray Sheriff Hartley, a similar skeptic who blocks Norliss's investigation and who tells his men, "I'm putting a lid on this one." Clearly, Curtis and Nolan are mining the same Kolchakian vein. The title *The Norliss Tapes* even recalls the original title of the first Kolchak movie—*The Kolchak Tapes*. Blogger Christopher Loring Knowles (*Weekend Matinee*) observed, "For my money, Thinnes suits the material better; his moody, brooding demeanor adds a somber realism to the proceedings that McGavin's wiseguy act could either embellish or undermine, depending on which way the wind was blowing."[75]

Before his death, the terminally ill James Cort made a pact with the dark gods that he would return to life every night after sunset in order to sculpt a body for the demon Sargoth (Bob Schott) to inhabit. Norliss tells Ellen, "The clay mixture is 40 percent human blood." The zombified Cort (Nick Dimitri, in Fred Phillips's ghoulish gray makeup) has been draining women's blood to mix with his clay. The blood ultimately is his undoing, for just as Cort brings Sargoth to life, Norliss traps both creatures inside "a blood circle" and sets it on fire.

Screenwriter Nolan's blending of vampire, zombie, golem, and Egyptian lore was quite innovative and memorable as was the film's nod to the demonology and downbeat endings so popular in early-1970s literature and film. Telecast on the heels of *The Night Strangler*, Nolan and Curtis's *Norliss Tapes* captivated the Kolchak fans who caught it, and it made a lasting impression—for decades a mythic one because *The Norliss Tapes* had never been available on VHS and did not come to DVD until October 2006.

Still attuned to Kolchakian concerns, the critics took notice of *The Norliss Tapes*. *The Hollywood Reporter* wrote, "The movie is a lot of fun, with a new twist on the old vampire story."[76] *Variety* offered, "Curtis directed film with an eye to tension, and that he manages. The idea behind Nolan's script has validity, with its open dependency on the supernatural. The basic thrust, to scare, is what counts, and there Nolan, Curtis, Thinnes, and company succeed."[77]

The *Miami News* opined, "This program confirms one basic television truth: excellence in execution can be more important than mere originality. The professional, technical, and acting job reflected in *The Norliss Tapes* is a tribute to all those involved in its production."[78]

"People still talk about *The Norliss Tapes* all these years later," marveled Roy Thinnes, who worked with Curtis again on *Supertrain* (1979) and the 1991 *Dark Shadows*.[79] In a 2002 interview, Curtis laughed, "*Norliss* was supposed to be a pilot for a series. I just left everyone up in the air. When they didn't pick it up as a series, I laughed my ass off. What do I think happened to [Norliss, the missing writer]? I have no idea."[80]

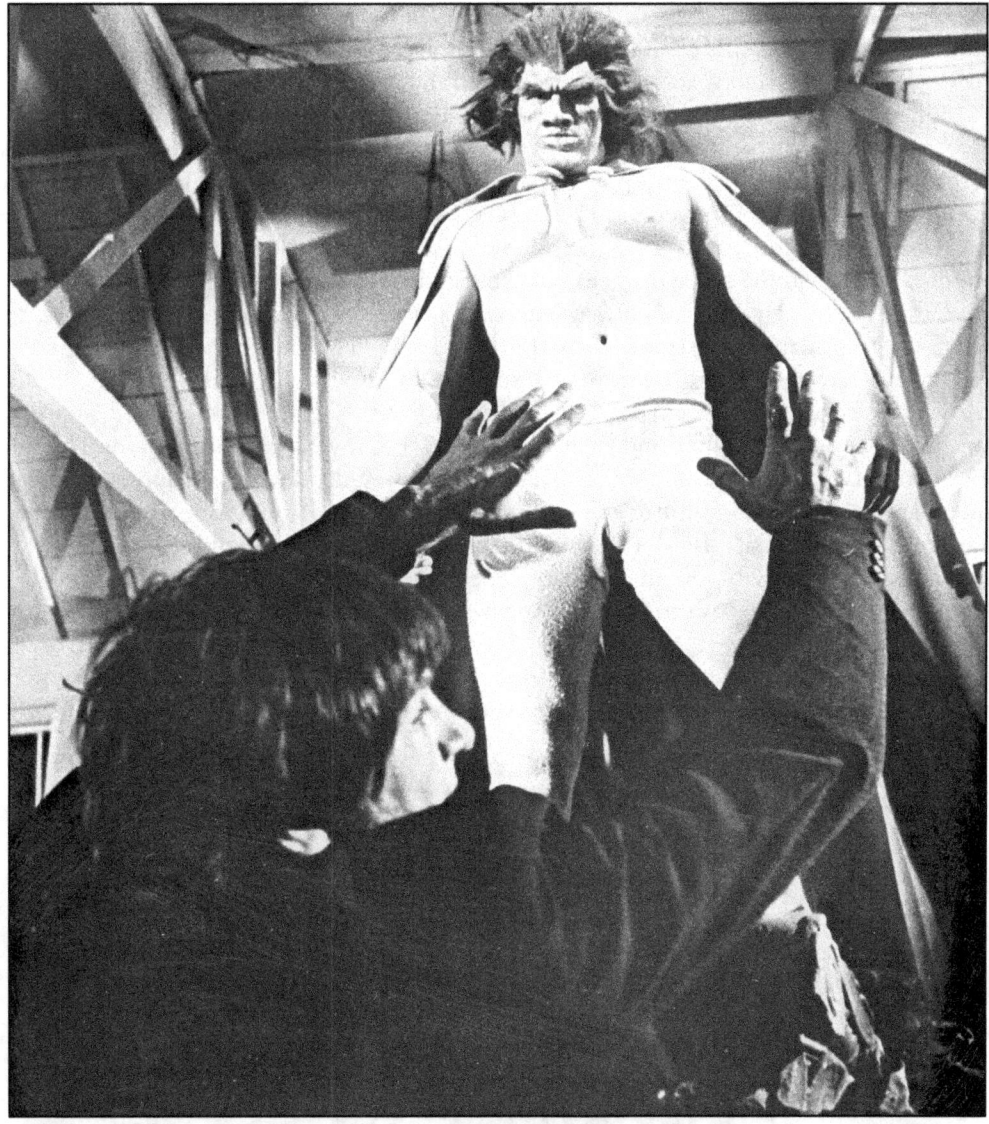

In *The Norliss Tapes* (1973), Bob Schott (as the demon Sargoth) menaces Nick Dimitri (as James Cort).

"Richard Matheson, Earl Wallace, and I were Dan's three favorite writers," William F. Nolan told me in a 2010 telephone conversation. "After *Norliss*, Dan wanted a series. Dan and six writers [including Nolan] sat around Dan's swimming pool and discussed ideas. I came up with *The Return*."[81] Nolan's promising follow-up adventure involved time travel, but a *Norliss* sequel or series never materialized.

Next came Curtis's late-night production of **The Picture of Dorian Gray** (ABC, Monday 23 & Tuesday 24 April 1973), adapted from Oscar Wilde's 1891 novel by John Tomerlin (*The Twilight Zone*) and directed by Glenn Jordan (Curtis's *Frankenstein*). *The Hollywood Reporter* noted that Tomerlin's adaptation "adheres closely to the original."[82]

Like Albert Lewin's 1945 MGM movie *The Picture of Dorian Gray*, Dan Curtis's 1973 adaptation takes a few liberties with Wilde's text, but Curtis's production is the most faithful adaptation of *The Picture of Dorian Gray* ever filmed. Tomerlin's script retains many of Lord Henry Wotton and Dorian Gray's famous aphorisms about beauty, love, marriage, and temptation—and the movie is more revealing of Dorian Gray's omnisexuality than the more discreet versions made in the 1910s, 1945, and the 1960s.

Whereas the action of Wilde's novel takes places over the course of 18 years, the events of this adaptation stretch from 1891 to 1911. The film begins with a Wildean epigraph—"Those who go beneath the surface do so at their peril"—just as Curtis's *Frankenstein* begins with an epigraph from *Paradise Lost*. *The Picture of Dorian Gray* does especially well in faithfully bringing to the screen the novel's first and second chapters (Basil and Henry's conversation about Dorian and the introduction of Dorian himself) and chapter 16 (Dorian's visit to the opium den and his confrontation with Sibyl Vane's brother James). Artist Basil Hallward (Charles Aidman) is suitably protective (and enamored) of young, blond, androgynously beautiful Dorian (Shane Briant), and Lord *Harry* Wotton (Nigel Davenport) is charismatically witty, seductive, and Svengaliesque toward this new object of his affection. Curtis regular John Karlen portrays Dorian's friend Alan Campbell, whom Dorian forces to do his dirty work by cruelly bringing up the names of three men with whom Campbell has had socially questionable relationships.

The Picture of Dorian Gray (1973): As Dorian's butler looks on, Shane Briant (in bed, as Dorian Gray) and John Karlen (as Alan Campbell) interact in Dorian's bedroom.

Again for *Dorian Gray*, Robert Cobert did not compose new music but oversaw the skillful use of his *Dark Shadows* cues, including several versions of "Quentin's Theme," as well as two cues from *The Strange Case of Dr. Jekyll and Mr. Hyde*. Cobert reused his emotional cue "Death of Hyde" for Dorian Gray's death scene just as he had done for the staking of Barnabas Collins in *House of Dark Shadows* (1970) and for the deaths of Victor and his creation in *Frankenstein* (1973).

Seventies-era movie-poster artist John Solie (*Soylent Green, Shaft's Big Score*) created six different portraits to trace the ruination of Dorian Gray's soul. Shane Briant, who played Dorian, revealed that he got to keep one of them (the beautiful one). Briant explained,

> On the last day, the prop man cut out the portrait—which was six feet long and four feet wide—and rolled it up and gave it to me, which was lovely. I went off to a party that Fionnula Flanagan was giving up in the [Hollywood] hills, and I left it in the back of the cab! I figured it was lost, [but] I rang up the cab company the next day, and they had it. So I still have it—but it hasn't changed! I used to stand in front of it and pray, "Please, I'm getting old! Isn't there something you can do?" But no, the picture is still as good as ever, and I'm getting old and wrinkled.[83]

The Picture of Dorian Gray, like Curtis's *Frankenstein*, was shot on videotape at the MGM Studios in Culver City, California. Briant remembered,

> We had eight days of rehearsal, and then we shot it in four. We did a three-hour program from start to finish in 12 days, which must be some kind of a record! We were really going! We rehearsed in the Culver City studios—not the ones now, but on the old *Gone with the Wind* lot, and then we shot it with four videotape cameras. We went from start to finish almost in order, from eight in the morning until eight at night, non-stop. Dan Curtis is a very strong character, strong-willed and a hard taskmaster. If he says you shoot it in four days, you shoot it in four days![84]

While Albert Lewin's 1945 MGM movie with Hurd Hatfield, Angela Lansbury, and George Sanders was Old Hollywood's gold-standard adaptation of *Dorian Gray*, Curtis's 1973 production became the definitive version for the modern era. *Variety* declared,

> Oscar Wilde's world of entertainment (London, 1891), stylishly produced by Dan Curtis Productions, revives the horror tale with insights entirely in keeping with the theme of the original book. Hints of malevolence, sensuality, and decadence, all played out with fine restraint by exotic young actor Shane Briant, give the story freshness and suspense. Wilde knew what he was talking about, and Dan Curtis's production, handsomely mounted, handles the tale with respect and care. Everyone associated with this production deserves kudos.[85]

Next, Dan Curtis exploited his own Kolchakian writer-investigates-murders sub-genre one last time in **Scream of the Wolf** (ABC, Wednesday 16 January 1974), telecast one year to the day after *The Night Strangler*. Richard Matheson once again wrote the teleplay, this time from the 1969 short story, "The Hunter," by David Case, author of *Fengriffin* (1970).

This movie's picturesque setting is Malibu, California, where John Weatherby (Peter Graves) has traded his big-game-hunting days for a more leisurely life as a men's-adventure novelist. Weatherby's girlfriend is Sandy (Jo Ann Pflug, playing a totally different type than her wacky Louise in *The Night Strangler*). Living near Weatherby is his old friend Byron Douglas (Clint Walker), a troubled, reclusive big-game hunter.

Scream of the Wolf (1974): Clint Walker (as Byron) reveals his plan to hunt Peter Graves (as John) in Dan Curtis and Richard Matheson's updating of "The Most Dangerous Game." At Curtis's memorial service, Matheson remarks, "Dan's firebrand temper was never directed at me."

The strangely nonchalant Byron is more concerned with hunting, arm-wrestling, and other manly pursuits than with the series of brutal, wolfen murders happening around town. In a change from the Kolchak adventures, all but one of the six victims are male. Sheriff Bell (Phil Carey) asks for Weatherby's help in the investigation after Byron gives Bell the brush-off. "The tracks go from four feet to two feet to nothing, period!" a baffled Weatherby observes—almost as if the wolf-like creature begins walking upright and gains enough human-like sentience to begin covering his tracks.

In a change from Claude Akins's skeptical-sheriff characterization, Sheriff Bell is just as eager to solve the mystery—whatever it turns out to be—as is Weatherby, who begins to wonder if an actual werewolf is stalking the woods. In a nod to the two *Night Stalker* movies, Bell and city officials hold a press conference, which a heckling reporter not unlike Carl Kolchak disrupts. However, in another switch, the local newspaper freely prints the headline, "WEREWOLF" KILLER STILL AT LARGE. This is one of Matheson's clever red herrings to lull the audience into the belief that a real werewolf is the culprit.

Curtis films the murders with his usual quick takes, low angles, and dark shadows, as well as quite a few zoom shots (popular in genre filmmaking at the time). Robert Cobert supplies suitably tense, eerie background music, plus a funky main title.

The most memorable scene in *Scream of the Wolf* is a staple of the 1970s-era woman-in-jeopardy TV-movie subgenre. The creature's frenzied chase of Sandy through her house is a precursor to Curtis and Matheson's perfection of that scenario one year later in Karen Black's *tour-de-force* dash through her apartment with the Zuni fetish doll literally on her heels in *Trilogy of Terror*. Sandy survives the attack but is convinced that Byron, who was bitten by a wolf in Canada, is to blame. The hunter's only response is, "In a way, these killings may be of benefit to everybody."

Matheson has a few more twists in store in this underrated, almost-forgotten TV-movie now relegated to public-domain DVDs. David Deal, author of *Television Fright Films of the 1970s* (McFarland, 2007), calls Clint Walker's enigmatic Byron "one of his finest performances." Deal adds,

> Curtis and Matheson have fashioned a sharp, fast-moving thriller with *Scream of the Wolf*. The many fog-shrouded night scenes lend atmosphere galore, and the killings are not drawn-out stalking affairs but swift, exciting set pieces. The use of the camera from the killer's point of view—fast and low to the ground—is properly suggestive of an animal and adds considerably to the action.[86]

Next, Curtis's late-night *Wide World Mystery* production **Shadow of Fear** (ABC, Monday 28 January 1974) was a contemporary, five-character mystery drama that had the look and feel of the daytime serials of the 1970s. Written by Larry Brody (*Bright Promise, The Bold Ones*) and directed by Herb Kenwith (*Star Trek, Strange Paradise*), *Shadow of Fear* concerns a man named Styron (Claude Akins), a former cop-turned-private investigator who tends to become too closely involved with his cases.

Styron comes to the aid of Danna Ballard Forrester (Anjanette Comer), the young wife of Pantronics Corporation president Martin Forrester (Jason Evers). Now that Styron has been thrown off the police force (Brody's script hints that Styron attacked or even killed one or more men who were seeing his wife Lil), he is working as the head of Pantronics plant security, and Martin Forrester asks for his help when Forrester's wife Danna appears to be the victim of a stalker. Styron uncovers the fact (omitted by Forrester) that Danna previously was hospitalized for D.I.D. (dissociative identity disorder) and suspects that, now, either Danna's malicious alter-ego "Donna" has returned, or someone is making it look that way.

When Forrester's artist-mistress turns up dead (off-camera), Styron tells his protégé Sgt. Lou Arnburg (Phil Carey), "This whole thing is an elaborate murder frame!" The story's final twist reveals exactly who is framing whom. The four actors who carry the show play well as an ensemble and make the most of their many sets (home, office, bank, police station, apartment, stairwell, etc.), which are the most lavish element of this otherwise small-scale production, shot on videotape at General Service Studios (later renamed Sunset Las Palmas Studios).

Shadow of Fear (1974): Anjanette Comer (as Danna) is not sure whether Tom Selleck (as Mark) is her friend or her enemy in Dan Curtis and Herb Kenwith's late-night mystery.

Robert Cobert uses a solo-piano theme for Danna, and the rest of the background music in *Shadow of Fear* is Cobert's well-loved *Dark Shadows* music cues. Cobert's distinctive brand of (in his words) "great spook music"[87] is always an immediate signal to viewers that a program is A DAN CURTIS PRODUCTION, and Curtis himself was always the first to credit Cobert with contributing to the success of their many collaborations, whether large (*The Last Ride of the Dalton Gang*), small (*Shadow of Fear*), or gigantic (*War and Remembrance*).

Making another ratings and critical splash for Curtis was **Dracula** (CBS, Friday 8 February 1974; rerun Saturday 28 November 1992), directed by Curtis, written by Richard Matheson, and starring Jack Palance as the vampire count. Originally scheduled to air on Friday 12 October 1973, *Dracula* was pre-empted by President Richard Nixon's speech concerning the resignation of Vice-President Spiro Agnew.[88] Much more information about *Dracula* appears in chapter two.

One of Robert Cobert's most haunting compositions, the harmonica theme from *Night of Dark Shadows* (1971), became the theme song of the next Curtis-produced *Wide World Mystery* episode, **The Invasion of Carol Enders** (ABC, Friday 8 March 1974), directed by Burt Brinckerhoff and written by Gene Raser Kearney from a story by Kearney and Merwin Gerard. Brinckerhoff, then a new director, went on to direct the controversial PBS program *Steambath* (1973) and television adaptations of *How to Succeed in Business without Really Trying* (1975) and *Brave New World* (1980). Gene Kearney had written and directed episodes of *Night Gallery* and *Kojak*, and Merwin Gerard had written for *M Squad* and *One Step Beyond*. Both writers were well suited to pen this supernatural—yet realistic—story of possession, set to Robert Cobert's *Dark Shadows* background music.

Meredith Baxter plays Carol Enders, who is assaulted and nearly dies. Elsewhere in the hospital where Carol has been taken, Diana Hastings Bernard (Sally Kemp), the new wife of Dr. Peter Bernard (Charles Aidman), *does* die of injuries from a suspicious car accident just as Carol is fading fast. Suddenly, Carol rallies miraculously and awakens with the consciousness of Diana Bernard. The spirit possessing Carol's body comes to realize that it is earthbound because Diana was murdered—perhaps by someone close to her—and Diana must use Carol to expose her murderer.

This clever plot—used again in the 2000s on *Medium* and *Drop Dead Diva*—may sound preposterous, but the excellent cast, led by Meredith Baxter and Christopher Connelly (as Carol's concerned fiancé Adam Reston), makes it believable and enthralling. Baxter succeeds in delivering lines such as, "I think I know who killed me," with complete seriousness and no camp or unintentional humor.

Another asset to the strong cast is, once again, John Karlen, who appeared in 14 of Dan Curtis's productions. A bit of 1970s-era social commentary occurs when Karlen's character, David Hastings, muses, "I was a space engineer making $30,000 a year when I married Diana. Then, the world got bored with the moon, and I got stuck in a field nobody needs. I liked what I did. There were some real thrills in those days." George DiCenzo, who appeared in four of Curtis's productions, plays Dr. Palmer, who is as baffled by the possession of Carol Enders as Lt. Carrea (Phil Pine) is.

The Invasion of Carol Enders (1974): To enhance the unusual love story enacted by Christopher Connelly (as Adam) and Meredith Baxter (as Carol), composer Robert Cobert sets it to his haunting theme from *Night of Dark Shadows*.

Dan Curtis, who served as an uncredited director of portions of *The Invasion of Carol Enders,* knew the value of an accomplished cast. "If you got good actors," he said in a 2003 DVD interview, "you don't have to tell them a damn thing."[89] The cast of *Carol Enders* makes this the best of Curtis's four single-night *Wide World* mysteries.

Having mastered horror, Curtis next began a two-picture foray into gangster movies. **Melvin Purvis, G-Man** (ABC, Tuesday 9 April 1974) co-starred Dale Robertson as the renowned Bureau of Investigation agent and Harris Yulin as Purvis's adversary "Machine Gun" Kelly. Released theatrically overseas as *The Legend of Machine Gun Kelly,* this Dan Curtis/American International co-production was an outgrowth of AIP's 1973 theatrical film *Dillinger,* co-starring Warren Oates as John Dillinger and Ben Johnson as Melvin Purvis. Please see chapter three for much more information about *Melvin Purvis, G-Man,* directed by Dan Curtis; its prequel, *Dillinger,* directed by John Milius; and its sequel, *The Kansas City Massacre,* directed by Curtis.

In 1973 and 1974, Dan Curtis productions had become a fixture on ABC-TV's late-night *Wide World Mystery* schedule. The most notable *Wide World Mystery* production of 1974 was **The Turn of the Screw** (Monday 15 & Tuesday 16 April), directed by Curtis himself on location at Hennick House in Essex, England. William F. Nolan adapted Henry James's 1898 novel and gave the unnamed governess a name. Nolan called *The Turn of the Screw* "one of my best scripts."[90]

The Turn of the Screw was always one of Dan Curtis's favorite ghost stories. The director admitted,

> A good deal of it went into *Dark Shadows*. I first saw it as *The Innocents* as a play in some regional theatre in New Jersey, and it scared the hell out of me. I was always fascinated by it. Right after I saw the play, I read James's *Turn of the Screw* and was even more fascinated by it. Then, I saw Jack Clayton's *The Innocents* [1961], which I thought was absolutely brilliant, and I was still in love with the story. I thought if I ever got the chance, I would love to do my own version of it.[91]

Curtis was so enamored of Megs Jenkins's portrayal of Mrs. Grosse in Clayton's *Innocents* that he could visualize no one else in the role, so he asked Jenkins to play the part again for him. Curtis cast Lynn Redgrave as the governess, named Miss Jane Cubberly in Nolan's script. (Redgrave's father Michael had appeared in *The Innocents*.) In the roles of the possessed children, Eva Griffith played Flora, and Jasper Jacob played Miles. Shakespearean actor James Laurenson and *Dark Shadows* star Kathryn Leigh Scott portrayed the ghostly Peter Quint and Miss Jessel.

Like all of his *Wide World* mysteries, Curtis's *Turn of the Screw* was shot on videotape. Curtis had to use the early-1970s-era, big, bulky cameras that barely fit into the rooms of Hennick House and were controlled by a mobile unit in a truck outside. "We didn't have anything back then," Curtis remarked about technology, but by ordering a special camera and a special dolly from the United States, he managed to give *The Turn of the Screw* "that low-angle look that I always feel brings more intimacy and texture to the picture."[92] Curtis enjoyed having a chance to perfect the soap-opera-style, live-on-tape, in-camera editing that he had learned when he had directed 21 episodes of *Dark Shadows* in the late 1960s. Additionally, nine short scenes were filmed, not videotaped, for logistical or technical reasons. This mixture of film and tape was not uncommon in

British television productions of the seventies (e.g. *Doctor Who; Blake's 7; Upstairs, Downstairs*). There was even one filmed exterior scene in Curtis and Lela Swift's otherwise videotaped *Dead of Night: A Darkness at Blaisedon* in 1969. Robert Cobert scored *The Turn of the Screw* with eerie music cues from *Dark Shadows* and *Night of Dark Shadows*.

William F. Nolan remembered that adapting Henry James's enigmatic novella was "difficult in that I had to 'extend' the material from a novelette to a two-night miniseries. I wanted to retain the mood and period atmosphere and to remain faithful to James's concept and characters. Apparently, I pulled it off because the critical reception to my teleplay was very positive."[93]

Lynn Redgrave had her own memories of *The Turn of the Screw*. In a DVD interview, she recalled,

> Dan Curtis is a larger-than-life character with a smile so broad, so extraordinary, that when he says, "You must do this," you think, "But of course!" He brings such enthusiasm to his projects. Boy, did he really get involved in this—so involved in the Henry James story, in where the location would be, in the costuming, in the whole thing of how to show the spirits of Peter Quint and Miss Jessel, who were possessing the young children. It was wonderful working with him. All sorts of peculiar things happened because it was the seventies and we were on location, but he always somehow made sure that everything ended up okay.[94]

As with *Frankenstein* and *Dorian Gray*, Curtis's efforts to present 19th-century literature to a *Wide World* audience met with critical approval. The *Los Angeles Herald-Examiner* wrote, "The Henry James story can still exert a magnetic pull, as witness the two-parter that will be screened by ABC tonight. The Dan Curtis production—he directed also—bears the glossy token of its English make. The acting has the glisteningly fine finish of the English period film."[95] *Variety* added,

> Dan Curtis traveled to England to produce and direct William F. Nolan's tele-adaptation of Henry James's chilling *Turn of the Screw*, two-parter late-night version. Curtis brings off several interesting touches, such as [actress Megs] Jenkins's explaining the evils of the house to Cubberly—without being heard [by the viewers]. Or the frightening appearances of Quint—and the insinuations of evil by the children as they half-mock Cubberly. It should hold late-night viewers who want their goosebumps served large.[96]

The Turn of the Screw (1974): Lynn Redgrave (as the governess) and Jasper Jacob (a last-minute replacement for *Oliver!* star Mark Lester) pose for a somber shot from the two-part ABC *Wide World Mystery*.

One month after *The Turn of the Screw* aired, Curtis produced **Come Die with Me** (ABC, Tuesday 14 May 1974), again directed by Burt Brinckerhoff (*The Invasion of Carol Enders*) and written by James Blumgarten (*Mister Rock and Roll*). In terms of cast, this claustrophobic drama is a treat for fans of *Route 66* (George Maharis), *Dark Shadows* (Kathryn Leigh Scott), *Batman* (Alan Napier), and *Blacula* (Charles Macaulay), but the main attraction is the outstanding performance by Eileen Brennan (*Laugh-In*) as Mary Thatcher, a repressed housekeeper who suddenly finds her manipulative side when she blackmails the rakish murderer Walter Burr (Maharis) into a love affair. Kathryn Leigh Scott is equally fine as Burr's New York girlfriend, Suzy Pratt, who urges Walter to get out from under Mary's thumb—with disastrous results. *Come Die with Me* is a fascinating study in the shifting power that people hold over each other, but after a well-written and well-acted build-up, the drama suffers from an unsatisfying, inconclusive ending.

Come Die with Me **(1974):** Eileen Brennan (as Mary) and George Maharis (as Walter) stand over Charles Macaulay (as Walter's brother Frank, whom Walter has murdered).

In terms of music, *Come Die with Me* is a veritable Robert Cobert hit parade. Cobert scores the drama with his music from *Dark Shadows* and many other Dan Curtis productions, including party music from *House of Dark Shadows*, the piano theme from *Night of Dark Shadows*, the music-box theme from *Dracula*, the piano theme from *Shadow of Fear*, and both sides of the Robert Cobert Orchestra's 1970 Roulette Records 45 RPM single ("Ode to Angelique" and "Missy").[97]

Three months later (Tuesday 20 August 1974, my parents' 20th wedding anniversary), on *Wide World Mystery*, Dan Curtis produced the seventh and last of his ABC late-night mysteries. Based on a true story, **Nightmare at 43 Hillcrest** was directed by Curtis's frequent collaborator Lela Swift and written by novelist and lyricist William Katz. Part family drama and part crime story, *Hillcrest* effectively conveys the truly nightmarish situation of an innocent family terrorized, arrested, and persecuted as "heroin dealers" when, in fact, the police have *planted* eight bags of heroin in the house to cover up a colossal mistake. The officers have raided the house at 43 Hillcrest when they should have busted the house at 43 *North* Hillcrest. To cover their blunder, the ruthless, ambitious deputy police commissioner Clarence Hartog (Peter Mark Richman) orders Detective Sanford Bates (Don Dubbins) to plant the heroin in the home of Esther and Greg Leyden (Emmaline Henry and Jim Hutton) and their daughter Nancy (Linda Curtis, Dan Curtis's daughter, who died tragically in 1975). Even after the Leydens' attorney Richard Estabrook (Richard Stahl) gives up on them, Officer Frank Linwood (John Karlen again) and Assistant District Attorney Sharon Reischauer ("special guest star" Mariette Hartley) continue to try to prove the family's innocence to District Attorney Michael Doran (Walter Brooke of *The Green Hornet*).

Robert Cobert's *Dark Shadows* music cues are minimal as much of *Nightmare at 43 Hillcrest* takes on a documentary feel, complete with closing crawls about the fates of the innocent and the guilty. The cast members give earnest performances, with Peter Mark Richman especially effective as the smarmy, arrogant Hartog. The highlight of the program is a long interrogation scene between the diligent assistant D.A. (Hartley) and the sexist Hartog, who is amazed and furious that a woman is making him squirm. The scene plays out like "live theatre," an observation that Robert Foxworth (in a 2006 DVD interview) made about his and Karlen's own *Frankenstein* miniseries.[98]

Curtis's final telefilm of 1974 was **The Great Ice Rip-Off** (ABC, Wednesday 6 November), a clever heist comedy written by Andrew Peter Marin (*Bad Ronald*). It is the story of four diamond thieves who use a Seattle-to-San Diego bus as their getaway vehicle. Unbeknownst to the thieves, one of the other passengers is a retired police officer.

Marin's script is clever, the music by Robert Cobert is innovative, and the cast is first-rate. "Special guest star" Grayson Hall (*Dark Shadows*) joins two fine actors who, like Hall herself, really do not have any present-day equivalents—Lee J. Cobb and Gig Young. Dan Curtis's direction is sharp, and this time, he mixes his trademark low camera angles with some exciting high angles—aerial shots of the Greyhound bus as it travels downs the picturesque coastline.

Cobert's music score signals that *The Great Ice Rip-Off* is an unusual Dan Curtis production as baritone saxophone and low brass (in unison), muted trumpet, flute, and percussion create a main-title theme that is playful and Mancini-esque.[99] After an opening sequence in which Curtis and Paul Lohmann's camera focuses on close-ups of hands manipulating safety-deposit boxes, the quartet of diamond ("ice") thieves is revealed in seriocomic style.

Harkey Rollins (Gig Young), the suave ringleader, dresses as a gray-haired old woman and steals $1,000,000 in diamonds from Klein's Jewelers in Seattle. (The jewelry store is named for Norma Mae Klein Curtis.) Rollins, in his smart business suit again, boards a Greyhound bus in Seattle and rides out of town with a briefcase full of "ice." Georgie (Matt Clark) poses as a security guard and steals $1,250,000 in diamonds from the San Francisco Museum of Modern Art. He, with the loot, boards the bus when it stops in San Francisco. Archie (Geoffrey Lewis) dresses as a machine-gun-toting mugger and holds up a Carmel society wedding for $1,500,000 in the guests' diamond jewelry. When the Greyhound bus stops in Carmel, Archie, with the swag, gets aboard. Checker (Robert Walden) poses as the night desk clerk at the Royal Palms Hotel in Pasadena and helps himself to $1,000,000 in diamonds from the hotel guests' safety-deposit boxes. Packing up the "ice" but running late, he takes a frantic cab ride from Pasadena to Hollywood and flags down the bus just in time to board. (A radio news report reveals that the head of security at the Royal Palms Hotel is one Daniel Cherkoss, which is the birth name of Dan Curtis.)

The Great Ice Rip-Off (1974): Lee J. Cobb (as Willy), Grayson Hall (as Helen), and Gig Young (as Harkey) take a rest stop during their characters' bus trip down the California coast. The working title of the movie is *A Break in the Ice.*

This clever and seemingly foolproof plan is marred by Willy Calso (Lee J. Cobb), a newly retired Seattle cop who, with his wife Helen (Grayson Hall), is riding the bus to his and Helen's new home in San Diego. Willy, along with Helen, latches on to Harkey, chats him up, plays cards with him, enlists his aid in foiling an unrelated on-board pickpocket, and even confides in Harkey his suspicions that the perpetrators of the systematic diamond thefts are on board this very bus. The interplay among Cobb, Hall, and Young is delightful and much more than enough to make an often static bus-ride scenario crackle with excitement. Grayson Hall's Helen Calso is warm to Harkey and solicitous of her cop-husband, who still has not processed the idea of retirement. Across the aisle from them, Harkey coolly reads *Poirot Investigates*, by Agatha Christie, and tries not to notice that the overzealous Willy Calso is coming closer and closer to ruining everything.

Dan Curtis was especially proud of this "quirky little story"[100] and was happy to see it generate good reviews. *The Hollywood Reporter* called *The Great Ice Rip-Off* "a caper picture that is highly entertaining."[101] *Variety* applauded the "light touch [. . .] applied by producer Dan Curtis at directorial reins of quadruple diamond caper. [. . .] Pic has enough sharp corners to keep viewers alter, and Curtis's eye for human foibles again manages to get laughs. [. . .] Curtis picks up credit for being able to derive amusement from a caper film after the onslaught of the genre in recent years."[102] In the months before this TV-movie's premiere, audiences had seen such theatrical capers as *The Hot Rock* (1972), *The Sting* (1973), and *Bank Shot* (1974).[103] Nevertheless, producer-director Curtis, writer Marin, and composer Cobert manage to craft something fresh and delightful. Cobert even uses "Quentin's Theme" as the background Muzak in the coffee shop in the Carmel, California, bus station where Willy, Helen and Harkey take a rest stop.

When television scholars and viewers alike think of the works of Dan Curtis, the programs that immediately come to mind are *Dark Shadows* (1966-1971), *The Night Stalker* (1972), *The Winds of War* (1983)—and **Trilogy of Terror** (ABC, Tuesday 4 March 1975), another ratings smash that made a huge impression on the popular-culture consciousness. Curtis, Richard Matheson, and William F. Nolan collaborated on this anthology of three of Matheson's short stories, all starring Karen Black. The actress had come to Dan Curtis's attention when he had seen her in *The Playroom* on Broadway. He later cast her as four different women in *Trilogy of Terror*.

The first story of the trilogy is "Julie," based on Matheson's 1962 short story "The Likeness of Julie" and adapted by Nolan. Julie Eldridge (Karen Black) is a seemingly shy, mousy English professor who exerts an unexplained, wicked influence over a series of her male students, including Chad Foster (Robert "Skip" Burton, Black's husband at the time) and Arthur Moore (Gregory Harrison).

The second segment of *Trilogy of Terror* is "Millicent and Therese," based on Matheson's 1969 short story "Needle in the Heart" and adapted by Nolan. Millicent and Therese Lorimor (both Karen Black) are vastly different sisters who uneasily share their childhood home after the death of their father. Nolan retains the feel of Matheson's epistolary short story by having the prim, proper, brown-haired Millicent write entries in her diary about Therese, her blonde, libertine, immoral sibling, who corrupts Thomas Anmar (John Karlen again) and confounds both women's psychiatrist, Dr. Chester Ramsay (George Gaynes).

The third segment of *Trilogy of Terror* is the one that viewers remember most strongly. "Amelia," based on Matheson's 1969 short story "Prey" and adapted by Matheson himself, is the story of a small, ferocious-looking Zuni fetish doll that comes to life and stalks Karen Black through her apartment. Black called *Trilogy of Terror* "a little legend all to itself."[104] That legend has lived on through reruns and home video in the 1980s, Curtis's *Trilogy of Terror II* in the 1990s, and a collectible Zuni fetish doll action figure in the 2000s.

With one exception, Matheson's "Amelia" teleplay is extremely faithful to his "Prey" short story. In the story, Amelia's mother and boyfriend speak several lines over the telephone; in the film, viewers hear only Amelia's side of the conversations. Karen Black declared,

> I rewrote some of the dialogue with the mother in the beginning with the director, Dan, because I wanted to make it very clear how the mother made Amelia feel. So at the end, it would be justified what she did [i.e. planned to kill her mother]. I wanted the audience to feel her suppression and the way she was made to feel inadequate. I thought that scene on the phone was very important to bring all of that out. Even though Amelia herself couldn't recognize it, the audience could.[105]

Of her director, Black added, "Dan is an excellent director and excellent at doing suspense. He knows just the right angles. Nobody is better at suspense. Dan should be applauded for his work with it."[106]

Curtis remembered that long before the days of CGI effects, he "did it all with smoke and mirrors. The Zuni doll was a little hand puppet. But it worked. The thing still holds up." Curtis explained,

> The first two stories were pretty straightforward, but when it came time to shoot the Zuni-doll story, I was scared out of my wits because I didn't know what we were going to do. How was I going to make this thing work? All we had was a hand puppet and a little model with hands and legs that could move. So what we did was to build the apartment set on risers. We cut lines into the floor that were covered by the shag carpet, and we had some idiot underneath running [and] moving the Zuni doll by means of a rod stuck up the puppet's ass. Well, forget it. It absolutely didn't work. It was the most awful thing you've ever seen. So I got the idea of chasing Karen Black with a hand-held camera about two inches off the ground. That was very effective, but I still didn't have anything with the doll. When it was over, everybody was going home, and I was sitting there in a total depression. I didn't know what to do. Then, I got one last thought, which saved the picture. I got hold of the puppeteer [Erick Von Buelow, co-creator of the Pillsbury Doughboy], and we hung a piece of black velvet. And I just shot a ton of close-ups of the doll: opening its mouth, thrashing around, exiting frame. I sent it to the lab and had it skip-framed, and before you know it, it was zipping around. I flipped the film over to make him go from left to right and right to left.

The knife would jump from one hand to another, but nobody has ever noticed that! It was against black. I could cut to it any time I wanted. I edited those into the scene, and it was very effective. It absolutely saved me.[107]

So does Walker Edmiston's performance of the terrifying voice of the Zuni doll. Edmiston later portrayed General Douglas MacArthur in *War and Remembrance*. Also adding to the horrifying effect of *Trilogy of Terror* is Robert Cobert's nerve-wracking music. "I wrote some of the most abstruse music that Dan's ever allowed me to write," Cobert exclaimed. "Really far-out!"[108] Among other instruments, Cobert uses vibraphone for Julie, oboes for Millicent and Therese, and clarinet, bass clarinet, trumpet, strings, and tambourine for Amelia. Cobert's music over the closing credits builds to a shattering climax. Karen Black remarked, "He does an incredible job with the music."[109] She continued,

> It's an interesting study as to *why* [the Zuni-doll story] is *so* scary. It seems to me that maybe it's the little things in life that kill you eventually. But, of course, I'm a woman, and I think it's fine to say this in 2006, but women are afraid of *entry*—you know, vaginal entry—and that's why rats, snakes, and mice are so incredibly frightening. If you watch women draw away from them, they generally close their knees, you see! I don't know if you think that consciously, but certainly you're vulnerable in a way that a man can't be. So I think that small things and women—and being chased by a small thing—might have something to do with why it's *so* scary.[110]

Trilogy of Terror received high ratings and high praise. *Variety* called the film "fodder for a virtuoso performance by Karen Black, who essays a quartet of women, and producer-director Dan Curtis, [who] displays his talents in the horror genre. The beginning and final scene, in which the devil doll prepares her for action, are separated by ghoulish work shrewdly manipulated, realistically managed."[111]

Curtis's other TV-movie of 1975 was another adventure of Melvin Purvis, G-man, as co-written by "Bronson Howitzer" (*Alias Smith and Jones*) and William F. Nolan (*Logan's Run*). ABC launched its 1975-1976 season with **The Kansas City Massacre** on Friday 19 September, and like *Trilogy of Terror* six months earlier, Curtis's film carried a PARENTAL DISCRETION IS ADVISED warning because of its violent, mature subject matter. After *The Kansas City Massacre*, Curtis considered another Purvis project, Nolan's *The Legend of Johnny Dillinger*, and/or a Melvin Purvis TV series, neither of which ever materialized. Please see chapter three for much more information about *The Kansas City Massacre* and the unproduced scripts of its possible sequels.

Instead, Curtis returned to his horror roots—and the big screen—with the 1976 United Artists feature **Burnt Offerings**, based on Robert Marasco's 1973 Gothic-horror novel of the same name. The impressive cast included Karen Black, Oliver Reed, Bette Davis, Burgess Meredith, and Eileen Heckart. In addition to directing *Burnt Offerings*, Curtis co-wrote the script with William F. Nolan. "I took the back half" of the script, Curtis remembered, "and Nolan wrote the first half."[112]

Trilogy of Terror (1975): Karen Black fights the Zuni warrior doll in this memorable scene from the climactic "Amelia" ("Prey") segment of the trilogy.

Burnt Offerings (1976): Oliver Reed (*The Assassination Bureau*) and Karen Black (*The Day of the Locust*) portray husband and wife in Dan Curtis's award-winning United Artists film. Curtis visits Black on the set of Alfred Hitchcock's *Family Plot* (1976) and asks her to star in *Burnt Offerings*.

The movie is an extremely accurate, faithful filming of the novel—up to a point. Virtually everything that is in the movie is in the book, and vice versa.[113] The only changes of any import come at the conclusion of the film—but they are significant changes. In the novel, the father and son meet their demises at the swimming pool on the estate, but in the movie, the mother rescues them. Ultimately, no one saves them from the much gorier, more spectacular finishes that Curtis and Nolan devise for them.[114] Nolan and Curtis forgo novelist Marasco's nebulous, abstract ending for a more cinematic conclusion, which is a cross between the climaxes of Alfred Hitchcock's *Psycho* (1960) and Curtis's own *Night of Dark Shadows* (1971).[115] Curtis admitted,

> Someone pointed out to me that I stole the ending from what I did in *Night of Dark Shadows*—the concept of the person going back into the house and the car horn beeping outside and the whole *waiting* thing. "What's taking so long?" All I know is I think the last 15 minutes of this film—and I did a lot of scary stuff in my day—is the scariest 15 minutes I have ever seen. Nothing beats the last 15 minutes of this picture.[116]

Nevertheless, until the final moments, *Burnt Offerings* is an extremely faithful filming of the novel. Even a great deal of Marasco's actual dialogue makes it into the screenplay. In both the novel and the film, homeowners Roz Allardyce (Eileen Heckart) and her brother Arnold (Burgess Meredith) tell Marian Rolfe (Karen Black) and her husband Ben (Oliver Reed) that the house is "practically immortal."[117] The elderly Allardyce siblings offer the house to Ben and Marian—or perhaps it is vice versa—for the entire summer for only $900.00.

At first, Ben, Marian, young David (Lee Harcourt Montgomery), and Aunt Elizabeth (Bette Davis) are overjoyed with their summer retreat, but soon, disturbing events cast a pall of uneasiness, suspicion, and even terror over 17 Shore Road. Ben tries to drown David in the pool, a rift grows between Ben and Marian, and Aunt Elizabeth loses her energy and begins to wither away. At the same time, Marian neglects her family as she becomes obsessed with caring for the house and possessively looking after the never-seen, 85-year-old Allardyce mother whom Roz and Arnold have left behind in the attic sitting room. According to Marasco's novel, "There was a malevolence in the house, and she [Marian] was being used as its agent."[118]

While a graying Marian becomes consumed by her housekeeping, Ben begins suffering a mental breakdown. These are perhaps the most frightening scenes in the film, as Ben abuses David and later Marian and suffers dreams and hallucinations involving a grim, long-ago funeral and a grinning chauffeur (Anthony James) driving a hearse-like Bentley—which now may be coming back for Ben and his failing aunt. The chauffeur's leering interest in the boy Ben (Todd Turquand) suggests a long-buried abuse which may be at the root of Ben's mistreatment of David and Marian and of the house's exploitation of Ben's fears. Bette Davis's death scene, which anticipates Sylvia Sidney's similar death scene in Don Taylor's *Damien—Omen II* (1978) by two years, is a memorable moment as Aunt Elizabeth and Ben, both terror-stricken, are paralyzed by their fear of what may be approaching the bedroom door. With each new death, the house revitalizes itself.

The Career of Dan Curtis: An Overview 73

Burnt Offerings (1976) director Dan Curtis and camera operator Sven Walnum film Oliver Reed and Lee H. Montgomery in the swimming pool at Dunsmuir House and Gardens in Oakland, California, in August 1975. *Burnt Offerings* airs on television for the first time on 23 September 1978 (on NBC's *Saturday Night at the Movies*).

The ending was inconsiderately revealed in United Press International's unsigned, lackluster review of the film. UPI also called *Burnt Offerings* "torturously slow,"[119] but almost all other reviewers understood the fact that the film works *because* it is slow-moving and the frights are spaced out along the two-hour running time. The *Fort Worth Star-Telegram* realized that "Curtis, the *Dark Shadows* creator, has done a masterful job of bringing to the viewer a tangible sense of dread and then punctuating it with jabs of pure terror."[120]

Films in Review agreed, "This story of a family menaced by psychic forces which plague their summer estate succeeds because producer-director Dan Curtis has enough confidence in his material to pitch the level of suspense at a low key."[121] The *New York Times* added, "Director Curtis times his audience immersions into the ice-bath of terror with skill."[122] Rex Reed, in *Vogue*, also complimented the film's "inwardly churning horror," "visually breathtaking splendor," and "enormous style."[123]

Much of that style comes from Curtis's most frequent use of low angles in any of his horror movies. Curtis claimed,

> I was always known as "Mr. Low Angle." I never want to shoot eye-level, with rare exceptions, because I think it's boring. Either you're going to shoot low, or you're going to shoot high, or you're going to shoot raking angles. I try not to get straight-on stuff because the low angle, to me, is more involving. You somehow feel, as a viewer, that you're in the picture, and you're looking *up* at it, and you are *there*. Visually, it seems to have more depth and be more interesting. You see ceilings, for example.[124]

Another hallmark of the film is Robert Cobert's tantalizing score. Cobert infuses *Burnt Offerings* with *Dark Shadows*-style trembling violins, ominous vibraphone, and harsh brass. He adds bells when the grinning chauffeur haunts Ben, and as in *Dark Shadows* and *Dracula*, Cobert uses a music-box theme to great effect.

"Little things" are what make the movie work, Curtis explained, "like finding the old, rusted bicycle by the graves and the glasses at the bottom of the pool."[125] *Burnt Offerings*, at its core, is the story of a family. Curtis and Nolan's script accentuates the family's happiness in the initial car ride to the house and the group's banter and warmth before the malevolence of the house unhinges Ben, enslaves Marian, and destroys Aunt Elizabeth. After a slowly paced build-up, the characters careen helplessly to their ghastly ends.

Burnt Offerings ranked number one at the box office for the week of 13-19 October 1976. Its business was boosted by Lawrence Van Gelder's oft-quoted blurb from the *New York Times*: "an outstanding terror movie [. . .] that does for summer houses what *Jaws* did for a dip in the surf."[126] Rex Reed called *Burnt Offerings* "an amazingly gripping horror film."[127] *Films in Review* noted, "Curtis is one of the few Hollywood producers to employ well-known sci-fi authors regularly to write scripts. This deserves applause at a time when most such movies are being entrusted to people who don't understand or respect the genre."[128] Over the years, *Burnt Offerings* has earned a reputation as being more sophisticated than most contemporary horror films. "The public loved it," William F. Nolan said.[129]

"I've been waiting for you, Ben": Karen Black appears in Al Fleming's old-age makeup as "Mrs. Allardyce." Black calls *Burnt Offerings* (1976) "a wonderful, scary movie."

George LaVoo, in *The Old, Dark House* genre magazine, wrote, "Bette Davis outdoes them all in the role of Aunt Elizabeth. Her death scene, with the chauffeur dragging the coffin up the stairs, is by far the best scene in the movie."[130] In 1977, Davis won the Saturn Award for best supporting actress from the Academy of Science-Fiction, Fantasy, and Horror Films. *Burnt Offerings* also won Saturns for best horror film of 1976 (beating *The Omen*) and best director (Dan Curtis). Bette Davis and Oliver Reed won acting awards for *Burnt Offerings* at the Antwerp Film Festival in Belgium, and Karen Black and Burgess Meredith won acting awards at the Sitges-Catalonian Film Festival. Curtis was named the best director at that festival in Spain.

Essential to the effect and the success of *Burnt Offerings* is Karen Black, whose portrayal of Marian goes from sympathetic to ambivalent to lethal. In a 1976 interview, Dan Curtis revealed that his daughter Tracy, who had acted with Black in *Trilogy of Terror*, "threatened to leave home if I didn't cast Karen Black in *Burnt Offerings*."[131] Curtis had high praise for Black's performances in both films. "She worked her tail off and never, ever let me down."[132] Thirty years later, in a DVD interview, Karen Black insisted, "There's no one better at this genre than Dan Curtis. He has certitude and reliability."[133]

However, after mastering horror for more than a decade, Curtis left the genre for more than a dozen years after his two 1977 telefilms. **Dead of Night** (NBC, Tuesday 29 March) was another trilogy of terror and the final full-fledged Dan Curtis/Richard Matheson collaboration. Two of the stories (about vampirism and black magic) were Matheson's, and Matheson adapted the third, about time travel, from a short story by Jack Finney, a respected fantasy author who since the 1950s had specialized in such tales (*Time and Again, From Time to Time, The Woodrow Wilson Dime*, "The Third Level"). Curtis's filming of the 1956 Finney story, "Second Chance," is an old-fashioned, Bradbury-esque tale of a restored 1923 Jordan Playboy automobile that carries its driver (Ed Begley Jr.) back in time to 1926 (1923 in Finney's story). This is a change-of-pace sweet film from Curtis and a warm-up for his two semi-autobiographical family dramas (1978 and 1980) and, much later (1998), his sensitive filming of Jack Finney's romantic time-travel short story "The Love Letter."

The second *Dead of Night* entry is Matheson's adaptation of his 1959 short story "No Such Thing as a Vampire." This segment actually was filmed for Metromedia in 1973 as the pilot of a weekly mystery anthology series. According to Jim Pierson, "Originally titled *Inner Sanctum*, it never aired, and Dan bought back the half-hour and folded it into his *Dead of Night* TV-movie pilot."[134]

"No Such Thing as a Vampire" co-stars Patrick Macnee, Anjanette Comer, and Horst Bucholz as a husband, a wife, and a family friend—one of whom may be a vampire. Macnee, star of *The Avengers* (1961-1969), gleefully plays against type in this clever—and frightening—tale. Indeed, *The Hollywood Reporter* acknowledged, "All of the performances are top-rate."[135]

Dead of Night (1977): In "Second Chance," Ed Begley Jr. (*Mary Hartman, Mary Hartman*) drives a restored 1923 Jordan Playboy automobile back to the year 1926 (192<u>3</u> in Jack Finney's short story).

Dead of Night **(1977): How is Anjanette Comer's character, Alexia Gheria, losing blood on a nightly basis if there is "No Such Thing as a Vampire"?**

Much scarier still is "Bobby," the final act that attempts to recapture the killer-chases-woman phenomenon of *Trilogy of Terror*. Matheson wrote this story especially for *Dead of Night,* so it is very much in tune with the times. It incorporates demonology (in vogue at the time) and perpetuates the 1970s-era trend of real horror in an everyday setting (e.g. *The Exorcist* [1973], *The Wicker Man* [1973], *The Texas Chainsaw Massacre* [1974], *Carrie* [1976], *Halloween* [1978]) as a woman named Alma (Joan Hackett) resorts to the dark arts to bring her drowned 12-year-old son Bobby (Lee Harcourt Montgomery of *Burnt Offerings*) back from his watery grave. The Bobby that returns is horrifyingly different and poses a deadly threat to Alma. "Bobby" continues a trend of evil-child movies (e.g. *The Bad Seed* [1956], *Village of the Damned* [1960], *The Innocents* [1961], *A Little Game* [TV-1971], *The Other* [1972]), but even more importantly, it belongs to the then-current sub-genre of films expressing female anxiety about reproduction, childbirth, and children (e.g. *Rosemary's Baby* [1968], *The Exorcist* [1973], *It's Alive* [1974], Matheson's *The Stranger Within* [TV-1974], *The Brood* [1979]).

In addition to being topical, "Bobby" is an extremely frightening cat-and-mouse game which builds relentlessly to a shocking climax. As always, Curtis's direction is full of low angles, and Robert Cobert makes excellent use of music *and silence*. Whenever either begins, the effect is nerve-jangling.

Six months after *Dead of Night,* ABC launched its 1977-1978 season with **Curse of the Black Widow** (Friday 16 September), Curtis's homage to 1950s-era monster movies. Anthony Franciosa headed a veteran cast (June Allyson, Sid Caesar, Jeff Corey, June Lockhart, and Vic Morrow) in a tale of a private investigator, a *femme fatale*, and a giant spider. Also starring were Patty Duke Astin, Donna Mills, Max Gail, and Roz Kelly. Curtis again included his daughter Tracy, as well as his neighborhood handyman Orin Cannon, whom Curtis used in small parts in five of his films.

Writer Robert Blees created the story of *Curse of the Black Widow*, and Blees and Earl Wallace co-wrote the script (with the working titles of *Dark Destroyer* and *Spider Lady*). Blees had co-written one of the actual giant-bug movies that *Curse of the Black Widow* evokes—*The Black Scorpion* (1957), about giant scorpions in Mexico City. More recently, Blees had co-written *Dr. Phibes Rises Again* and *Frogs* (both 1972). Earl Wallace went on to write *Supertrain* and *The Last Ride of the Dalton Gang* (both 1979) for Curtis. In the 1980s, Wallace was the story editor of *The Winds of War*, and he was a full-fledged co-writer (with Dan Curtis and Herman Wouk) of *War and Remembrance*. Between the two *War* miniseries, Wallace won the Academy Award for the Best Original Screenplay of 1985 for co-writing *Witness*, directed by Peter Weir.

Dead of Night (1977): Joan Hackett (*The Last of Sheila*) plays Alma, who is so desperate to bring her drowned son "Bobby" back to life that she resorts to the dark arts.

In *Curse of the Black Widow*, Mark Higbie (Tony Franciosa) is a private investigator who is drawn into a baffling series of gruesome murders somehow tied to the fraternal twins Leigh and Laura Lockwood and a mysterious brunette named Valerie Steffan. The film pays homage to *film noir* in the scene in which Leigh (Donna Mills) comes to Higbie's office and hires him. Countless *film-noir* thrillers, from *The Maltese Falcon* (1941) to *Chinatown* (1974), have included such a scene in which the beautiful, enigmatic female client hires the gumshoe. *Curse of the Black Widow* also toys with Curtis's Kolchakian formula as Higbie butts heads with Lt. Guillermo "Gilly" Conti (Vic Morrow) and delivers lines such as, "What are you guys trying to hide?" and "I'm going to stay on this thing, and I'm going to find out what you're so scared of!"

Phil "Rags" Ragsdale (Max Gail), one of Higbie's allies in the police department, surreptitiously aids Higbie in his investigation of these full-moon murders in which men's chests are ripped open and "the bodies drained of blood." "Rags" tells him of a Chinese legend of "an enchanting woman who appeared to weary travelers and took them to a cave to rest." There, she transformed into a giant spider and fed on them. He adds that certain "North American Indians" have a similar legend. Higbie and his outspoken secretary, Florence Ann "Flaps" Parsons (Roz Kelly), research a belief held by "Northern California Indians" of "a spider curse transferred down the female line" and causing transformations, from woman to spider, during the full moon.

The aforementioned characters, with their unusual names and distinctive personalities, lend texture and characterization to *Curse of the Black Widow*. Sid Caesar provides comic relief as Lazlo Cozart, Higbie's ornery neighbor in the office building. H.B. Haggerty plays Marion "Popeye" Sykes, an alcoholic gymnastics coach who witnessed one of the first documented spider-murders. Jeff Corey has a memorable scene as Aspa Soldado, a Native American who rescues Higbie after he has a terrifying accident. Dan Curtis's gymnast daughter Tracy even turns a flip in one scene.

While Mark Higbie's storyline is unfolding, the heart of *Curse of the Black Widow* is the story of the Lockwood family. "Flaps" learns that Leigh and Laura's mother gave birth to the twins in 1947 in the desert after surviving a plane crash that killed their father. Before Aspa Soldado found the woman and her newborns, one of the girls had been bitten numerous times by spiders. Leigh and Laura's mother later died under mysterious circumstances in Rome in 1965. Their family estate is now home to Olga (June Allyson), the twins' former nanny, and Jennifer (Rosanna Locke), a young girl of unspecified parentage. Jennifer calls Laura (Patty Duke Astin) "Aunt Laura" and thinks of Olga as her "grandmother." Whenever Laura stays at the house, she goes upstairs to a locked attic room and visits a shadowed figure.

Meanwhile, Leigh Lockwood, Higbie's client, lives in a fashionable beach house. At the beginning of the film, Leigh is engaged to Frank Chatham (James Storm), and Laura is engaged to Jeff Wallace (Robert "Skip" Burton). In the past, each man was linked to the opposite sister. Before the end of the film, both fiancés (and a third man, who encountered Valerie Steffan) have died from the bite of the giant spider.

Curse of the Black Widow (1977): Tony Franciosa (*The Name of the Game*) and Roz Kelly (*Happy Days*) flee the murderous spider.

This family melodrama becomes even more complicated when it is revealed that the spider-bitten twin is cursed, like a werewolf, to transform into a giant spider under the full moon—and that her mother (June Lockhart) did not die in Rome but went mad after seeing her daughter change. It is Mrs. Lockwood who languishes in the attic room. One of the twin sisters is revealed to be the spider-woman, and secrets about Valerie and Jennifer come out, too. The surprisingly layered *Curse of the Black Widow*—much more than just a giant-spider movie—is one of Curtis's most entertaining horror films.

"Cinematically speaking," author David Deal adds, "this is actually a well photographed movie," thanks to Curtis's director of photography Paul Lohmann (*Nashville, High Anxiety, Time After Time*). In *Television Fright Films of the 1970s* (McFarland, 2007), Deal writes,

> Higbie's fall through the floor of an old house (unleashing a bevy of creepy crawlers) is nicely done, as is the shot of Olga (June Allyson) trapped in a web near the end of the film. The scenes shot from the point of view of the spider will evoke images of the fabled science-fiction films of the 1950s.[136]

Robert Cobert's music is a Kolchakian blend of "detective jazz" (a jazz-riff *leit-motif* for Higbie) and his trademark scary music (along with two disco instrumentals as source music). In a change of pace, Cobert scores one scene with solo acoustic guitar (an idea that he considered for *Night of Dark Shadows* but discarded).

Curse of the Black Widow was another ratings winner for ABC. Before receiving a deluxe VHS treatment in 1999, it was released on early home video under the softer title *Love Trap*. Patty Duke, who played Laura Lockwood, laughingly admitted that *Curse of the Black Widow* was one of her sons' favorites of her movies when they were growing up.

Dan Curtis's own personal golden age of horror (1966-1977), beginning with *Dark Shadows* and *The Strange Case of Dr. Jekyll and Mr. Hyde*, now concluded with *Dead of Night* and *Curse of the Black Widow*. Curtis felt that he had reached the point where he "didn't want to try to squeak another door."[137]

Curtis next turned his directorial attention to **When Every Day Was the Fourth of July** (NBC *Big Event*, Sunday 12 March 1978), a nostalgic, semi-autobiographical film about the Cooper family of Bridgeport, Connecticut, in June of 1937. Attorney Ed Cooper (Dean Jones) and his wife Millie (Louise Sorel) are the parents of Daniel (Chris Petersen) and Sarah (Katy Kurtzman). The character of young Daniel Cooper is based on Daniel Cherkoss (Dan Curtis) himself. Charles Aidman narrates the film as Daniel, remembering that turbulent summer when his father defended Sarah's friend, Albert "Snowman" Cavanaugh (Geoffrey Lewis), a brain-damaged Great War veteran, when "Snowman" was accused of murdering his employer.

When Every Day Was the Fourth of July (1978): The characters played by Katy Kurtzman and Geoffrey Lewis share a special but misunderstood friendship.

All of the principals deliver fine performances in this successful combination family-and-courtroom drama. Scott Brady (*Shotgun Slade, The Kansas City Massacre*) is especially noteworthy as the unsympathetic character Officer Mike Doyle. Geoffrey Lewis's kindly character Albert cannot speak, so Lewis performs eloquently with his face and body. When Lewis (*Dillinger, The Great Ice Rip-Off*) died in April 2015, his actress-daughter Juliette Lewis mentioned on Facebook that *When Every Day Was the Fourth of July* was one of her favorite performances of her father's. Writer Lee Hutson (*The Children Nobody Wanted*) scripted the film, from a story by Hutson and Curtis. Mr. Hutson's teleplay was nominated for an Edgar Award. Walter Scharf (*The Man from U.N.C.L.E.*) composed the music.

In its glowing review of the telefilm, the *Los Angeles Herald-Examiner* declared, "It's an absolute gem. It will touch all of your emotions. It will grip you with suspense. It will amuse you. It will warm your heart."[138] The *Los Angeles Times* concurred that *When Every Day Was the Fourth of July* was "pretty wonderful."[139] Curtis told the *L.A. Times* that this was the movie that he had wanted to make for the last 20 years.[140] The film won the 1978 Golden Halo Award for Family Film Entertainment from the Southern California Motion-Picture Council, as well as a Certificate of Commendation from the Horizon House Institute in Philadelphia "for exemplary work in bringing mental-health issues to the American public."[141] Indeed, the film does explore issues of bigotry, bullying, alcoholism, and family dysfunction in ways that family members of all ages can appreciate. An award-winning sequel appeared, this time on ABC, two years later.

Curtis ended his extremely successful decade of the 1970s with two acclaimed TV-movies—and his only real television flop. NBC-TV's **Supertrain** (Wednesday 7 February to Saturday 28 July 1979) was one of the most expensive and high-profile failures in the history of television—"the biggest money-loser in TV history at the time," according to Jim Pierson.[142] Designed as an answer to ABC-TV's *The Love Boat* (1977-1986), *Supertrain* was an anthology series of comedy, drama, and mystery about the passengers and crew of a futuristic, atomic-powered locomotive that crossed the country in 36 hours at a speed of 200 miles per hour. Some of the show's elaborate sets were of the train's 14' X 22' swimming pool, the gymnasium and steam room, and the seventies-style discotheque. The sets, along with detailed miniatures of the train, inflated the show's budget to ten million dollars.

Supertrain (1979): Dan Curtis steers the multi-million-dollar vehicle through only the two-hour pilot "Express to Terror" and four subsequent hour-long episodes. Curtis—and many of the viewers—leave *Supertrain* before episodes 5-9 are made.

"Frankly, I thought *Supertrain* was the worst idea I'd ever heard," Curtis remembered. "I thought they were out of their minds. But a good friend at NBC said, 'Everybody wants you to do this thing called *Supertrain*.' And they convinced me to do it—against my better judgment."[143]

Curtis executive-produced the first five of the show's nine episodes, but he directed only the February 7 pilot episode (later released on VHS as *Express to Terror*), featuring music by Robert Cobert. After that highly-rated debut episode (starring Steve Lawrence, Don Meredith, and Robert Alda), *Supertrain* plummeted in the ratings, and NBC pulled the show after only four more Wednesday-night episodes (February 14, 21, 28, March 14).

Supertrain (1979): Dan Curtis (left) directs Steve Lawrence (as Mike) and Char Fontane (as Cindy) in "Express to Terror," the two-hour premiere.

The guest stars in the five episodes executive-produced by Curtis included Stella Stevens and Vicki Lawrence in "Express to Terror" (February 7; never rerun); Dick Van Dyke and Barbara Rhoades in "And a Cup of Kindness, Too" (February 14; rerun June 2); Nehemiah Persoff and Paul Sand in "The Queen and the Improbable Knight" (February 21; rerun June 9); Roy Thinnes (in a dual role) and Scott Brady in "Hail to the Chief" (February 28; rerun June 16); and Bo Hopkins and Mills Watson in "Superstar" (March 14; rerun June 30).

Supertrain **(1979): Keenan Wynn (left), Edward Andrews, and Don Meredith co-star in "Express to Terror."**

At this point, Curtis left the show, and NBC brought back a slightly revamped *Supertrain* for four additional new episodes and eight reruns (7 April-28 July 1979) on Saturday nights (opposite ABC's popular *Love Boat* companion, *Fantasy Island*). Jim Pierson observed, "NBC wanted *Supertrain* to be more escapism like *Love Boat*, but Dan wanted more mystery and intrigue with a touch of violence."[144] In later years, whenever anyone asked Dan Curtis about *Supertrain*, his reply was, "Super *what?*"[145] Curiously, in the 2010s, a super-fast train figured into the plots of episodes of *Human Target* and *Supergirl*. In June 2018, the long-lost Supertrain miniature seen on the 1979 TV series was found in a barn, and a *Supertrain* fan bought it for $25,000.

Curtis quickly rebounded from the *Supertrain* experience by directing two notable TV-movies later in 1979. The first, **Mrs. R's Daughter** (NBC, Wednesday 19 September 1979), produced by Joseph Stern, showcased a *tour-de-force* performance by Cloris Leachman as a mother determined to bring her daughter's rapist to justice. The lives of Ellie Pruitt (Season Hubley), her mother Ruth Randall (Leachman), and her stepfather Frank Randall (Donald Moffat) are shattered when Ellie is beaten and raped. Mrs. Randall exclaims, "Her life's been changed—and *he* did it!" The punishment for serial rapist Carl Bergson (John Fitzpatrick) proves to be elusive even after his capture because of scared witnesses, continuances, and mistakes. The tenacious Mrs. Randall goes through several lawyers before Joseph Barron (Ron Rifkin) helps her bring Ellie's rapist to trial after a year-long delay. *TV Guide* called the film "intense." Emmy Award-winning writer George Rubino (*The Last Tenant*) based his teleplay on an actual incident.

Mrs. R's Daughter **(1979): Season Hubley of** *Family* **and Cloris Leachman of** *Phyllis* **play daughter and mother in Joe Stern and Dan Curtis's bleak drama.** *TV Guide* **calls the telefilm "intense."**

As in his horror movies (especially *Burnt Offerings*), Curtis's extremely low camera angles in *Mrs. R's Daughter* effect a tone of claustrophobia and despair. Robert Cobert's somber music, augmented by Moog synthesizers, adds to the melancholy mood.

Two months later, during the crucial November-sweeps period, NBC aired the three-hour event, **The Last Ride of the Dalton Gang** (Tuesday 20 November 1979), Curtis's only Western and one of his personal favorites of his films. The film's VHS tape box described it as "an epic tale of outlaws running out of time." Much more information about this film appears in chapter four, as well as in *Dalton Gang* star Larry Wilcox's foreword to this book.

The Cooper family of Bridgeport, Connecticut, returned in **The Long Days of Summer** (ABC, Friday 23 May 1980), another semi-autobiographical work, directed by

Curtis, produced by Joseph Stern (*Mrs. R's Daughter*), and co-written by Lee Hutson (*Killing at Hell's Gate*) and Hindi Brooks (*Family*). Walter Scharf (*Mission: Impossible*) composed the music.

Dean Jones reprises his role of attorney Ed Cooper, husband to Millie (Joan Hackett) and father to Daniel (Ronnie Scribner) and Sarah (Louanne Sirota). Whereas Sarah is one of the protagonists of *When Every Day Was the Fourth of July,* this sequel shifts the focus mostly to Daniel. Charles Aidman returns to narrate Daniel's memories of the summer of 1938.

The Coopers, who are Jewish (like Curtis's own Cherkoss family of Bridgeport), confront anti-Semitism from the local German-American Club. The family is further distressed when Josef Kaplan (Donald Moffat), a German Jewish man, escapes to America and reveals Nazi Germany's growing atrocities against the Jews. Ed Cooper tries to help Kaplan, whose dire message falls on indifferent ears around town. A highlight of the film is a scene in which Ed's WASP employers (Andrew Duggan and Dave Shelley) pressure Ed to cut his ties with Kaplan. This film's historic subject matter—the Holocaust, a whistle-stop appearance by President Franklin Roosevelt (Stephen Roberts), the June 22 Joe Louis-Max Schmeling fight, and a Golden Gloves boxing match between young Daniel Cooper and an older boy (David Baron)—begins to evoke an era that Curtis, several years later, brought fully to life in his two epic *War* miniseries. *Dark Shadows* actors John Karlen and Michael McGuire play supporting roles, and Gloria Calomee returns as the Coopers' housekeeper Clementine.

The Long Days of Summer (1980): Dean Jones (as Ed Cooper) smiles alongside Joan Hackett (as Millie Cooper). At Dan Curtis's memorial service, Jones calls Curtis a powerful "prayer warrior" for his friends in need.

Like its predecessor (*When Every Day Was the Fourth of July*), *The Long Days of Summer* received the Golden Halo Award for Family Film Entertainment from the Southern California Motion-Picture Council. The *Los Angeles Herald-Examiner* ranked the "extraordinarily good" film number three in the top ten television programs of 1980.[146] *The Los Angeles Times* declared that the film "has the sort of honesty and reality that is lacking in most TV series."[147] Once again, this sequel is not afraid to tackle difficult issues such as race, bigotry, politics, and ethics.

Both *The Long Days of Summer* and *When Every Day Was the Fourth of July* were unsold pilots for a *Waltons*-style family TV series to be called *The Coopers*. Later in the 1980s and even in the 1990s, Curtis and Hutson kept alive hope for a *Coopers* series by preparing at least three episode scripts: "A Christmas Story" (by Dan Curtis, Lee Hutson, Tim Kring, and I.C. Rappoport), "For the Love of Ginger Parker" (by I.C. Rappoport), and "A Little Girl across the Room" (by Mr. Hutson).[148]

On Tuesday 3 March 1981, after *Guiding Light*, CBS-TV's *Afternoon Playhouse* presented **I Think I'm Having a Baby**, a teenage drama starring David Birney, Shawn Stevens, Shane Sinutko, and several up-and-coming actresses: Jennifer Jason Leigh, Tracey Gold, Ally Sheedy, and Helen Hunt. Leigh plays a high-school student who fears that she is pregnant after one sexual experience with Stevens's character. David Birney is excellent as Mr. Fenning, a dynamic teacher who asks his students tough questions about life, love, and sex.

Although Dan Curtis did not produce or direct *I Think I'm Having a Baby*, the program was made under his Dan Curtis Associates banner. Joseph Stern (*The Long Days of Summer*) was the executive producer, Blossom Elfman (*The Girls of Huntington House*) was the writer, and Arthur Allan Seidelman (*Children of Rage*) was the director. The music composer was Curtis mainstay Robert Cobert, who was nominated for a Daytime Emmy Award for his music score, which makes good use of flute and harp. Cobert lost the Emmy to Dick Hyman for "Sunshine's on the Way" (*NBC Special Treat*). Elfman won an Emmy for writing the show.[149]

Two years after *The Long Days of Summer*, writer Lee Hutson, producer Joe Stern, and executive-producer Dan Curtis re-teamed for another unsold pilot, **The Big Easy** (ABC, Sunday 15 August 1982), directed by Jud Taylor (*The Last Tenant*). According to Jim Pierson, "Joe [Stern] reminded me that Dan was barely involved with it like *I Think I'm Having a Baby*. *The Big Easy* was Joe's project."[150]

If it had become a series, *The Big Easy* would have starred William Devane as New Orleans private investigator Jake Rubidoux, Nicholas Pryor as newspaperman Walker Garrett, Lane Smith as policeman Frank Medley, and Ja'net Dubois as nightclub owner Gloria Chenier. Between P.I. jobs, Jake plays clarinet in Gloria's French Quarter club, The Big Easy, "a lived-in joint that's been here for a while—like before the Louisiana Purchase," as Jake remarks in his ongoing voice-over narration. Mr. Hutson's teleplay effects a *film-noir* feel through this narration, Jake's wisecracking personality, and such hard-boiled lingo as "racket," "dough," "frail," "stiff," and "doll." Jake characterizes himself by observing, "Good thing I'm an easygoing guy," and by constantly referencing old movies (*The Postman Always Rings Twice, Desert Fury, Dial M for Murder, One-Eyed Jacks*) as if he and the people in his orbit could be a part of them.

William Devane (*Knots Landing*) and Ja'net DuBois (*Good Times*) co-star in *The Big Easy*, an unsold pilot. *The Big Easy* (1982) and *The Winds of War* (1983) come about through a production deal between Dan Curtis and Paramount Pictures.

Rubidoux is hired by a client (Hugh Gillin) who claims to be Texas oilman Nunnally Hayes, the father of Cynthia Hayes (Mary Crosby), a woman who has gone missing. Only after Jake finds Cynthia with her gambler-boyfriend Jean Laveau (Crofton Hardester) and tells "Hayes" does he discover that "Hayes" is *not* Cynthia's father but a hit man hired to "chill" her. Adding to the intrigue is Cynthia's ex-boyfriend, gigolo Jeb Taylor (Jared Martin), who is being "kept"—and quite possessively—by Lorri Fitzgerald (Barbara Babcock), a *femme fatale* whom Jake compares to "the blonde in *Desert Fury*" (apparently, Lizabeth Scott). Along the way, Emmy Award-winning director of photography Charles Correll (*The Dark Secret of Harvest Home* et al.) captures atmospheric shots of Bourbon Street, Jackson Square, Audubon Park, and the Superdome. Composer J.J. Johnson (*Lucan, CHiPs*) provides minimal background music but a pleasing main-title theme and plenty of source music ("Hello Dolly," "Love Letters," "The Nearness of You," "Tangerine," et al.).

After surviving a dramatic shoot-out with the hit man at journalist Walker Garrett's house, Jake solves his case at Lorri Fitzgerald's home in the Garden District. NOPD Lt. Frank Medley asks Jake, "What are you going to do next?" and Rubidoux replies, "Take a nap."

Variety was complimentary of William Devane and *The Big Easy*. The trade paper declared, "A veteran actor and far more skilled than most TV stars, Devane demonstrated a capacity for the insouciant charm so necessary to carry off a private eye who spends his spare time in a New Orleans jazz joint. [. . .] If ABC comes up short some time in mid-winter, *The Big Easy* would be resurrected with profit."[151]

Chapters five and six of this book chronicle the pair of gigantic ABC-TV miniseries that occupied Dan Curtis's time for almost the entire decade of the 1980s— **The Winds of War** (February 1983; rerun September 1986) and **War and Remembrance** (November 1988 and May 1989). Planning and directing the two mammoth productions seemed impossible, yet Curtis succeeded at every turn and made an indelible mark on television storytelling. In the 2019 documentary *Master of Dark Shadows,* producer Barbara Steele calls *War and Remembrance* "the pinnacle of Dan's existence."

In 1986, Curtis took a very short break from filming *War and Remembrance* to shoot a live performance of his good friend Dean Jones's one-man show **St. John in Exile**. Written by Don Berrigan and directed on stage by Lory Basham Jones, *St. John in Exile* presents Dean Jones as the 86-year-old last surviving Apostle, John, who tells his inspiring story while he is detained on the Greek island of Patmos. The *Arizona Republic* called *St. John in Exile* "magnificent! One is reminded of unforgettable roles played by Henry Fonda as Clarence Darrow and Hal Holbrook as Mark Twain." After directing a special live videotaping (in Van Nuys, California) of Dean Jones's *tour de force* as St. John, Dan Curtis called it "the best performance I've ever seen."[152] Dean Jones passed away on Tuesday 1 September 2015.

The 1990s began for Curtis with NBC-TV's Sunday 29 July 1990 airing of **Johnny Ryan**, an unsold pilot movie. Curtis served as executive producer of *Johnny Ryan* but left the producing to Christopher Chulack and the directing to Robert Collins. Chulack went on to produce and direct *Homefront, Third Watch,* and *ER* after *Johnny Ryan*. Collins had directed *Police Story, Gideon's Trumpet,* and *Savage Harvest* before *Johnny Ryan*. The teleplay was by Mark Rodgers, who had written for *Police Story, Eischied,* and *T.J. Hooker*.

Johnny Ryan, originally titled *Against the Mob,* pits a special NYPD task force against five crime families in 1949 New York City. Heading the squad is Detective Johnny Ryan (Clancy Brown), a former Marine who answers to New York's District Attorney, Frank S. Hogan (J. Kenneth Campbell). While Johnny Ryan is a fictional character, Frank Hogan (1902-1974) was New York's real-life, long-time DA from 1941 until his resignation (after a stroke) in late 1973. The inclusion of a few real-life personalities, such as the incorruptible Hogan and the gangsters Frank Costello (Victor Argo) and Meyer Lansky (Michael Fairman), gives *Johnny Ryan* a docudrama feel. Adding to the verisimilitude is the period detail of the clothes and the cars, as well as stock footage of Times Square from decades ago. Jack Benny is heard on the radio, and a "Sugar" Ray Robinson fight airs on an early television set in a bar.

Unfortunately, too much of a period-docudrama feel, along with the absence of Dan Curtis's more dynamic directing style, makes *Johnny Ryan* rather stodgy in places. Mark Rodgers's script, while well written, is a rehash of countless cops-and-robbers movies that had come before: the murder of an informant, a kindly old Irish cop who mentors Johnny Ryan, Johnny's unwise romantic entanglement with a gangster's girlfriend, the revelation of a "good" cop's collusion with the gangsters, etc. There is even a *Casablanca*-esque good-bye scene at an airport. Art Durbano of *TV Guide* called Johnny Ryan "a routine exercise in the genre."[153]

The cast of *Johnny Ryan* (1990) includes (seated) **Teri Austin and Clancy Brown** and (standing, from left) **Cameron Thor, Bruce Abbott, Eugene Clark, and Nestor Serrano.**

On the other hand, a well-done highlight of *Johnny Ryan* is an ambush and shootout on the road to Utica, New York. Other assets are the excellent performances of J. Kenneth Campbell as DA Hogan, Robert Prosky as Captain Miles Fitzgerald, and Julia Campbell as Eve Manion, the showgirl who has the bad luck of being caught between gangster/club owner Steve Lombardi (Paul Rossilli) and Johnny Ryan. Teri Austin of *Knots Landing* is underused as attorney Paula Westridge, a potentially interesting character. In the limited time that he appears, Jason Beghe of *Intruders* also shines as Peter Howard, an alcoholic, suicidal police officer who ultimately helps Ryan and his partner Tom Kelly (Bruce Abbott) make their case against Lombardi and Anthony "Tough Tony" Cardini (Robert Miranda), who together threw an informant out of a window to his death.

A crucial element missing from *Johnny Ryan* is Robert Cobert's music. Director Bob Collins selected as his composer Chris Boardman, who had written the music for Collins's 1989 TV-movies *The Hijacking of the Achille Lauro* (NBC, Monday 13 February) and *Prime Target* (NBC, Friday 29 September). Boardman's music score is a mixture of *noir*-ish muted-trumpet and tenor-saxophone cues, big-band swing interludes, and vintage songs such as "Sing, Sing, Sing," which opens the film; "Satin Doll," to which Eve Manion and the other showgirls dance at Steve Lombardi's Havana Club; and "Body and Soul," which "Mel Torme" (actually a lookalike actor) sings at the club. Boardman's scores for *Achille Lauro* and *Johnny Ryan* were nominated for Emmy Awards but lost to the music from *Lonesome Dove* (Basil Poledouris) and *Stephen King's IT* (Richard Bellis), respectively. Poledouris won his Emmy over not only Chris Boardman for *The Hijacking of the Achille Lauro* but also Robert Cobert for *War and Remembrance*.

As the single Dan Curtis production between *War and Remembrance* (1988, 1989) and *Dark Shadows* (1991), *Johnny Ryan* (1990) is enjoyable but far from one of the strongest Curtis productions. With Curtis's *auteur* directing and script-doctoring—and Cobert's music—*Johnny Ryan* possibly could have been another *Kansas City Massacre* (1975). Without them, it is an admirable but ordinary programmer. *TV Guide* gave the telefilm two stars (out of four). As the pilot came and went, Curtis was hard at work on the next milestone in his career: a nighttime revival of *Dark Shadows*.

In both 1988 and 1989, before and after the broadcasts of *War and Remembrance*, NBC entertainment president Brandon Tartikoff had approached Dan Curtis about resurrecting *Dark Shadows* as a lavish nighttime dramatic serial—a kind of *Dynasty* with fangs. At first skeptical about revisiting *Dark Shadows* after two decades, Curtis ultimately decided to remake the show, this time with the luxuries of time, money, and film (instead of videotape). He resolved to produce **Dark Shadows** in the much grander, more opulent way that he "and the fans had always wanted to see the series," in his words.[154]

The new *Dark Shadows* was filmed in and around Los Angeles from March to December 1990. After directing the pilot from Monday 19 March to Wednesday 11 April 1990, Curtis directed episodes two, three, and four between Monday 23 July and Tuesday 28 August 1990. Armand Mastroianni (*Tales from the Darkside*), Paul Lynch (the 1980s *Twilight Zone*), Rob Bowman (*Star Trek: The Next Generation*), and Mark Sobel (*Quantum Leap*) directed hours six through 13, with a few retakes directed by Curtis for the 12th and 13th hours. Robert Cobert, of course, returned to furnish the show with his 1960s *Dark Shadows* music cues, as well as many new, eerie, synthesized compositions, performed by a 25-piece orchestra under his direction.

As Curtis was preparing the new *Dark Shadows* in 1989 and 1990, he drew as much inspiration from *House of Dark Shadows* as he did from the television series. With an order first for just a pilot, then for six hours, and finally for 13 hours, the director knew that he would have to condense and streamline the 1967 Barnabas storyline and the 1795 epic, which together had taken a full year's worth of daily episodes to tell. Curtis realized that he, Sam Hall (on board for the new series), and the late Gordon Russell had already condensed the original Barnabas/Maggie story for *House of Dark Shadows*, so he patterned some of the four-million-dollar pilot after that film. Curtis and Hall co-wrote the series with eight other writers: Hall's novelist son Matthew Hall, *Beauty and the Beast* writers M.M. Shelly Moore and Linda Campanelli, Jon Boorstin (*Dream Lover*), Steve Feke (*When a Stranger Calls*), William Gray (*The Changeling*), Hall Powell (*B.L. Stryker*), and Bill Taub (*Supertrain*).

Dark Shadows (1991): Roy Thinnes (as Roger Collins) consoles Jean Simmons (as Elizabeth Collins Stoddard).

Daphne Budd, the Collinwood employee whom Barnabas attacks in her car at the beginning of *House of Dark Shadows,* becomes Daphne Collins for the 1991 series. Since she is a niece to both Roger Collins (Roy Thinnes) and Elizabeth Collins Stoddard (Jean Simmons), the Roger and Elizabeth of 1991 must have a brother somewhere. Daphne Collins (Rebecca Staab) is attacked in her car by the vampire and then follows the path of the Carolyn Stoddard character in *House of Dark Shadows.* It is Daphne who becomes the vampire, and Curtis shoots her funeral, her undead appearance to young David Collins (Joseph Gordon-Levitt), and her staking by Professor Woodard (Stefan Gierasch) very similarly to the corresponding scenes in *House of Dark Shadows.*

The new Barnabas Collins, played by Ben Cross (*Nightlife*), is more sinister and ferocious than Jonathan Frid's TV Barnabas but not quite the rampaging evildoer of the 1970 movie. Cross's Barnabas has a tortured, vulnerable, romantic side which allows him to fall in love with Victoria Winters (Joanna Going), whom he sees as the reincarnation of Josette DuPres, and which causes him to seek a cure for his vampirism from Dr. Julia Hoffman (Barbara Steele). In the new series, Victoria, not Maggie, resembles Josette and captures Barnabas's heart. In a sign of the times, the new Maggie Evans (Ely Pouget) is a New Age mystic who is having an affair with Roger Collins—something unthinkable on the original series![155] After the Harmonic Convergence in the year 1987, devotees of mysticism believed that a new era had dawned, and their New Age beliefs received a great deal of attention in various media. In a logical step in the updating of *Dark Shadows,* Dan Curtis and his writers acknowledged the new philosophy by reshaping the Maggie character into a New Age psychic.

Other considerable changes occur in the characters of Willie Loomis and the Reverend Trask. Jim Fyfe portrays Willie much more comically than even John Karlen did, and Roy Thinnes unwisely plays Trask as a foppish dandy instead of as the frightening, dangerous witchfinder that Jerry Lacy portrayed. Other surprises in Curtis's 13-hour remake of the 1967 and 1795 storylines are the death of Joe Haskell (Michael Weiss), the manner in which Barnabas becomes a vampire (Josette's doppelganger, not a bat, bites him), the family's use of a Ouija-type board (something that never happened on the original series), and Dr. Hoffman's possession by the spirit of the witch Angelique (played by Lysette Anthony of *A Ghost in Monte Carlo*). The outstanding sixth episode (Friday 1 February 1991) features a lavish costume party at Collinwood and climaxes with the séance that sends Victoria Winters back in time to 1790 and leaves Phyllis Wicke (Ellen Wheeler) in her place.

One of the hallmarks of the series is the dramatic, emotional, and tragic mood that the show almost always maintains (thus why Willie and especially Trask are so jarring). *Terror Television* (McFarland, 2001) author John Kenneth Muir notes that "a sense of overwhelming tragedy dominates this *Dark Shadows* in an almost poetic manner."[156] Except for a few missteps, *Dark Shadows* '91 is a worthy successor to the original series.

Curtis filmed much of *Dark Shadows* '91 at Greystone mansion in Beverly Hills, California. The 55-room mansion on 18 acres of land was built in 1928 by the oil millionaire Edward Doheny, who earlier in the 1920s had played a role in the Teapot Dome scandal. The city of Beverly Hills assumed ownership of Greystone in 1965, and since 1971 it has opened the grounds (but not the house) as a public park. Since

1963, Greystone has been seen in countless movies and TV shows, including *The Disorderly Orderly*, *The Loved One*, *Mannix*, and *General Hospital*. Greystone served admirably as Collinwood for *Dark Shadows* (and would again in the 2000s).

Dark Shadows (1991): Ben Cross (*The Unholy*) stars as Barnabas Collins in NBC's prime-time revival. *Star Trek* fans know Cross as Sarek, Spock's father, in the 2009 film.

The first four hours of NBC-TV's *Dark Shadows* aired as a miniseries on Sunday 13 & Monday 14 January 1991. The show garnered respectable ratings, especially from the coveted 18-34 and 25-54 demographics, and favorable reviews. The *Fort Worth Star-Telegram* called the series "dark, slick, and expertly acted and executed" and "beautifully photographed."[157] *The Hollywood Reporter* complimented the show's "wonderful sets and stately surroundings."[158] *Variety* called it "bloody good" and observed, "Fans will get a rush from the new *Dark Shadows* because, in many ways, it's faithful to the original, and new viewers looking for something to sink their teeth into won't be disappointed, either. Ben Cross and Joanna Going are excellent."[159] The *Chicago Sun-Times* proclaimed, "This Gothic chiller is bound to enchant TV viewers who are swayed by a lovingly designed experiment in style and flavor. [. . .] The vampire's kiss is irresistible!"[160]

Dark Shadows (1991): Roy Thinnes (as Roger), Joseph Gordon-Levitt (as David), and Joanna Going (as Victoria) are involved in a never-resolved subplot about David's mother Laura. In 2012, Gordon-Levitt (David Collins '91) and Gulliver McGrath (David Collins '12) play the President's sons in Steven Spielberg's *Lincoln*.

The new *Dark Shadows* seemed destined for success—but then, fate intervened and dealt the show a mortal wound. Before the fifth hour could air in its regular Friday-night timeslot on January 18, the Persian Gulf War broke out. News coverage blanketed the TV networks for much of the week, and *Dark Shadows* was lost in the shuffle. Although the Friday 18 January episode aired on the East Coast, it was pre-empted by war coverage on the West Coast and did not air until Friday 25 January, one hour before that night's regularly scheduled episode. A nationwide pre-emption in favor of a showing of *The Empire Strikes Back* (1980) on 22 February did not help, and neither did Brandon Tartikoff's departure from NBC for Paramount Pictures. The new NBC entertainment president, Warren Littlefield, did not seem interested in *Dark Shadows*, and despite fans' "Save *Dark Shadows* Day" demonstrations across the country on Wednesday 8 May 1991, *Dark Shadows* did not appear on NBC's fall schedule. The final episode had aired on Friday 22 March 1991 and had ended with a cliffhanger: Victoria Winters returns from her travels through time with the knowledge that the Barnabas Collins of 1790 and the Barnabas of 1991 are one and the same—and a vampire.

Dan Curtis and the fans were crestfallen that a promising new beginning for *Dark Shadows* had ended so abruptly. Curtis, who had fought NBC for the go-ahead to film 13 hours instead of a mere six, considered keeping the new show alive through a made-for-TV movie or a theatrical feature, but no such sequel materialized. (The mythos of the new series did live on for another two years in the form of a comic-book series from Innovation Comics.) The TV show received the Saturn Award for Best Genre Television Presentation from the Academy of Science-Fiction, Fantasy, and Horror Films, and it won Dee-Dee Petty (*The Last Ride of the Dalton Gang, The Outsiders*) and four other stylists an Emmy Award for hairstyling for the thrilling eighth episode (Friday 15 February 1991), in which Barnabas and his brother Jeremiah (Adrian Paul) fight a duel over Josette and suffer the disastrous effects of Angelique's witchcraft. *Dark Shadows* '91 later reran several times on the Sci-Fi, TNT, and Chiller channels.

One year after the NBC-TV nighttime series, Curtis, in his foreword to Jim Pierson's book, *Dark Shadows Resurrected* (Pomegranate Press, 1992), wrote,

> After a quarter of a century, no one is more surprised than I with the devotion that *Dark Shadows* still commands. I can't believe that it's been going on all these years. When the original daytime series ended in the spring of 1971 and we finished the second theatrical film shortly thereafter, I figured that *Dark Shadows* was a thing of the past.
>
> As the years passed, it became apparent that *Dark Shadows* was much more than just a fond memory. The undying fascination and loyalty for the series were astonishing, and in 1990 I found myself back in the dark corridors of Collinwood, producing a new incarnation of *Dark Shadows* for primetime, weekly television.
>
> I never intended to do *Dark Shadows* again, but the show refused to die, kept alive by legions of passionate fans. Although the new series was given a network life of only 12 episodes, I think we were able to recreate and reinvent the magic that first enthralled viewers so many years ago.[161]

The year 1992 saw two new Dan Curtis productions on network television. On Saturday 1 February 1992, ABC-TV aired **Angie the Lieutenant**, a half-hour dramatic pilot starring Angie Dickinson. One of writer-producer-director Robert Collins's greatest accomplishments was his creation of the classic TV series *Police Woman* (NBC, 1974-1978), starring Dickinson as Sgt. Suzanne "Pepper" Anderson. Bob Collins had written "The Gamble," the Tuesday 26 March 1974 episode of NBC-TV's *Police Story* that had introduced Angie Dickinson as a police officer named Lisa Beaumont. The "Gamble" pilot was retooled, Earl Holliman was added to the cast, and *Police Woman* premiered on NBC on Friday 13 September 1974 (opposite "The Ripper," the debut episode of *Kolchak: The Night Stalker*, on ABC).

Now, Robert Collins and Angie Dickinson were together again as writer-producer-director and star, respectively, of *Angie the Lieutenant*, executive-produced by Dan Curtis. *Angie* was the pilot for a potential half-hour dramatic series about Lt. Angela "Angie" Martin (Dickinson), a recently promoted Washington DC policewoman who assumes the leadership of a multicultural, all-male squad of plainclothes detectives. Under Lt. Martin's command are her old friend Carl Koenig (Michael MacRae), overachieving Georgetown graduate Elliott Chase (Jesse Dabson), Oliver Jackson (Harold Sylvester), and Ernesto Mendez (Geoffrey Rivas)—all of whom are disconcerted that their new boss is a woman.

The cast of *Angie the Lieutenant* (1992) includes (left to right) Jesse Dabson, Harold Sylvester, Angie Dickinson, Michael MacRae, and Geoffrey Rivas.

Providing local color are scenes of Washington DC landmarks and a cameo appearance by Congressman William D. Lowery (R-California), who was a member of the United States House of Representatives from 1981 to 1993. As the pilot episode begins, Lowery's statement to the press is being covered by newswoman Zee Campbell (Sarah Carson) of WDBX-TV 8 in Washington DC. Later, the reporter is raped, beaten, and left for dead in "Crack City" by a gang of four men—and Lt. Angie Martin and her detectives begin their first case together.

Angie Dickinson, certainly no stranger to playing gun-wielding policewomen, brings believability and a natural ease to her role. She is suitably authoritative, forceful, and even sarcastic when she needs to be. At other times, she adds a woman's touch to her work, such as bringing Zee Campbell's favorite TV makeup and a hairbrush to her bedside and suddenly embracing Det. Carl Koenig in order to hide his face from some crooks who would recognize him. Dickinson also wears three different stylish outfits in the episode, and in the final moments, she goes to the Capitol and meets an unnamed undersecretary (Michael Tolan) who is the man in Lt. Angie Martin's life.

Robert Collins's script, set to synthesized music by Stanley Clarke (*The Five Heartbeats*), is fast-paced and full of characterization, and his direction is much more energetic than that of the often languorous *Johnny Ryan*. Angela Bassett makes the most of her small role as Zee Campbell's nurse. A moment of hilarious comic relief is provided by Dyanna Ortelli as Juanita Gallegoes, a self-proclaimed "streetwalker" whom Angie Martin recruits as an informant. "In my business," Juanita remarks, "you meet a lot of people, but you don't see much of their faces." To be convinced to become a "snitch," Juanita insists on having Angie's smart alligator purse. Upon closer examination of her new handbag, Juanita protests, "Hey, this isn't real alligator!" Angie matter-of-factly replies, "Oh, in our business, we learn to fake things, too, Juanita."

According to Jim Pierson, "*Angie* was a half-hour pilot idea for ABC to return to the old half-hour drama format like *Adam-12, Felony Squad*, etc. Dan was only moderately involved with *Angie*."[162] Around the time of *Angie*, Curtis was making plans with Richard Matheson and Darren McGavin to revive Carl Kolchak in a *Night Stalker* reunion movie for ABC. That network, as well as two others, passed on the idea.

Next, Curtis combined his horror and miniseries expertise for the two-part CBS event **Intruders: They Are Among Us** (Sunday 17 & Tuesday 19 May 1992), which he directed and co-executive-produced. Based on the book of the same name by Budd Hopkins, *Intruders* was a horror/sci-fi docudrama based on 600 actual case studies of alien abduction. Please see chapter seven for much more information about *Intruders* (which CBS reran on 30-31 May 1995).

While his made-for-television accomplishments were numerous, Dan Curtis made only four theatrical films, including *House of Dark Shadows* (MGM, 1970), *Night of Dark Shadows* (MGM, 1971), and *Burnt Offerings* (UA, 1976). His fourth and final feature, **Me and the Kid** (Orion, 1993), was a bittersweet experience for the director. Because of its uneven (but refreshing) mix of broad comedy, crime drama, and kids' adventure, *Me and the Kid* under-performed in theatres and greatly disappointed Curtis. He recalled,

> While I was doing *The Winds of War*, a fellow who worked with me, Joe Stern, came across this book called *Taking Gary Feldman*, by Stanley Cohen. He showed it to me, and I thought it was a good story although I felt certain things needed to be done to it. But we sold it to CBS, and they developed a screenplay while I was off doing the miniseries. Unfortunately, it never worked out—the option lapsed, and that was that. But I always remembered that story. It's really a problem finding material. It limits me as it limits everybody else. And I'm very tough on material—there's not a lot of stuff I like, particularly after I finished those two giant epics, *The Winds of War* and *War and Remembrance*. I mean, everything paled by comparison, and nothing appealed to me. It was awful; I was in a very depressed state. I thought, "I'll never find anything else I want to do." Then, I remembered the *Gary Feldman* script. It was a sweet little movie, a direct departure from the epics I'd been making. So I optioned it again and developed the screenplay—without talking to any studios. I just developed the material myself, and I thought I would try to put it together and make a deal. I took it around to a few places and met a lot of people who felt the central relationship needed to be developed more, but I said, "Hold the phone; I believe this works—I'll make it myself!" And that's what happened.[163]

Curtis spent four million dollars of his own money filming *Me and the Kid* in California, New York, and New Jersey from mid-October to early December 1992. Producer-director Curtis had some input into Richard Tannenbaum's script, and Robert Cobert supplied the jaunty background music (as well as a song, "Goin' to Mexico"). Tracy Curtis served as associate producer.

Neglected by his parents (David Dukes and Anita Morris), Gary Feldman (Alex Zuckerman) is a sheltered rich boy who walks in on two inept burglars, Harry Banner (Danny Aiello) and Roy Walls (John Karlen lookalike Joe Pantoliano), cracking his father's safe. When the safe is devoid of cash, the crooks kidnap Gary instead. This is the most fun that Gary has had in his whole life! He would rather stay with the criminals, especially Harry, than return home.

After parting with the cruel Roy, the kind-hearted Harry takes Gary with him on a cross-country adventure that leads them to an out-of-the-way motel and amusement park run by Rose Farrell (Cathy Moriarty). As the police, the FBI, and Gary's parents close in, the boy does something outlandish that allows Harry to escape. The final scene takes place "six months later."

The cast of *Me and the Kid* is excellent—it also includes Demond Wilson, Abe Vigoda, Robin Thomas, Ben Stein, and Rick Aiello—but the story, of a boy who befriends a crook and travels with him, was difficult to sell. Curtis was aiming for a latter-day *Kid* (1921) or *Champ* (1931, 1979)—with elements of buddy movies, road movies, and his own 1974 *Great Ice Rip-Off* caper movie—but *Me and the Kid* became lost amid the many *Home Alone* (1990) imitations of the early 1990s. Perhaps the worst blow was that *Me and the Kid* (released on Friday 22 October 1993) appeared at essentially the same time (24 November) as Clint Eastwood's much higher-profile film

A Perfect World (1993), which itself was the story of a boy who accompanies a criminal (Kevin Costner) on his capers.

Despite favorable audience response at early screenings, *Me and the Kid* made no impression at the box office and vanished quickly. (By Wednesday 30 March 1994, it was available on VHS. It came to DVD in 2004. I showed it to my Tennessee State University students in 2007.) The *Los Angeles Times* called the film "an amiable family entertainment for the undemanding, but it has the potential to be much more."[164] *Variety* noted young Alex Zuckerman's "unaffected acting,"[165] but the *Orange County Register* criticized the film's "weak" script and "major flaws in feasibility."[166] Granted, the beginning and the end of *Me and the Kid* could be considered weak or implausible, and a nevertheless very strong, delightful middle could not counteract those flaws. The *Los Angeles Times* praised the "lovable duo" of Danny Aiello and Alex Zuckerman but lamented, "You really want their picture to be better."[167]

***Me and the Kid* (1993): Danny Aiello (left) shares a moment between takes with director Dan Curtis.**

In an interview in the Thursday 9 December 1993 *Wire*, Dan Curtis blamed Orion Pictures for "opening and closing *Me and the Kid* in a week." He insisted, "The promotion was all wrong. It opened as a well-kept secret. Nobody came to see it. It broke my heart. I lost my tail on it. Never, never again will I finance a movie with my own money."[168] As *Me and the Kid* found a small cult audience on home video, Curtis put his noble experiment behind him and refocused his attention on television—and *Dark Shadows*.

Still yearning for a full-fledged revival of his Gothic serial, Curtis, in June 1993, toyed with the idea of making two *Dark Shadows* movies. However, no such movies materialized. In July, Curtis made plans to film a four-hour miniseries of Richard Matheson's 1991 Western novel *Journal of the Gun Years* for TNT. Sadly, in early 1994, he shelved his plans for this promising, change-of-pace Curtis/Matheson collaboration. Thursday, June 2, of that year found Curtis reunited with Herman Wouk as they and members of Congress gathered at the Library of Congress to commemorate the 50th anniversary of D-Day (four days early). Clips from *War and Remembrance* were a part of the program.

In mid-1995, Curtis again considered remaking *The Night Stalker*, an idea that would prove to be another ten years away from fruition. On Thursday 7 December 1995 (Pearl Harbor Day), the *War* filmmaker was the guest speaker at a University of Southern California directing class. Finally, in the spring of 1996, Curtis traveled to Toronto to make another TV-movie—and another horror TV-movie at that.

Because the Zuni fetish doll had become so much a part of popular culture over the years—even being spoofed on an episode of *The Simpsons* and made into a collectible action figure—Curtis decided to film **Trilogy of Terror II** for the USA Network in 1996. It turned out to be his final horror presentation on television. (The 2004 *Dark Shadows* pilot for WB never aired.) *Trilogy of Terror II*, seen on Wednesday 30 October 1996, proved to be a powerful finale to Curtis's unique brand of horror television. This latter-day sequel is perhaps scarier than either *Trilogy of Terror* (1975) or *Dead of Night* (1977).

Trilogy of Terror II (1996): Lysette Anthony (*Dark Shadows* '91) plays Alma in "Bobby," the second segment.

Stepping into Karen Black's role as the woman around whom each story is built is Lysette Anthony, Angelique from the 1991 *Dark Shadows*. The first story, adapted by

William F. Nolan and Dan Curtis, is "The Graveyard Rats," based on the March 1936 *Weird Tales* story by fantasy author Henry Kuttner (*Dr. Cyclops*, "The Twonky," "Mimsy Were the Borogroves"). It tells a terrifying, *noir*-ish story of a rich old man (Matt Clark), his trophy wife (Anthony), her lover (Geraint Wyn Davies), and a gravedigger (Geoffrey Lewis), all devoured by greed, lust, or rats.

The second story is a shot-for-shot remake of "Bobby," Richard Matheson's story from *Dead of Night* (1977). Lysette Anthony assumes Joan Hackett's role of Alma. Dan Curtis faithfully follows Matheson's script and almost all of his own camera angles and shots from his earlier filming of Alma's ordeal at the hands of her demonic son. This time, however, the storm outside is even fiercer, Robert Cobert's dire music adds eerie synthesized effects, and the climax is even scarier. "Bobby" still packs a punch and explores Richard Matheson's trademark theme of one person, alone, against insurmountable odds (e.g. the last man on earth, the shrinking man, the time traveler, the motorist in *Duel*, Amelia in *Trilogy of Terror*, Bobby's mother Alma, etc.).

William F. Nolan explained that Matheson was not involved with *Trilogy of Terror II*. "Dan simply reshot Matheson's 'Bobby' from his earlier script and put it in as the middle story. Then, he and I wrote the other two as a team. I had always wanted to have a crack at writing about the Zuni doll—since it was all anybody ever talked about from the first *Trilogy*—so it was very satisfying being able to do it at last."[169] Curiously, the third story, "He Who Kills," is both a sequel to and a remake of Matheson's "Amelia" story about the Zuni fetish doll in *Trilogy of Terror*. This story begins soon after Amelia's story has ended. Amelia has died (off-camera), and the police take the charred Zuni doll to Dr. Simpson (Lysette Anthony again), a scientist who examines it at her office in a natural-history museum after hours. The Zuni doll comes back to life and stalks her through the museum, and what follows is a close remake of the original segment's frantic, bloody battle of wits between woman and doll.

In an interview in the November 1996 *Cinefantastique*, Curtis called *Trilogy of Terror II* "scarier" than the original, "and it has more humor in it."[170] *USA Today* raved that *Trilogy of Terror II* is "not only the best and spookiest new offering of the TV season, but it is also a wonderful and worthy nod to an old TV classic. Revisiting *Trilogy of Terror* was a clever choice. Equally clever was casting Lysette Anthony."[171] *USA Today* also dubbed these three stories "more ambitious" than the 1975 stories and added, "From its morbid opening credits to its final shock sequence, *Trilogy of Terror II* is a treat all the way."[172]

The *New York Daily News* declared that the Zuni fetish doll had "lost none of its menace—or teeth—in the intervening years. If you enjoyed the original *Trilogy of Terror*, you'll want to scope out the sequel as well."[173] On New Year's Eve of 1996, the *N.Y. Daily News* named *Trilogy of Terror II* one of the best made-for-TV movies of '96.[174] Months later, makeup artist Rick Stratton (*Edward Scissorhands*, *Batman Forever*) was nominated for an Emmy Award for his *Trilogy of Terror II* makeup and prosthetics.

Trilogy of Terror II, with its strict remake of "Bobby," its loose remake of "Amelia," and its outstanding new Henry Kuttner adaptation, serves as a synthesis of *Dead of Night* and *Trilogy of Terror*, with new tips of the hat to *Weird Tales* and *film noir* as well. William F. Nolan expressed only one regret: "In my opinion, the best segment of all would have been my adaptation of Philip K. Dick's 'The Father-Thing,' but it got dropped at the last moment and replaced with Matheson's 'Bobby.' My Dick teleplay was very frightening, but no one ever got a chance to see it."[175]

In a 2010 telephone conversation with me, Nolan revealed that *Trilogy of Terror II* (1996) had been germinating for 17 years. In 1979, Dan Curtis had wanted to produce an anthology TV series called *House of Terror*, and Nolan had written the first drafts of his "Graveyard Rats" and "Father-Thing" scripts at that time. *House of Terror* never materialized, and ten years later (1989), Curtis first made plans with Nolan to make *Trilogy of Terror II*. Curtis finally made the film in early 1996. Nolan remembered that he met with Curtis in May 2000 about making another story about the Zuni doll, but they decided against it. Nolan last saw Curtis in April 2004 at the Museum of Television and Radio in Los Angeles.

In 1996-1997, Dan Curtis and Morgan Creek Productions planned a theatrical version of *The Night Stalker*—with a new, perhaps younger actor to play reporter Carl Kolchak. Nick Nolte expressed an interest in playing Kolchak but was never officially cast. On Thursday 12 December 1996, the headline on the front page of *The Hollywood Reporter* proclaimed, "NIGHT STALKER ON PROWL IN PIC." However, in February 1997, Morgan Creek reneged on the deal, and Kolchak hibernated for another eight-and-one-half years until the short-lived ABC-TV remake in the fall of 2005.[176]

Curtis's next telefilm became the seventh-highest-rated *Hallmark Hall of Fame* presentation in history when it was watched by 20,920,000 viewers. **The Love Letter** (CBS, Sunday 1 February 1998) was a critically acclaimed adaptation of time-travel master Jack Finney's short story about kindred spirits who exchange passionate letters across two centuries. The story first appeared in the 1 August 1959 edition of *The Saturday Evening Post*.

In the updated film version, set in Massachusetts, Scott Corrigan (Campbell Scott) lives in 1998 while the poet Elizabeth Whitcomb (Jennifer Jason Leigh) lives in 1863. Scott buys an antique desk that happened to belong to Elizabeth, and inside a secret compartment he finds a letter that Lizzie has written to her unknown soulmate, whoever, wherever, and *whenever* he is. Scott begins mailing letters to Lizzie at an 1857-era U.S. Post Office still in use. She sends letters to him by leaving them in the secret compartment of the desk that both of them own, 135 years apart.

Lizzie's father (Gerrit Graham) is forcing Lizzie into a marriage to Everett Reagle (Curtis regular David Dukes) until she flees to Boston and meets Colonel Caleb Denby (Campbell Scott) at the very moment that Scott, in 1998, has suffered a bicycling injury and is unconscious. Scott's fiancée Debra (Daphne Ashbrook) and his mother Beatrice (Estelle Parsons) wait for him to recover, and he does. Lizzie loses Colonel Denby in the Battle of Gettysburg, and Scott loses Debra because of his obsession with Lizzie and her world. The final scene takes place at the grave of Elizabeth Whitcomb (1834-1901) as Scott Corrigan begins a new chapter in his life.

The Love Letter is exquisitely romantic and heartfelt, and Robert Cobert's music is especially wistful and sentimental. One of the most sublime moments occurs when Scott and Lizzie feel each other's presence when they traverse the same staircase in their respective times. *Love Letter* scriptwriter James Henerson (*Love on a Rooftop*, *The Second Hundred Years*) won the Writers Guild of America award for the Best Long-Form Screenplay of 1998.

The Love Letter (1998): Between *Somewhere in Time* and *The Lake House,* there is Dan Curtis's love letter to romantic fantasy. Campbell Scott and Jennifer Jason Leigh co-star in one of the highest-rated *Hallmark Hall of Fame* presentations.

Curtis directed the Hallmark movie in and around Richmond, Petersburg, and Manakin, Virginia, during the fall of 1997. Lizzie's house was actually the Tuckahoe historic home in Manakin. Curtis admitted that he had wanted to film Finney's time-travel romance for two decades. *The Love Letter* "is the most magical love story I've ever come across," he uncharacteristically gushed. Curtis explained,

> It transcends time and will enchant the audience. It reaches into your heart because it's about two people yearning for each other, separated by almost 150 years, who exist simultaneously and communicate through letters. Watching this movie is going to be the equivalent of curling up in front of the fireplace on a winter's night with a wonderful, engaging romantic novel. You just know it's going to make you feel good, and that's what *The Love Letter* does. It tells us that romance is always possible in our lives—even though it may occur in very unusual ways![177]

USA Today observed, "Producer-director Curtis, who gingerly moved between time periods and parallel dimensions on the classic soap *Dark Shadows,* is up to his old tricks."[178] *Entertainment Weekly* awarded *The Love Letter* the grade of **A-** and added, "It's like that rarest of Hallmark cards: unabashedly romantic yet surprisingly light on cheese."[179] The *Christian Science Monitor* called *The Love Letter* "a delightful high romance; the movie spins a fantastic story of love that transcends time itself; beautifully acted and directed, it creates a world that is entirely engaging."[180] *Variety* praised the film's "well-executed script, based on a Jack Finney short story, that melds romance, fantasy, and quasi-time travel and is enhanced by endearing performances from its principals," including Scott, Leigh, Parsons, and Dukes. According to *Variety*,

> Director Dan Curtis keeps the pace brisk, knowing when to move the tale along or to slow down for some weepy moments that are crucial but never indulgent. He is aided by Eric Van Haren Norman's camerawork, which uses the striking shades of autumn to backdrop the story and its emotional underpinnings while soaking in Jan Scott's lush production design. Bill Blunden's editing makes it all seamless. The only quibble is this Hallmark card should have been saved for airing closer to Valentine's Day [instead of 13 days prior to the date].[181]

Jennifer Jason Leigh of *I Think I'm Having a Baby* and *The Love Letter* declared, "I love Dan Curtis. With everything he's done—all those huge miniseries like *War and Remembrance*—I mean, he's a legend. But he's got a great young attitude and a really sweet heart. He's got this tough-guy exterior and this deep, gruff voice, but he really is a marshmallow."[182]

Curtis's softer side did shine through in his sensitive direction of *The Love Letter*. Indeed, one wonders how *Somewhere in Time* (1980), Richard Matheson's gold-standard time-travel romance, would have been different if Dan Curtis, not Jeannot Szwarc (*The Devil's Daughter, Jaws 2, Supergirl*), had directed it. Matheson named a *Somewhere in Time* character Professor Finney, after Jack Finney, and the 2000 South Korean film *Il Mare* (and its 2006 American remake *The Lake House*) appropriated Finney's actual plot of lovers separated by time but connected by their letters.

One also wonders about the possibilities of a project mentioned by Matthew Bradley in *The Richard Matheson Companion* (Gauntlet, 2008): "As early as 1973, Matheson had adapted 'The Love Letter' into a half-hour script for the abortive *Dead of Night* series, but it was never filmed, and a quarter-century later, Curtis and screenwriter James Henerson expanded the story into a two-hour *Hallmark Hall of Fame* presentation."[183] Perhaps, in some parallel band of time, there is a *Love Letter* adapted by Richard Matheson or a *Somewhere in Time* directed by Dan Curtis. There also could be a Dan Curtis production called *I Love Harrisburg in the Springtime*, an unproduced script that Jack Finney wrote for Curtis in mid-1974.

The Love Letter was Curtis's final film before a seven-year-long absence from the screen. On Tuesday 3 March 1998, one month after CBS aired *The Love Letter*, Curtis received the Golden Laurel Award from the Producers Guild of America. On Wednesday 27 January 1999 in Los Angeles, Curtis participated in the Museum of Television and Radio's seminar about film and television portrayals of the Holocaust from the 1950s to the 1990s. *War and Remembrance*, of course, held its own with *The Diary of Anne Frank* (1959) and *Schindler's List* (1993). On Monday 23 October 2000, the Museum of Television and Radio honored Curtis, Karen Black, Robert Cobert, Richard Matheson, and William F. Nolan at its seminar, "Monster in the Box: Horror on Television" (or, more accurately, Dan Curtis's horror on television). The audience and the honorees watched *Trilogy of Terror* and then engaged in a question-and-answer session.

On Thursday 8 March 2001, Curtis once again appeared at the Museum of TV and Radio for what would be a once-in-a-lifetime gathering of *Dark Shadows* stars and fans. The Dark Shadows Festival fan conventions had been held around the country every year since 1983, but Curtis had never attended one. Finally, he did participate in this momentous *Dark Shadows* 35th-anniversary reunion with composer Robert Cobert, director Lela Swift, designer Sy Tomashoff, and actors Nancy Barrett, Roger Davis, Kate Jackson, John Karlen, Jerry Lacy, Alexandra Moltke, Lara Parker, Christopher Pennock, Robert Rodan, Mitchell Ryan, Kathryn Leigh Scott, David Selby, and James Storm. It was the most highly and enthusiastically attended gathering in the museum's series of classic-TV reunion seminars. Surrounded by his cast, Dan Curtis marveled,

> The greatest fun in the world was hiring all of these people. I just hired people I liked. I couldn't tell if they could act or they couldn't. But I'll tell you something: they all learned. I've never seen anything like it. I remember when Katie [Jackson] came on, she could barely say her own name, but by the time she started to work in the story every day, she became great. *Everybody* became wonderful in this, and I would have a great time. I'd show up at this place [the *Dark Shadows* studio], and it felt like home. It was a big repertory company. In reality, that's what it was. The one thing I wanted to do and I never did—we just never got around to doing it—during the Christmas holidays, when there are no ratings, but we were booming along and I didn't want to waste the story that we had, I thought, why shouldn't we put the whole group together and for two weeks do Charles Dickens's *A Christmas Carol* with the *Dark Shadows* Players, and I really was going to do it. Each Christmas came along, and I never got to do it, and that's the one thing I regret.[184]

Later in 2001, Curtis considered making films about the Civil War, Franklin Delano Roosevelt's "Four Freedoms" speech, and the 1951 scandal involving the West Point football team. Development agreements for *Four Freedoms* scripts by Joyce Carol Oates, Tom Rickman, Steven DeSouza, and Frank Deford exist, as does sportswriter Deford's actual 2002 script of *The Price of Honor*, but none of these projects came to fruition.

In the early 2000s, Norma Klein Curtis began showing signs of the Alzheimer's disease which (along with heart disease) would end her life in March 2006. Ironically, Curtis's next-to-last film was about a man's struggle with his wife's debilitating neurological disease.

First, *Dark Shadows* occupied the director's attention once again. Ever since the short-lived 1991 revival, Curtis had been seeking a way to reincarnate the show yet again. He had considered a theatrical film, a nighttime TV series, a daytime series, an animated series, and even a Broadway musical (with music by Robert Cobert and Rupert Holmes). In early 2002, the Fox network considered making a new, nighttime *Dark Shadows* based on a script by Eric Bernt, writer of the 2000 films *Romeo Must Die* and *Highlander: Endgame*, but Fox eventually passed on the idea.

Finally, in 2003, the WB network, which had enjoyed considerable success with its shows about vampires, super-heroes, and teenagers, greenlighted the pilot for a new, younger, hipper **Dark Shadows**. Executive producers Dan Curtis and John Wells (*ER, The West Wing*) asked Rob Bowman, one of the directors of the 1991 series, to direct the lavish, six-million-dollar pilot film. The scriptwriter was Mark Verheiden, who had written for *Timecop* (1997-1998) and *Smallville* (2001-2011).

Verheiden prepared for the job by watching some 1967 episodes of *Dark Shadows*, the two movies, and all of the 1991 series. Although Dan Curtis wanted to restage the 1967 Barnabas-out-of-the-coffin storyline and the 1795 saga, Verheiden desired a new approach, perhaps one focusing on young David Collins. His ideas brought him into conflict with both Curtis and the WB. "I hate it" is what Verheiden reported that Curtis said to him several times.[185]

Another idea that Verheiden devised was Victoria's witnessing Collinsport locals engaging in an ancient Halloween ritual around a bonfire. Verheiden explained,

> I really wanted to set it in a different world, but that collided with what the network wanted. They were very concerned that it *not* be like a different place. They wanted it to feel like this was a town in "real Maine, USA." It was a valid request but a bit hard to make come together because on *Dark Shadows*, the characters *are* in kind of a strange place—it's just the nature of the Gothic.[186]

Finally, Verheiden crafted a script that once again launched *Dark Shadows* with the arrival via train of Victoria Winters (Marley Shelton) and with Willie Loomis's release of Barnabas Collins (Alec Newman) from the chained coffin. This time, Willie (Matt Czuchry) has a girlfriend, Kelly Greer (Alexis Thorpe), who is present at the unchaining and who becomes Barnabas's first victim. Verheiden was pleased and proud when Peter Roth, head of Warner Brothers, called him and said that the script was "the best he'd read all year."[187]

The 41-minute pilot, filmed at Greystone Mansion in Beverly Hills, also introduces Roger Collins (Martin Donovan), intended to be the J.R. Ewing-like villain to

Barnabas's hero; Elizabeth Collins Stoddard (Blair Brown); Carolyn Stoddard (Jessica Chastain); David Collins (Alexander Gould); Dr. Julia Hoffman (Kelly Hu); and several other Collinsport citizens. Curtis wanted to introduce even more characters in the pilot, but Verhdeiden protested that the script was overcrowded. Therefore, there is no Professor Stokes or Professor Woodard character, and there is no Maggie Evans. There is, however, Angelique (Ivana Milicevic), who for the first time is introduced simultaneously with Barnabas and Victoria. The pilot's final, unfinished scene, in which Angelique crashes through the windshield of Victoria's car, would have had to have been redone or even excised before it matched the more serious tone of the rest of the pilot.

A definite misstep is Blair Brown's wrong-headed portrayal of Elizabeth Collins Stoddard. Brown lacks the majesty of Joan Bennett and Jean Simmons, and she does further disservice to the character by playing her as wacky and scatterbrained. Her sitcom-like portrayal does not complement the more serious efforts by Donovan and Newman in their interpretations of Roger and Barnabas. In the early stages of the pilot, the Internet hummed with fans' wishes that Kathryn Leigh Scott, Marie Wallace, or Kate Jackson could have played Elizabeth. In fact, Scott, as well as Susan Sullivan, did audition for the role, but co-producer John Wells pushed for Blair Brown (*Captains and the Kings*).

Because this is a WB television production, the young men and women are fashionably beautiful as required by the network's distinctive look. Willie Loomis and Joe Haskell (Jason Shaw) could be models, Victoria and Carolyn are extremely attractive, and even Barnabas and Julia have been made more youthful. The reduction in Barnabas's age actually is a wise move because Jonathan Frid and Ben Cross (both in their early forties when they played Barnabas) had been too old for the part. Barnabas had become a vampire when he had been a young man in his early twenties, so it is logical that he would have retained a more youthful appearance in un-death.

Rob Bowman had bowed out of the WB project in order to direct *Elektra* (2005), and last-minute replacement director P.J. Hogan, while able to helm an excellent version of *Peter Pan* in 2003, did not quite capture the essence of *Dark Shadows*. Mark Verheiden recalled that Hogan attempted a colorful, overly artistic, "Dario Argento/*Suspiria* look" that Verheiden called "nerve-wracking because the Argento style can be emotionally distancing."[188] Argento was the stylish Italian director of *Deep Red* (1975), *Suspiria* (1977), *Inferno* (1980), *Opera* (1987), and *Trauma* (1993). Critic Mark Dawidziak stated the situation more harshly when he observed, in his talk at the 2005 Dark Shadows Festival, that much of the pilot was "lighted like a French whorehouse." Victoria's overcoat is yellow, the side of a building is blue, and many walls are lighted red. Adding to the weird effect was the musical temp track, which temporarily scored the pilot with cues from *Klute* (1971), *Deep Red* (1975), and *Jennifer Eight* (1992). Post-production work on the pilot never progressed to the point of adding (or even commissioning) Robert Cobert's all-important compositions.

Dark Shadows (2004): Ivana Milicevic and Alec Newman portray Angelique and Barnabas in the unsold pilot for the WB network. In 2006, both Milicevic (Angelique '04) and Eva Green (Angelique '12) appear in the James Bond film *Casino Royale*. In 2008, Newman re-enters the world of *Dark Shadows* as a voice artist in Big Finish Productions' *Dark Shadows* CD audio dramas *Clothes of Sand* and *The Ghost Watcher,* both co-starring Kathryn Leigh Scott.

Despite these drawbacks, *Dark Shadows* '04 displayed great promise for a contemporary reinvention of the series. Most of the cast, especially the young women, played their roles very well, and Alec Newman displayed the definite potential for developing into a strong, romantic Barnabas. Having portrayed Paul Atreides in two *Dune* miniseries (2000, 2003) for the Sci-Fi Channel and Victor Frankenstein in the Hallmark Channel's superb 2004 *Frankenstein* miniseries, Newman had proven that he could play a tortured soul. Also, for the first time, the cast of *Dark Shadows* was multicultural. The original series had included only one Asian American and two African Americans in minor, short-term roles, and the 1991 remake had featured one African-American actor in the small role of a police officer. For *Dark Shadows* '04, Dr. Hoffman (Kelly Hu) was Asian-American, Sheriff George Patterson (Michael D. Roberts) was African-American, and the young housekeeper "Sophia" (Jenna Dewan)—not the middle-aged Mrs. Johnson of the two previous series—was described as Latina. Curtis looked forward to a spot for his new show on the WB's fall 2004 schedule.

Nevertheless, when Curtis and co-producer John Wells screened the unfinished pilot for Warner Brothers executives in June 2004, the executives rejected it out of hand and expressed no interest in retooling it. In July, WB chairman Garth Ancier said, "We had a new director [Hogan] come in who was accomplished in movies but frankly didn't do a particularly good job, and the rest is history." Ancier added, "The script was terrific, [but] creatively, the end result did not come out the way we'd all hoped for."[189] The WB had driven a stake through the heart of *Dark Shadows* '04. Lacking post-production, titles, and music, the pilot never was telecast or released on video or DVD. Its only public exhibitions have taken place at Dark Shadows Festival fan conventions.

Dan Curtis, although terribly disappointed, was philosophical. "*Dark Shadows* refuses to die," he declared. "I can never escape it. The new pilot didn't work out, but we're still looking at other possibilities. We've considered a stage version, and it would make a great feature film, so who knows what might happen next?"[190]

The WB later regretted its decision to shelve *Dark Shadows,* for the show's fall 2004 debut would have caught the wave of the similarly mystical and quirky *Lost* and *Desperate Housewives,* which premiered that fall, as well as *Medium* (which began in January 2005) and the *six* horror/sci-fi-themed TV series (including *Supernatural, Invasion,* and *Ghost Whisperer*) that debuted in the fall of 2005. Dan Curtis and replacement director P.J. Hogan had never quite gelled in their visions for *Dark Shadows,* and Curtis felt that a Rob Bowman-directed pilot (if not a Dan Curtis-directed one) would have stood a better chance of successfully reimagining *Dark Shadows* for the 21st century.

On Thursday 22 April 2004, Curtis made his final appearance at the Museum of Television and Radio in Los Angeles for "*War, Shadows,* and *The Night Stalker*: A Conversation with Dan Curtis." Near the end of his career, Curtis finally was receiving the kind of recognition that his Gothic-horror projects, his Western, and his two *War* miniseries had always warranted.

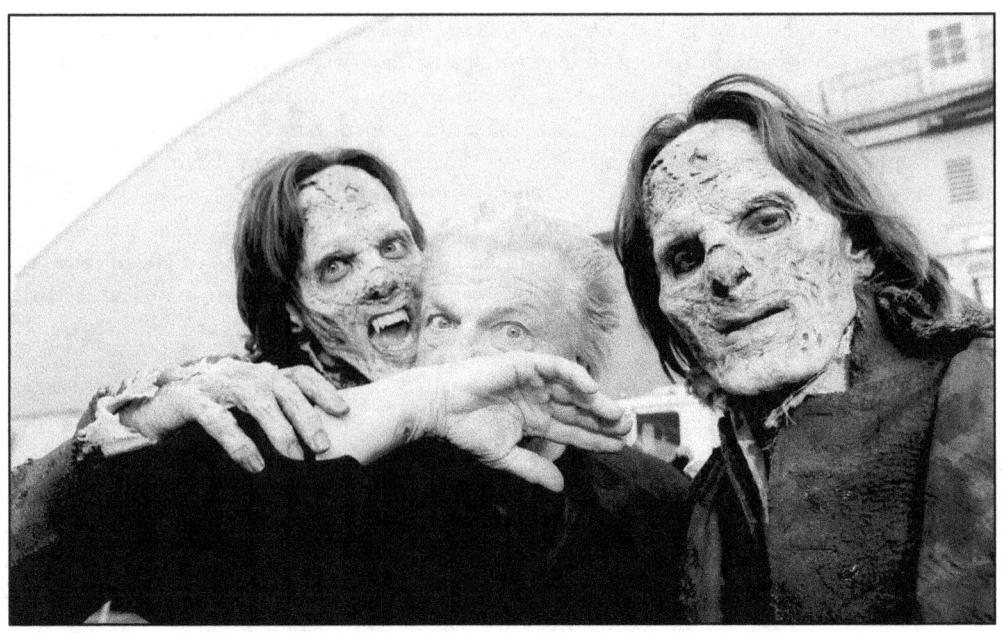

Dark Shadows (2004): Original *Dark Shadows* actor John Karlen is attacked by "vampires" when he visits the set of the unsold pilot. Karlen does not appear in the pilot film (although he *could* have played the old man on the train).

On 22 April 2004, Dan Curtis (now 76 years old) poses for a picture at the Museum of Television and Radio in Los Angeles. Curtis is at the museum to be honored for his 41 years as a producer—from *Challenge Golf* '63 to *Dark Shadows* '04.

In mid-2004, Curtis directed a heartbreakingly beautiful PSA (**public-service announcement**) for the Alzheimer's Association. The four-minute film depicts an elderly couple walking along a beach as Barbra Streisand's recording of Marvin Hamlisch's song "The Way We Were" is heard on the soundtrack. Home-movie-style flashback footage shows the woman and man much younger and living through the milestones of their lives. According to Jim Pierson, "Dan was frustrated as he never saw it shown anywhere. Ironically, the PSA's voice artist, Peter Falk, later suffered from Alzheimer's disease."[191] So did my mother, Sonia Anne Young Thompson, who passed away in May 2018 as I was preparing the revised second edition of *The Television Horrors of Dan Curtis*.

Curtis's final two films recalled the heartrending drama of his two semi-autobiographical TV-movies and the issue-oriented fare of *Mrs. R's Daughter* (1979). **Saving Milly** (CBS, Sunday 13 March 2005; rerun Sunday 9 July 2006), filmed in Vancouver, was based on political journalist Mort Kondracke's non-fiction best-seller of the same name. As adapted by Jeff Arch (*Sleepless in Seattle, Iron Will*), *Saving Milly* is the story of Kondracke's 38-year-long love affair with his activist/therapist wife Millicent "Milly" Martinez Kondracke (d. 22 July 2004), who is diagnosed with an especially severe form of Parkinson's disease. Bruce Greenwood and Madeleine Stowe play Mort and Milly as they meet, fall in love, marry, raise two daughters, deal with his alcoholism, and face her devastating illness. The story is framed by Mort's testimony before a Congressional subcommittee on behalf of Parkinson's research, and it is tagged by remarks by Michael J. Fox (*Family Ties*) and the real-life Mort Kondracke (*The Beltway Boys*). Madeleine Stowe, who gives a brilliant and heartbreaking performance, won an Imagen Award for Best Television Actress. Jeff Arch's emotional script was nominated for the Humanitas Prize. Lee Holdridge (*Beauty and the Beast, The Dreamer of Oz*) composed the music.

Curtis admitted that he was drawn to the project because Alzheimer's disease had touched his family and he wanted to raise the public's awareness of all debilitating neurological diseases. "I'm usually never happy to hear about people crying," Curtis told *USA Today*. "This time, I am. *Saving Milly* is not a disease-of-the-week movie. If we can get the word out there, without it being a lesson or homework, and tell a great, moving love story, a ten-handkerchief picture, then I'll do it."[192] He did.

The *New York Daily News* called *Saving Milly* "challenging," "well-acted," and "tender," as well as "part passionate romance, part advocacy piece, and definitely worth a look."[193] The Parents Television Council named it "the best TV show of the week."[194] *The Hollywood Reporter* called *Saving Milly* "a beautifully acted, deeply moving film that manages to be at once inspirational and grueling."[195] Susan Stewart of *TV Guide* observed, "*Milly* may rely on the conventions and clichés of the issue movie, but it also boasts moments of unusual intimacy and candor. My score (0-10): **7**."[196]

Two months later, Curtis was back on television with another hard-hitting topical work—and his swan song. **Our Fathers** (Showtime, Saturday 21 May 2005) was a fact-based examination of the Boston Catholic diocese's sex-abuse scandal as it was first exposed in 2000. Christopher Plummer portrayed Cardinal Bernard Law and received Emmy and SAG Award nominations. Brian Dennehy, as Father Dominic Spagnolia, also received an Emmy Award nomination.

Director Dan Curtis and *Back to the Future* star Michael J. Fox smile on the set of *Saving Milly* (2005). Fox appears as himself at the end of Curtis's next-to-last film.

Boston attorney Mitchell Garabedian (Ted Danson) organizes more and more victims of sexual abuse until 86 plaintiffs sue the diocese and Cardinal Law. Among the victims, now grown men, are Angelo DeFranco (Daniel Baldwin), Patrick McSorley (James Oliver), and Gary Bergeron (Thomas Mitchell). Garabedian interviews Mary Ryan (Ellen Burstyn), the mother of seven sons, *all* of whom were abused by Father John Geoghan (played by Damien Atkins [young] and Steven Shaw [old]), who is convicted, imprisoned, and ultimately murdered in his jail cell.

One of the highlights of the film is the scene in which another victim, Olan Horne (Chris Bauer of *The Wire*), confronts Cardinal Law at his residence and shames Law into facing the men in a support group for sex-abuse victims. The cast also includes Kenneth Welsh, Jan Rubes, Will Lyman, Kathleen Laskey, Hugh Dillon, and Wayne Best. Colin Fox of *Strange Paradise* plays Law's advisor Daniel Kibbe.

Curtis's film was based on the book *Our Fathers: The Secret Life of the Catholic Church in an Age of Scandal,* by *Newsweek* writer David France (himself a victim of abuse). The screenplay by Thomas Michael Donnelly (*Quicksilver, Talent for the Game*) was nominated for a Writers Guild of America award for Best Long-Form Adapted Screenplay. Robert Cobert composed the music.

    Curtis sought to make a non-sensational, balanced look at both the church and the victims. "It had everything that I thought would make a really riveting picture," he noted. "Then comes the difficulty of doing something that's as touchy as this. How do you do it? It's kind of simple in a strange way. You just tell the truth."[197] Indeed, *USA Today* observed, "Curtis never allows a trace of salaciousness to enter the film. He sets the tone without showing anything explicit."[198] Nevertheless, the *Boston Herald* conceded, "If your heart hasn't already been broken by the priest sex-abuse scandal, then Showtime's strong film *Our Fathers* will finish the job."[199]

    The San Jose *Mercury News* proclaimed that *Our Fathers* was "everything most TV docudramas about recent events are *not*: thoughtful, restrained without sacrificing emotion, and with a clear ring of truth to it." The *News* added, "The real emotional core is the way *Our Fathers* handles the effect the abuse had on the victims. Without being explicit, the film captures the horror these young men went through as their innocence, faith, and trust were ripped away."[200]

    TV Guide's Matt Roush noted, "Dan Curtis knows all about *Dark Shadows*, and there are plenty to be found in the conspiracy of silence that is shattered in *Our Fathers*, a forceful and sorrowful docudrama."[201] Ten years later, Stanley Tucci played Mitchell Garabedian, and Len Cariou played Cardinal Law, in Josh Singer and Tom McCarthy's film *Spotlight*, which won the Academy Award for the Best Picture of 2015.

    In the fall of 2005, ABC attempted a remake of its 1974-1975 series *Kolchak: The Night Stalker*, based on Dan Curtis and Richard Matheson's TV-movies *The Night Stalker* (1972) and *The Night Strangler* (1973). In this new series, titled simply *Night Stalker*, Stuart Townsend (*Queen of the Damned*) played a much younger, more upscale Carl Kolchak, who, along with a team of crime reporters, investigated paranormal events in southern California. A brief, almost subliminal clip of Darren McGavin as Kolchak appeared in the first episode (Thursday 29 September 2005), as did McGavin's trademark straw hat on the new Kolchak's coat rack. There, the similarities between the incarnations ended. The dark, humorless *Night Stalker* was much more like *The X-Files*, *CSI*, and everything else on 1990s/2000s television than the unique, seriocomic *Kolchak: The Night Stalker* of yore. *Entertainment Weekly* and *Variety* summed up the lackluster series perfectly when the former wrote, "This remake of the 1970s cult classic [. . .] has an eerie, *X-Files* vibe,"[202] and the latter added, "It lacks the flavor of the original."[203]

    Also, *Night Stalker* was too affluent and stylish to be like its predecessor, which had reveled in Kolchak's shabbiness. The remake lacked the original's wit, as well as (according to *Syndicated*) "heart, drama, and—most inexcusably—horror."[204] In November, ABC unceremoniously dropped the series after airing six of its ten episodes. Ironically, the unaired eighth episode, "Into Night," promisingly evoked *The Night Stalker* (1972) in its story of a vampire-like killer, and the ninth and best episode, "Timeless," was practically a remake of *The Night Strangler* (1973) as an ageless woman commits murders in 1900, 1935, 1970, and 2005 in order to retain her youth. Those and all of the other episodes of *Night Stalker* finally aired on the Sci-Fi Channel in the summer and fall of 2006. Dan Curtis, who had not been associated with the 1974-1975 series, was involved with the 2005 effort as a consulting producer who merely offered some script suggestions.

On Saturday 25 February 2006, Darren McGavin, the original and definitive Kolchak, died at the age of 83. It was a sad foreshadowing of two more imminent deaths. In November 2005, Dan Curtis was diagnosed with brain cancer. Norma Mae Klein Curtis, his wife of 54 years, was already in an advanced stage of Alzheimer's disease. Kathryn Leigh Scott—Maggie and Josette on *Dark Shadows* four decades earlier—remembered,

> My last memory of Dan is an afternoon spent in his garden not too long before he passed away. He was no longer the big, gruff lion who used to terrify us. His illness had weakened him. He could no longer speak, but he could enjoy his favorite dark chocolates I'd brought. We sat together paging through the beautiful coffee-table book Jim Pierson had put together on the occasion of Dan's 75th birthday. As we sat there in the afternoon sun, his hand would fall across the page, pointing to a particular actor or a scene from one of his films—horror, Westerns, dramas, romances, mysteries—all of them great stories, well told by a master storyteller. I am so grateful I had that precious time with Dan, to tell him how much he inspired me, encouraged me, gave me so many rare opportunities—and how much I appreciated all of it.[205]

On Tuesday 7 March 2006, Norma died of complications from Alzheimer's and heart disease. Twenty days later—Monday 27 March 2006—Dan Curtis succumbed to brain cancer at his home in Brentwood, California. Cathy and Tracy Curtis were dealt the unimaginable blow of losing both of their parents in less than three weeks' time.

The funeral for Dan Curtis was held on Thursday 30 March 2006 at Eden Memorial Park in Mission Hills, California. Rabbi Abraham Cooper conducted the service. Speakers at the funeral included Cathy Curtis, Tracy Curtis, Norma's physician and Alzheimer's researcher Dr. Jeffrey Cummings, producer Barbara Steele, and author Herman Wouk. Pallbearers were Daniel Blatt, Hart Bochner, John Karlen, David Kennedy, John McMahon, Jim Pierson, David Selby, and Robert Singer. In attendance were Robert Cobert, Roger Davis, Jerry Lacy, Lara Parker, Robert Rodan, Kathryn Leigh Scott, and James Storm (*Dark Shadows*); Karen Black (*Trilogy of Terror, Burnt Offerings*); Dean Jones (*When Every Day Was the Fourth of July, The Long Days of Summer, St. John in Exile*); Lisa Eilbacher and Peter Graves (*The Winds of War*); Barry Bostwick and Jane Seymour (*War and Remembrance*); Bruce Greenwood (*Saving Milly*); Frank Spotnitz (*X-Files* and *Night Stalker* producer); and many others.

Herman Wouk told the mourners that Dan Curtis was the only man who could have brought the truth of the Holocaust so unforgettably to life in his *War* miniseries. The other speakers remembered the director as driven, creative, indefatigable, sometimes impatient, often generous, always inspiring, and determined to succeed. His daughters shared reminiscences of their father and his exhortation to them never to give up and always to believe in themselves.[206]

On Saturday 13 May 2006, approximately 100 people attended a memorial service for Curtis at the Directors Guild in Los Angeles. A tribute video, compiled by Tracy Curtis and Dark Shadows Festival chairman Jim Pierson, presented still pictures from

Curtis's personal and professional life, followed by clips from *Dark Shadows; The Night Stalker; Dracula; Melvin Purvis, G-Man; Trilogy of Terror; When Every Day Was the Fourth of July; The Last Ride of the Dalton Gang; The Love Letter; Our Fathers;* and *Saving Milly.* Extensive clips from *The Winds of War* and *War and Remembrance* followed, as well as clips of Curtis on *Entertainment Tonight* (1983) and at the Emmy Awards (1989). Marcy Robin's *Shadowgram* #108 (June 2006) provided an in-depth report about the occasion.

In his remarks, Jim Pierson called Curtis "a world-class motivator, mentor, and creative genius" and "the ultimate fearless leader." Former ABC executive Brandon Stoddard, who had greenlighted *Dark Shadows,* cancelled *Dark Shadows,* and overseen Curtis's TV-movies and epic miniseries, called *The Winds of War* and *War and Remembrance* "the greatest achievement by one man in the history of TV or movies." Richard Matheson remembered Curtis's "creative fervor" and his eager acceptance of Matheson's last-minute changes to the script of *Dracula* (1974). Daniel Blatt recalled that in his 50-year-long friendship with Curtis, Blatt went from being Curtis's teenage golf caddy to a fellow producer (*The Howling, Cujo*), thanks to Curtis's mentoring of him and the director's "enormous largesse."

Robert Singer, like Blatt, began as Curtis's teenage caddy and became one of his associate producers (*Trilogy of Terror, Burnt Offerings*). "I'll never forget these words Dan said to me many years ago—'Kid, I'm tired of yelling; *you* yell for a while.'" Singer added that Curtis's direction of the two *War* miniseries was "the most underrated feat in the history of television." Dan Curtis Productions executive David Kennedy, who had run the company after Curtis no longer could, said that his "second father" Dan Curtis had been on an "eternal quest for excellence" and had "a never-give-up spirit."[207] Earlier, Kennedy had declared in print that Curtis's "wondrous love affair with Norma" made "Romeo and Juliet pale in comparison,"[208] and at the memorial service Kennedy compared Dan Curtis to Hamlet's father and declared, "This was a man."[209]

Kathryn Leigh Scott spoke for her *Dark Shadows* castmates when she said, "Dan gave so many of us our very first jobs [. . .] a great, rare opportunity to experiment and get paid while learning on the job." She continued,

> Every day, Dan had us climbing out on a new limb, risking failure doing a live half hour on kinescope with tons of special effects and scant rehearsal. We'd race to change costumes during commercial breaks; doorknobs came off in our hands; sets collapsed; a candle flame blew out, but the room stayed bright as day; dead bodies moved; and on a stroll through the cemetery, your cape would drag Styrofoam tombstones in your wake. And this was an era long before "bloopers" were considered funny! We begged, we wept, we pleaded for a chance to redo the show before we lost air time to the four-o'clock news, but Dan would say, "Whad d'ya kidding me? It'll air once, and no one will ever see it again." How wrong he was! The show has [almost] never been off the air. Thanks to DVDs, you can watch *Dark Shadows* on your laptop in a Brazilian jungle—and yes, *Dark Shadows* actors still earn residuals. To Dan, we were family. He wouldn't let any of us go. If the character we were playing was killed off, he'd bring us back as another character. After work, he'd join us for drinks at the pub on the corner, and sometimes he'd

take the whole gang to dinner. With *Dark Shadows* as his proving ground, Dan went on to produce and/or direct four motion pictures, 30 television films, four TV pilots, six series and miniseries, and his crowning achievements, 18 hours of *The Winds of War* and 29 hours of *War and Remembrance*. *Dark Shadows* actors continued to pop up regularly in his other productions over the years, and in the case of Bob Cobert, who composed the music for *Dark Shadows,* he went on to compose [almost] all of Dan's scores for 40 years. Many of us here today have 40 years' worth of wonderful memories of Dan. I will forever be indebted to him and will miss him—as we all will.[210]

Cobert, of course, was in attendance at the DGA memorial service, as were *Dark Shadows* actors Lara Parker, Christopher Pennock, Robert Rodan, and David Selby. Representing the 1991 *Dark Shadows* were actress-producer Barbara Steele, writer William Gray, and directors Paul Lynch and Armand Mastroianni. Other celebrities paying their respects included Ben Murphy (*The Winds of War*), Ian McShane (*War and Remembrance*), and Madeleine Stowe (*Saving Milly*). *The Winds of War* actress Ali MacGraw sent a letter "admiring [Dan's] vision and superhuman energy."[211]

In 1980, film historian and theatrical agent David Del Valle had met Curtis through Barbara Steele, who was his client. In 1987, Del Valle remembered, "I vividly recall sitting in a small screening room with Barbara and Dan watching the rushes of John Gielgud on his way to the gas chambers in *War and Remembrance*. When the lights went up, Dan stood up and raised his fist heavenward: 'Steven Spielberg, eat your heart out!'"[212]

That same night, Curtis had mused, "You know, when I die, even if this show wins a truckload of Emmys, they will end up saying, 'Dan Curtis, creator of daytime television's *Dark Shadows,* died today.'"[213] It was an observation that Curtis repeated, privately and publicly, several times. In March and April 2006, all of his many obituaries mentioned both *Dark Shadows* and the *War* miniseries, and most of them mentioned his many Gothic-horror projects and his professional and personal involvement with golf. The great producer-director himself had remarked,

> People have always said to me since I've finished *War and Remembrance,* "How are you going to top yourself?" That's crazy. I don't plan to try. There's nothing I can do to top myself. I will never completely recover from it. I'm not destroyed by it, but it's something that will live with me forever. It's always in my mind. The images and moments run through my mind all the time. It will never leave me—never, never. This is something I'll be proud of until the day I go.[214]

In terms of quality, ratings, and influence, the television works of Dan Curtis command a very special place in popular culture. The words, A DAN CURTIS PRODUCTION, will not soon be forgotten. Curtis's legacy will be felt for many years to come. In fact, in the mid-2010s, the Academy of Science-Fiction, Fantasy, and Horror Films gave an annual Saturn Award called the Dan Curtis Legacy Award. The Academy presented the Dan Curtis Legacy Award to a writer/producer/director who, like Curtis, delivers excellent genre entertainment. The 2013, 2014, 2015, 2016, and 2018 winners were, respectively, Vince Gilligan (*Breaking Bad, Better Call Saul, Battle*

Creek), Bryan Fuller (*Pushing Daisies, Mockingbird Lane, Star Trek: Discovery*), Carlton Cuse (*Lost, Bates Motel, The Strain*), Eric Kripke (*Supernatural, Revolution, Timeless*), and Sarah Schecter (*Supergirl, Riverdale, Black Lightning*). No award was given in 2017 or 2019, but a deserving recipient would have been Roberto Orci (*Fringe, Sleepy Hollow, Scorpion*).

Six years after the producer-director's death, the name Dan Curtis once again flashed across movie screens when Tim Burton's 2012 film *Dark Shadows* was "dedicated to the memory of Dan Curtis." Curtis's daughters Tracy and Cathy, as well as Jim Pierson, acted as consultants, and *Saving Milly* and *Our Fathers* producer David Kennedy was one of the producers. Although the music score is composed by Danny Elfman (*Batman Returns, Mars Attacks!*), the very first sound in the film is a bit of Robert Cobert's *Dark Shadows* music cue "The Secret Room." Unfortunately, Cobert's *Dark Shadows* theme, Collinwood theme, Josette's Music Box theme, or other cues are *not* heard in the film, which nevertheless features a dynamic Elfman score and early-1970s-era songs by the Carpenters, Donovan, Elton John, T. Rex, and others.

After an outstanding eight-minute prologue covering the years 1760-1776 and the origin of the relationship between Barnabas Collins (Johnny Depp) and Angelique Bouchard (Eva Green), the action moves ahead to October 1972. The residents of a Collinwood in disrepair are Elizabeth Collins Stoddard (Michelle Pfeiffer), Roger Collins (Jonny Lee Miller), Carolyn Stoddard (Chloe Grace Moretz), David Collins (Gulliver McGrath), Dr. Julia Hoffman (Helena Bonham Carter), caretaker Willie Loomis (Jackie Earle Haley), and housekeeper Mrs. Johnson (Ray Shirley). For the fourth time (1966, 1991, 2004, 2012), Dan Curtis's dream of the governess riding the train is shot—only this time, the governess is Maggie Evans, who adopts the spurious name "Victoria Winters" as the Moody Blues' "Nights in White Satin" is heard. (Simon and Garfunkel's "The Sounds of Silence" was considered for this scene.)

Bella Heathcote plays "Victoria Winters" and the ghost of Josette DuPres, and Josephine Butler plays the ghost of Laura Collins. Collinwood is a cursed house of dark shadows, full of "vampires, ghosts, and witches," in the sarcastic words of an unbelieving Elizabeth Stoddard. However, Liz soon becomes a believer when Barnabas Collins returns to Collinwood and immediately reveals his secret to her and her alone. The vampire proceeds to revitalize the great house and the Collins fish-canning business, which has been all but eclipsed by the preternaturally prosperous Angel Bay Seafood, run by the ageless "Angie" (actually, Angelique). The great Christopher Lee plays an old fisherman employed by Angie until Barnabas hypnotizes him into switching sides.

What *Dark Shadows* '12 does well, it does very well. The dramatic prologue, the design of Collinwood and Collinsport, the period music and costumes, and the scattered moments of drama, romance, and horror are outstanding and in the spirit of the 1966-1971 and 1991 incarnations of *Dark Shadows*. These serious moments are remnants of the original 2008 script by John August (*Big Fish, Corpse Bride*) before Seth Grahame-Smith (*Vendettas, The Hard Times of R.J. Berger*) wrote a new, overly comical revision in late 2010. Now, Mrs. Johnson, Willie, Julia, and sometimes even Barnabas and Angelique are played for laughs. Mrs. Johnson, who never speaks, cleans around Barnabas as he hangs upside down like a bat or sleeps in cupboards. Willie and Julia are alcoholics. Barnabas befriends a group of hippies but then slaughters them. Angelique seduces Barnabas in an utterly out-of-control scene that has the lovers hurling each other against walls, breaking furniture, and rolling around on the ceiling as Barry White's 1974 song "You're the First, the Last, My Everything" blares on the soundtrack. At one point, Angelique has a lizard's tongue. "The scene doesn't even make sense," according to the *Boston Globe*.[215]

In the final 20 minutes of the film, *Dark Shadows* '12 goes completely out of all reason as Angelique spews green vomit on Barnabas, Liz totes a shotgun, the paintings and sculptures in Collinwood come to life, Angelique cracks and crumbles like a porcelain doll, Collinwood is wrecked and burned, Angelique pulls her heart out of her body, and a character turns into a werewolf! Barnabas and Victoria, whose courtship is not given nearly enough screen time, share a life-changing experience, and the final shot shows another character turning into a vampire. Most viewers are left exhausted after these head-spinning, overblown events. Justin Chang of *Variety* noted the "FX-laden climax that desperately conjures up everything from *Rebecca* to *Death Becomes Her*."[216] Ty Burr of the *Boston Globe* observed that "the last half-hour is a traffic jam of silly ideas like a werewolf out of nowhere."[217] Granted, both the original *Dark Shadows* and the 1991 revival had a few comic characters and a few funny moments (intentional or unintentional), but Dan Curtis and Art Wallace's concept of the show was that of a serious drama and not a sitcom or a farce.

A highlight of the 2012 film—in addition to the serious prologue—is the grand party that the Collins family throws at Barnabas and Carolyn's urging. Since this is 1972, Alice Cooper (playing himself) entertains the guests with his songs "No More Mr. Nice Guy" and "The Ballad of Dwight Fry." The latter song is introduced by Carolyn in a sly nod to the original show's mystery surrounding her absent father—"Mommy, where's Daddy? He's been gone for so long. Do you think he'll *ever* come home?"

Fans of Curtis's original series were delighted to see Jonathan Frid, Lara Parker, Kathryn Leigh Scott, and David Selby as four party guests whom Elizabeth and Barnabas welcome. The four *Dark Shadows* stars journeyed to England in early July 2011 and filmed the party scene at Pinewood Studios where the Collinwood and Collinsport sets were housed. Jonathan Frid, the first and definitive Barnabas, died nine months after he filmed his cameo role and just one month before this film was released.

Needless to say, reactions to *Dark Shadows* '12 ran the gamut from love to indifference to disappointment to hate. Many diehard fans disliked the silly elements, but many others were more receptive to the tongue-in-cheek treatment. Some fans concluded that DS '12 succeeds as an entertaining vampire movie (especially to viewers who have no knowledge of *Dark Shadows*) but it fails as a *Dark Shadows* movie because of the rampant silliness and excess. In other words, *Dark Shadows* '12 is a typical Tim Burton movie, but it is not a *Dark Shadows* movie. At least, there are a half-dozen shots of the familiar waves crashing against the rocks (but no Cobert theme song to go with them).

The New York Times called Tim Burton's *Dark Shadows* "Mr. Burton's most pleasurable film in years" and praised the director's "exquisite detail work, his playfulness, and his macabre wit. [. . .] There is also something of a story, mostly involving Barnabas's true love, if anyone's interested, though traditional storytelling has never been Mr. Burton's specialty or perhaps interest. What counts in his work is the telling, not the tale."[218]

At Pinewood Studios in July 2011, original *Dark Shadows* stars Jonathan Frid (left), Lara Parker, Kathryn Leigh Scott, and David Selby (standing), wearing their 1972-era costumes, are ready to shoot the party scene in Tim Burton's *Dark Shadows* (2012). Frid dies on 14 April 2012, one month before the May 11 release of Burton's film.

Barnabas, Quentin, and the Rock Star: Jonathan Frid (left), Alice Cooper, and David Selby prepare to shoot the party scene in Tim Burton's *Dark Shadows* (2012).

Variety noted, "Burton and Depp have cited Curtis's creation as a formative influence, and together with scenarist Seth Grahame-Smith, they have paid tribute to the show's legacy in predictably whimsical, irreverent fashion." Reviewer Justin Chang continued,

> With a smirk and a wink, the filmmakers have inflated an enduring relic into an extravagantly empty postmodern artifact, an object lesson in the perils of camping up a property that had no shortage of camp to begin with. [. . .] Outfitting ABC's cult-worshipped, occult-themed soap opera with super-slick production values and a tone that veers unsteadily between kooky comedy and Gothic horror, this bizarre but weirdly bloodless retro-camp exercise is neither funny nor eerie enough to seduce the uninitiated and will court bemused reactions at best from the series's still-estimable fan following. The picture's pedigree could intrigue audiences for a spell, but long-term box-office bewitchment seems unlikely.[229]

Boston Globe reviewer Ty Burr, while finding some fault with the movie, declared, "Tim Burton has got his groove back [. . .] after the cluttered pointlessness of *Alice in Wonderland* and *Charlie and the Chocolate Factory*. [. . .] *Dark Shadows* doesn't pretend to be anything more than an entertainment, but it recaptures the experience of watching the Gothic daytime soap opera with rapturous comic bliss."[220]

Michael Logan of *TV Guide* quoted *Night of Dark Shadows* star and 2012 party guest David Selby:

> Burton not only dedicates the film to Dan Curtis, the late creator of *Dark Shadows*, but he also casts some of the show's top stars in cameo roles, including Jonathan Frid (who died at 87 just last month), David Selby (Quentin), Kathryn Leigh Scott (Josette), and Lara Parker (Angelique). They have become the film's biggest boosters. "I have complete confidence in Tim Burton's vision," says Selby. "It's good to put a fresh perspective on what we did so many years ago. The fans who are upset have to remember that when we made the series, we screwed with beloved monster movies and turned them upside down! We were hardly reverent ourselves."[231]

Jay Stone, in the St. John, New Brunswick, *Telegraph-Journal*, called *Dark Shadows* "something unusual: a long and scattered romp,"[222] and Lisa Kennedy, in the *Denver Post*, dubbed the film "an often amusing, teasingly naughty lark."[223] In *Shadowgram* #122/123 (January 2014), editor Marcy Robin reported the *Entertainment Weekly* review of the movie trailer that premiered both on TV's *Ellen* and on the Internet on Thursday 15 March 2012.[224] Without even seeing the entire film, *E. Weekly* seemed to grasp its problems:

> Ultimately, it "plays for laughs" but starts as "straight-up Gothic horror: an 18th-century romance, a jealous witch, a freshly-born vampire craving blood, a hushed ghost whispering, 'He's coming.'" It then "turns on the laugh track" and "takes its source material not so seriously. When the buried undead bloodsucker Barnabas is freed from his tomb in the year

1972, he finds the time period…a little funky," and later "things even get a little kinky" with "a surreal love scene."

It "sets up a kind of comedic, supernatural version of *Fatal Attraction* as Barnabas and Angelique war with each other, with his decadent Me Decade family caught in the crossfire…. Those craving serious treatment of the material may be disappointed, but fans of Burton's twisted sense of humor who don't come with major expectations may be surprised to find this movie is more farce than horror."[235]

Shades of *Night of Dark Shadows*: Burton's film seemed incomplete because certain scenes seemed to be missing. *Shadowgram* #122/123 revealed a very illuminating *Syndicated* report from Thursday 20 September 2012:

Warner Brothers has released a set of deleted scenes. Now, we've got some idea of what happened to some of that missing character development as apparently several key scenes were cut in favor of other, more dramatic scenes or perhaps more humorous scenes. These seem like they were perhaps meant to be funny but didn't quite turn out. The character-driven scenes: 1. An important interaction between Barnabas and David as they discuss prehistoric dinosaurs and early Collins family history. 2. Dr. Hoffman is shown to hold some concern for Victoria. 3. Hoffman and Elizabeth discuss Barnabas's eccentricities, which not only deepens the relationship between these two characters but also shows a little more of the distrust for Barnabas's story that any rational person would have had in their situations. 4. The conversation between Carolyn and Victoria which is hinted at later, but we never see. It also foreshadows the transformation of her character at the film's climax, something that was sorely lacking in the final cut. 5. A scene that shows that the townspeople actually noticed that people were getting killed out in the woods. These are all outstanding, and I question the decision to remove any of them. Perhaps, the scenes showed poor pacing where they sat—it'd be hard to tell without rewatching the film with them in it—or perhaps it wasn't Burton's decision to remove any of them. Either way, even just watching them after the fact, they improve the film immensely and make the greater vision of *Dark Shadows* more apparent.[236]

Because of the film's mid-level performance at the box office (especially in the United States), no sequel to *Dark Shadows* materialized. Nevertheless, the Gothic serial has returned from the dead, time and again, in movies, novels, comic books, Big Finish CD dramas, and even a ballet, so Dan Curtis's 55-year-old dream of the governess on the train may yet resurface in multimedia. *Dark Shadows* is only one of the indelible marks that the versatile director has made on popular culture.

That impact was celebrated in 2019 with the release on DVD and Blu-Ray of **Master of Dark Shadows: The Gothic World of Dan Curtis.** Presented by "MPI Media Group, in association with Severin Films and Dan Curtis Productions," *Master of Dark Shadows* is a feature-length work, scored to Robert Cobert's music, *about* the great producer-director and his spooky brainchild. The documentary is narrated by Dan Curtis's friend Ian McShane (*War and Remembrance, Deadwood*) and directed by David

Gregory (*Plague Town, The Theatre Bizarre*). The prolific Gregory has directed more than 200 DVD/Blu-Ray extras, featuring interviews with Dario Argento, Karen Black, Christopher Lee, Richard Matheson, Franco Nero, Paula Prentiss, Charlotte Rampling, Ken Russell, Barbara Steele, Raquel Welch, and dozens of other genre luminaries. Gregory is also the director of the 2014 documentary feature *Lost Soul: The Doomed Journey of Richard Stanley's "Island of Doctor Moreau,"* about the troubled 1996 production starring Marlon Brando, Val Kilmer, and Ron Perlman.

The 2019 Dan Curtis documentary reveals a bit of information about and pictures of the young Curtis although daughter Tracy Curtis reveals in her interview that Curtis did not talk about his early family very often. Both she and her sister Cathy Curtis mention that their mother Norma Curtis always gave her opinions about Curtis's ideas and projects and Curtis listened to her. Tracy Curtis adds that her father was "always working—always reading scripts and books" for his next big idea. Some of those books came from his New York secretary Rita Fein, who in the late 1960s would bring horror books back to her boss from her travels. "He had a frightening intensity," Fein remembers in her interview, but she knew that Dan Curtis also was very sensitive. In fact, she mentions a moment in the mid-1960s when she looked over at him and saw that he "was crying." Barbara Steele concurs: "Behind that cloak of largesse, there was a very vulnerable person. He couldn't have been so intuitive without it."

Master of Dark Shadows (2019) features a rare ABC *Dark Shadows* promo (narrated by Paul Frees) featuring Alexandra Moltke running away from Seaview Terrace, the cliffside mansion in Newport, Rhode Island.

In addition to rare family pictures and home movies, *Master of Dark Shadows* affords viewers clips of Curtis's *CBS Match-Play Golf Classic*, Art Wallace's television play "The House," ABC's early promos for *Dark Shadows*, and Jonathan Frid's public appearances. The late Frid and Curtis appear in archive footage from the 1990s and the 2000s, but the other 30 interviewees appear in new footage shot since 2016. Some of the *Dark Shadows* stars are seen sitting inside Lyndhurst in Tarrytown, New York, or the Vista Theatre in Los Angeles, California. *Dark Shadows* writer Joe Caldwell sits for his interview inside the now demolished *Dark Shadows* TV studio that stood (until September 2017) at 433 West 53rd Street in Manhattan. Robert Cobert appears in his Southern California home while his unmistakable music for *Dark Shadows*, *The Great Ice Rip-Off*, *Supertrain*, and other Dan Curtis productions artfully underscores the entire documentary.

Cobert declares that "*Dark Shadows* changed the face of daytime television." Former ABC-TV executives Michael Brockman and Leonard Goldberg further discuss the Gothic serial as do *Dark Shadows* stars Nancy Barrett, Roger Davis, John Karlen, Jerry Lacy, Lara Parker, Christopher Pennock, Kathryn Leigh Scott, David Selby, James Storm, and Marie Wallace. Pictures or clips of other *Dark Shadows* performers (including Grayson Hall) and writers (including Ron Sproat) appear in the film.

David Gregory's documentary, produced by Jim Pierson, reveals Dan Curtis to be a tireless and determined *auteur* of *Dark Shadows* and his other horror and war productions. *Dark Shadows* writer Malcolm Marmorstein, who wrote 80 episodes, claims that the writers sometimes had "24-hour story sessions" in order to keep the ideas and plots flowing, and fellow writer Joe Caldwell, who wrote 63 episodes, remembers, "Dan kept saying, 'How can we make it better?'" Lara Parker acknowledges that Dan Curtis "gave us all our starts," and James Storm insists that Curtis "was always on my side, and I really was incredibly indebted to him."

David Selby discusses his "theme song," "Quentin's Theme" (originally written by Cobert for *The Strange Case of Dr. Jekyll and Mr. Hyde*), and his gratitude for having been on *Dark Shadows* and having played the unique role of Quentin Collins. "It was a respite to go to the studio because of what was going on around us" (i.e. news of the Vietnam War, social unrest, and assassinations). Selby playfully adds, "The actors were just as eccentric as the characters they played!"

The documentary also covers *The Winds of War*, *War and Remembrance*, and all incarnations of *Dark Shadows*, including the 1970, 1971, and 2012 films. Barbara Steele, Ben Cross, and director Armand Mastroiani discuss the 1991 *Dark Shadows* series, and Alec Newman and writer Mark Verheiden remember the never-aired 2004 WB pilot. Steele remarks that her co-star Cross "was great because he looks like a medieval gargoyle." Cross reveals, "I felt lucky and blessed to be on *Dark Shadows*. No one on the set worked harder than Dan Curtis, [and] if he didn't like something, boy, did you know it!"

Fifteen years after the project, Alec Newman still feels terribly disappointed that the 2004 WB pilot—"a sure thing, certain to be picked up" as a series, everyone believed—was rejected and never finished. Nevertheless, Newman says, "I loved being a tiny part of that world [of *Dark Shadows*] that people are really passionate about." Ironically, Alec Newman is the embodiment of writer Malcolm Marmorstein's vision for the character of Barnabas Collins back in 1967 when Marmorstein urged Dan Curtis to "get a young blond guy" to play the vampire! Marmorstein did *not* want "a Bela Lugosi type." The writer says that his premise was that no one in Collinsport, Maine, had ever read *Dracula* or seen a Bela Lugosi movie. Vampires were unknown there.

Also seen in *Master of Dark Shadows* are Paley Center for Media curators David Bushman and Ron Simon, former *16* magazine associate editor Nola Leone, Jonathan Frid's business partner Mary O'Leary, Dan Curtis's frequent collaborator William F. Nolan, and long-time *Dark Shadows* fan Whoopi Goldberg, who claims that the original series was "right up my alley" because "these were characters that were talking to *you*," i.e. us the young viewers. The Oscar-winning comedian admits that she loved Barnabas and Quentin. "Jonathan Frid's picture was on my wall because I wanted to get bit!" As for the werewolf, "I would have taken that bite, also," she laughs.

Master of Dark Shadows is an outstanding tribute to a producer-director who had an impact on many lives and definitely left his mark. As Nancy Barrett exclaims, "If you were in the middle of the Atlantic Ocean, in a leaky rowboat with one oar, you would want Dan Curtis in that boat with you because he would figure out a way to save your neck!"[227]

Premiere screenings of *Master of Dark Shadows,* attended by *Dark Shadows* stars and fans, took place at the Los Angeles Airport Westin Hotel on Saturday 20 October 2018 and at the Paley Center for Media in New York City on Saturday 13 April 2019. October 2018 proved to be a momentous month for all things Dan Curtis. First, the New York branch of the Miskatonic Institute of Horror Studies celebrated made-for-TV horror in general and Dan Curtis in particular. At the Brooklyn Horror-Film Festival on October 13, author and TV-movie expert Amanda Reyes presented "Big Scares on the Small Screen: A Brief History of the Made-for-TV Horror Film." Then, back at the Paley Center for Media in NYC on October 25, curator David Bushman presented "Dan Curtis: Old School/New School." Bushman discussed how the scary productions of Dan Curtis blended elements of classic horror and modern horror and went on to influence today's horror properties and their creators. Finally, on Monday 29 October 2018, the Decades television network began airing *Dark Shadows* weeknights at midnight (11:00 PM Central time).[228]

More and more viewers in the 2020s are being exposed to *Dark Shadows*. Although the show is readily available on VHS, DVD, and various streaming media, the Decades network, like the Sci-Fi Channel 20+ years earlier, is providing fans the excitement of seeing their favorite show *on* television again. "Tune in tomorrow" is what *Dark Shadows*—and soap operas in general—are all about.

The Productions of Dan Curtis

Challenge Golf (1963)
The CBS Golf Classic (1963-1973)
Dark Shadows (1966-1971)
The Strange Case of Dr. Jekyll and Mr. Hyde (1968)
Dead of Night: A Darkness at Blaisedon (1969)
House of Dark Shadows (1970)
Night of Dark Shadows (1971)
The Night Stalker (1972)
The Night Strangler (1973)
Frankenstein (1973)
The Norliss Tapes (1973)
The Picture of Dorian Gray (1973)
Scream of the Wolf (1974)
Shadow of Fear (1974)
Dracula (1974)
The Invasion of Carol Enders (1974)
Melvin Purvis, G-Man (1974)
The Turn of the Screw (1974)
Come Die with Me (1974)
Nightmare at 43 Hillcrest (1974)
The Great Ice Rip-Off (1974)
Trilogy of Terror (1975)
The Kansas City Massacre (1975)
Burnt Offerings (1976)
Dead of Night (1977)
Curse of the Black Widow (1977)
When Every Day Was the Fourth of July (1978)
Supertrain (1979)
Mrs. R's Daughter (1979)
The Last Ride of the Dalton Gang (1979)
The Long Days of Summer (1980)
I Think I'm Having a Baby (1981)
The Big Easy (1982)
The Winds of War (1983)
St. John in Exile (1986)
War and Remembrance (1988, 1989)
Johnny Ryan (1990)
Dark Shadows (1991)
Angie the Lieutenant (1992)
Intruders (1992)
Me and the Kid (1993)
Trilogy of Terror II (1996)
The Love Letter (1998)
Dark Shadows (2004)
Alzheimer's Association PSA (2004)
Saving Milly (2005)
Our Fathers (2005)

In 1973, Dan Curtis is 45 years old when he directs *Dracula* (CBS, 1974).

CHAPTER II
Dracula

In 1973, Dan Curtis traveled to England and Yugoslavia to direct his acclaimed version of *Dracula*, based on Bram Stoker's 1897 novel. The film, sometimes known as *Bram Stoker's Dracula* or *Dan Curtis's Dracula*, aired on CBS-TV on Friday 8 February 1974 after the fifth episode of *Dirty Sally* and the first episode of *Good Times*. *Dracula* aired opposite *The Six-Million-Dollar Man*, *The Odd Couple*, and *Toma* on ABC and *The Girl with Something Extra*, *The Brian Keith Show*, and *The Dean Martin Show* on NBC.

Dracula was the fourth of six collaborations between Curtis and author Richard Matheson (1926-2013), who had written about vampires in such 1950s stories and novels as "Blood Son," "The Funeral," and *I Am Legend*. Matheson's 1959 short story "No Such Thing as a Vampire" had been filmed for the 19 April 1968 premiere episode of BBC-TV's *Late-Night Horror*—one of the very first BBC productions filmed in color—before Dan Curtis remade it in 1973.

Matheson recalled that his and Curtis's *Dracula* (whose running time is 1 hour, 38 minutes) aired in a two-hour timeslot. He added,

> [It] turned out quite well, I thought, but it was even better at the three hours originally shot. I wrote a script for three hours, and Dan shot a three-hour version, but the network would give us only two hours. So Dan had to edit it down. I would have loved to have seen it at three hours. It was the first one that tried to follow the book and the first one to use the Vlad the Impaler material. To this day, I think we came the closest.[1]

What Matheson includes in his adaptation *is* an accurate reproduction of Bram Stoker's novel, especially the novel's first four chapters (relating Jonathan Harker's stay at Castle Dracula), as well as the shipwreck of the *Demeter* (chapter 7), Dracula's release of a wolf from the zoo (chapter 11), Mina's drinking of Dracula's blood from an open wound (chapter 21), and Van Helsing's hypnosis of Mina (chapter 23). However, Matheson omits the characters of Quincey Morris (often absent from film adaptations), Dr. John Seward, and the mad R.M. Renfield. The adaptation works without the Seward/Renfield subplot as it focuses fully on Jonathan Harker (Murray Brown), Mina Murray (Penelope Horner), Arthur Holmwood (Simon Ward), Lucy Westenra (Fiona Lewis), Mrs. Westenra (Pamela Brown), Dr. Abraham Van Helsing (Nigel Davenport), and Count Dracula (Jack Palance).

Dan Curtis's Dracula makes two significant changes, one of which makes this adaptation so distinctive and influential. In the novel, Jonathan's opening storyline leaves him (at the end of chapter 4) a prisoner of Castle Dracula and at the mercy of Dracula's three vampire brides (played in the movie by Sarah Douglas, Barbara Lindley, and Virginia Wetherell). Four chapters later, Mina receives word that Jonathan is in a hospital in Budapest. Stoker never explains exactly how Harker managed to escape the castle. In Curtis's version, Jonathan does *not* escape. When Arthur and Van Helsing arrive at Castle Dracula, they find that their friend has become a vampire.

Hanna-Maria Pravda and Murray Brown play a scene from Richard Matheson and Dan Curtis's *Dracula* (1974).

Count Dracula's vampire brides (including Virginia Wetherell Bates of *Demons of the Mind*) attack Jonathan Harker.

The more important change is the revisionist explanation of why Dracula comes to England in the first place. Stoker does not offer a reason until chapter 24 when Van Helsing assumes that Dracula is "leaving his own barren land—barren of peoples—and coming to a new land where life of man teems 'til they are like the multitude of standing corn."[2] In other words, Dracula may as well relocate to the world's largest city (London) in order to have an endless supply of victims. Curtis insisted,

> Richard Matheson, who's a wonderful writer, and I adapted the Bram Stoker novel and brought to it something that wasn't in it. I ripped myself off. I took the *Dark Shadows* love story and put it in our *Dracula* because in the novel, Dracula leaves Transylvania and goes to England for no reason at all. Stoker says he's sucked virtually everybody dry down there, and he had to find new blood. We didn't do that. I always felt that was ridiculous, so we came up with the central love story to *Dracula* that never existed in the novel but that has *since*, I might add, been *copied* by other *Draculas*, the most recent one, for instance.[3]

Curtis referred to Francis Ford Coppola's *Bram Stoker's Dracula* (1992).[4] However, the animated adventures *The Batman vs. Dracula* (2005) and *Highlander: The Search for Vengeance* (2006) also fit this description. So do Fred Olen Ray's vampire serial *The Lair* (2007-2009) and the popular CW series *The Vampire Diaries* (2009-2017). Curtis added,

> In our movie, he [Dracula] saw a picture of a girl [Lucy] in the newspaper, and we established that she was the reincarnation of this woman he was in love with in the 1400s. She's in England, and he goes to England to get her back. It's a little *Dark Shadowy*, but it worked. It was perfect. That's why our *Dracula* was as good as it was. It brought to the monster a degree of sympathy. Instead of making him just this marauding vampire, he was a haunted figure. You really cared about him even though you were terrified of him. Jack [Palance] is extraordinary. Jack is the best Dracula there ever was. He was the most frightening Dracula that ever put on that cape.[5]

The *Los Angeles Times* agreed. "This two-hour version of the classic horror story made for television by Dan Curtis and offered tonight on CBS would chill the bones of a plaster saint. It's as flesh-crawling an experience as you've ever had."[6] The *Times* proclaimed, "If the late [Bela] Lugosi was the definitive Count Dracula, it's no longer true. It's now Jack Palance."[7]

In a 2000 DVD featurette, Palance, who died on 10 November 2006 at age 87, mused that Count Dracula was "the only character I ever played that frightened me even in the doing of it. But I never thought of the character as being evil. He was someone who was trapped in a situation." Palance added that with Curtis at the helm of the movie, "I knew it would be done very well and with great authenticity."[8] Donald F. Glut, author of *The Dracula Book* (Scarecrow, 1975), agreed: "The film surely ranks with the best movie adaptations of Stoker's *Dracula*, and it firmly establishes director Curtis and actor Palance among the genre's upper echelon."[9]

In 1973, Jack Palance (*Oklahoma Crude*) is 54 years old when he plays Count Dracula.

That newfound authenticity is the other hallmark of Curtis's *Dracula*—and the other ingredient that Coppola's 1992 blockbuster appropriated from its 1974 predecessor. Except for one line in Mehmet Muktar's 1953 Turkish film *Drakula Istanbul'da* (*Dracula in Istanbul*)—"The locals believe that I, like my ancestor Voyvodo Drakula, am ruthless"—Curtis's *Dracula* is the first Dracula film to make an explicit connection between Count Dracula and the real-life Vlad the Impaler of the 15th century. Matheson's screenplay reflects the scholarship of the time in Raymond McNally and Radu Florescu's *In Search of Dracula* (Houghton Mifflin, 1972) and *Dracula: A Biography of Vlad the Impaler, 1431-1476* (its 1973 follow-up).

Twenty-first-century film audiences take for granted that the Dracula character is based on the real-life story of a ruthless warrior, but at the time of Curtis's *Dracula*, such an idea was just coming into the popular consciousness. Vlad Dracula, also known as Vlad Tepes, was born in Sighisoara (a.k.a. Schassburg), a village in Transylvania, in late 1430 or early 1431. His father Vlad Dracul had been prince of Wallachia and a member of the Order of the Dragon, a Christian brotherhood founded by King Sigismund I of Hungary in 1418 and dedicated to fighting the Turkish people. "Drac" is a Romanian word meaning "dragon" or "devil." Vlad Dracul's son was called Dracul**a**, or "son of the dragon" or "son of the devil." In later life, Vlad Dracula also was called "Tepes," which means "impaler," because of his penchant for skewering as many of his enemies as possible. Vlad had many of them, for he spent his life attacking the Turkish people and fighting to acquire and keep the throne of Wallachia. After putting to death 40,000 of his enemies (four times more than Ivan the Terrible), Vlad fell to an assassin in December 1476 or early January 1477.[10]

Some evidence of Count Dracula's having been patterned after Vlad Tepes exists in Bram Stoker's novel. In chapter 3, Harker notes that Dracula sounds "like a king speaking"[11] when the Count talks knowingly of his family's "guarding of the frontier of Turkey-land."[12] Dracula declares,

> Who was it but one of my own race who as Voivode crossed the Danube and beat the Turk on his own ground? This was a Dracula indeed! [. . .] Was it not this Dracula, indeed, who inspired that other of his race who in a later age again and again brought his forces over the great river into Turkey-land; who, when he was beaten back, came again, and again, and again, though he had to come alone from the bloody field where his troops were being slaughtered, since he knew that he alone could ultimately triumph! They said that he thought only of himself. Bah! What good are peasants without a leader? Where ends the war without a brain and heart to conduct it? Again, when, after the battle of Mohacs, we threw off the Hungarian yoke, we of the Dracula blood were amongst their leaders, for our spirit would not brook that we were not free.[13]

Later, in chapter 18, as Van Helsing is explaining the rules of vampirism to Mina and the others, he reports his own findings about Dracula's origins.

> Thus, when we find the habitation of this man-that-was, we can confine him to his coffin and destroy him, if we obey what we know. But he is clever. I have asked my friend Arminius, of Buda-Peth University, to make his record; and, from all the means that are, he tells me of what he

has been. He must, indeed, have been that Voivode Dracula who won his name against the Turk, over the great river on the very frontier of Turkeyland. If it be so, then he was no common man; for in that time, and for centuries after, he was spoken of as the cleverest and the most cunning, as well as the bravest of the sons of the "land beyond the forest." That mighty brain and that iron resolution went with him to his grave, and are even now arrayed against us. The Draculas were, says Arminius, a great and noble race, though now and again were scions who were held by their coevals to have had dealings with the Evil One. They learned his secrets in the Scholomance, amongst the mountains over Lake Hermanstadt, where the devil claims the tenth scholar as his due. In the records are such words as "stregoic"—witch, "ordog," and "pokol"—Satan and hell; and in one manuscript, this very Dracula is spoken of as "wampyr," which we all understand too well.[14]

Dracula (1974): Simon Ward (*The Three Musketeers*) and Nigel Davenport (*The Picture of Dorian Gray*) portray Arthur Holmwood and Abraham Van Helsing.

Van Helsing's "friend Arminius" is the real-life Hungarian historian Arminius Vambery, author of *Hungary in Ancient, Medieval, and Modern Times* (1886) and other books of history and travel. Bram Stoker met Vambery at the Beefsteak Room, behind the Lyceum Theatre, in 1890 when Stoker was 43 and Vambery was 58. (The restaurant is mentioned in *Masterpiece Theatre*'s 2007 reimagining of *Dracula*.) At the time that he met Vambery, Stoker had begun to write *Dracula,* and it is possible that Vambery told Stoker stories of Vlad the Impaler—stories that the leading Hungarian scholar doubtless knew even though he himself never wrote about Vlad Tepes in any of his own books.[15] "The land beyond the forest" refers both to the literal translation of "transylvania" and to Emily Gerard Laszowska's 1888 book, *The Land Beyond the Forest: Facts, Figures, and Fancies from Transylvania,* which Stoker is known to have read when he was gathering information about the region.

The Scholomance is a legendary school of occult sciences and necromancy—a kind of antediluvian Hogwarts—where Count Dracula studied and perhaps where he lost his soul to the powers of darkness and became a vampire. (Stoker offers no concrete explanation as to how Dracula became undead centuries ago, but he strongly hints that sorcery was involved.) Students at the Scholomance are taught by a dragon and/or the devil how to affect the weather and how to transform themselves into animals.[16] Dracula's name suggests both "dragon" and "devil."

In Curtis and Matheson's groundbreaking film, Count Dracula is seen as a medieval warrior prince in two brief flashbacks and in an enormous painting. The nameplate below the painting of the kingly soldier on horseback even names him as "Vlad Tepes, Prince of Wallachia, 1475." In one scene, Dracula refers to himself as "me, who commanded armies hundreds of years before you were born." Indeed, in the summer of 1475, Vlad had regained the throne and then led armies to Serbia and Turkey.[17]

Finally, after Van Helsing and Arthur succeed in destroying the vampire, an epigraph in red letters on the screen proclaims,

> In the 15th Century, in the area of Hungary known as Transylvania, there lived a nobleman so fierce in battle that his troops gave him the name <u>Dracula</u>, which means devil. Soldier, statesman, alchemist, and warrior, so powerful a man was he that it was claimed he succeeded in overcoming even physical death. To this day, it has yet to be disproven.

Richard Matheson's words echo Dr. Seward's diary entry in chapter 23 of Stoker's novel:

> He was in life a most wonderful man. Soldier, statesman, and alchemist—which latter was the highest development of the science-knowledge of his time. He had a mighty brain, a learning beyond compare, and a heart that knew no fear and no remorse. He dared even to attend the Scholomance, and there was no branch of knowledge of his time that he did not essay. Well, in him, the brain powers survived the physical death.[18]

The film takes place near Bistritz, Hungary, in May 1897; "five weeks later" near Whitby, England; and finally, back in Hungary. The scenes of Jonathan Harker's captivity in Castle Dracula are atmospheric and frightening. Count Dracula and his vampire brides show a feral side that is quite unnerving. The scares continue in England as a wolf attacks Arthur Holmwood and Dracula vampirizes Lucy Westenra, who seems to be the reincarnation of Dracula's lost love. The scenes of Lucy's macabre death and rainy funeral are reminiscent of the corresponding scenes with Carolyn Stoddard in *House of Dark Shadows* (1970).

Simon Ward, who plays Arthur in *Dracula* (1974), also appears in *The Monster Club* (1981) as George and in *Supergirl* (1984) as Zor-El.

One of the most chilling moments of *Dracula* is Arthur's sighting of Lucy, now a vampire, plaintively rapping on the window and begging Arthur to let her come in. Another scary highlight is the mayhem that the superhuman Count Dracula causes at the George Hotel where Mina Murray and Mrs. Westenra are staying.

One of the most shocking moments (especially for 1974-era television) is Dracula's opening a wound on his torso and forcing Mina to drink *his* blood while Arthur Holmwood and Dr. Abraham Van Helsing stand by helplessly. The overseas theatrical cut of *Dracula* (for England, France, Japan, South America, et al.) is even gorier. Blood gushes from the mouths of Lucy and one of the vampire brides when they are staked, and blood bursts from Dracula's mouth when he is impaled in the sunlight. Curtis's film editor was Richard A. Harris, who also edited *Scream of the Wolf, The Great Ice Rip-Off,* and the two Melvin Purvis movies before he edited two *Bad News Bears* movies, two *Fletch* movies, and three Arnold Schwarzenegger movies. Harris won the Academy Award for editing James Cameron's *Titanic* (1997).

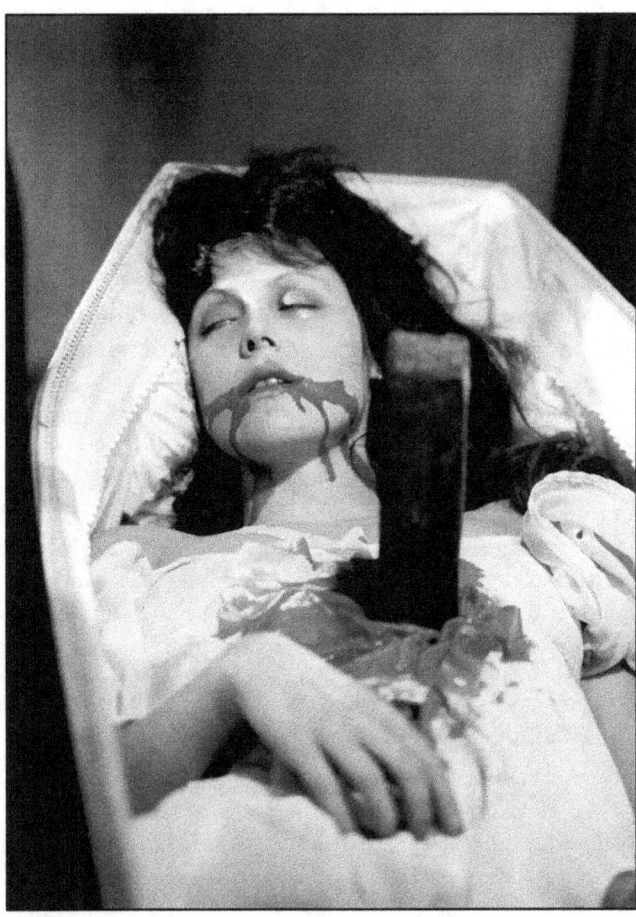

The bloodier cuts of a staked Fiona Lewis (as Lucy) appear in the 2014 *Dracula* Blu-Ray release from MPI Home Video.

For *Dan Curtis's Dracula*, Robert Cobert wrote a majestic, martial fanfare for the former warrior prince, as well as a dynamic main-title theme in the key of C minor. Cobert explained, "I wrote a love theme for *Dracula* that came from a music box. [. . .] I was the first composer to write a love theme for Dracula because Dan's *Dracula* had a love story in it.[19] [. . .] I wrote something modal, with a Romanian accent, the kind of music box that he might have had."[20] By "modal," Cobert meant something evocative of medieval church music.

"In a number of movies we did," Cobert added, "I had a music box somewhere."[21] Indeed, *House of Dark Shadows* (1970), *Come Die with Me* (1974), and *Burnt Offerings* (1976) feature music-box themes, continuing a practice begun on the *Dark Shadows* TV series with Josette's Music Box. "When I wrote the Dracula music-box theme, I played it for Dan, and at first he didn't like it. He said, 'It sounds sad.' I said, 'Of course it sounds sad. He's Dracula. He's sad!' It was a Hungarian music box rather than a Mozartian music box. Then, that music-box theme becomes the love theme, with full orchestra, and it morphs into danger halfway through."[22]

Cobert was given three weeks to write the music for Dracula. "That was a longer time than usual," he remembered.

> I usually got two weeks to write a movie score. I wrote the *Dracula* music at my beach house in the Hamptons. Writing it was a happy, rewarding experience.
>
> Whenever I did a movie with Dan, he and I sat down with a music editor, who took notes, and Dan showed me the movie. Then, we decided where the music should go. He'd say, "We need something here," and I'd say, "We need something there," and we worked it out. Dan said, "You gotta write something big for the death of Dracula," so I did. I ended with the theme for Dracula as the warrior and then the music box.[23]

The music, recorded by a 40-piece orchestra in London, was only one of many elements that made Curtis's *Dracula* an important addition to the nearly 200 film adaptations of Bram Stoker's novel since 1920. Of all of the actors who have portrayed the vampire, Jack Palance brought unique ferocity to the role and pioneered Dracula's cinematic portrayal as Vlad the Impaler. Radu Florescu and Raymond McNally later noted Palance's portrayal of Vlad Dracula and declared, "The best scene is where Dracula, upon finding that his long-lost love has been destroyed, groans like a wild animal as he smashes the funeral urns. In the final scene, Dracula is killed by a huge lance as the sun is coming up."[24] J. Gordon Melton, author of *The Vampire Book: The Encyclopedia of the Undead* (Visible Ink, 1994), added,

> Knowledge of the historical Dracula has had a marked influence on both Dracula movies and fiction. Two of the more important Dracula movies, *Dracula* (1974), starring Jack Palance, and *Bram Stoker's Dracula*, a recent [1992] production directed by Francis Ford Coppola, attempted to integrate the historical research on Vlad the Impaler into the story and used it as a rationale to make Dracula's actions more comprehensible.[25]

Jack Palance (left), Nigel Davenport, and Simon Ward perform the staking scene at the conclusion of Matheson and Curtis's *Dracula* (1974).

At this point, Richard Matheson's *Dracula* script calls for gold coins to fall from the impaled vampire's pockets.

Dan Curtis confidently insisted that his, Matheson's, and Palance's film "is the best *Dracula* that was ever made! It was very erotic, without showing a hell of a lot, and very scary and done with a lot of classic style. We had a wonderful director of photography, Ossie Morris, and we shot it in England and Yugoslavia. It was a really good production."[26] *Variety* called it "a tribute to Palance, Curtis, and Matheson that it comes off as logically as it does." *Variety* continued,

> Curtis and Matheson, ignoring previous flourishes made out of Bram Stoker's Victorian novel, approach the tale with a fresh, realistic fashion, designed to chill. With Jack Palance turning in one of the finest performances of his career as the bloodthirsty nobleman, Matheson has brought out the essential elements of the story [. . .] Stoker, Sir Henry Irving's business manager as well as a novelist, would be delighted.[27]

Dracula benefits from beautiful cinematography by Oswald "Ossie" Morris (1915-2014), who recently had won the Academy Award for his cinematography of *Fiddler on the Roof* (1971). Morris photographed notable movies from *Moulin Rouge* (1952) to *Lolita* (1962) to *Sleuth* (1972) to *The Dark Crystal* (1982), and he imbued *Dracula* with gorgeous shots of the Yugoslavian countryside, high-angle shots of running wolves, and Curtis's trademark low-angle shots of the actors. Oswald Morris photographed *Dracula* around the time that he shot *The Mackintosh Man* (1973), *The Odessa File* (1973), and *The Man with the Golden Gun* (1974), the James Bond movie that co-starred another one of the best movie Draculas, Christopher Lee.

***Dracula* (1974): Oswald Morris's camera looks down on Nigel Davenport (left) and Simon Ward.**

CBS reran *Dracula* in prime time and late-night in the mid-1970s, and A&E and local TV stations showed it in the 1980s and 1990s. CBS re-re-aired it on Saturday 28 November 1992 (opposite a football game on ABC and sitcoms and a Bob Hope special on NBC). CBS was taking advantage of the momentary upswing of interest in Dracula—especially Dracula as Vlad Tepes—because of the release of Francis Ford Coppola's *Bram Stoker's Dracula* (1992) on November 13. Fans were delighted to see 1992 end with a Dan Curtis classic to complement the new productions *Angie the Lieutenant* (February 1) and *Intruders: They Are Among Us* (May 17 & 19). When *Dracula* re-aired on November 28, Dan Curtis was busy filming *Me and the Kid* (1993).

As excellent as *Dracula* is as a two-hour movie, it would have been even more epic as the three-hour film that Curtis and Matheson had envisioned. Sadly, almost all of the extra, unused footage for a three-hour *Dracula* was lost some time in the 1980s. The MPI Blu-Ray of *Dracula* features the only remaining extra footage, "a few odd scraps" that Jim Pierson found "in a can of trailer outtakes" as Pierson was restoring the film for the Blu-Ray release and a gala screening at the Vista Theatre in Los Angeles on 30 April 2014.[28] The scraps reveal nothing new: they are soundless shots of Jack Palance posing as Dracula, Arthur and Van Helsing protecting Lucy as she sleeps, and Van Helsing hypnotizing Mina and staking Lucy and one of the brides.

Luckily, Matheson's three-act "screen treatment" (plot synopsis) and 140-page script (dated 7 August 1972) do exist and were published in Mark Dawidziak's 2006 book *Bloodlines: Richard Matheson's* Dracula, I Am Legend, *and Other Vampire Stories*. Dawidziak dedicated the book "to Dan [Curtis] and Darren [McGavin], both legends."[29]

Matheson's typewritten script is that of a nearly three-hour-long film that very closely resembles the finished *two*-hour movie—with a few significant exceptions. In the first scenes at Castle Dracula, Matheson's script calls for Count Dracula to appear as an old man with his fingernails "cut to a point"[30] as in Bram Stoker's novel. It is only after biting Lucy that "Dracula now looks like a vigorous man in his forties."[31]

In the scene in which Dracula prevents his three wives from feeding on Jonathan, Dracula "has a moving sack in his hands."[32] The script calls for "a momentary glimpse of a half-dead little girl," upon whom "the hideous trio" pounces.[33] Next, the little girl's parents are standing outside the castle and screaming for Dracula to give them back their child. The vampire summons a pack of wolves to attack the parents.[34]

Other elements that do not transfer from script to screen are several more shots of Dracula's driving his carriage to and from the George Hotel, an image of the undead Lucy's tempting Arthur by showing her breasts to him, and a glimpse of Lucy's severed head. (Van Helsing does not cut off Lucy's or any vampire's head in the finished film.) In the scene in which Dracula bursts in to Mina and Mrs. Westenra's hotel room, Matheson calls for Mrs. Westenra's death at Dracula's hands, but Curtis leaves her alive.

A major difference between the script and the film is that Matheson, like Stoker, allows Jonathan Harker to escape from Castle Dracula. Mina receives a letter from "the Hospital of St. Joseph and St. Mary, its address in Buda-Pesth. CAMERA MOVES DOWN on one of the lines in the handwritten letter. He has been under our care for nearly six weeks, suffering from a violent brain fever."[35]

When Mina arrives at the hospital in Budapest, Hungary, a nun takes her to the Mother Superior, who tells her that Jonathan has *died*. "Two days ago," she informs Mina. "We sent another telegram, but, obviously, you'd left already."[36]

Mina sobs, begins to cry. The Mother Superior puts her hand on her shoulder. After a while, Mina looks up.

                  MINA
May I see him?

                  MOTHER SUPERIOR
I'm afraid that's impossible.

                  MINA
Why?

                  MOTHER SUPERIOR
His…body was…disposed of.

                  MINA
Dis<u>pos</u>ed of? What do you mean?

The Mother Superior swallows nervously, braces herself, then speaks again.

                  MOTHER SUPERIOR
It was burned.

CAMERA MOVES IN QUICKLY ON Mina's stunned expression.[37]

Other differences emerge at the end of the script when Arthur Holmwood and Abraham Van Helsing close in on the vampire at Castle Dracula. Matheson calls for the novel's horde of rats, as well as Dracula's gold coins that spill from his pockets after his impaled body begins "to atrophy as he dies."[38]

CAMERA APPROACHING his dead body as, like ancient dust, it starts to drizzle greyly to the floor, leaving his shirt and coat suspended on the pike. As they begin to sag, gold coins start to drop from the pockets. CAMERA down-tilts to the coins as they fall on the floor.
MOVING SHOT—CLOSE ON COIN as it rolls across the floor to Van Helsing and stops. His hand reaches INTO FRAME and picks it up, CAMERA RISING TO REVEAL him gazing at the coin.
P.O.V. SHOT—GOLD COIN—CAMERA MOVES IN ON the ancient gold coin. On its face is the head of Dracula; beneath it, his name and the date, in Roman numerals, 1410. Faint CROWD NOISES begin.[39]

The script, as well as the movie, ends with the crowd noises, the shot of Dracula's portrait, and the "crawl title" in red letters. Matheson and Curtis's film is largely faithful to Stoker's novel, but the additions of Old Dracula, Jonathan's escape (but *not* death), the rats, and the gold coins would have made the movie even *more* faithful.

Fiona Lewis (*Dr. Phibes Rises Again*) and Jack Palance (*Bronk*) perform a brief flashback love scene. In *Dracula* (1974), Lewis plays both Dracula's lost love and Lucy Westenra.

What the typewritten script does *not* include is the creative input of director Dan Curtis. In Matheson's script, there is no scene in which Harker, now a vampire, attacks Holmwood and Van Helsing; there is no music box; there are no flashbacks to the life (brief love scene) and death (brief deathbed scene) of Dracula's long-lost love (Fiona Lewis); and there is no all-important moment (as in *Horror of Dracula* [1958] and several *Dark Shadows* episodes [1968 et al.]) when the vampire slayers flood the room with sunlight and stun the monster before they destroy him. Apparently, these scenes in the movie were devised by Dan Curtis (with input from Robert Cobert and Richard Matheson).

Mark Dawidziak's aforementioned *Bloodlines* book (Gauntlet Press, 2006) published Matheson's extremely detailed "screen treatment," which reveals the plot of the *three-hour-long* script and film that might have been. The treatment, too, first describes Count Dracula as "a tall, old man, clean-shaven except for a long, white moustache, [and] dressed entirely in black."[40] After Dracula goes to England and begins feeding on Lucy, he is "a very different Dracula, no longer old but seemingly, incredibly, becoming young again."[41] Later, after several nights when Arthur and his godfather Van Helsing prevent Lucy from going to Dracula, "the infuriated vampire [is] starting to age again."[42]

According to Dawidziak, Matheson lamented the shortening of his and Curtis's *Dracula* from three hours to two hours because (in Matheson's words) "it needed that extra hour" to be the nearly complete and definitive *Dracula* adaptation that Matheson had envisioned.[43] Dawidziak added,

> Nowhere is this more evident than in the downward spiral experienced by the character of Jonathan Harker. In Matheson's screen treatment, Jonathan is sent to Transylvania, where he is imprisoned by Dracula. He escapes from Castle Dracula and, as in the book, is reunited with his fiancée, Mina, in a Budapest hospital operated by nuns. Jonathan and Mina join Arthur and Van Helsing in the hunt for Dracula, a hunt that leads back to Castle Dracula. Fittingly, it is Jonathan who administers the death blow, thrusting a medieval pike through the vampire's heart.
>
> That's all pretty much in keeping with Stoker's novel. In the script written for a three-hour timeslot, though, Jonathan is killed off in Budapest. He manages to escape from Dracula's castle, only to die before Mina can make it to the hospital.
>
> Can things get any worse for poor Jonathan? Well, sure. He was played by Keanu Reeves in the [1992] Coppola version, and that was a fate worse than death. Curtis also had a nasty fate for him. In the director-producer's final cut, Jonathan disappears from the story, only to rush out of the darkness at the end as a vampire lurking in Castle Dracula. He went from impaling Dracula to getting staked himself. He went from conquering hero revisiting Castle Dracula to never having escaped the Transylvanian fortress.
>
> Jonathan's shocking reappearance definitely is a "made-you-jump" moment in the film, yet it hardly adheres to the kind of fidelity that Matheson advised in the screen treatment.

In 1974, Murray Brown appears in both Dan Curtis's *Dracula* (as Jonathan) and José Ramon Larraz's *Vampyres* (as Ted).

Still, even if the two-hour version of [Dan Curtis's] *Dracula* (actually 100 minutes plus commercials) falls short of being definitive, it does meet two of the essential goals stated by Matheson in the screen treatment.

"What cannot be eliminated—*must not* be eliminated—is the overwhelming sense of credible, intimate horror which the book transmits to its readers," he maintained. Curtis and his team certainly captured that.

The other goal stated by Matheson and achieved by this *Dracula* is that it convinces the viewer that "an attempt is being made to present a literate, intelligent, adult version of a marvelously terrifying story." From screen treatment to screenplay to screen, this attempt distinguishes the Matheson take on *Dracula*.[44]

If Dan Curtis had had that extra hour (for the Harker story arc, which included a hypnosis scene), a bigger budget (for the rats, the coins, Old Dracula, and other touches), and more freedom (for the horrifying moment with the little girl and her parents), *Dan Curtis's Dracula* (TV-1974) would have been *the* definitive version of the oft-filmed story. As it is, it ranks with Gerald Savory and Philip Savile's *Count Dracula* (TV-1977) and one or two other films as *one of* the most nearly definitive adaptations of *Dracula*. Like Curtis's mostly faithful versions of *The Strange Case of Dr. Jekyll and Mr. Hyde* and *The Picture of Dorian Gray*, Matheson and Curtis's *Dracula* is a major touchstone in horror television. According to Richard Matheson,

> I think it came as close as you could with just two hours, but there was quite a bit missing. I would have loved to have seen it at three hours. [. . .] That would have been dandy. Then, we could have really done it to a fare-thee-well. But even at the shorter time, it still came off very well. [. . .] It was the first one that tried to follow the book and the first one to use the Vlad the Impaler material. To this day, I think we came the closest.[45]

Dan Curtis certainly agreed. *Dracula* (1974) and *Burnt Offerings* (1976) are two of his greatest achievements in horror. In the early 2000s, Curtis reflected on his rich legacy of television and movie horror. He revealed,

> Horror stories are the most difficult type of things to do because you need imagination and humor, and you can never make a mistake. The first screw-up, you lose all credibility, and you're dead with the audience. Most people say, "Well, it's a ghost, so we can do whatever we want with it." They're the people who are dead before they start. A logic lapse or the wrong kind of laugh can sink you. Every single word is a deathtrap. That's the worst part of it. Every single line in a horror picture becomes dangerous. A simple "hello" at the wrong place can bring an unwanted laugh. You don't want *any* unwanted laughs. You want chuckles in the right places. You want people smiling with you when you do certain things. So if you can do these kinds of pictures, you can do anything. Most people think just the opposite—that if you can do these kinds of pictures, you can't do anything else. Well, I've proven them wrong.[46]

Dracula (CBS, 8 February 1974). Producer: Dan Curtis. Associate producer: Robert Singer. Director: Dan Curtis. First assistant director: Derek Kavanaugh. Teleplay: Richard Matheson (based on the novel by Bram Stoker). Music: Robert Cobert. Director of photography: Oswald Morris. Production designer: Trevor Williams. Makeup: Paul Rabiger. Costumer: Ruth Myers.

Cast: Jack Palance (Count Dracula), Nigel Davenport (Dr. Abraham Van Helsing), Murray Brown (Jonathan Harker), Penelope Horner (Mina Murray), Simon Ward (Arthur Holmwood), Fiona Lewis (Lucy Westenra), Pamela Brown (Mrs. Westenra), Reg Lye (Zookeeper), Sarah Douglas (Bride), Barbara Lindley (Bride), Virginia Wetherall Bates (Bride). 100 minutes. Available on VHS, DVD, and Blu-Ray.

Dan Curtis Significa: In his foreword to *The Vampire Archives: The Most Complete Volume of Vampire Tales Ever Published* (Vintage Books, 2009), *Anno Dracula* author Kim Newman pays tribute to Dan Curtis's *Dracula* (1974) and Jack Palance's count when he writes,

> Gradually, with stage and then film adaptations, *Dracula* became a standard, then a classic, then an all-pervasive cultural phenomenon. The Dracula who survives to this day isn't strictly Bram Stoker's but a mélange of Lord Ruthven, Varney, Stoker, Max Schreck's Nosferatu, Bela Lugosi, Christopher Lee, Gary Oldham, Jack Palance, Frank Langella, Count Chocula, Jamie Gillis in *Dracula Sucks,* Fred Saberhagen, Gene Colan's *Tomb of Dracula* artwork, Anne Rice's Lestat, Raymond McNally and Radu Florescu's Vlad the Impaler, Stephen King's Barlow, Heathcliff, Byron himself, Henry Irving, Jack the Ripper, those hobby kits (and much other Universal Pictures merchandise), and many, many other onion layers.[47]

Newman adds, "I detect a rasp of Jack Palance's count in Daniel Day-Lewis's whispery, cajoling threats as he plans to suck the lifeblood from a parched land"[48] in Day-Lewis's Oscar-winning performance as oilman Daniel Planview in Paul Thomas Anderson's *There Will Be Blood* (2007).

Dan Curtis Significa: The original titles of the Dan Curtis horror productions *The Night Stalker* (1972), *The Norliss Tapes* (1973), *Scream of the Wolf* (1974), and *Trilogy of Terror* (1975) were *The Kolchak Tapes, Demon, The Hunter,* and *Trilogy in Terror,* respectively. All four productions were written by Richard Matheson (*Dracula*) and/or William F. Nolan (*The Norliss Tapes*).

"Richard Matheson, Earl Wallace, and I were Dan's three favorite writers," Bill Nolan told me in a 28 February 2010 telephone conversation. "After *Norliss,* Dan wanted a series. Dan and six writers [including Nolan] sat around Dan's swimming pool and discussed ideas. I came up with *The Return.*"[49] Nolan's promising follow-up adventure involved time travel, but a *Norliss* sequel or series never materialized. Instead, Nolan and Curtis made two crime dramas about real-life Bureau of Investigation agent Melvin Purvis (1903-1960).

Richard B. Matheson (*What Dreams May Come*) died in 2013 and Earl W. Wallace (*Witness*) in 2018, but William F. Nolan (*Sky Heist*) was alive and well—and writing—in the early 2020s.

Six years before he plays Dracula, Jack Palance transforms from Henry Jekyll into Edward Hyde in the 1968 Dan Curtis production *The Strange Case of Dr. Jekyll and Mr. Hyde* (1968). Makeup artist Dick Smith goes on to win an Academy Award for *Amadeus* (1984).

After *Dracula,* Dan Curtis turns his attention to his and William F. Nolan's two Melvin Purvis crime dramas (1974, 1975).

CHAPTER III

Melvin Purvis, G-Man, *The Kansas City Massacre*, and More

In addition to horror films, a cinematic genre that continues to fascinate audiences is gangster movies. In the mid-1970s, at the peak of his mastery of fright films, Dan Curtis put his *auteur's* stamp on the gangster genre, too. The central figure of Curtis's pair of TV shoot-'em-ups was a real-life, and controversial, agent of the Bureau of Investigation. (The agency did not become the Federal Bureau of Investigation until 1935.)

Much has been written, alleged, disputed, misrepresented, and verified about Melvin Purvis (1903-1960), the lawyer and star G-man (Government man, as Bureau agents were called) who is credited (and sometimes discredited) with capturing some of America's most wanted criminals in the early 1930s. On film and especially on television, more than one dozen actors have portrayed Purvis. They include Steven Hill (1960), Geoffrey Binney (1974), Will Patton (1991), Dan Cortese (1996), Scott Brooks (2008), and Christian Bale (2009), but the three most notable portrayals are by Ben Johnson, once, in John Milius's *Dillinger* (1973), and Dale Robertson, twice, in Dan Curtis's *Melvin Purvis, G-Man* (1974) and *The Kansas City Massacre* (1975). In fact, Curtis's pair of classic TV crime dramas was an outgrowth of the *Dillinger* theatrical film produced by Samuel Z. Arkoff's American International Pictures (*Wuthering Heights, The Abominable Dr. Phibes, Frogs*).

Roger Corman's protégé John Milius, a writer (*Jeremiah Johnson, The Life and Times of Judge Roy Bean*) and a director (*The Wind and the Lion, Big Wednesday*), performed both duties for *Dillinger*, a hard-hitting account of gangster John Dillinger's 1933-1934 crime spree and agent Melvin Purvis's relentless pursuit of "Public Enemy Number One." The *San Francisco Chronicle* called the film "brilliant,"[1] the *New York Times* praised the film's "beautiful action sequences,"[2] and *Robbing Banks* author L.R. Kirchner agreed that "the gun battles in this film are extraordinary."[3] *Dillinger* is a worthy successor to Arthur Penn's *Bonnie and Clyde* (1967) despite its occasional borrowing from that film (e.g. some getaways are similarly staged, an enthusiastic amateur joins the gang, a young couple's car is commandeered, a gangster near death becomes delirious, and the film ends abruptly). *Dillinger* eschews most of the 1967 classic's rollicking tone for a more fatalistic one, especially in Dillinger's burial of a friend in an unmarked grave, the worrying suffered by the gangsters' loved ones, Dillinger's telephone call to Melvin Purvis, and Purvis's farewell note to Dillinger.

Some of the events in *Dillinger*, as well as almost all "true" gangster movies, are apocryphal, but writer-director Milius understandably gives his film a few Hollywood tweaks that make for more drama. Many events in the film are compressed to give the impression that Melvin Purvis (Ben Johnson) and his G-men captured John Dillinger (Warren Oates) and his confederates at essentially the same moment in 1934. In reality,

Dillinger died on Sunday 22 July, Homer Van Meter (Harry Dean Stanton) perished on Thursday 23 August, Charles Mackley (John Ryan) died on Saturday 22 September, Harry Pierpont (Geoffrey Lewis) was executed on Wednesday 17 October, "Pretty Boy" Floyd (Steve Kanaly) died on Monday 22 October, and "Baby Face" Nelson (Richard Dreyfuss) perished on Tuesday 27 November 1934. (Bonnie Parker and Clyde Barrow, who are mentioned twice in *Dillinger*, were gunned down in a completely separate incident on Wednesday 23 May 1934.) In that eventful year of 1934, the American public got the news of the death of a glamorous public "enemy" on an almost monthly basis.

Historical liberties aside, *Dillinger* effectively captures the hopeless *milieu* of the Great Depression and the ambiguous heroes and villains that it spawned. Additional cast members are Roy Jenson as Purvis's Bureau of Investigation colleague Samuel P. Cowley (1899-1934); Michelle Phillips (billed as "Introducing Michelle Phillips") as Billie Frechette, who loves Dillinger; Cloris Leachman as Ana Sage, the "Lady in Red" who contributes to the outlaw's downfall outside the Biograph Theatre in Chicago; and Tennessee State University graduate and Chicago Bears defensive tackle Frank McRae as Reed Youngblood, a convicted murderer whom Dillinger frees from prison and takes into his gang. Barry DeVorzon's music score, while short on original background cues, makes outstanding use of "We're in the Money," "Red River Valley," "Honey," "It's Easy to Remember," and other standards.

Dillinger could just as easily have been named *Purvis and Dillinger*, for Ben Johnson as the famous G-man narrates the film and drives the plot as much as Purvis's nemesis does. Johnson portrays "Midwest Bureau Chief" Purvis as well dressed, obsessed with keeping his cigar lighted, mindful of his responsibility to the public, and extremely resolute—self-assured at best and self-centered at worst. One of the highlights of the film is Purvis's lecture about "cops and robbers" and right and wrong to a young boy while Purvis gets his shoes shined. In an unguarded moment, Purvis mentions to the fatherless boy that "I don't have anybody, either." However, another scene shows Purvis at dinner with his fiancée. (Purvis was briefly engaged to Lucky Strike model Janice Jarrett in the spring of 1937 but not during the 1933-1934 time frame of this movie.)

Unfortunately, Milius's usually excellent cinematic portrait of Purvis and Dillinger ends on a disappointing note when a closing billboard reveals whatever-happened-to information about Purvis—and gets it all wrong. According to the billboard,

> Melvin Purvis quit the FBI after the Dillinger case and went into private business. He shot himself in 1961 [sic] with the same gun [sic] he used to kill Dillinger.

Purvis, who did retire from the Bureau in 1935 and served as an army colonel in World War II and as the part owner of radio station WOLS in Florence, South Carolina, may have shot himself, intentionally or accidentally, on the morning of Monday 29 February 1960. However, the gun in question was a Colt .45 automatic pistol that had belonged to Gus Winkler, a Chicago hit man who had served as one of Purvis's informants a quarter-century earlier. Purvis's "suicide" is also highly questionable, for he left no note, and it is possible that his gun accidentally discharged as he prepared to clean it. As Purvis's biographer-son Alston Purvis wrote, "It is true [my father] told me he intended to lend Gus Winkler's pistol to a friend, Lyle McKain, to use in a display at a gun show. The idea that the shooting was accidental is entirely plausible."[4]

Another theory, although unlikely, is that Purvis was murdered by one of the many enemies that he had made on both sides of the law. As Alston Purvis, author of *The Vendetta*, asked, "Why was the pistol found near his left hand when he was right-handed? Did the amount of powder burns indicate the pistol had been fired from a distance?"[5]

Alston Purvis's 2005 book does not mention John Milius's *Dillinger* (1973) or the other Melvin Purvis movies. While *Dillinger* is in no way a Dan Curtis production, its art director was Trevor Williams, a Curtis regular who would serve as art director on Curtis's two Purvis films. Also, the movie's set decorator was Charles Pierce, who would dress the sets for three of Curtis's 1974 *Wide World Mystery* segments and for his second Purvis film in 1975. *Dillinger* aired several times in October, November, and December 2009 on the cable-TV movie channel called This TV.

Dale Robertson (*The Iron Horse*) stars as the real-life Bureau of Investigation agent, *Melvin Purvis, G-Man* (1974).

When ABC wanted to bring Melvin Purvis to television, the house of *Blacula* (AIP) joined with the house of *Dark Shadows* (DCP) to produce **Melvin Purvis, G-Man**, seen on the *ABC Tuesday Movie of the Week* on 9 April 1974 between *Happy Days* and *Marcus Welby, M.D.* John Milius co-wrote the teleplay with William F. Nolan (*The Norliss Tapes, The Turn of the Screw*), and *Dillinger* production manager Elliot Schick served as executive production supervisor of *Melvin Purvis*. Donald C. Klune returned as assistant director. Dan Curtis produced and directed *Melvin Purvis*, with plenty of low-angle shots, and Robert Cobert, of course, composed the music, a change-of-pace mixture of rowdy bluegrass and melancholy solo harmonica

Melvin Purvis, G-Man, which takes place in December 1933-January 1934, is a prequel to *Dillinger*, which is set mostly in the summer of 1934. Oddly, *Melvin Purvis* dramatizes events which actually occurred in July-September 1933 when George "Machine Gun" Kelly and his gang kidnapped Oklahoma City oil millionaire Charles Urschel and held him for ransom. In the telefilm, Kelly (Harris Yulin) kidnaps millionaire "Thatcher Covington" (Dick Sargent); collects a $500,000 ransom; releases Covington; but is captured by Purvis (Dale Robertson) in his sixth-floor room in the Monarch Hotel in Memphis, Tennessee (Kelly's hometown). In Curtis's remake of a scene from *Dillinger*, "Machine Gun" Kelly pleads, "Don't shoot me, G-man," and thereby gives Melvin Purvis and all Government men their catchy name. In subsequent decades, the anecdote has been attributed to Kelly's wife Kate Thorne, Kelly himself, FBI publicity, or legend.

Other similarities to *Dillinger* are Purvis's voice-over narration, mentions of the Barrow and Barker gangs, Purvis's assistance from his right-hand man Sam Cowley (Steve Kanaly), and a Chicago World's Fair poster that appears in both films. One difference is in the portrayal of women. In *Dillinger*, Billie Frechette (Michelle Phillips) is passive and only slightly involved in John Dillinger's criminal activities. In *Melvin Purvis*, Kate Ryan Kelly (as Margaret Blye's fiery character is named) is a full-fledged member of the Kelly Gang. She can handle firearms more skillfully than some of the men in the gang, such as Anthony Redecci (John Karlen), and (in the Monarch Hotel scene) she is even portrayed as the backbone behind her much softer husband and his doltish henchmen—"a collection of inept buffoons," in the words of TV-movie expert Alvin Marill.[6]

Noting this film's seriocomic tone, the *Los Angeles Herald-Examiner* called *Melvin Purvis, G-Man* "a whimsical throwback to 1930s gangsterdom, country style. It advances in a delightfully bouncy rhythm. It has more the effect of a sly, tongue-in-cheek folk tale than the ache of real bullet holes" as *Dillinger* had.[7] The *Los Angeles Times* went so far as to call "ABC's spunky, provocative" telefilm "far superior to *Dillinger*, the theatrical film that preceded it." The *L.A. Times* continued, "Here, motivation and character are made to count for much more than mere violence. Its development creates confrontations both revealing and ambiguous, which have been directed by Dan Curtis with a sense of edginess and insight."[8] Two of those confrontations are a very personal machine-gun "duel" between Kelly and Redecci and a tender exchange between an unusually compassionate Purvis and the wounded, frightened Kelly Gang member Thomas "Buckwheat" Longaker (played by Elliott Street of *The Harrad Experiment*).

Melvin Purvis, G-Man (1974): Dale Robertson (seated, as the title character) poses with members of Purvis's team, including Steve Kanaly (left, as Sam Cowley).

Variety had similar praise for "AIP's first TV venture, and under the imaginative banner of Dan Curtis Productions." It reported, "Curtis's direction is creative [and] makes a strong script by John Milius and William F. Nolan come to life without tripping over [the] nostalgia theme."[9] While an exciting shoot-out between the Bureau agents and the Kelly Gang is a highlight, the centerpiece of *Melvin Purvis, G-Man* is Dale Robertson's charismatic, larger-than-life portrayal of the unflappable clothes-horse who spouts self-assured observations on human nature between tokes on his ever-present cigar. The telefilm ends with Purvis getting another shoe shine and chuckling to himself over his capture of Kelly and his new "G-man" moniker. Adding further flair to the proceedings are the aforementioned Karlen as Redecci and Street as "Buckwheat," Matt Clark as Charlie Parlmetter, David Canary as Gene Farber, and Don Megowan as a smart-aleck short-order cook.

Critic Leonard Maltin characterized *Melvin Purvis, G-Man* as "a wonderful send-up of the type of gangster movie they don't make any more."[10] Curtis's sequel, *The Kansas City Massacre,* followed on ABC one-and-one-half years later, but first, *The Fugitive* creator Roy Huggins followed Curtis's lead by executive-producing the 1974 TV-movie *The Story of Pretty Boy Floyd* (ABC, Tuesday 7 May). Later in 1974, Quinn Martin, another famous executive producer, joined the trend with *The FBI vs. Alvin Karpis, Public Enemy Number One* (CBS, Friday 8 November).

Melvin Purvis, G-Man (1974): Harris Yulin (center, as "Machine Gun" Kelly) and John Karlen (right, as Anthony Redecci) face the G-men in a shoot-out.

Interestingly, there was quite a bit of interchange among the casts of these 1970s gangster movies. A pre-*Dallas* Steve Kanaly played "Pretty Boy" Floyd in *Dillinger* and Sam Cowley in *Melvin Purvis*. John Karlen portrayed Anthony Redecci in *Melvin Purvis* and replaced Kanaly as Cowley in *The Kansas City Massacre*. Mills Watson played Shine Rush in *The Story of Pretty Boy Floyd* and Frank Nash in *The Kansas City Massacre*. Matt Clark portrayed Charlie Parlmetter in *Melvin Purvis* and Vernon Miller in *The Kansas City Massacre*. Elliott Street played "Buckwheat" Longaker in *Melvin Purvis* and "Baby Face" Nelson in *The Kansas City Massacre*. Harris Yulin portrayed "Machine Gun" Kelly in *Melvin Purvis*, J. Edgar Hoover in *The FBI vs. Alvin Karpis*, and Johnny Lazia in *The Kansas City Massacre*. Don Megowan and Jim Hill played small roles in both of Curtis's Purvis movies, but surprisingly, Geoffrey Lewis, who portrayed Harry Pierpont in *Dillinger* and had roles in three of Dan Curtis's productions (including 1974's *Great Ice Rip-Off*), did not appear in either *Melvin Purvis, G-Man* or *The Kansas City Massacre*.

ABC launched its 1975-1976 season with **The Kansas City Massacre** on Friday 19 September, and like *Trilogy of Terror* six months earlier, Curtis's film carried a PARENTAL DISCRETION IS ADVISED warning because of its violent, mature subject matter. Dale Robertson returned as the epicurean fashion-plate to smoke out more public enemies in America's heartland—but also to stop and show compassion for a criminal's wife (Sally Kirkland) and young son (Ike Eisenmann).

Chapter III: *Melvin Purvis, G-Man; The Kansas City Massacre*, and More   159

Dan Curtis directs a shoot-out in *The Kansas City Massacre* (1975). William F. Nolan, the co-writer of the two Melvin Purvis TV-movies, calls his friend Curtis "cantankerous" but terrific.

The Kansas City Massacre, which is set in April, May, and June of 1933, once again moves backward in time from the events of *Melvin Purvis, G-Man* (December 1933-January 1934) and *Dillinger* (summer 1934). It dramatizes the watershed event that spurs on Purvis's efforts to round up the public enemies and that ushered in the important change of allowing Bureau of Investigation agents to carry firearms and make arrests. A machine-gun attack on criminal Frank "Jelly" Nash and several law enforcers and bystanders occurred at the Union Station railroad depot in Kansas City, Missouri, on Saturday 17 June 1933. According to Robertson's voice-over narration as Purvis,

> In addition to our prisoner, Frank Nash, and one of the gunmen, Solly Weissman, five officers were killed that morning at Union Plaza Station: Frank Hermanson and W.J. Grooms of the Kansas City Detective Bureau, Mike Fanning and Lyle Gage of the federal penitentiary, and Ed Martin of the Bureau. Twelve innocent bystanders were also seriously wounded in that violent exchange of gunfire which came to be known as the Kansas City Massacre.

AIP had no involvement with *The Kansas City Massacre*, which was strictly a Dan Curtis production. William F. Nolan co-wrote the script with *Lawman* and *Rawhide* writer "Bronson Howitzer" (Richard Hardman), and Curtis produced and directed. Curtis mixed his trademark low camera angles with some high shots (i.e. looking down from the tops of stairwells) and even a few crooked angles reminiscent of ABC-TV's *Batman* (1966-1968).

In *The Kansas City Massacre*, Purvis, along with his aide Sam Cowley (John Karlen), battles a veritable rogues' gallery of more than one dozen criminals, loosely organized as the "Karpis/Barker/Floyd Gang": Alvin Karpis (Morgan Paull), Doc Barker (Gary Sandy), Fred Barker (Hunter Von Leer), "Pretty Boy" Floyd (Bo Hopkins), Adam Richetti (Robert Walden), "Baby Face" Nelson (Elliott Street), Frank "Jelly" Nash (Mills Watson), Vernon Miller (Matt Clark), Homer Van Meter (Brion James), Harry Pierpont (Larry Manetti), Wilbur Underhill (W.T. Zacha), Larry DeVol (James Storm), and John Dillinger (William Jordon). Harris Yulin plays crime boss Johnny Lazia, and Western and *film-noir* veteran Scott Brady portrays Commissioner Hubert Tucker McElwaine, who is not what he seems. Brady was one of Dan Curtis's favorite actors. The director recalled,

> I remembered Scott Brady from years ago, and I got him to play the cop in *The Night Strangler*. He was so happy to play the cop, and I would say to him, "Hang around the set, Scott, and if there's anything else I can think of to stick you into, I'll do it." And he did it. He was always there for pick-up scenes in the picture because he would do anything just to be in the picture. I kept Scott around, and from that point on, Scott Brady became a part of my stock company. I used him in a million pictures [actually, six]. I loved him; he was great.[11]

The Kansas City Massacre (1975): Scott Brady (as Hubert McElwaine), John Karlen (as a recast Sam Cowley), and Dale Robertson (as Melvin Purvis) perform a scene in William F. Nolan and Dan Curtis's second Purvis film.

Curtis's self-proclaimed "stock company" of actors was one of his *auteur* hallmarks. Just as Orson Welles before him, Robert Altman and Woody Allen alongside him, and Joe Dante after him had done, Curtis populated his movies with many of the same actors time and again. Roy Thinnes (*The Norliss Tapes, Supertrain, Dark Shadows*) remarked, "Dan's honest, and he wants everyone around him to be honest, so he hires people and puts together this great repertory company. You see a lot of the same people working with him down the line—a faithful group."12

The Kansas City Massacre (1975): Bo Hopkins (left, as "Pretty Boy" Floyd) and others stick their hands up in this climactic scene from the film, based on the true story of the 17 June 1933 massacre.

In Curtis's television mysteries and crime dramas, Charles Aidman, Orin Cannon, Matt Clark, Jim Hill, Norman Honath, Don Megowan, Dale Robertson, Elliott Street, Robert Walden, Mills Watson, and Harris Yulin appear in at least two of them, and the *Dark Shadows* actors who make return appearances are Thayer David, Louis Edmonds, Grayson Hall, John Karlen, Kathryn Leigh Scott, and James Storm. Jim Storm appeared in five additional Dan Curtis productions after *Dark Shadows,* and Johnny Karlen appeared a record 13 more times after *Dark Shadows*. In his talk at the 2005 Dark Shadows Festival, Karlen quipped, "Dan knew a good actor when he saw one!"

The Kansas City Massacre has no shortage of fine actors as the *Los Angeles Times* noted when it declared, "The casting is inspired."13 *Variety* added, "Splendid cast, with Robertson again portraying suave, humorless FBI Midwest chief, abetted by producer Dan Curtis's inventive direction, reconstructs era [of the 1930s] with relentless authenticity."14

Indeed, *The Kansas City Massacre* surpasses *Melvin Purvis, G-Man* in plot, characterization, action, music, and period detail. With a running time only eight minutes shorter than John Milius's *Dillinger*, Curtis's *Kansas City Massacre* has a longer time to establish plotlines than the shorter *Melvin Purvis* movie of the week. Although William F. Nolan and "Bronson Howizter" (Ric Hardman) seemingly overcrowd their teleplay with far more bad guys than are needed, their detailed script allows the audience to learn something about the character of each of them. The all-out firefight between the overzealous, bungling Oklahoma Highway Patrol and the outlaw legion concentrated at "Pretty Boy" Floyd's farmhouse tops the smaller-scale gunfight in *Melvin Purvis, G-Man*. Robert Cobert's music is an effective blend of bluegrass, Dixieland, and solo-clarinet cues, as well as the use of such vintage songs as "Life Is Just a Bowl of Cherries," "You Belong to Me," "With Plenty of Money and You," "Paradise," and "If You Knew Susie." Lynn Loring's character Viola Moreland, as "Sally Strand," sings "Am I Blue?" at Johnny Lazia's nightclub. Adding to the period detail are striking 1930s-era clothes and cars, plus radio broadcasts of *Little Orphan Annie* and *The Shadow*. According to *TV Guide*, this "tongue-in-cheek retrospection makes for solid entertainment."[15]

This time, the criminals are much smarter and more fearsome, and the comic relief comes from the Oklahoma Highway patrolmen, led by future *Mary Hartman, Mary Hartman* star Philip Bruns as Captain Ralph "Jimbo" Jackson. A light note late in the film is that "Pretty Boy" Floyd escapes in Captain Jackson's automobile. Essentially, Purvis, who has captured the Kansas City Massacre's mastermind Vernon Miller, *allows* Floyd to escape because Purvis realizes that Floyd apparently was not responsible for, or even aware of, the impending massacre. Although this theory is backed up by certain historical findings, Purvis's actions here do not match the events of *Dillinger*, in which Purvis (Ben Johnson) still blames Floyd (Steve Kanaly) for the massacre one year later. We fans of *Dark Shadows* and Dan Curtis movies can attribute this discrepancy to the notion that *Dillinger* takes place in parallel time and the two Curtis films occur in "our" time band.

The Kansas City Massacre is a rousing climax to the Milius/Curtis trilogy of Melvin Purvis adventures. Dan Curtis considered making more Purvis TV-movies and/or a weekly series, and he amassed numerous promising (albeit historically inaccurate) scripts, none of which were produced later in the 1970s (*or in the mid-1990s when Curtis wanted to remake Melvin Purvis, G-Man*). Here is some information about those leftover scripts.

"Machine Gun Kate," by Jock MacKelvie (*The Rookies*). 8-page treatment dated Friday 14 February 1975. Kathryn Kelly, née Cleo Coleman Shannon, is sent to the women's prison in Coffeyville, Kansas, and her husband, "Machine Gun" Kelly, is sent to Alcatraz. Kate assembles a gang behind bars, and the women escape from prison and hide out with "Ma" Barker in Tulsa, Oklahoma. Kate and her all-girl gang rob a few banks before Melvin Purvis and Sam Cowley capture them in Iola, Kansas.

"Death Wears a Baby's Face," by Jock MacKelvie (*Charlie's Angels*). 13-page treatment dated Wednesday 5 March 1975. "Baby Face" Nelson manages to escape Melvin Purvis and his G-men at the Little Bohemia Lodge and makes his way across the country. He robs banks, takes hostages, and gets run out of several towns by mobsters; even *they* don't want him around. Meanwhile, Nelson and his wife Helen hear the sobering news of John Dillinger's death outside the Biograph Theatre. Finally, Purvis, Cowley, and the Bureau agents track "Baby Face" Nelson to a cornfield in Niles Center, Illinois. Purvis's voice-over narration explains that after a shoot-out, Nelson has 17 lead slugs in him and his 123 days as Public Enemy Number One are over.

"Mrs. Machine Gun Kelly," by Robert Lewin (*Bracken's World*). 7-page synopsis dated Friday 25 April 1975. 34-page outline dated Tuesday 27 May 1975. This proposed sequel to *Melvin Purvis, G-Man* focuses on Kathryn Elizabeth Ryan, who is sent to prison after she and her husband "Machine Gun" Kelly kidnap Thatcher Covington. Suddenly, Kate is paroled, and she learns that a smitten Covington has bought her out of jail. Covington wants a relationship, but Kate throws the millionaire over for Al Capone! When George Kelly hears that his wife has taken up with Capone, he breaks out of jail and reclaims her. Meanwhile, Melvin Purvis meets Eliot Ness and offers to work with him, but Ness rebuffs Purvis. Ultimately, Purvis captures the Kellys and sends them back to prison, but Ness loses Capone.

"Mrs. Machine-Gun Kelly," by Robert Schlitt (*The Monkees*). 27-page outline dated Monday 21 July 1975. Katherine Kelly breaks her husband out of Joliet prison, but George Kelly is soon recaptured. Katherine carves out a place for herself in the Chicago underworld; eventually, she becomes Al Capone's mistress. When "Machine-Gun" Kelly hears the news, he escapes from Joliet in a laundry truck. The Kellys reunite and scheme to rob Capone's safe. Melvin Purvis and Sam Cowley foil their plans and send them to jail. Purvis informs Capone that the safe is evidence and Capone must come to the police station and sign an affidavit stating that the safe and its contents are his. The safe contains $300,000, and when Al Capone declares the cash to be his, Purvis has the grounds for a charge of income-tax evasion against the gangster!

"The Legend of Bonnie and Clyde," by Richard Guttman (*Back Door to Hell*). 32-page treatment dated Tuesday 27 May 1975. 34-page treatment dated Friday 30 May 1975. 37-page treatment dated Thursday 5 June 1975. 97-page complete script dated Tuesday 26 August 1975 (revised Monday 3 November 1975). The Barrow Gang's shoot-out in Joplin, Missouri, brings the gang to the attention of Melvin Purvis—and Texas Ranger "Black" Jack Ryan, who is bent on catching and killing the gangsters before Purvis apprehends them. Clyde Barrow, Bonnie Parker, and Blanche and Buck Barrow are joined by W.D. Jones, who becomes their driver. The Barrow Gang robs banks in Minnesota and Arkansas and has a serious automobile accident in Oklahoma. Later, Blanche and Buck are wounded and captured, and W.D. Jones turns himself in. Bonnie and Clyde break Clyde's friend Henry Methvin out of jail, and the new trio robs a bank in Indiana. *The Legend of Bonnie and Clyde* concludes with the famous ambush of Bonnie and Clyde on the road to Arcadia, Louisiana, on Wednesday 23 May 1934, after Henry Methvin and his father have given up the pair. Purvis is furious that "Black" Jack Ryan and his men have gunned down Bonnie and Clyde before Purvis could take them alive. In the final scene, Melvin Purvis and Sam Cowley visit Bonnie Parker's grave in Dallas. Purvis muses, "She wrote they'd be buried side by side, but Clyde's 12 miles on the other side of town." Except for the obvious but necessary fiction of inserting Purvis into the story, Guttman's teleplay often adheres to the documented facts about Bonnie, Clyde, Blanche, and Buck, as well as Jones and Methvin, who were real people (unlike "C.W. Moss" of Arthur Penn's 1967 masterpiece *Bonnie and Clyde,* a film that this script takes pains not to mimic too closely).

"Melvin Purvis, G-Man," a.k.a. "The Great Chicago Raid," a.k.a. "The Legend of Johnny Dillinger," a.k.a. "Dillinger," by Earl Wallace (*The Last Ride of the Dalton Gang*) and Dan Curtis. 127-page script dated Friday 18 March 1994. 127-page revised script, circa mid-1994. 200-page revised two-part script dated Monday 29 August 1994. Curtis and Wallace perfectly recapture the rollicking, seriocomic feel of *Melvin Purvis, G-Man* (1974) twenty years later in this impressive script for a three- or four-hour TV-movie. The highly fictionalized story takes place between February and December 1934. Period detail includes mentions of Jack Benny, Ronald Colman, baseball teams, the CCC, and the NBC Red and Blue radio networks. Purvis's easygoing voice-over narration and folksy dialogue complete the mood. Purvis even has a love interest—Sheriff Lillian Holly of Crown Point, Indiana. The script begins with John Dillinger and Herbert Youngblood's escape from Sheriff Holly's jail. Johnny and Herbie soon join forces with Homer Van Meter, Harry Pierpont, Fred and Doc Barker, and other wanted criminals and they rob banks in Indiana, Illinois, and Kansas. Then, other public enemies (Alvin Karpis, Larry DeVol, John Hamilton, Wilbur Underhill, Charles Mackley, et al.) join the rogues' gallery and help Dillinger and "Baby Face" Nelson rob the Chicago Mint in an armored-car mock-up that they use as a battering ram. Melvin Purvis receives several phone calls from Dillinger and Nelson and subtly gleans information from them. Purvis and Sam Cowley also visit Johnny Dillinger's father and win him over. The script dramatizes the shoot-out at Little Bohemia Lodge, and it also includes a scene in which Billie Frechette pays Dr. Wilhelm Loesser to perform plastic surgery. After the obligatory Biograph Theatre sequence in which "Dillinger" is killed, the script's twist is that it was look-alike Jimmy Lawrence, *not* Dillinger, who was gunned down! Purvis deduces the ruse and follows the real Dillinger and "Baby Face" Nelson to Old Man Dillinger's farm where Johnny has stashed the ten million dollars stolen from the Chicago Mint. Nelson dies, but Dillinger gets away. In the final scene, set on Christmas Eve 1934, Purvis receives a phone call from Dillinger in South America where Johnny and Billie have settled and gone straight. Purvis tells Cowley that Dillinger has gone into the banking business and adds, "If John Dillinger can't succeed in the banking business, who can?" Purvis then leaves to go on a date with Sheriff Lillian Holly. This enjoyable 1994 teleplay would have reintroduced America to Melvin Purvis, G-Man (albeit a fictionalized version) 14 or 15 years before Michael Mann's more serious *Public Enemies* (2009).

This script is inspired by William F. Nolan's 1974 outline and/or Nolan's 1976 script "Dillinger," a.k.a. "The Great Dillinger Manhunt," a.k.a. "The Great Dillinger/Nelson Manhunt," a.k.a. "The Legend of Johnny Dillinger." In a Sunday 17 January 2010 letter to me, Bill Nolan revealed that his outline featured "a great *true* twist: Dillinger was *not* killed at the Biograph in '34. A 'stooge' died in his place. All factual!" According to Nolan's research, look-alike James Lawrence died in Dillinger's place outside the theatre, and the real Dillinger lived a long life in Northern California. Nolan maintains that the East Chicago police and the Bureau of Investigation were responsible for the hoax.

On 19 September 1975, *The Kansas City Massacre*, starring Dale Robertson, airs on the *ABC Friday Night Movie* opposite *Hawaii Five-O* and *Barnaby Jones* on CBS and *The Rockford Files* and *Police Woman* on NBC.

Over the years, Dan Curtis certainly had plenty of ideas ready for a possible Melvin Purvis TV series and/or revival. Other Purvis concepts that Curtis was considering (as early as 1974) were pitting Purvis and Cowley against Ma Barker, bootleggers, Billy the Bomber, rioting prisoners, Frank Nash, the operators of a floating casino, the Reilly gang, a murderer on an American Indian reservation, and Tex Harmony. In addition to his "Legend of Johnny Dillinger," William F. Nolan submitted outlines involving Melvin Purvis with Wilbur Underhill ("The Tri-State Terror") and "Baby Face" Nelson ("The Great Nelson Manhunt"). In some other, parallel band of time, a book like this would include an episode guide to ABC-TV's *Purvis—FBI* (January 1976?-August 1977?). The possibilities are endless.

In reality, three-and-one-half decades after the Milius/Curtis trilogy, Melvin Purvis and his outlaw foes recaptured the public's interest in a very big way when *Heat* and *Collateral* director Michael Mann's $80 million Universal motion picture *Public Enemies* was released on Wednesday 1 July 2009. Christian Bale and Johnny Depp co-star as Purvis and Dillinger, respectively, in a sprawling tale that spans Dillinger's entire year-long crime spree. J. Edgar Hoover, who does not appear in the Milius/Curtis trilogy, is played here by Billy Crudup. Richard Short's Agent Sam Cowley is a minor character.

The theatrically staged bank-robbery scenes in *Public Enemies* are highlights as are Dillinger's arraignment in Crown Point, Indiana, and his subsequent escape from jail on Saturday 3 March 1934. Depp captures Dillinger's arrogance in the gangster's nonchalant appearances in public places, such as the club where Billie Frechette (Marion Cotillard) checks coats and a movie theatre where he watches himself in newsreels. As in Milius's film, Dillinger is keenly aware of his public image and does not want to mar his Robin Hood persona by doing something *really* bad, like kidnapping.

The scenes set inside the Biograph Theatre on Sunday 22 July 1934 are especially gripping as Dillinger avidly watches Clark Gable, Myrna Loy, and William Powell in W.S. Van Dyke's *Manhattan Melodrama* (1934) moments before his doom. The following sequence, outside the Biograph, as Bureau agents close in on Dillinger and gun him down, is well played and historically accurate in the number of bullets that hit Dillinger (three, by most accounts) if not exactly in the location of his death (in the alley next to the theatre and not on the sidewalk in front). According to Michael Sragow of the *Baltimore Sun*, "Mann and Depp's rendering of Dillinger's last night, spent in and outside of a Chicago movie theatre, attains the soaring intensity of hard-guy opera."[16]

One of the film's minor flaws is the poorly staged scene in which Billie Frechette is apprehended. Dillinger's placement on the street is far too conspicuous for him not to have been seen by countless people around him. (In reality, he remained in his car as Bureau agents, led by Purvis, arrested Frechette and her contact Larry Strong at Chicago's Tumble Inn.) Another quibble is a couple of wildly apocryphal—but very Hollywood—sequences near the end of the film.

The only real failing of *Public Enemies* is its often confusing nature. There are dozens of characters, and many of them do not have enough screen time or enough clear explanation to register with the audience. Michael Mann could have used John Milius's and Dan Curtis's devices of on-screen titles and voice-over narration to introduce the many good guys and bad guys. Regrettably, Mann's filming of the all-important shoot-out between Purvis's agents and Dllinger's gang at the Little Bohemia Lodge in Manitowish, Wisconsin, on Monday 23 April 1934 suffers from quick, jerky, hand-held camera shots and the nighttime darkness on the screen.

Christian Bale plays Melvin Purvis as a much less eccentric but fiercely loyal, no-nonsense company man who is acclimating himself to his Herculean task of capturing "Public Enemy Number One." Bale's Purvis is *never* seen smoking except for the fateful lighting of his cigar outside the Biograph Theatre. Like Milius's *Dillinger,* Mann's *Public Enemies* concludes with a whatever-happened-to billboard that states that Purvis left the Bureau one year after Dillinger's capture and "died in 1960 by his own hand."

The 1933-1934 detail in *Public Enemies* is outstanding. The clothes, the hats, the cars, the trains, the guns, and the ornate bank buildings perfectly evoke the era as do the sounds of Lowell Thomas and Will Rogers on the radio and the inclusion on the soundtrack of Benny Goodman's "King Porter Stomp," three Billie Holiday recordings, and several other vintage songs. Elliot Goldenthal's elegiac music score, heavy on strings, mixes in a few bluesy cues, and Diana Krall sings "Bye Bye Blackbird," a song that Dillinger and Frechette adopt as their own. The end result is a strong sense of style. According to *Salon* critic Stephanie Zacharek, "The glamour quotient in *Public*

Enemies is high, and in a landscape of contemporary movies in which 'sophistication' is seemingly a dirty word, it's a relief to see actors in period dress rather than outlandish *Willy Wonka* get-ups and super-hero costumes."[17]

At the Hollywood premiere of *Public Enemies* on Tuesday 23 June 2009—23 months after *Shadowgram* and *Variety* had announced the news of a *Dark Shadows* feature film—Johnny Depp spoke officially about the project and director Tim Burton's involvement. "*Dark Shadows*, with Tim, will also be down the line," Depp revealed. He continued,

> Tim has to finish [*Alice in*] *Wonderland* before he can start work on the next film. I love what he did with that. I think people are going to be so excited and satisfied when they see that film. Some of his best work. And I will be thrilled to work with him again on *Dark Shadows*. I was a big fan of it when I was a kid, and I think it is another of those perfect projects for Tim to reimagine.[18]

One month later, at the San Diego Comic-Book Convention (23-24-25-26 July), when Burton and Depp appeared at an *Alice in Wonderland* preview event, the director told the crowd that he was looking forward to getting started on *Dark Shadows* when he finished making *Alice in Wonderland*. In an interview with MTV, Burton added that *Dark Shadows* was something that he and Depp "both love and are excited about. [. . .] It was such a weird soap opera. Part of the energy of it was the tone and weirdness of it. That's our challenge: to try to capture that vibe. [. . .] It's one of the more interesting things about it."[19] The results of Burton's and Depp's efforts—*Dark Shadows* (2012)—are discussed in chapter one of this book.

Dillinger (AIP, 1973). Executive producer: Samuel Z. Arkoff. Producer: Buzz Feitshans. Director: John Milius. First assistant director: Donald C. Klune. Screenplay: John Milius. Music: Barry DeVorzon. Director of photography: Jules Brenner. Art director: Trevor Williams. Set decorator: Charles Pierce. Makeup: Tom Ellingwood. Costumers: James George and Barbara Siebert.

Cast: Ben Johnson (Melvin Purvis), Warren Oates (John Dillinger), Michelle Phillips (Billie Frechette), Roy Jenson (Sam Cowley), Harry Dean Stanton (Homer Van Meter), Geoffrey Lewis (Harry Pierpont), Richard Dreyfuss (Lester Gillis "Baby Face" Nelson), Steve Kanaly (Charles Arthur "Pretty Boy" Floyd), John Ryan (Charles Mackley), Frank McRae (Reed Youngblood), Michelle Phillips (Polly Hamilton), Cloris Leachman (Ana Sage, the "Lady in Red"). 107 minutes. Available on VHS and DVD. (*Dillinger* is not a Dan Curtis production.)

Melvin Purvis, G-Man (ABC, 9 April 1974). Executive producer: Paul Picard. Producer: Dan Curtis. Director: Dan Curtis. First assistant director: Donald C. Klune. Teleplay: John Milius and William F. Nolan (from a story by John Milius). Music: Robert Cobert. Director of photography: Jacques Marquette. Art director: Trevor Williams. Makeup: no credit given. Costumer: no credit given.

Cast: Dale Robertson (Melvin Purvis), Harris Yulin (George "Machine Gun" Kelly), Margaret Blye (Kate Ryan Kelly), Steve Kanaly (Sam Cowley), John Karlen

(Anthony Redecci), Dick Sargent (Thatcher Covington), Woodrow Parfrey (Nash Covington), Matt Clark (Charlie Parlmetter), David Canary (Eugene Farber), Elliott Street (Thomas "Buckwheat" Longaker), Jim Hill (J.D. Longaker), Don Megowan (hamburger-stand man), Eddie Quillan (Monarch Hotel clerk), Hank Rolike (shoeshine man). 74 minutes. Available on VHS only.

The Kansas City Massacre (ABC, 19 September 1975). Producer: Dan Curtis. Associate producer: Robert Singer. Director: Dan Curtis. First assistant director: Art Levinson. Teleplay: Bronson Howitzer (Richard Hardman), William F. Nolan (from a story by Bronson Howizter). Music: Robert Cobert. Director of photography: Paul Lohman. Art director: Trevor Williams. Set decorator: Charles Pierce. Makeup: Mike Westmore. Costumer: John Perry. Choreographer: Ellen Halpen.

Cast: Dale Robertson (Melvin Purvis), Bo Hopkins (Charles Arthur "Pretty Boy" Floyd), Lynn Loring (Viola Moreland), John Karlen (Sam Cowley), Robert Walden (Adam Richetti), Matt Clark (Vernon Miller), Mills Watson (Frank "Jelly" Nash), Scott Brady (Commissioner Hubert T. McElwaine), Elliott Street (Lester Gillis "Baby Face" Nelson), Harris Yulin (Johnny Lazia), Philip Bruns (Captain Ralph "Jimbo" Jackson), William Jordon (John Dillinger), Brion James (Homer Van Meter), Larry Manetti (Harry Pierpont), W.T. Zacha (Wilbur Underhill), Morgan Paull (Alvin "Creepy" Karpis), Sally Kirkland (Wilma Floyd), Gary Sandy (Doc Barker), Hunter Von Leer (Fred Barker), James Storm (Larry DeVol), Ike Eisenmann (Jackie Floyd), Don Megowan (Boss Slinger), Orin Cannon (Leroy Merkee), Jim Hill (bank teller), Lester Maddox (Governor Patrick Burns). 99 minutes. Available on VHS only.

Public Enemies (Universal, 2009). Executive producers: Jane Rosenthal, G. Mac Brown, and Robert De Niro. Producers: Kevin Misher and Michael Mann. Director: Michael Mann. Assistant directors: Bob Wagner, Michael Waxman, Bryan Carroll, Kwame Amoaku, Traci Lewis, Lucille OuYang, et al. Screenplay: Ann Biderman, Ronan Bennett, Michael Mann (based on the book by Bryan Burrough). Music: Elliot Goldenthal. Director of photography: Dante Spinotti. Art directors: Nathan Crowley, Patrick Lumb, William Skinner. Makeup: Deborah Dee, Vicki Fischer, Chantelle Johnson, Vicki Vacca, et al. Costumer: Colleen Atwood (2012 *Dark Shadows* costumer).

Cast: Christian Bale (Melvin Purvis), Johnny Depp (John Dillinger), Marion Cotillard (Billie Frechette), Richard Short (Sam Cowley), Stephen Dorff (Homer Van Meter), Channing Tatum (Charles Arthur "Pretty Boy" Floyd), Stephen Graham (Lester Gillis "Baby Face" Nelson), David Wenham (Harry Pierpont), Giovanni Ribisi (Alvin Karpis), Billy Crudup (J. Edgar Hoover), Chandler Williams (Clyde Tolson), Rebecca Spence (Doris Rogers), Emilie de Ravin (Barbara Patzke), Christian Stolte (Charles Mackley), Bill Camp (Frank Nitti), Steve Key (Doc Barker), Lili Taylor (Sheriff Lillian Holley), Michael Bentt (Herbert Youngblood), Stephen Lang (Charles Winstead), Ed Bruce (Senator Kenneth McKellar [D-Tennessee]), Shawn Hatosy (Johnny Madala), Diana Krall (torch singer), Leelee Sobieski (Polly Hamilton), Branka Katic (Ana Sage, the "Lady in Red"). 143 minutes. Available on DVD and Blu-Ray. (*Public Enemies* is not a Dan Curtis production.)

Dan Curtis Significa: The working titles of *Melvin Purvis, G-Man* (1974) and *The Kansas City Massacre* (1975) were *Purvis—FBI* and *The Return of Melvin Purvis, G-Man*, respectively. *Melvin Purvis, G-Man* (1974) was released internationally as *The Legend of Machine Gun Kelly*. A Mexican lobby card for *La Leyenda del Ametralladora Kelly* pictures Dick Sargent held at gunpoint by Margaret Blye.

Although Thayer David (*Dark Shadows, Nero Wolfe*) did not appear in either of Dan Curtis's Melvin Purvis movies, he did play Connelly opposite Mickey Rooney as Nelson in Don Siegel's *Baby Face Nelson* (1957). In that film, Homer Van Meter was played by Elisha Cook Jr. (*The Night Stalker, Dead of Night*), and John Dillinger was played by Leo Gordon (*The Winds of War, War and Remembrance*). Ten years later, when Thayer David was on *Dark Shadows*, he remarked, "Dan Curtis, our producer, has the idea that people like to see a stock company of actors."[20]

Dan Curtis Significa: In addition to the never-produced *Purvis—FBI* scripts, Dan Curtis collected quite a few other teleplays that ultimately were never filmed. Curtis himself wrote or co-wrote a few of them, including *The Hoods* (1975), *Making It* (1989, 1999, 2005), *The Raid on 330 Park* (1993, with Earl Wallace), *The Last Summer* (undated, with Barbara Steele), and *Komine, Pike, and W.D. Baldry* (undated, with Jerry Renert and Jeff Wilhelm). As early as 1969-1970 and as late as 1976, Curtis considered filming *The Last of the Crazy People*, based on Timothy Findley's 1967 novel about a troubled family. Curtis also considered the scripts *RFK: Between the Gunshots* (1976), by Lee Hutson (*When Every Day Was the Fourth of July*); *Deathwork* (1992), by Robert Carrington (*Wait Until Dark*); *Command Performance* (1995), by James Henerson (*The Love Letter*); *Condemned* (2001), by Lee Hutson (*The Long Days of Summer*), and *The Price of Honor* (2002), by sportswriter Frank Deford (*Trading Hearts*).

Perhaps the three biggest missed opportunities among the unproduced scripts were the time-travel trilogy *I Love Harrisburg in the Springtime*, by Jack Finney (*From Time to Time*); the Western epic *Diary of a Gunfighter*, by Richard Matheson (*Scream of the Wolf*); and *Wuthering Heights*, adapted in the early 1970s by Sam Hall (*Dark Shadows*) and again in the late 1970s by Julian Mitchell (*The Mysterious Stranger*). Curtis also considered remaking *The Strange Case of Dr. Jekyll and Mr. Hyde* (on film, not videotape) and *The Night Stalker* (and directing it himself).[21]

In the late 1970s, Dan Curtis directs *Express to Terror*, *Mrs. R's Daughter*, and *The Last Ride of the Dalton Gang*.

CHAPTER IV

The Last Ride of the Dalton Gang

In a 2005 DVD interview, Dan Curtis revealed that he "always loved Westerns." He added, "I always wanted to make a Western. I just love the whole feel of Westerns and the look of Westerns. At that point [1979], I had reached *my style* in terms of shooting, and my style was accommodated very nicely by the Western genre because I jammed frames with gun butts and everything had dust in it!"[1]

On Tuesday 20 November 1979, NBC presented the three-hour event, **The Last Ride of the Dalton Gang**, Curtis's only Western and one of his personal favorites of his films. The movie (whose running time is 2 hours, 26 minutes) aired in a three-hour timeslot opposite *Happy Days, Angie, Three's Company, Taxi,* and *Family* on ABC and *Raggedy Ann & Andy* and *Young Love, First Love* on CBS. Curtis originally planned *The Last Ride of the Dalton Gang* as a two-part, four-hour miniseries called *The Raid on Coffeyville*, but he (not the network this time) decided to reshape it as a tighter, one-night feature. (The extra footage still exists.) Curtis remembered, "The only reason it ended up the length it was is I didn't think that the four hours would *hold* over two nights. It probably would have, and it was a mistake to cut it down, but the cut-down version was great, playing as three hours in one night."[2]

The Last Ride of the Dalton Gang (NBC, 1979) stars (standing, from left) Matt Clark, John Fitzpatrick, Cliff Potts, Sharon Farrell, Larry Wilcox, James Crittenden, Eric Lawson (and kneeling, from left), Bo Hopkins, Randy Quaid, and Dennis Fimple.

The Last Ride of the Dalton Gang, written by future Oscar winner Earl W. Wallace (*Witness*), tells the often light-hearted story of the Dalton brothers' misadventures as deputy marshals-turned-horse thieves, train bandits, and bank robbers. Curtis mixes the rollicking tone of *Bonnie and Clyde* (1967) with the fatalism of *The Wild Bunch* (1969) and the nostalgia of classic Hollywood Westerns. He filmed the movie in and around Los Angeles, Columbia, Jamestown, Placerville, Sacramento, Sonora, and Stockton, California.

The Last Ride of the Dalton Gang features one of the best credits sequences of all of Curtis's movies: a fast-moving montage of covers of Western pulp magazines, such as *The Pecos Kid Western*, *Ace-High Western Stories*, *Fifteen Western Tales*, *Ranch Romances*, and *Thrilling Western*. According to Curtis,

> The title sequence in this picture is one of my favorite things in the movie. The picture is very reminiscent of the feel that you get from reading those old pulp Westerns, and I used to love the covers of those pulp westerns. So in order to get that feel for this picture—let the audience know what's coming—I thought if we took those covers and did a montage of those covers, doing camera moves on those covers, on those great paintings, it would tell the audience, "This is the kind of movie you're about to see," and the music that Cobert wrote to go with it really hammered that home.[3]

Over the last 130+ years, magazines and movies have transformed the real lives of the Dalton brothers and their accomplices into the stuff of pulpy Western adventure-romances. After all, their mother, Adeline Younger Dalton (1835-1925), was the aunt of Cole Younger, another famous outlaw, whose partners were Frank and Jesse James. Adeline and her husband Lewis Dalton (1826-1890) lived in Coffeyville, Kansas, from 1886 to 1890 and were the parents of 15 children, most of them upstanding citizens. Thirteen of the children lived to adulthood, with the last surviving sister, Leona, living until 1964. In Curtis's movie, Mr. and Mrs. Dalton are played by Royal Dano and Trudi Brenon.

The Last Ride of the Dalton Gang focuses on five of the Dalton brothers. Don Collier briefly plays Frank Dalton (1858-1888), who became a Deputy U.S. Marshal but was killed in the line of duty three years later. Bronze Wrangler Award winner Randy Quaid plays **Gratton Dalton** (1861-1892), who also became a Deputy U.S. Marshal for a time. Mills Watson plays Bill Dalton (1866-1894), who ran for the California State Legislature but turned to a life of crime himself after the death of his brothers. Bronze Wrangler Award winner Cliff Potts plays **Bob Dalton** (1869-1892), the self-appointed leader of the Dalton Gang and the mastermind of the raid on Coffeyville. *CHiPs* star Larry Wilcox plays **Emmett Dalton** (1871-1937), who establishes the frame story of the movie by telling his life story to a newspaper reporter (Terry Kiser) in Hollywood, California, on 6 June 1934.

Chapter IV: *The Last Ride of the Dalton Gang*

Larry Wilcox (left) and Cliff Potts play brothers Emmett and Bob in Dan Curtis's only Western, *The Last Ride of the Dalton Gang* (1979). *CHiPs* star Wilcox writes about the film in his foreword to this book.

The real-life Bob and Emmett followed Grat's lead and became U.S. Deputy Marshals. They worked for the famous "Hanging Judge," Isaac Parker (1838-1896; Dale Robertson in the movie), but the brothers soon became disenchanted and decided that the other side of the law—outlawry—was the place where their talents and fortunes lay. They graduated from lesser crimes (1890-1891) to four spectacular train robberies (May 1891-July 1892), all the while being pursued by U.S. Marshal Heck Thomas (1850-1912; in Curtis's movie, only a minor character, played by Bill Jelliffe). The last ride of the Dalton Gang was into Coffeyville, Kansas, where Bob Dalton led his brothers and two of their confederates in a failed mission to rob *two* banks at the same time in broad daylight.

Before the Coffeyville raid, the actual Dalton Gang numbered ten or more as shown in the film. Other gang members included George "Bitter Creek" Newcomb (played by Matt Clark), Bill "Billy" Doolin (portrayed by Bo Hopkins), "Blackfaced" Charlie Bryant (played by Dennis Fimple), "Cockeye" Charley Pierce (not a character in the film), Bill McElhanie (called "Hugh MacElhenie" in the movie and portrayed by James Crittenden), **Bill Power** (called "Willie Powers" in the movie and played by Eric Lawson), and **Dick Broadwell** (called "'Texas Jack' Broadwell" in the movie and portrayed by John Fitzpatrick). All of the aforementioned outlaws met their deaths between 1891 and 1895; however, Dan Curtis and Earl Wallace take the liberty of allowing "Bitter Creek" Newcomb to live on and run in to Emmett Dalton on the street in Hollywood in 1934. They draw guns on each other, which attracts the attention of the reporter Mr. Nafius, but then they make peace and sit down with Nafius to talk about the infamous Dalton Gang of '92.

In reality, the five Dalton Gang members who rode into Coffeyville on Wednesday 5 October 1892 to rob the First National Bank and the C.M. Condon Bank were Bob, Emmett, and Grat Dalton; Bill Power; and Dick Broadwell. The men wore unconvincing fake beards and openly carried rifles as it was hunting season. Under their coats, each man carried two guns (most of them Colt .45 revolvers) except Bob Dalton, who carried a British Bulldog .38 in addition to his two Colts.[4] For years, there was a rumor of a sixth accomplice, possibly Bill Doolin, but there is little or no evidence of a sixth outlaw in Coffeyville that day.

Bo Hopkins (*The Kansas City Massacre, Supertrain*) portrays the often disgruntled Dalton Gang member Billy Doolin.

The five outlaws assumed that they could breeze into town, rob the banks, and make a clean getaway, but the shrewd Coffeyville citizens immediately saw through their disguises and spread the word that the Daltons were striking the First National and the

Condon. The townspeople—two shoemakers, a barber, a stable owner, Town Marshal Charles Connelly, and many others—quickly fetched their personal firearms or were quietly issued rifles from the Isham Hardware Store next door to the First National. The townsmen took up positions along the street, in windows, and on rooftops and waited for the robbers to emerge.

Bob and Emmett had stormed into the First National Bank while Grat, Bill Power, and Dick Broadwell had invaded the Condon Bank. Bob and Emmett efficiently stole more than $20,000 from the First National, but the tellers at the Condon Bank were giving their three robbers a harder time by gathering the silver coins very slowly and claiming that the vault where the paper money was kept was on a timed lock and could not be opened "for another 15 minutes." The townspeople outside the banks were making good use of those minutes and began shooting the criminals when they ran out of the banks. The Dalton Gang returned fire.

Randy Quaid (*The Last Detail, Midnight Express*) plays Gratton "Grat" Dalton.

Photographs taken later that same day (5 October 1892) show the results of the huge gun battle that ensued: bank windows riddled with bullet holes, dead horses, and the corpses of Bill Power (who died first), Dick Broadwell, Bob Dalton, and Grat Dalton. Emmett Dalton, who tried to rescue his dead or dying brothers, was shot 23 times but did not die. In addition to the four dead outlaws and several dead horses, the smoky, hellish gunfight killed four Coffeyville citizens (including Town Marshal Connelly, shot by Grat) and wounded three.[5]

Emmett Dalton (1871-1937) lived to serve 14 years in prison and another 30 years as a free man. In 1907, he married Julia Johnson Dalton (played by Julie Hill in Curtis's movie) and settled in Los Angeles where he worked in real estate and filmmaking. He also wrote two books about his brothers and himself.

Both of his books, *Beyond the Law* and *When the Daltons Rode*, were made into movies. Emmett played himself in the 1918 six-reel silent film *Beyond the Law*. Frank Albertson played Emmett in the 1940 feature *When the Daltons Rode*. Surprisingly, *Beyond the Law* was a commercial failure despite Emmett's participation,[6] and *When the Daltons Rode* (made three years after his death) took the inexplicable liberty of killing off Emmett in the Coffeyville incident that he alone had survived.

After those two films, the Daltons and/or Bill Doolin popped up in movies and TV shows several more times in the mid-20th century (e.g. *You Are There* and *Stories of the Century* in the 1950s) and even after Curtis's 1979 film (e.g. *Cattle Annie and Little Britches* in the 1980s, *Lucky Luke* in the 1990s, *Les Dalton* in the 2000s, and *When the Storm God Rides* in the 2010s). *The Daltons Ride Again* (1945) featured Lon Chaney Jr. as Grat Dalton. *Badman's Territory* (1946) included the Daltons and their gang members in small roles. In *The Cimarron Kid* (1952), Audie Murphy played Bill Doolin, a member of the Dalton Gang. *Jesse James vs. the Daltons* (1954) was directed in 3-D by William Castle. *The Dalton Girls* (1957) was a fanciful story of the Dalton sisters' picking up where their slain brothers left off.

The year 1949 was a big one for the Dalton brothers and Bill Doolin on the silver screen. *The Dalton Gang* featured Robert Lowery, Batman of that year's *Batman and Robin* movie serial, as "Blackie Dalton." *The Doolins of Oklahoma* starred Randolph Scott as Bill Doolin and opened with a re-enactment of the Coffeyville incident. In his 2000 Castle book *Robbing Banks*, L.R. Kirchner singles out Gordon Douglas's *Doolins of Oklahoma* (1949) and Dan Curtis's *Last Ride of the Dalton Gang* (1979) as films that, while exaggerated, "have the distinctive Western feel of the time period and are legitimate movies as far as decent acting and scripts are concerned."[7]

Curtis's film, while historically accurate on many points, does not stick to the facts at all times. In addition to keeping "Bitter Creek" alive for the fictitious 1934 reunion, the movie has Bill Dalton running for governor of California. Judge Isaac Parker (Dale Robertson) is involved in the movie, but Heck Thomas is replaced by a new character, "U.S. Marshal Will Smith," played by Jack Palance. In this movie, "Smith" is the one who doggedly pursues the Dalton Gang and shows up in Coffeyville in time to shoot Emmett before Judge Parker shoots him. (In actuality, Heck Thomas was not present for the gun battle.) In a major (and perhaps unwise) deviation from reality, "Smith" brings 50 men with him to Coffeyville, and it is they, not the townspeople, who battle the Daltons.

Chapter IV: *The Last Ride of the Dalton Gang* 177

Dracula star Jack Palance (left) and Elliott Street (who appears in both of Dan Curtis's Melvin Purvis movies) play a tense scene in *The Last Ride of the Dalton Gang* (1979).

Another major character in the film is (more or less) real: "Virginia Wade," a.k.a. Eugenia Moore, a.k.a. T. King, a.k.a. Flo Quick (Sharon Farrell), a schoolteacher-turned- "businesswoman" who falls for Bob Dalton, runs with the Dalton Gang, and forms her own gang of outlaws after the Coffeyville incident. Old Emmett tells the reporter that Flo and her gang "got killed robbin' a bank down in Las Cruces in '93." Sharon Farrell, a familiar face in 1960s and 1970s television, gives a multi-faceted performance as the tough madam whose heart melts for Bob Dalton (Cliff Potts).

Curtis's often light-hearted film begins with the playful legend, "What follows here is not intended to be an accurate re-creation of historical fact. Not that it matters." This disclaimer, along with the montage of pulp magazines and Robert Cobert's rollicking opening theme, effectively clues-in the audience. Curtis remarked, "As you see from the legend at the beginning of the film, that's basically the feeling that we had throughout the picture."[8] There are moments of hilarity along the way, and even a Buffalo Bill Wild West Show that the Dalton Gang disrupts, but the final gun battle, which took Curtis four days to shoot, packs an emotional punch. By then, the audience has come to know and care about the cocky Bob, the naïve Emmett, and the slow-witted Grat and their friends and lovers.

Sharon Farrell (*The Eyes of Charles Sand*, *The Cloning of Clifford Swimmer*) plays Flo Quick in Dan Curtis's *Dalton Gang* movie.

Chapter IV: *The Last Ride of the Dalton Gang* 179

Cliff Potts (left) and Randy Quaid play Bob and "Grat," in death, at the sobering conclusion of Dan Curtis's otherwise rollicking Western.

By 1979, Curtis, now having shot *Dracula, Burnt Offerings, Curse of the Black Widow,* and two Melvin Purvis crime dramas, had matured and refined his *auteur*'s style of filmmaking. Curtis explained,

> I was pretty ready to shoot this picture. I knew it was going to be loaded with action, but those Melvin Purvis movies I had done showed me that I could handle that stuff with ease. This picture was tougher than any movie I've ever made—including *The Winds of War* and *War and Remembrance*. It was supposed to be four hours long, a two-parter. I had a 31-day shooting schedule. It was the most difficult thing I've ever had to do because, as you see from the film, it was just loaded with action and loaded with texture and a million characters. It was a very difficult picture to make, but it turned out great.[9]

Despite stiff competition from the ABC comedies, *The Last Ride of the Dalton Gang* was a ratings success. Judith Crist of *TV Guide* wrote,

> For those who delight in later Americana, strictly dime-Western, romantic version, there's *The Last Ride of the Dalton Gang*, produced and directed for TV by Dan Curtis, written by Earl W. Wallace, and offered with the warning that "What follows here is not intended to be an accurate re-creation of historical fact. Not that it matters." What follows is a boisterous, shoot-'em-up account of the law-manning, horse-stealing, train-and-bank-robbing career of the four of five brothers who "just couldn't stay on the right side of the law."

Only Em Dalton [Larry Wilcox], who recounts their adventures to a reporter in 1934, died (in 1937) with his boots off. The virtue of this entertainment is that the outlaws, though appealing, are not glorified but are seen clearly as the not-too-bright hoodlums they were.[10]

The Last Ride of the Dalton Gang won the Western Heritage Bronze Wrangler Award, for Outstanding Fictional Television Program of 1979, from the National Cowboy Hall of Fame. "This picture really got me ready for *The Winds of War*," Curtis observed, because of its large cast, complex action sequences, and period detail.[11]

The National Cowboy Hall of Fame also honored composer Robert Cobert, whose *Dalton Gang* music score won the Bronze Wrangler Award for Best Western Music Score of 1979. Cobert's music is by turns playful, romantic, comedic, and suspenseful. Cobert achieves an authentic Western sound through his use of harmonica, guitar, snare drum, player piano, and sentimental strings. In an interview on the 2005 MPI Home Video *Dalton Gang* DVD that also includes 14 tracks (40 minutes) of Cobert's music, Dan Curtis declared,

> Cobert once again astounded me. It was our first Western, his *and* mine, and from a guy who had never written anything for a Western score, for a picture that was loaded with action and humor, it could be one of the greatest scores he's ever written. Every single cue in it was absolutely wonderful.[12]

A decade later, Cobert briefly returned to the Western genre when he scored William Claxton's 1988 syndicated TV-movie *Bonanza: The Next Generation*. It was also in the 1980s that Cobert received his two Emmy Award nominations for his music for Arthur Allan Seidelman's *I Think I'm Having a Baby* and Dan Curtis's *War and Remembrance*.

Cobert's happy/sad music propels *The Last Ride of the Dalton Gang* from initial exuberance to ultimate catastrophe, and it unifies the shorter cut of the movie. Director Dan Curtis and film editor Dennis Virkler's three-hour cut of the four-hour *Raid on Coffeyville* is tight, fluid, and engrossing. Virkler had edited *Burnt Offerings, Dead of Night, When Every Day Was the Fourth of July*, and other productions for Curtis. He went on to edit *Xanadu* (1980), *Under Siege* (1992), *Daredevil* (2003), and *The Wolf Man* (2010). Dennis Virkler received Academy Award nominations for his work on *The Hunt for Red October* (1990) and *The Fugitive* (1993).

The deleted scenes—or, usually, just single lines in a scene—appear in Earl Wallace's original two-part *Raid on Coffeyville* script, dated 10 April 1978 and revised on April 25 & 27 and May 3, 4, & 10. Usually, only a few lines of dialogue here and there are cut in order to shorten and smooth out a scene. For example, some lines are dropped from the scene of the Dalton brothers as boys, the preacher's remarks at Frank Dalton's funeral are shortened, a few lines are deleted from the Christmas Eve scene, the dialogue during the shoot-out at Archuletta's gambling house is trimmed, and Bill Dalton loses a few lines of his campaign speech.

In three longer (but still very short) scenes missing from the final cut, the Dalton Gang discusses raiding Archuletta's casino, Flo Quick and Bill Dalton exchange a few words about Bob and Grat, and Judge Parker and Mr. Smith disagree over the best way to capture the gang. Plus, two brief scenes of Bob and Flo in bed together are cut. In one (page 48), Bob says, "Y'know, I could [get] used to all this," and Flo replies, "Well, I'll let you in on a little secret...So could I." Later (page 86), after Flo has returned to Bob after a break-up, the lovers' pillow talk begins with Bob's line, "You never did tell me just what made you send that telegram." Flo replies, "Oh, it was rainin' all the time back there. I just decided I needed a change of climate." Bob remarks, "Oh...'change of climate,' was it[?]"[13]

A few scenes earlier, as seen in the *Dalton Gang* movie, Bob, Emmett & Julia, and Grat have met Flo's train, and Bob and Flo have a tender reunion that ends in an embrace and a kiss. At this point (62 minutes into the film), the scene fades to a commercial break, but pages 83, 83A, and 84 of the *Raid on Coffeyville* teleplay call for an amusing scene that does not appear in the final cut.

> Bob comes out of the station with Flo on his arm, followed by Em & Julia and Grat. The porter, staggering under his load, brings up the rear.
>
> BOB
> ...so, all we've got to do is wait until Billy gets himself elected in November, and then he's gonna make us inspectors!
>
> FLO
> Inspectors? He's going to be governor of this state, and that's the best he can do for his own brothers[?]
>
> In the b.g. [background], Julia gives Em a surprised look.
>
> BOB (a warning)
> Now, Flo—
>
> FLO
> Bob Dalton, don't you know anything? If you're governor, there's all kinds of things you can get into—
>
> BOB
> Is that so? Like what?
>
> FLO
> For instance...governors appoint judges, don't they?
>
> BOB
> Well, yes—
>
> FLO (impatient)
> Don't you understand? You don't just <u>give</u> away good jobs like that. You <u>sell</u> them!

Bob and Em exchange a look, shake their heads. Flo notices, breaks off the lecture.

>   FLO (continuing)
> What's wrong—?

Bob stops, turns to face her:

>   BOB
> Y'know, Flo, you sure musta missed tellin' us what to do, travelin' fifteen hundred miles to start all over again.

HOLD as Flo suddenly realizes they're right. She begins to blush with embarrassment. A beat, and then they all start to laugh. ON JULIA: she's been listening to Flo with a puzzled expression; now, she smiles timidly.

>   JULIA
> You know, you sure don't talk like a schoolteacher—

Flo gives her a surprised look, turns to look at Bob and Em. They grin, shrug helplessly, and we CUT TO [the scene, *included* in the movie, in which Bob shows Flo a "quintessential, white-picket-fenced, vine-covered cottage"].[14]

Every once in a while, some of Emmett Dalton's narration is deleted from the film. For example, on page 21 of Earl Wallace's 205-page typewritten script, Em (Larry Wilcox of *CHiPs*) recalls, "Now, in my opinion, it wasn't exactly fair the way Frank always expected us to follow his example. Y'see, it was *his nature* always to do the right thing—which wasn't exactly the way Bob an' Grat an' me was put together." Much later (page 112 of the script), Em reveals, "[Bob] seemed to blame himself for Grat's gettin' killed, and there wasn't nothing anyone could say to make him feel any different. But the worst part was—he didn't just take it out on himself—he was makin' life miserable for everyone else."[15]

Part I of *The Raid on Coffeyville* ends with the gang members' discussing the (inaccurate) news that Grat has died. Bob is more determined than ever to accelerate their lives of crime and make the railroads and everybody "pay." Part II begins with "a recap of scenes from Part I" and a montage of the gang's train robberies.

One hour and 57 minutes into the finished film, pages 155, 156, 157, and 157A of Earl Wallace's script call for an emotional scene between Emmett (Larry Wilcox of *Trail of Danger*) and Julia (Julie Hill of *Dallas Cowboys Cheerleaders II*). As the gang members ride up to their cave hide-out, "Flo and Julia step out to meet them. We should note the boys are carrying packages of clothing. As Em swings down from the saddle with a grin, we should note a troubled frown on Julia's face."

> EM
> Wait'll you see the new outfits we got, Julie! Them Coffeyville banks'll be proud to get robbed by us!

But Julia just gives him a look, turns, and walks away. Em shoots Bob a troubled glance, but Bob only shrugs and follows the boys on up into the cave. Flo hangs back and motions for Em to go after Julia. As Em catches up with Julia, [she] turns to face him:

> EM
> Julie—! Hey, what's wrong, hon?

She gives him a look, then blurts it out:

> JULIA
> Em, I don't want you to go into Coffeyville with Bob!

Em shakes his head, confused.

> EM
> What're you talkin' about? It's all settled—

> JULIA
> No, it's not! It's not settled 'til you do it! Em, I keep thinking about what Billy said about you all getting killed. I'm so afraid they'll kill you!

> EM (soothingly)
> Hon, you're just scaring yourself. Don't you see—

> JULIA (determined)
> No, I'm not scaring myself. It's gonna end up bad. I know it is!

Em takes her by the shoulders:

> EM
> Now, you listen to me, sweetheart: This ain't any more dangerous than robbin' trains. And anyway, you know it's gonna be our last job—

She gives him a look, says nothing.

> EM (continuing)
> And besides, look at Flo. <u>She</u> ain't worried...

> (trying to convince himself)
> And you know Flo's a pretty smart lady.

Julia just stares at him, then:

> JULIA
> Don't you understand anything? Flo's scared to death!
> She just won't show it around Bob 'cause she knows
> it won't do any good.
> (then, intensely)
> But I'm not Flo, Em! I'm just not! And I don't want
> you to go!!

And with that, she turns away. Em stares after her, then frowns:

> EM
> Hey, wait a minute, Julie. I never wanted you to be
> like Flo. I want you just like you are. [a beat]
> An' maybe you're right about it bein' dangerous.
> An' maybe I'm a bit scared, too... [a beat]
> But what if I didn't go because you asked me not to?
> An' then somethin' did happen? You think we'd ever be
> able to live together after that?

> She looks at him, stricken by the truth of what he's said. A beat, and then she begins to cry softly. He crosses to her and holds her close, and as he does so, we begin to CRANE UP and PULL BACK from the two solitary figures, and then finally we DISSOLVE THROUGH TO [a scene, *included* in the movie, between Mr. Smith and Mr. Kermit].[16]

In 2016, *CHiPs* and *Dalton Gang* star Larry Wilcox told me that he did not remember shooting this scene and felt that it must not have been filmed. Wilcox continued,

Reading this scene now makes me think it was a typical [...] form of writing that attempts to set up the audience with more fear—and then killing [us] all as was predicted. [...] Audiences are way too savvy for this kind of so-called *character premonition* outlined in dialogue. I am glad this scene was not in the film as it lacks the subtlety of really well thought out *innuendo and inference*. Anyone can write parallel themes and counterpoint, but few can weave them into the tapestry with hints and shades and hues.[14]

With a few exceptions, the *Raid on Coffeyville* scenes and individual lines that were cut from *The Last Ride of the Dalton Gang* do not advance the plot and perhaps would have confirmed Dan Curtis's initial fear of dragging out the story. Instead, the two-and-one-half-hour movie is efficient and eminently watchable. In a 2005 DVD interview, Curtis stated that he felt that his *Dalton Gang* TV-movie could have been released theatrically, "as is," and succeeded. The film lives on through occasional showings on the Encore Western cable-TV channel and through its VHS and DVD releases.

The Last Ride of the Dalton Gang (NBC, 1979) stars (standing, from left) Julie Hill, Larry Wilcox, Cliff Potts, Sharon Farrell, Bo Hopkins, James Crittenden, Matt Clark (and kneeling, from left), Dennis Fimple, Randy Quaid, Eric Lawson, and John Fitzpatrick.

The Last Ride of the Dalton Gang (NBC, 20 November 1979). Executive producer: Dan Curtis. Producer: Joseph Stern. Director: Dan Curtis. First assistant director: Penelope Foster. Teleplay: Earl Wallace. Music: Robert Cobert. Director of photography: Frank Stanley. Production designer: Ned Parsons. Makeup: Jack Petty, Dee-Dee Petty. Costumer: James George.

Cast: Larry Wilcox (Emmet Dalton), Cliff Potts (Bob Dalton), Randy Quaid (Grat Dalton), Sharon Farrell (Flo Quick), Matt Clark ("Bitter Creek" Newcomb), Royal Dano (Lewis Dalton), Dale Robertson (Isaac Parker), Jack Palance (Will Smith), Julie Hill (Julia Jonson), Mills Watson (Bill Dalton), Terry Kiser (Mr. Nafius), Bo Hopkins (Bill Doolin), John Fitzpatrick ("Texas Jack" Broadwell), Eric Lawson (Willie Powers), Dennis Fimple ("Blackfaced" Charlie Bryant), James Crittenden (MacElhenie), Don Collier (Frank Dalton), Harris Yulin (Jesse James), Bill Jelliffe (Heck Thomas), Scott Brady (Jay Gould), John Karlen (Mr. Kermit), H.M. Wynant (James Hill), Derek Wilcox

(Young Emmet), Bubba Smith (Lothar), Orin Cannon (bartender). 146 minutes. Available on VHS and DVD.

Dan Curtis Significa: Forty-five years before Barnabas Collins of *Dark Shadows* emerged from his chained coffin and found a lookalike for his lost love Josette—and ten years before a similar scenario occurred in Karl Freund's *The Mummy*—Harry Houdini wrote and starred in director Burton L. King's *The Man from Beyond*. Released on 2 April 1922, the film concerns "Howard Hillary," who comes back to life after being frozen in the Arctic for 100 years and finds a modern-day reincarnation of his lost love ("Marie," played by Nita Naldi of *Dr. Jekyll and Mr. Hyde*).

On ABC-TV's *Dark Shadows* (1966-1971), the interiors of the Collinwood mansion were Sy Tomashoff's beautiful sets inside the *Dark Shadows* studio at 24 West 67th Street (1966)—and later 433 West 53rd Street (1966-1971)—in New York City. The exterior of Collinwood was Seaview Terrace, now known as the Carey Mansion, on Ruggles Avenue in Newport, Rhode Island. The 65-room mansion is situated near The Breakers and other famous Gilded Age homes along Newport's seaside "Cliff Walk."

In 1927-1929, Washington DC businessman Edson Bradley built up Seaview Terrace around James Kernochan's former residence "Seaview," which had been constructed in 1885. Architect Howard Greenley designed the new house for Mr. and Mrs. Bradley. Greenley also designed the Prince George Hotel in New York City and the Corning Free Academy in Corning, New York.

For much of the 1930s, Seaview Terrace was home to the Bradleys' daughter Julia and her husband Herbert Shipman. In the 1940s, the great house became the quarters for World War II army officers, and around 1950, it became a private school for girls. In 1974, the Carey family of New York purchased Seaview Terrace and renamed it the Carey Mansion. The French Renaissance manor house still belongs to the Careys, who for decades leased it to Salve Regina University as a recital hall and a student dormitory. Then, in mid-2009, the Careys ended their affiliation with Salve Regina and turned Seaview Terrace back into a private residence. In 2009-2010, Denise Carey refurbished most of the house. In 2016, writer-director Charlie McDowell filmed part of his 2017 Netflix film *The Discovery*, starring Robert Redford and Mary Steenburgen, at Seaview Terrace.[18]

Dan Curtis Significa: *House of Dark Shadows* and *Night of Dark Shadows* first aired on network television on the *CBS Late Movie*. *HODS* aired on Friday 16 July 1976. *NODS* aired on Monday 13 June 1977 after a rerun of *Kojak*.

In *House of Dark Shadows* (1970) and *Night of Dark Shadows* (1971), the interiors and exteriors of the great house of Collinwood were filmed at Lyndhurst, the magnificent Gothic Revival mansion on the banks of the Hudson River in Tarrytown, New York. It was designed and built in 1838 by the famous 19th-century architect Alexander Jackson Davis. Earlier in the 1830s, Davis had designed the Indiana state capitol, the Federal Customs House in New York City, and several buildings on the campus of the University of Michigan.

Davis built Lyndhurst (first called "Knoll") as a country villa for William Paulding, a brigadier general in the War of 1812 and a mayor of New York in the 1820s. In 1864-1865, Davis doubled the size of the house for its second owner, George Merritt, a New York City merchant. Merritt renamed the mansion "Lyndenhurst" (soon "Lyndhurst") after the linden trees which he planted on the 67-acre estate.

Between 1880 and his death in 1892, Lyndhurst was the summer home of the railroad magnate Jay Gould, who controlled the Union Pacific Railroad, the New York Elevated Railway, and the Western Union Telegraph Company. Gould ran a spur line of his railroad behind the mansion on the riverbank. A huge portrait of Gould is seen in *House of Dark Shadows*, and Gould's railroad track is the scene of a fight to the death in *Night of Dark Shadows*. Actor Scott Brady portrayed Jay Gould in a few scenes in *The Last Ride of the Dalton Gang* (1979).

After Gould's death, Lyndhurst became the home of Gould's daughter Helen Gould Shepard and her family until her death in 1938. For the next 23 years, Gould's other daughter, Anna, Duchess of Talleyrand-Perigord, resided there. Upon her death in 1961, Lyndhurst passed to the National Trust for Historic Preservation. Nine years later, *House of Dark Shadows* became the first of several movies, including *The Worst Witch* (1986), *Reversal of Fortune* (1990), *Gloria* (1999), and *Winter's Tale* (2014), to shoot scenes at Lyndhurst—all while daily tours of the house were still conducted. *Reversal of Fortune* is notable in that both the interior of Lyndhurst and the exterior of Seaview Terrace may be glimpsed in the film.[19]

Dan Curtis spends the 1980s bringing *The Winds of War* and *War and Remembrance* to life.

CHAPTER V

The Winds of War

"Dan Curtis is the man who kept television horror alive in the 1970s," John Kenneth Muir stated in his 2001 book *Terror Television*.[1] The seventies saw Curtis dominate TV horror as the producer-director of *The Night Strangler, The Norliss Tapes, Scream of the Wolf, Dracula, The Turn of the Screw, Trilogy of Terror, Dead of Night,* and *Curse of the Black Widow* (1973-1977). The 1980s propelled Curtis even higher in the television firmament as he became king of the miniseries. He spent almost the entire decade on the two greatest achievements of his career and two of the most impressive filmmaking feats in history: the ABC miniseries *The Winds of War* (1983) and *War and Remembrance* (1988, 1989), based on the best-selling novels by Herman Wouk (1915-2019).

Playing the Henry family in *The Winds of War* (ABC, 1983) are (standing, from left) Deborah Winters, Polly Bergen, Robert Mitchum, Lisa Eilbacher, Ali MacGraw (and kneeling, from left), Ben Murphy, and Jan-Michael Vincent.

In 1980, ABC executive Barry Diller asked Curtis to take on the Herculean task of bringing to television **The Winds of War**, Wouk's sprawling novel of an American Naval family in the years 1939-1941. Wouk himself was against the idea after being greatly displeased by Hollywood's filmings of his novels *The Caine Mutiny* in 1954 and especially *Marjorie Morningstar* in 1958 and *Youngblood Hawke* in 1964. Wouk claimed that Hollywood had "trivialized" the latter two works, and he did not want to see a watered-down screen version of his 1971 masterpiece *The Winds of War*, an 888-page opus which he had begun researching in 1960.

Nevertheless, Curtis, once a Naval Reserve officer, and Wouk, a four-year naval officer on minesweepers, met and convinced each other to film *The Winds of War* from a screenplay by Wouk. Unaccustomed to writing for the screen, Wouk gladly accepted pointers from Curtis, by now a master at doctoring the scripts of his projects. Earl W. Wallace (*Curse of the Black Widow, The Last Ride of the Dalton Gang, Witness*) served as story editor. "We all worked closely on the screenplay," Curtis recalled, "with Herman having the final word on everything. He even told ABC how many commercials and *what kind of* commercials they could run during the thing!"[2]

The miniseries's running time of 15 hours (scheduled in an 18-hour block on ABC) was the equivalent of seven motion pictures. Curtis originally planned to direct only parts of the epic and use other directors to fill in the rest, but ABC wanted a single director—Curtis—and his singular *auteur's* vision. Curtis remembered,

> I kept thinking, "What am I going to do?" I talked to my wife about it, and then I said, "I'll just start directing this thing, and then when I start to wear myself out, I'll bring in other directors and fight about it then. Norma said, "As long as you promise me you won't direct the whole thing!" I said, "Promise you? There's no way I could direct the whole thing." Well, I directed the whole thing.[3]

Curtis filmed the $40 million production for more than one year (1 December 1980 to 8 December 1981) at 267 locations in six countries: the United States, England, West Germany, Austria, Italy, and Yugoslavia. "We shot as much as we could in Yugoslavia," Curtis explained in a DVD interview. He remembered,

> The people were wonderful in Yugoslavia. It was still a communist country, and the people were very impoverished. But it had this tremendous innocence. Wherever you went, people were happy to see you. We found quaint villages like where we shot the Jewish wedding, and we actually used the real rabbi and the real cantor. Ali [MacGraw] loved the flower markets and the food markets. The food was great.[4]

At that time the most enormous project in television or film history, *The Winds of War* consisted of 4000 camera set-ups, more than one million feet of film, and 1785 scenes in Wouk and Curtis's 962-page script. There were 285 speaking roles and thousands of extras spread across Europe. Curtis had actualized the Old Hollywood expression, "a cast of thousands." Heading the cast, along with Ali MacGraw, were Robert Mitchum, Polly Bergen, Jan-Michael Vincent, Victoria Tennant, David Dukes, Peter Graves, Chaim Topol, Jeremy Kemp, and John Houseman. Character actors from Anton Diffring, Andrew Duggan, Jerry Fujikawa, and John Karlen to Charles Lane, Ferdy Mayne, Barry Morse, and Richard X. Slattery made appearances, and Ralph Bellamy reprised his 1960 *Sunrise at Campobello* role of President Franklin Delano Roosevelt.

In *The Winds of War* (1983), Victoria Tennant and Robert Mitchum play slow-burning lovers who meet in London.

Playing Morse's on-screen wife was Barbara Steele, an icon of 1960s-era European cinema (*8½, The Hours of Love, Young Torless*) and Italian horror (*Black Sunday, The Horrible Dr. Hichcock, An Angel for Satan*). Steele was living in Los Angeles after the 1980 death of her husband, Oscar-winning screenwriter James Poe (*Around the World in 80 Days; Lilies of the Field; They Shoot Horses, Don't They?*). She met Curtis through a mutual friend, British ICM agent Maggie Abbott, and he hired Steele to peruse stock footage of World War II for possible use in *The Winds of War*. Curtis and Steele began a successful professional relationship which lasted until his death. Steele became associate producer of *The Winds of War* (1983), full producer of *War and Remembrance* (1988, 1989) and *Saving Milly* (2005), co-producer of *Our Fathers* (2005), and co-star of the 1991 *Dark Shadows* revival.

"*The Winds of War* and *War and Remembrance* were such vast projects of staggering complexity, covering all of World War II and the events leading up to it," Steele observed. She explained,

> This involved years of shooting, pre-production, and post-production. It was the equivalent of making 18 motion pictures back to back, involving so many people, countries, currencies, and shifting world events that it seemed unimaginable and even mad to me that one man could have the desire and the passion—let alone the energy—to be able to translate these two epic books to the screen with a commitment involving years and years of work. But Dan never faltered in his vision. He was like a rabid wolf in his intensity and determination. Of course, the whole operatic landscape suited his personality so perfectly; it's as if he were born for these projects. They were both beautiful and terrible.[5]

Robert Mitchum, who starred as Captain Victor "Pug" Henry, described Dan Curtis to reporters as a director of "complete and total ferocity."[6] In *People* magazine in 1983, Curtis called Mitchum "the biggest pro in the world."[7] Ali MacGraw, who played Natalie Jastrow Henry, told *Entertainment Tonight* that Dan Curtis was "the best director" with whom she had ever worked.[8]

Polly Bergen was well suited for the role of Rhoda Henry, Victor's restless wife. Bergen, a voracious reader, had read both *The Winds of War* and its 1042-page sequel, *War and Remembrance* (1978), and strongly desired to play Rhoda. She received Emmy Award nominations for her work in both miniseries. "I loved working with Dan," Bergen recalled. "He was enormously supportive, a terrific and very loud director, and I had complete trust in him. He could be very difficult, but he never was with me. I would work with him any day of the week."[9]

Once fearful that he would tire of shooting *The Winds of War*, Curtis later declared, "It was the toughest thing I ever did, but I *never* got tired. I could have kept shooting forever. Making *The Winds of War* was one of the greatest experiences of my life. Recreating history where it actually happened was the most exciting experience."[10] Curtis remembered with special fondness shooting the meeting between Roosevelt (Ralph Bellamy) and Churchill (Howard Lang) aboard the *Prince of Wales* (actually, the U.S.S. *Missouri*) and recreating the attack on Pearl Harbor (actually, the Oxnard, California, naval base)—*on 7 December* 1981—two decades before Michael Bay's *Pearl Harbor* (2001) and well before the conveniences of CGI special effects.

Director Dan Curtis converses with actress Ali MacGraw on location for *The Winds of War* (1983).

Curtis's efforts paid off remarkably when *The Winds of War*, broadcast on ABC-TV on February 6-7-8-9-10-11 and 13 of 1983, commanded more than 140 million viewers. It delivered a 38.6 rating and a 53 share, and it remains the third-most-watched miniseries of all time, after *Roots* in 1977 and *The Thorn Birds* later in 1983. *The Winds of War* appeared on 17+ different magazine covers and made headlines around the world. "The reviews were phenomenal," Curtis beamed. "I'd never even *seen* reviews like the ones we got."[11] *Variety* called *The Winds of War* "striking television" and "an impressive look at history in the making" and praised its "enormous sweep" and "unerring ring of truth."[12] *Newsday* called it "really something extraordinary and special,"[13] and the *Philadelphia Enquirer* proclaimed it to be "television in its finest hour."[14] "Cancel all your engagements" and "try not to miss it," urged *TV Guide*.[15] The *Detroit News* added,

> Producer-director Dan Curtis treads knowingly between the television form known as docudrama and the old movie romances. He tastefully employs 1940s movie conventions (the recurring, heavy love-theme music; the camera turning around the kissing couple), but he knows he's directing for the little screen, not the big one. His emphasis is on the telling close-up, the intimate set piece. His action sequences are just enough to convey cold or smoke or carnage. Some of the outdoor shots are beautiful—a

delicately lighted Geneva, the Kremlin as seen from a frozen hill, the leafy richness of Siena. The total effect is remarkably evocative of the period.[16]

Robert Cobert's music score, with its love theme, marches, waltzes, and ethnic music, ran longer than 2000 manuscript pages. The love theme joined Cobert's equally haunting "Quentin's Theme" from *Dark Shadows* as a staple on what the broadcasting industry calls beautiful-music radio stations.

Writing for *The World of Dark Shadows* #36 (December 1983), I called *The Winds of War* "a grandiose tale" and added, "Herman Wouk's teleplay and Dan Curtis's direction did a marvelous job of explaining the situations, events, philosophies, cultures, and emotions which together hurled the planet into the awesome maelstrom that took years to resolve."[17]

The Winds of War, **episode #1, "The Winds Rise,"** written by Herman Wouk and directed by Dan Curtis, premiered on ABC-TV on Sunday 6 February 1983 in a three-hour timeslot (the actual running time is 2 hours, 28 minutes) following *Ripley's Believe It or Not.* The setting of show #1 is Berlin, Germany; New York, New York; Siena and Rome, Italy; Warsaw and Krakow, Poland; et al. from 31 March 1939 through 1 September 1939.

Paramount Home Entertainment DVD liner notes: "Spring 1939. The winds of war that will soon engulf the world are starting to stir. It's also a time of change for United States Navy Commander Victor 'Pug' Henry [Robert Mitchum], who, accompanied by his wife Rhoda [Polly Bergen], arrives in Berlin to assume his new appointment as naval attaché to the U.S. Embassy. 'Pug' is unaware that he and his family—scattered around the globe, from Poland to the Pacific—are about to experience the most harrowing and adventurous years of their lives. An uneasy sign of the growing adversity is Pug's encounter with a madman named Adolf Hitler [Gunter Meisner]."

Curtis makes his *auteur's* mark with this first episode, which climaxes with Germany's invasion of Poland and the plight of Byron Henry (Jan-Michael Vincent) and Natalie Jastrow (Ali MacGraw), who are trapped in the Polish countryside. Curtis's close-ups are intimate and telling, and his wide shots are rich and cinematic. *TV Guide* critic Robert MacKenzie declared, "Dan Curtis has produced and directed for Paramount with creative finesse and a large vision" that transcends the so-called small screen.[18]

Curtis once said, "I love going back in time. I love recreating history."[19] This episode and all of the subsequent shows effectively balance scenes of recreated historical events, such as the German military officials' plans for "Case White" (the invasion of Poland), with scenes that propel the personal stories of Wouk's characters, such as the first meeting of Victor "Pug" Henry and Pamela Tudsbury (Victoria Tennant); the complicated relationships among Byron, Natalie, Aaron Jastrow (John Houseman), and Leslie Slote (David Dukes); and the dangerous attraction between Rhoda Henry and Palmer Kirby (Peter Graves). The historical scenes are narrated ably and urgently by William T. Woodson, whose voice also was heard on *The Invaders, The Odd Couple,* and *Super Friends.*

Chapter V: *The Winds of War*

Dan Curtis directs Ali MacGraw (as Natalie Jastrow) and David Dukes (as Leslie Slote) in this scene from *The Winds of War* **(1983).**

In an especially poignant scene, set in Berlin, Victor seeks answers from Ludwig Rosenthal (Ferdy Mayne), the owner of a spectacular mansion which Mr. and Mrs. Rosenthal have vacated and which the German government is offering to rent to "Pug" and Rhoda for a mere $78.00 per month. Victor learns that a new German ordinance does not allow Jewish citizens to own property. Indeed, the winds of war are rising, judging from everything that "Pug" observes as a U.S. attaché to Berlin.

Stefan Gierasch, who would play Professor Woodard and Joshua Collins in Dan Curtis's 1991 nighttime *Dark Shadows*, portrays Herr Knoedler, a realtor, and Herman Wouk himself appears in the cameo role of the archbishop of Siena, Italy. "The Winds Rise" received a 39.1 rating and a 53 share.

The Winds of War, **episode #2, "The Storm Breaks,"** written by Herman Wouk and directed by Dan Curtis, premiered on ABC-TV on Monday 7 February 1983 in a three-hour timeslot (the actual running time is 2 hours, 25 minutes). The setting of show #2 is the Polish countryside; Pensacola, Florida; Warsaw, Poland; New York, New York; Berlin, Germany; Siena, Italy; et al. from early September to early November 1939.

Paramount Home Entertainment DVD liner notes: "The storm breaks in Europe as the German-Soviet pact—one that 'Pug' had warned American officials about—has come to pass, prompting U.S. President Franklin Delano Roosevelt [Ralph Bellamy] to request that 'Pug' be his 'eyes and ears' in Germany. Among the millions affected by Hitler's lightning-fast sweep into Poland are Pug's son, Byron, and the woman Byron loves, Natalie Jastrow, the niece of Jewish-American author Aaron Jastrow and fiancée of American diplomat Leslie Slote."

Because of the way Herman Wouk wrote them and stipulated their format to ABC, many scenes in *The Winds of War* are very long ones that climax and resolve before there is ever a commercial break. This suspension maintains the tension and realism of each scene and even simulates live theatre. The *Dark Shadows* television series and Curtis's seven *Wide World Mystery* episodes, often shot in live-on-tape style, certainly suggest an ongoing stage play, and many interludes in Curtis's two *War* masterpieces come across in the same way. An example in episode #2 is the agonizing, seemingly endless stretch when Byron, Natalie, and a group of Jewish and Christian refugees are being interrogated and threatened by an S.S. officer, played by Arthur Brauss of the 1977 war film *The Cross of Iron*.

The terrifying interrogation is especially hard on Byron's refugee friend "Mark Hartley," whose real name is Marvin Horowitz. He is played with great emotion by Ron Rifkin (*Mrs. R's Daughter, Alias*). His performance is dramatic and heart-wrenching, and a touching moment comes when Byron helps Marvin pass as Christian by giving Marvin his Bible and inscribing it to "Mark Hartley." Episode #2 climaxes in early November 1939 as Adolf Hitler prepares for the oft-postponed "Case Yellow," or the invasion of France. "The Storm Breaks" received a 40.2 rating and a 54 share.

The Winds of War, **episode #3, "Cataclysm,"** written by Herman Wouk and directed by Dan Curtis, premiered on ABC-TV on Tuesday 8 February 1983 in a two-hour timeslot (the actual running time is 1 hour, 37 minutes) following *Happy Days* and *Laverne and Shirley*. The setting of show #3 is Rome, Italy; Berlin, Germany; Miami Beach and Pensacola, Florida; Paris, France; New York, New York; London, England; et al. from mid-December 1939 to mid-May 1940.

Paramount Home Entertainment DVD liner notes: "Chaos erupts in Europe as Warsaw falls and a defiant Adolf Hitler declares, 'The only road to peace is through German victory.' 'Pug' Henry, in his role as an unofficial observer for President Roosevelt, travels to Rome to meet Mussolini [Enzo Castellari]. The objective is to arrange a peace conference between 'Il Duce' and U.S. delegate Sumner Welles [Ben Hammer], but 'Pug' is alarmed by the Italian dictator's thirst for power, which belies his conciliatory gestures."

This especially enthralling episode covers the (in Rhoda's words) "grim Christmas" of 1939, Hitler's 1940 invasions of Norway and France, Byron and Natalie's engagement, and the Pensacola wedding of Warren Henry (Ben Murphy) and Janice Lacouture Henry (Deborah Winters). Especially well written and well-acted scenes are Rhoda's spat with radio newsman Fred Fearing (*Dark Shadows* alumnus Michael McGuire) at a Christmas Eve dinner, Rhoda and Victor's conversation about it as they drive home, Victor's tense lunch at a Miami boat dock with Byron and Natalie, and Victor's meeting with Hitler at a country estate outside Berlin.

Chapter V: *The Winds of War* 197

Dan Curtis directs Gunter Meisner (as Adolf Hitler) in *The Winds of War* **(1983).**

Another outstanding scene is Victor's discussion of the power structures of Germany and America with several German businessmen and politicians. One of them is the powerful and unscrupulous banker Wolf Stoller (Barry Morse of *The Fugitive* and *Space: 1999*), who is responsible for bankrupting countless Jewish businessmen in Germany. Stoller's wife is played by none other than the *Winds* associate producer Barbara Steele, the classic horror-movie star and future *Dark Shadows* (1991) star who would collaborate with Dan Curtis on several more productions in the 1990s and the 2000s. "Cataclysm" received a 38.7 rating and a 54 share.

The Winds of War, **episode #4, "Defiance,"** written by Herman Wouk and directed by Dan Curtis, premiered on ABC-TV on Wednesday 9 February 1983 in a two-hour timeslot (the actual running time is 1 hour, 37 minutes) following *The Fall Guy*. The setting of show #4 is Washington, DC; Stratford and New London, Connecticut; Compiegne, France; Rome and Florence, Italy; Berlin, Germany; London, England; the Isle of Wight; et al. from May to August 1940.

Paramount Home Entertainment DVD liner notes: "Great Britain is soon reeling under German air assaults as the country—blitzed and desperately short of supplies and weapons—stands heroically alone against Hitler's might. Reassigned to London, 'Pug' Henry becomes involved in two secret British projects and meets the charismatic Winston Churchill [Howard Lang]. He also finds moments of quiet tranquility in a world gone mad in the form of Pamela Tudsbury, the beautiful daughter of an old friend."

The middle episode of the miniseries focuses on the ever-growing war across Europe as Captain Victor "Pug" Henry meets with the President and Mrs. Roosevelt (Elizabeth Hoffman), and later with Winston Churchill, and visits England to study the latest breakthroughs in radar and other war technology. Meanwhile, a notable scene takes place in Washington DC as Natalie Jastrow assures her ex-fiancé Leslie Slote that she is in love with Byron Henry, she will marry him, and she knows what she is doing. Later, Natalie squares off with August Van Winaker II (John Harkins of *Dark Shadows*), a pompous and crooked bureaucrat, as she tries to solve her uncle Aaron Jastrow's passport problems and get him out of Italy, which has just declared war on France. In her 1991 autobiography *Moving Pictures,* Ali MacGraw (Natalie) wrote, "I felt proud to be a part of this film. I thought it was going to be a masterpiece."[20] It was.

TV Guide declared, "Much of the hoopla [over *The Winds of War*] is well-earned, particularly in informative, re-created scenes with the likes of Roosevelt, Churchill, and Hitler, and in such evocative big sequences as the strafing of a Polish-refugee caravan and the pandemonium of the London blitz."[21]

A welcome sight in a scene with Robert Mitchum and Jan-Michael Vincent is Western and *film-noir* character actor Scott Brady, a recurring player in Dan Curtis's productions. Curtis's self-proclaimed "stock company" of actors was one of his *auteur* hallmarks. Just as Orson Welles before him, Robert Altman and Woody Allen alongside him, and Joe Dante after him had done, Curtis populated his productions with many of the same actors again and again. The producer-director recalled,

> I remembered Scott Brady from years ago, and I got him to play the cop in *The Night Strangler.* He was so happy to play the cop, and I would say to him, "Hang around the set, Scott, and if there's anything else I can think of to stick you into, I'll do it. And he did it. He was always there for pick-up scenes in the picture because he would do anything just to be in the picture. I kept Scott around, and from that point on, Scott Brady became a part of my stock company. I used him in a million pictures [actually, six]. I loved him; he was great.[22]

Indeed, one wonders what *The Winds of War* would have been like if Scott Brady had played "Pug" Henry. Robert Mitchum, while effective as Henry, sometimes underplays his scenes so much that he comes off as aloof or bored. Mary Jane Brown, television critic for the *Nashville Banner,* observed, "Mitchum plays him stiffly and tough, without emotion even when it's needed."[23] Other reviewers called him "stoic" or "poker-faced."[24] Perhaps, in some alternate universe—Parallel Time, the concept familiar to *Dark Shadows* fans—Victor Henry was portrayed by Robert Alda, Edward Asner, Scott Brady, MacDonald Carey, Kirk Douglas, Charlton Heston, Howard Keel, Robert Preston, Mitchell Ryan, or Efrem Zimbalist Jr. Ed Asner was considered for the "Pug" Henry role before Mitchum won the part. James Coburn was considered for *War and Remembrance* if Mitchum had not returned.

To be fair, Mitchum comes alive in this episode's climactic scene of "Pug" Henry's ride-along, as a neutral observer, on a British bomber carrying out a nighttime bombing mission over Berlin. At one point, Mitchum, as Henry, lets out an exuberant "Yahoo!"

when a bomb finds its target. Later, when the plane is in danger of going down, he begins praying the Lord's Prayer to himself. "Defiance" received a 39 rating and a 57 share.

The Winds of War, **episode #5, "Of Love and War,"** written by Herman Wouk and directed by Dan Curtis, premiered on ABC-TV on Thursday 10 February 1983 in a two-hour timeslot (the actual running time is 1 hour, 36 minutes) following the first episodes of *Condo,* starring McLean Stevenson, and *Amanda's,* starring Beatrice Arthur. The setting of show #5 is London, England; Fairfield County, Connecticut; New York, New York; Berlin, Germany; Estoril and Lisbon, Portugal; the Caribbean Sea; et al. from September 1940 to January 1943.

Paramount Home Entertainment DVD liner notes: "In Germany, a murderous scheme is underway as Hitler makes plans to invade Russia. Byron Henry, now a naval submarine officer, elopes with Natalie Jastrow. Rhoda Henry's relationship with A-bomb developer Palmer 'Fred' Kirby threatens her marriage to 'Pug,' while 'Pug' finds that he's increasingly drawn to Pamela Tudsbury, who openly adores him."

This episode shines a forlorn spotlight on Leslie Slote, who is on the losing side of a love triangle worthy of W.S. Maugham's *Of Human Bondage.* Slote must stand by and watch Natalie, the inaccessible love of his life, reunite with Byron in Portugal and *marry* him there in a highly unconventional wedding "ceremony" that Slote has helped to make possible. Slote sends a note to Natalie and writes that he is "yours 'til death" as she and Byron begin their turbulent marriage.

Meanwhile, *Space: 1999* hero Barry Morse returns as the smarmy villain Wolf Stoller in one of the episode's most memorable scenes. In another very long and in-depth conversation reminiscent of the kind of "live theatre" that Dan Curtis can capture on film, Stoller butters up "Pug" Henry and promises him the lavish sum in a Swiss bank account—"after the war"—if Henry will be *a good friend* to Germany, i.e. spy for the Fatherland when he returns to England and America. Additional scenes with "Pug" and Pamela in Europe, and Palmer and Rhoda in America, make this outstanding episode live up to its title. "Of Love and War" received a 36.1 rating and a 50 share.

The Winds of War, **episode #6, "The Changing of the Guard,"** written by Herman Wouk and directed by Dan Curtis, premiered on ABC-TV on Friday 11 February 1983 in a three-hour timeslot (the actual running time is 2 hours, 26 minutes). The setting of show #6 is Lisbon, Portugal; Silver Spring, Maryland; Norfolk, Virginia; Washington, DC; the North Atlantic Ocean; Berlin and Berchtesgaden, Germany; San Francisco, California; Buckinghamshire, England; Rome, Italy; East Prussia; Minsk and Moscow, Russia; Zurich, Switzerland; Placentia Bay, Newfoundland; Pearl Harbor, Hawaii; et al. from January-February to late September 1941.

Paramount Home Entertainment DVD liner notes: "'Pug' Henry embarks on a perilous mission when President Roosevelt places him in command of 16 naval destroyers 'unofficially' escorting a shipment to war-torn England. Meanwhile, Natalie Jastrow Henry, who is pregnant and trapped in Italy with her uncle, is horrified to uncover evidence of Hitler's 'Final Solution' and fears, like so many others, that this 'solution' may include her and her family."

The quite eventful penultimate episode spotlights the on-again, off-again relationships of Rhoda and Palmer and of Pamela and Victor, as well as a tense game of brinkmanship between a U.S. Navy ship (carrying Victor) and German U-boats in the choppy North Atlantic. A highlight of the episode is the Henry family's April 26 dinner at the White House with President and Mrs. Roosevelt, as well as a few other guests, including "Willie" Somerset Maugham himself (Duncan Ross). The dinner is a reality check for Victor's wife Rhoda and a perfect opportunity for Byron to ask FDR to help his wife Natalie and her uncle Aaron Jastrow, who are going back and forth between Rome and Zurich but are not being allowed to return to the United States.

Polly Bergen, Peter Graves (middle), and Dan Curtis converse on location for *The Winds of War* (1983).

One of the most majestic scenes in *The Winds of War* is this episode's meeting (on 10 August 1941) of President Roosevelt and Prime Minister Churchill aboard the *Prince of Wales* (actually, the U.S.S. *Missouri*). Again, director Curtis allows this stirring scene to play out in real time as if the viewers were watching this historic event on stage or on C-Span. The excellent episode concludes in Hawaii where Byron, his brother Warren, and their sister Madeline (Lisa Eilbacher) have converged for Madeline's on-location radio show for her employer CBS. These scenes provide much-needed character development for Warren, his wife Janice, and Madeline Henry, who have appeared infrequently in the miniseries so far. "The Changing of the Guard" received a 35.2 rating and a 50 share.

The Winds of War, **episode #7, "Into the Maelstrom,"** written by Herman Wouk and directed by Dan Curtis, premiered on ABC-TV on Sunday 13 February 1983 in a three-hour timeslot (the actual running time is 2 hours, 28 minutes) following *Ripley's Believe It or Not*. The setting of show #7 is Moscow, Russia; Washington, DC; Manila and Cavite Bay, Philippine Islands; Rome and Naples, Italy; and Pearl Harbor, Hawaii, from October 8 through December 11 of 1941.

Auteur **director Dan Curtis spends almost all of the 1980s making his masterpieces,** *The Winds of War* **(1983) and** *War and Remembrance* **(1988, 1989).**

Paramount Home Entertainment DVD liner notes: "Unbeknownst to America, a 'Day of Infamy' is approaching. In Russia, 'Pug' Henry smooths over a diplomatic-military problem with Josef Stalin [Anatoly Chaguanian] and then heads for Hawaii and his new command: the battleship U.S.S. *California*. Other members of the Henry family are also on the move. Byron is at sea. His wife, Natalie, sets sail for Palestine with her uncle. And Pug's son, Warren, flies a mission out of Pearl Harbor, Hawaii. The date is December 7, 1941. For the Henrys—and the rest of the world—the winds of war have become a swirling, cataclysmic hurricane."

Of course, the most memorable scene in this final episode is the attack on Pearl Harbor. Dan Curtis filmed the organized mayhem, with eight cameras running simultaneously, at the Oxnard, California, naval base on the 7th of December, 1981, the 40th anniversary of the actual event.

The focus shifts to Janice and Warren Henry, who are stationed at Pearl Harbor and who live through the attack (although Warren is injured). Victor, hoping to take command of the *California,* soon joins them at Pearl, only to find his ship sinking.

Before the episode ends, Victor has finagled a new appointment: commander of the U.S.S. *Northampton*. Meanwhile, he has written Dear Jane letters to two women and received a Dear John letter from one of them, but unexpected circumstances change the plans for everyone concerned.

This episode features numerous character actors (e.g. Andrew Duggan, Jerry Fujikawa, Hugh Gillin, Richard X. Slattery, et al.), including the frequent *Petticoat Junction* and *Bewitched* guest star Charles Lane, who provides a bit of humor at the beginning of the episode. Plus, three of Dan Curtis's "stock company" players make appearances, including Scott Brady, who returns as Captain "Red" Tully. Matt Clark, who appears in a half-dozen Dan Curtis productions, plays "Torpedo Man Hansen," whose actions during the attack on Pearl Harbor earn him a promotion. *Dark Shadows* star John Karlen, who appears in more than one dozen of Curtis's works, plays "Ed PBY Pilot," who flies "Pug" Henry to Hawaii.

In the final scene, as Victor Henry stares out at the Pacific Ocean, the words THE END appear on the screen when the words THE BEGINNING would be more appropriate. Many of the characters' fates are left unresolved, and the Second World War has now only just begun. "Into the Maelstrom" received a 41 rating and a 53 share.

The Winds of War was nominated for the Emmy Award for Outstanding Limited Series, and Dan Curtis was nominated for Outstanding Directing in a Limited Series or Special for his direction of "Into the Maelstrom." *The Winds of War* received 11 other Emmy nominations in various Limited-Series categories: cinematography, art direction, special visual effects, costumes, film editing, film sound editing, film sound mixing (three separate nominations), supporting actress (Polly Bergen), and supporting actor (Ralph Bellamy). Bergen and Bellamy lost to Jean Simmons and Richard Kiley, both of *The Thorn Birds*, and Curtis lost to director John Erman for *Who Will Love My Children?* The TV-movie, starring Ann-Margret, ran on ABC on Valentine's Day 1983, the night after the final episode of *The Winds of War*.

In one of the most startling upsets in Emmy history, *both* the high-profile *Winds of War* and *Thorn Birds* lost the Outstanding Limited Series award to the Royal Shakespeare Company's syndicated TV adaptation of Charles Dickens's *Nicholas Nickleby*, a production that ABC, CBS, and NBC had turned down. However, *The Winds of War* did win Emmy Awards for cinematography (Charles Correll), costumes (Tommy Welsh et al.), and special visual effects (Roy Downey et al.). Although it did not win any of its four Golden Globe nominations, the miniseries won Spain's TP de Oro award for best foreign series, and Dan Curtis himself received the Torch of Liberty award from the Anti-Defamation League.[25]

Months after *The Winds of War* had aired and made television history, Dan Curtis lamented, "I just feel blank, with an edge of depression sneaking in, now that it's over. It's been a part of my life for four years."[26] By 1984, he had found his new passion and had begun work on the continuation of his decade-long masterpiece.

The Winds of War (ABC, 6-11 & 13 February 1983; rerun 7, 9-10, & 12-14 September 1986). Producer: Dan Curtis. Associate producer: Barbara Steele. Director:

Dan Curtis. First assistant director: Penelope Foster. Teleplay: Herman Wouk (based on his novel). Story editor: Earl Wallace. Music: Robert Cobert. Director of photography: Charles Correll. Art directors: John Cartwright, Mike Minor, Tom Roysden. Makeup: Wes Dawn, Jim Kail, Silvia Abascal. Costumers: Tommy Welsh, John Napolitano, Paul Vachon, Johannes Nikerk, Heidi Wujek.

Cast: Robert Mitchum (Victor "Pug" Henry), Polly Bergen (Rhoda Henry), Jan-Michael Vincent (Byron Henry), Ali MacGraw (Natalie Jastrow Henry), John Houseman (Aaron Jastrow), Victoria Tennant (Pamela Tudsbury), David Dukes (Leslie Slote), Ben Murphy (Warren Henry), Deborah Winters (Janice Henry), Lisa Eilbacher (Madeline Henry), Peter Graves (Palmer Kirby), Jeremy Kemp (Armin Von Roon), Chaim Topol (Berel Jastrow), Barry Morse (Wolf Stoller), Ralph Bellamy (Franklin D. Roosevelt). 923 minutes. Available on VHS and DVD.

Dan Curtis Significa: Robert Mitchum, who was paid one million dollars for starring in *The Winds of War* (1983), was born in Bridgeport, Connecticut, on Monday 6 August 1917. Ten years later, Dan Curtis was born in Bridgeport on Friday 12 August 1927. Curtis's nostalgic films *When Every Day Was the Fourth of July* and *The Long Days of Summer* were based on Curtis's childhood in Bridgeport. *When Every Day Was the Fourth of July*, which takes place in June-July 1937, aired on NBC on Sunday 12 March 1978 after *The Wonderful World of Disney* and *Project U.F.O.*

The Long Days of Summer is set in Bridgeport in the summer of 1938. On the night of Friday 23 May 1980, ABC paired *The Long Days of Summer* with another 90-minute TV-movie, *Reward*, directed by E.W. Swackhamer (*Death at Love House*), written by Jason Miller (*That Championship Summer*), and starring Michael Parks (*Then Came Bronson*) as a bounty hunter. *Reward* was not a Dan Curtis production.

When Every Day Was the Fourth of July and *The Long Days of Summer* were unsold pilots for a *Waltons*-style family TV series to be called *The Coopers*. Later in the 1980s and even in the 1990s, Dan Curtis and writer Lee Hutson kept alive hope for a *Coopers* series by preparing at least three episode scripts: "A Christmas Story" (by Curtis, Hutson, Tim Kring, and I.C. Rappaport), "For the Love of Ginger Parker" (by Rappaport), and "A Little Girl Across the Room" (by Hutson).[27]

Dan Curtis Significa: In late 1974, Gary Gerani's prose article "The Many Horrors of Dan Curtis" appeared in the premiere issue (January 1975) of Atlas/Seaboard's black-and-white comics magazine *Weird Tales of the Macabre*. Sandwiched between advertisements for model kits and super-8mm movies and the comic-book stories "Time Lapse" and "A Second Life," Gerani's article praised *House of Dark Shadows* (with its "careful lighting, upward angles, and, most of all, properly-paced editing"[28]), *The Night Stalker* ("truly novel"[29]), and *The Night Strangler* ("superior" to *Stalker*[30]). Gary Gerani called Dan Curtis "a quality-minded American producer whose personal interest and pride in the field of horror movies is clearly evident in his fine productions."[31] Gerani also named Curtis as "one of the most respected creative forces in horror films today."[32]

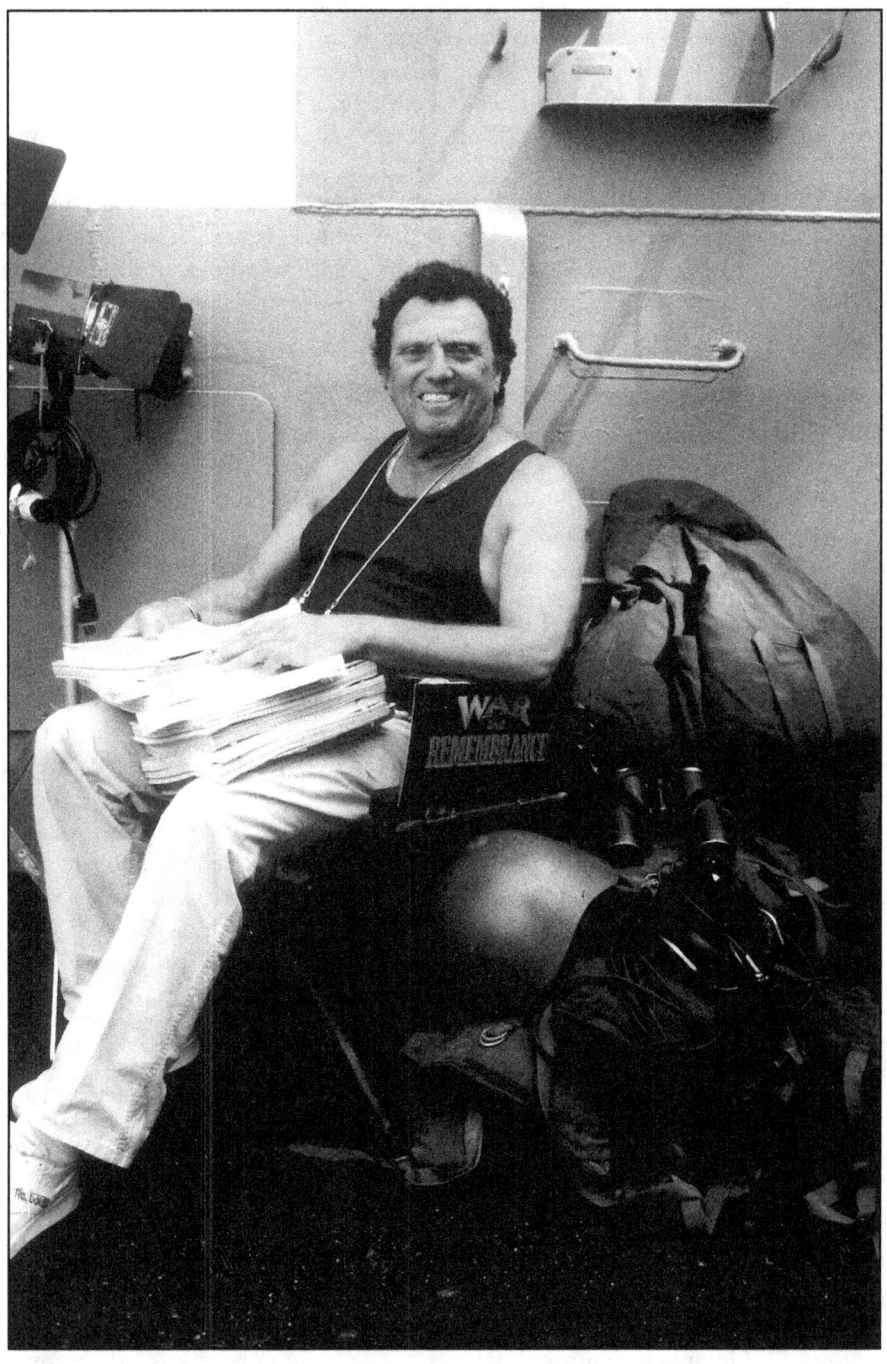

Dan Curtis shoots *War and Remembrance* all over the world in 1986 and 1987.

Chapter V: *The Winds of War*

Dan Curtis (middle) directs Jane Seymour and John Gielgud in a scene from *War and Remembrance* (1988, 1989).

Author Herman Wouk (left) greets actress Victoria Tennant and director Dan Curtis on location for *War and Remembrance* (1988, 1989).

Somewhere in Time star Jane Seymour portrays Natalie Jastrow Henry in Dan Curtis's *War and Remembrance* (seen on ABC in 1988 and 1989).

CHAPTER VI

War and Remembrance

By the time that ABC-TV reran *The Winds of War* on September 7, 9-10, and 12-13-14 of 1986 (three hours each night) as a kick-off to its 1986-1987 season, Curtis was already two-and-a-half years into his work on the miniseries's even more staggering sequel, *War and Remembrance,* again based on a Herman Wouk novel. This time, Curtis and Earl W. Wallace wrote the dramatic, personal scenes involving the novel's characters, and Wouk wrote the historical scenes. Returning as sole director was, of course, Dan Curtis, who remembered,

> When I finished *The Winds of War,* which turned out to be 18 hours, I swore I would never, ever do *War and Remembrance*. But *Winds* was such a huge hit that I knew *War and Remembrance* was going to be made. I wasn't going back into television. I figured I had done all the television I was ever going to do. I could never be able to top myself. I might as well get into the feature business, which is where I wanted to be. [ABC executive] Brandon Stoddard kept after me [to direct *War and Remembrance*], and I kept saying, no, no, no, no, no. One day, my wife and I were driving to Palm Springs. I was an unhappy guy, and she said to me, "You want to do *War and Remembrance,* don't you? I know you really want to do it." I said, "Yeah, maybe I do; I miss all the action and the excitement." Norma said, "Well, then, why don't you do it?"[1]

Curtis went to *War* again in early 1984 and began pre-production on the continuing story of the Victor Henry family in the years 1941-1945. This miniseries would recreate the most crucial events of World War II with stunning accuracy and power. History-making moments at Midway, Guadalcanal, Stalingrad, Yalta, El Alamein, the Battle of the Bulge, Babi Yar, Leyte Gulf, Iwo Jima, and Hiroshima would live again under Curtis's meticulous direction. The 21-month-long shooting schedule began in January 1986 in France and Poland and finally ended in September 1987 in Mobile, Alabama. A cast/crew dinner and wrap party aboard the *Queen Mary* in Long Beach, California, took place on Friday 8 January 1988.

While viewers found the naval battle sequences thrilling, the submarine sequences technically impressive, and the characters' romantic entanglements satisfying, the defining segments of *War and Remembrance* were the devastating recreations of the Holocaust—filmed at one of the actual places where the genocide occurred. After two years of delicate negotiations with the Polish government, Curtis and his cast and crew were allowed to film harrowing Holocaust scenes at the Auschwitz concentration camp in January and May of 1986.

War and Remembrance **director Dan Curtis (left) and star Robert Mitchum were born in Bridgeport, Connecticut, ten years apart: Mitchum in August 1917 and Curtis in August 1927.**

"Auschwitz was the worst," Curtis admitted. "There's no way to describe the feeling" of recreating the unspeakable horrors of the Nazis' "final solution" on the very ground where it happened—and with some of the actual survivors.[2] Curtis's associate producer Branko Lustig had been imprisoned in Auschwitz. Many of the extras who played the doomed Jews, herded naked into gas chambers, were also survivors of the camps. In January 1986, Herman Wouk himself visited Curtis in Poland and observed one night of the grueling filming at Auschwitz. The writer came away deeply moved and convinced that he and Curtis had captured the atrocity exactly as it must have happened.[3]

"When we do the extermination of 30,000 Jews at Babi Yar, you'll never see anything like it in your life," Curtis told the *Los Angeles Times* in September 1986. "As tough as it was for us, it was even tougher for the German crew because they couldn't come to terms with the fact that their forebears really did this."[4]

The Holocaust scenes were unflinching in their brutality, nudity, and horror. "One of the conditions that I had before I agreed to do *War and Remembrance*," Curtis stipulated, "was that ABC had to give me *carte blanche*." He insisted,

> I would not be *edited* in terms of pulling punches because I felt that to show the Holocaust in anything but its most brutal form would be a crime—and I didn't want to be part of that—so what I needed to know was there wasn't going to be anybody who was going to be censoring me or anybody who was going to stop me from doing what I had to do. ABC

agreed to that. I met with the Standards and Practices people, and we had an understanding.⁵

Herman Wouk is the author of *The Winds of War* **(Little, Brown, 1971) and** *War and Remembrance* **(Little, Brown, 1978). Wouk dies on 17 May 2019 at age 103.**

While *The Winds of War* was the equivalent of seven motion pictures, *War and Remembrance*—more than 23 hours of footage spread across 29 hours of television—approximated 11 movies in one. The final cost of the gigantic miniseries was $140 million, at that time the most expensive motion picture ever made and exceeded only in later years by *Titanic* (1997) and numerous fantasy films and super-hero movies which have cost more than $200 million each. Wouk, Curtis, and Wallace's 1492-page script contained 2070 scenes which took 1,852,739 feet of film to shoot.

ABC touted the miniseries as having been filmed in more than ten countries: England, France, West Germany, Switzerland, Austria, Poland, Yugoslavia, Italy, Canada, the United States (including Hawaii), and the Bahamas. Although 757 sets were built and used, many scenes were filmed at the actual locations, such as "The Eagle's Nest" and "The Wolf's Lair" (two of Adolf Hitler's headquarters), the Paris Opera House, and the Auschwitz death camp. Rummaging through some filing cabinets at Auschwitz, Curtis found the actual blueprints and specifications for the death camp's crematoria, whose interiors were then rebuilt almost perfectly to scale on a soundstage. Curtis and Wouk's goal was to tell the story of the Holocaust more vividly and accurately than ever before. "It's a way to make sure it never happens again," Curtis insisted.[6]

Steven Berkoff (looking at a map) portrays Adolf Hitler in *War and Remembrance* (1988, 1989).

Most of the principal actors of *The Winds of War* reprised their roles in *War and Remembrance*, and the several recastings were changes for the better, making a good cast great. Heading the cast were Robert Mitchum, Polly Bergen, Hart Bochner (replacing Jan-Michael Vincent), Jane Seymour (replacing Ali MacGraw), Victoria Tennant, David Dukes, Peter Graves, Chaim Topol, Jeremy Kemp, John Gielgud (replacing John Houseman), Sharon Stone (replacing Deborah Winters), Barry Bostwick (replacing Joseph Hacker), Steven Berkoff (replacing Gunter Meisner), and Ralph Bellamy. Once again, the supporting cast was a movie-and-TV who's who: Eddie Albert, Brian Blessed,

Mike Connors, John Dehner, Howard Duff, Nina Foch, Pat Hingle, E.G. Marshall, Ian McShane, Robert Morley, Dennis Patrick, Addison Powell, William Prince, John Rhys-Davies, William Schallert, and others. In all, there were 358 speaking roles, 2257 bit players, and 41,720 extras. Counting the almost 1700 crew members, Dan Curtis commanded an army of 46,000 people marching across Europe and North America. Curtis worked indefatigably with decommissioned or still-active ships, aircraft carriers, submarines, and planes; with 35-foot-long miniature ships on a wet set at Pinewood Studios in England; and with the thousands of extras playing the difficult roles of refugees, soldiers, prisoners, and corpses.

Terror Train **star Hart Bochner portrays Byron Henry in Dan Curtis's** *War and Remembrance* **(seen on ABC in 1988 and 1989).**

Producer Barbara Steele (who also played the small role of Elsa McMahon) had nothing but praise for the director. She remarked,
> There were moments when I thought the demands would kill all of us, but never Dan, because he was working from the center of his very big heart. It's as if we were living in Beethoven's Ninth Symphony. I don't believe there is another filmmaker on the planet who could have done [the two miniseries]. It was a moment of brilliant synchronicity, and it was wonderful to witness someone work at the height of his powers in a state of sustained enthrallment. Dan knew this was his "moment," and he could put his signature so beautifully and powerfully on a devastating period of history.[7]

Polly Bergen added, "I don't think there is any other television show, movie, or miniseries that has captured the incredible scope and majesty of *The Winds of War* and *War and Remembrance*. Dan never received the kind of recognition that he deserved."[8] Associate producer and Auschwitz survivor Branko Lustig declared, "Dan Curtis can be put in the category with Steven Spielberg and Ridley Scott. Nobody recreated the Holocaust better than Dan Curtis. He did it with his heart."[9] Lustig went on to produce Curtis's *Intruders* (1992), Spielberg's *Schindler's List* (1993), and six of Scott's films, including *Gladiator* (2000) and *American Gangster* (2007).

Michael Woods (left), Barry Bostwick, and Hart Bochner pose with Sharon Stone (left) and Victoria Tennant in this ABC publicity still for *War and Remembrance* (1988, 1989).

Also adding heart to *War and Remembrance* was the 11 hours of music—3500 manuscript pages—composed and conducted by Curtis's musical mainstay Robert Cobert. At ABC's request, Cobert repeated his *Winds of War* theme as the main-title theme of *War and Remembrance*; additionally, he composed what he called "everything from pure, romantic music to all kinds of military music to jazz."[10]

Despite Cobert's success with *The Winds of War* and essentially all of Dan Curtis's productions, Cobert initially was not guaranteed the job of scoring the sequel. In a DVD interview, the composer recalled,

> When they started *War and Remembrance*, they said, "Let's get Leonard Bernstein," or "Let's get John Williams." But Dan wanted me and *only me*. He called me up and said, "You're doing it!" Curtis asked me if I could write five minutes of music a day, and I thought about it and said, "Yeah, but I won't do it for free." When Dan told me that money was no object, I called my agent and said, "Go get 'em!"[11]

While many composers manage to perfect only one to three minutes of programmatic music per day, Cobert wrote five minutes of music each day. He dutifully worked 12 to 14 hours a day, seven days a week, from August through October 1988 in order to meet the deadline for the November 1988 episodes of *War and Remembrance*. With Curtis present in the recording studio and deliberating over every note, Cobert conducted a 50-piece orchestra in the recording of his background music. Except for a few quibbles, Curtis enthusiastically approved of every theme.

"I think Cobert's a genius, no question about it," Curtis declared. "He has an incredible knack for writing clever background music that enhances my movies all the time. He stands up there with the greatest, and somebody should start to recognize him."[12]

Finally, after almost five years in the making, *War and Remembrance* aired on ABC-TV on November 13, 15-16-17, 20, and 22-23 of 1988 (parts 1-7), and May 7-8-9-10 and 14 of 1989 (parts 8-12, called *War and Remembrance: The Final Chapter*). Because of the overwhelming length of the miniseries, its unwise division into two segments six months apart, and the ever-increasing alternative programming available on cable television, *War and Remembrance* attracted only about one-half of the 140 million viewers of *The Winds of War*. Nevertheless, commanding 55 to 75 million TV viewers is still impressive and admirable whether in 1988-1989, the 1990s, or the 21st century.

Once again, the reviews were spectacularly positive. The *Washington Post* called *War and Remembrance* "monumental," "mammoth," and "tremendous."[13] *Newsday* called it "super TV,"[14] and the *Newark Star Ledger* proclaimed the "masterwork" miniseries "very simply television's finest hours."[15] Newspapers from Los Angeles to Kansas City praised Dan Curtis's brilliant directing, and *TV Guide* singled out Curtis's "unparalleled combat footage."[16] Curtis especially enjoyed the Associated Press's assessment: "Curtis has himself a masterpiece of a war movie [. . .] the battle scenes are stunning [. . .] some of the best submarine scenes since *Das Boot*. The Battle of Midway [is] worthy of a theatrical film. The concentration-camp scenes are the most powerful such depictions television has ever seen."[17]

Curtis's personal goal with the submarine scenes was to top *Das Boot* (1981), and he also strove to surpass *Midway* (1976), all other World War II movies, and NBC-TV's

Emmy Award-winning *Holocaust* (seen in April 1978). According to the *Kansas City Star*, "Curtis did not fail."[18]

Howard Rosenberg of the *Los Angeles Times* agreed: "*War and Remembrance* takes its place at the top of all TV drama." Rosenberg added, "Volume one of ABC's *War and Remembrance* is more than just a dazzling achievement in historical storytelling. It is the best serialized drama in the history of American television. This is important, landmark TV—hard to take, but even harder to ignore. ABC should be proud."[19]

Indeed, in a rich British and American television landscape that had already produced *The Forsyte Saga* (1967); *Elizabeth R* (1971); *Upstairs, Downstairs* (1971-1975); *Rich Man, Poor Man* (1976); *Captains and the Kings* (1976); *The Moneychangers* (1976); *Roots* (1977); *Shogun* (1980); *The Winds of War* (1983); and *The Thorn Birds* (1983), being canonized by the *Los Angeles Times* as the greatest serialized drama in the history of American television was perhaps the ultimate accolade.

Writing for *Lone Star Shadows* vol. 2, no. 7/8 (summer/fall 1989), I concurred that *War and Remembrance* was even better than *The Winds of War*, and I called Robert Cobert's new music "superb, possibly even better than his music for *The Winds of War.* [. . .] Cobert's *War and Remembrance* theme song has been recorded by the likes of easy-listening instrumentalist Lex de Azevedo and 1940s bandleader Ray Anthony."[20] I played those records, as well as "Quentin's Theme," many times on WAMB-AM & FM in Nashville from the 1980s to the 2010s.

War and Remembrance, **episode #1,** written by Dan Curtis, Earl Wallace, and Herman Wouk and directed by Curtis, premiered on ABC-TV on Sunday 13 November 1988 in a three-hour timeslot (the actual running time is 2 hours, 26 minutes) following *Incredible Sunday*. The setting of show #1 is Pearl Harbor, Hawaii; Washington, DC; Marivales Bay, Philippine Islands; Naples, Italy; southwest Poland; K.L. Auschwitz camp; Singapore; the South China Sea; Rastenburg, East Prussia; et al. from 15 December to 27 December 1941.

MPI Home Video DVD liner notes: "Captain Victor 'Pug' Henry [Robert Mitchum] takes command of the cruiser U.S.S. *Northampton* after the Pearl Harbor attack. Adolf Hitler [now played by Steven Berkoff] continues his assault in Europe. Franklin Delano Roosevelt [Ralph Bellamy] orders a bombing raid on Japan and meets with Winston Churchill [now played by Robert Hardy]."

Once again narrated by William T. Woodson (*This Is Your FBI*), the global saga of the Henry and Jastrow families continues. It is still mid-December 1941 for the characters although five-and-one-half years have passed for the viewers. In the interim, several roles have been recast, and Sami Frey, Ian McShane, John Rhys-Davies, and Bill Wallis play new characters. *Dark Shadows* actor Addison Powell plays Admiral Harold Stark in this episode.

Christmastime of 1941 is exceedingly dismal although Churchill is at the White House with the President and Mrs. Roosevelt (Elizabeth Hoffman) for the lighting of the White House Christmas tree. Victor Henry and Byron Henry (now played by Hart Bochner) are at sea: "Pug" on a ship and Byron in a submarine. Rhoda Henry (Polly Pergen) is in Washington DC and once again gravitating toward Palmer Kirby (Peter Graves). Aaron Jastrow (now played by John Gielgud), his niece Natalie (now played by

Somewhere in Time star Jane Seymour), and her and Byron's baby Louis are still trapped in Italy. Pamela (Victoria Tennant) and her father Alistair Tudsbury (Robert Morley) find themselves in Singapore as the Japanese military approaches.

Dan Curtis demonstrates his skills as a teller of horror tales in this first episode and especially in episode number two (and again in five, seven, ten, et al.). This episode features a very long, tense scene of mounting horror as Byron and his fellow sailors aboard the submarine *Devilfish* are attacked on the ocean floor by a Japanese warship above them. When the captain of the *Devilfish* has a nervous breakdown and is injured during the attack, Byron and his friend Carter "Lady" Aster (Barry Bostwick) must take charge. Also aboard the *Devilfish* is Derringer, played by Mills Watson, a Curtis "stock company" player, making his fourth appearance in a Dan Curtis production.

Academy Award winner John Gielgud is in his early 80s when he plays Aaron Jastrow in *War and Remembrance*.

The *Fugitive* star Barry Morse returns but as a different character, General Franz Halder. Likewise, the *War* producer Barbara Steele makes a cameo appearance as a new character, Elsa McMahon, at a Christmas party in Singapore. Also making a cameo appearance in this and several *Winds of War* and *War and Remembrance* episodes is Greystone, the Beverly Hills mansion that would become Collinwood in Dan Curtis's 1991 and 2004 revivals of *Dark Shadows*.

Another moment of horror occurs at Auschwitz as the camp officials conduct a rehearsal for Hitler's "Final Solution" by gassing a group of Russian prisoners. As narrator Woodson explains, the poison gas is Zyklon B, a hydrogen/cyanide insecticide. This event foreshadows some unbearable and unforgettable moments in episode number two and others when Curtis directs powerful reenactments of a sad and very *real* horror story. This initial episode of *War and Remembrance* received a 21.8 rating and a 31 share.

War and Remembrance, **episode #2,** written by Dan Curtis, Earl Wallace, and Herman Wouk and directed by Curtis, premiered on ABC-TV on Tuesday 15 November 1988 in a three-hour timeslot (the actual running time is 2 hours, 23 minutes). The setting of show #2 is Siena and Rome, Italy; Bern, Switzerland; the South Pacific; southwest Poland; Washington, DC; Auschwitz camp; Birkenau camp; et al. from 27 January to 6 May 1942.

MPI Home Video DVD liner notes: "The Russian and German armies clash as the war grows fierce in Europe. Hitler announces new offensives against Leningrad and Stalingrad as his madness intensifies. The United States launches a bombing raid over Tokyo" (in a black-and-white sequence effectively blending actual World War II footage with new footage of the actors).

Leslie Slote's storyline in Bern comes to the forefront in this episode as Leslie, always unlucky in love, meets, loves, but loses Selma Archer (Mijou Kovacs), a young Jewish woman whose father is sending her to New York to marry a man she does not love. Meanwhile, Slote uncovers more evidence of Hitler's "Final Solution." David Dukes, the *79 Park Avenue* star who plays Slote in both miniseries, is perhaps the unsung Most Valuable Player of the productions. As I wrote in *Lone Star Shadows* in 1989, "One of film and TV's finest, yet inexplicably overlooked, actors, Dukes played Slote excellently throughout the entire saga."[21] David Dukes went on to co-star in Curtis's productions of *Me and the Kid* (1993) and *The Love Letter* (1998).

In Siena, Natalie is not fooled by the charming, helpful German official Werner Beck (played by Peter Lorre lookalike Bill Wallis), but Aaron *is* taken in by his former student who is seeking to keep the Jastrows under his thumb in Italy, *not* help them to leave. However, Aaron comes to his senses when Beck shows his true colors by urging Aaron to make radio broadcasts for the Axis.

In Auschwitz, the ultimate horror story, far more disturbing than any of Curtis's scary movies, unfolds before the visiting Adolf Eichmann (Milton Johns) and other Nazi brass: the methodical gassing of Jewish women, men, and children and the dispassionate dumping of the bodies in mass graves. These are some of the scenes that Curtis demanded be shown in their full horror, including nudity, violence, screaming, and death—all very painful to watch. Episode #2 received a 19 rating and a 29 share.

War and Remembrance, **episode #3,** written by Dan Curtis, Earl Wallace, and Herman Wouk and directed by Curtis, premiered on ABC-TV on Wednesday 16 November 1988 in a two-and-one-half-hour timeslot (the actual running time is 1 hour, 57 minutes) following *Growing Pains.* The setting of show #3 is Pearl Harbor, Hawaii;

the Pacific Ocean; Midway Island; Los Angeles, California; London, England; Siena, Italy; et al. from 26 May to 25 July 1942.

MPI Home Video DVD liner notes: "'Pug' Henry and Pamela Tudsbury are reunited in Honolulu. The American forces engage the Japanese fleet near Midway, changing the course of the war. Winston Churchill and Harry Hopkins [William Schallert], representing FDR, decide that combined American and British forces will engage the Germans in North Africa."

In what is almost a stand-alone episode, the majority of show number three dramatizes the decisive Battle of Midway (3-7 June 1942)—and two Henry men are in the thick of it. "Pug" captains the U.S.S. *Northampton* in the Pacific while his son Warren Henry (now played by Michael Woods of *Texas* and *Our Family Honor*) is a pilot stationed on the aircraft carrier U.S.S. *Enterprise* (actually, the U.S.S. *Lexington*). In an ultimately Emmy Award-winning feat of editing and special effects, actual footage of the Battle of Midway is blended with Dan Curtis's dynamic shots of sea and air combat using decommissioned ships, active destroyers, and various Navy airplanes. Narrator William Woodson, reading words written by Herman Wouk himself, gives the viewers a superb explanation of the events of the Battle of Midway—especially the "five minutes" that changed the course of World War II.

Dan Curtis (bending) directs William Schallert (left) and Ralph Bellamy (as FDR) in the *War and Remembrance* Oval Office set.

Aboard the *Enterprise,* a little war seems to be taking place among the officers. *Dark Shadows* alumnus Michael McGuire returns as a different character, Captain Miles Browning, who, along with other officers, clashes with the interim commander, Admiral Raymond Spruance (G.D. Spradlin), over tactics and strategy. Warren Henry voices his opinion, too, not long before tragedy strikes the Henry family. A highlight of the episode is Victor's heartfelt letter to Rhoda and her reaction to the sad news.

A high point of the entire miniseries so far is (in Pamela's words) "a bizarre conversation" between Pamela and Rhoda when they meet by chance in Los Angeles a couple of weeks later. Written by Earl Wallace and Dan Curtis, this scene is much more than the typical wife-meets-the-other-woman scenario. In a DVD interview, Victoria Tennant remarked that it is one of her personal favorites of her scenes in *War and Remembrance*.

Of all of the aforementioned Curtis mainstays (e.g. Matt Clark, John Karlen, Mills Watson, et al.), the *most* regular of Curtis's regulars—composer Robert Cobert—makes a cameo appearance as a bandleader. On Thursday 25 June 2015, Cobert, who composed the music for almost all of Curtis's four dozen productions, received a lifetime-achievement Saturn Award from the Academy of Science-Fiction, Fantasy, and Horror Films. Presenting the award to the then-90-year-old composer were *Dark Shadows* stars Kathryn Leigh Scott and David Selby.

Tuxedo-clad composer-conductor Robert Cobert laughs with Dan Curtis during the filming of Cobert's cameo appearance in *War and Remembrance* (1988, 1989). Cobert is nominated for the Emmy Award for his music.

The third episode of *War and Remembrance*, on 16 November 1988, received a 19.8 rating and a 31 share. It was the second-highest-rated episode of the miniseries. The premiere episode was the highest-rated of all.

War and Remembrance, **episode #4,** written by Dan Curtis, Earl Wallace, and Herman Wouk and directed by Curtis, premiered on ABC-TV on Thursday 17

November 1988 in a two-hour timeslot (the actual running time is 1 hour, 23 minutes) following the second episode of *Knightwatch*, starring Benjamin Bratt. The setting of show #4 is Siena, Follonica, and Piombino, Italy; Bern, Switzerland; Chicago, Illinois; Vinnitsa, Ukraine; Marciana, Elba; Gibraltar; Washington, DC; Corsica; Marseilles, France; et al. from 25 July to 2 November 1942.

MPI Home Video DVD liner notes: "In Europe and North Africa, Hitler's forces are racking up victories, but they are also suffering seriously in Russia. Rhoda meets Palmer Kirby and tells him she has decided to stay with 'Pug.' Byron travels to France as a diplomatic courier, and he and Natalie reunite briefly in Marseilles."

At Adolf Hitler's "Werewolf" headquarters in Ukraine, General Franz Halder (Barry Morse) quarrels with Hitler over the Fuhrer's megalomania. Hitler is trying to command his army himself, from 600 miles away, and when Hitler fires Halder, he decides to do *his* job, himself, too.

Rhoda's on-again, off-again relationship with Palmer seems to end for good in this episode when Rhoda meets Palmer for lunch as she is passing through Chicago on her way to Washington DC. The next possible complication in her life arises in the form of Colonel Harrison "Hack" Peters (*Mannix* star Mike Connors), a womanizer who notices Rhoda in Chicago and turns up in Washington to pursue her.

Robert Mitchum as "Pug" does not appear in this episode. Most of the show follows the desperate migration of Natalie, Louis, and Aaron from Siena to Elba to Corsica to Marseilles. For the moment, they have eluded the persistent Werner Beck, but they are still far from America and freedom. A wonderfully romantic moment caps the episode as Byron, who has been searching Europe for his family, finds Natalie in Marseilles, and they rush into each other's arms. Episode #4 received a 16.8 rating and a 25 share.

War and Remembrance, **episode #5,** written by Dan Curtis, Earl Wallace, and Herman Wouk and directed by Curtis, premiered on ABC-TV on Sunday 20 November 1988 in a two-hour-and-five-minute timeslot (the actual running time is 1 hour, 37 minutes) following *Incredible Sunday* and *Mission: Impossible*. The setting of show #5 is Marseilles and Lourdes, France; Tel El Aqqaqir and Alexandria, Egypt; Lisbon, Portugal; Munich, Germany; Auschwitz camp; Birkenau camp; Tassafaronga Point, Guadalcanal; et al. from 2 November to 1 December 1942.

MPI Home Video DVD liner notes: "Natalie, Louis, and Aaron are interned in Lourdes. The Allies invade North Africa and are victorious at El Alamein. The Germans eradicate evidence of mass graves at Auschwitz by building crematoriums. The American forces are poised to intercept Japanese trying to re-supply troops at Tassafaronga Point."

Natalie and Byron's reunion in France is short-lived because of the political vagaries of the Vichy government and the fighting in North Africa, of all things. Meanwhile, in Egypt, Pamela suffers a tragedy and narrowly escapes death herself. At Hitler's *Wolfsschanze* ("Wolf's Lair") headquarters, new chief of staff General Kurt Zeitzler (Peter Vaughan), Halder's replacement, provokes the Fuhrer into another rash decision.

This episode concludes by revealing the calamities facing *Northampton* captain "Pug" Henry at the nighttime Battle of Tassaforanga. Japanese torpedoes hit and badly damage the *Northampton* and her crew: 54 sailors are dead or missing, and 217 are wounded. Ultimately, "Pug" must give the order to abandon ship. Captain Henry is the last man off the burning, listing ship, and from a lifeboat, "Pug" watches his ship sink. "Stock company" member Matt Clark (seen in *Winds* show #7) now plays Chief Clark aboard the *Northampton,* and *Dark Shadows* and *Dallas* actor Dennis Patrick plays Admiral Mahlon Tisdale, with whom "Pug" confers by radio-phone.

Dan Curtis directs Robert Mitchum (right, at the podium) in a naval scene in *War and Remembrance* (1988, 1989).

Throughout this somber episode, which includes another very disturbing sequence at Auschwitz, Robert Cobert's Emmy Award-worthy music is especially effective as it evokes the nostalgia, romance, hardship, tragedy, and horror of World War II. Episode #5 received a 17 rating and a 26 share.

War and Remembrance, **episode #6,** written by Dan Curtis, Earl Wallace, and Herman Wouk and directed by Curtis, premiered on ABC-TV on Tuesday 22 November 1988 in a two-hour-and-twenty-minute timeslot (the actual running time is 1 hour, 51 minutes) following *Who's the Boss?* and *Roseanne.* The setting of show #6 is Washington, DC; Baden-Baden and Berlin, Germany; Honolulu, Hawaii; Casablanca, Morocco; Nuomea, New Caledonia; Moscow and Leningrad, Russia; Paris, France; et al. from 20 December 1942 to 3 April 1943.

MPI Home Video DVD liner notes: "Roosevelt asks 'Pug' to go to Russia as a military aide. Roosevelt and Churchill meet in Casablanca to map Allied war strategy. The German forces face crushing defeat in Stalingrad. An assassination plot against Hitler is uncovered. 'Pug' tours the Russian front."

Victor and Rhoda give their marriage another try when he spends Christmas and New Year's in Washington DC with her. Nevertheless, Rhoda still is drawn to "Hack" Peters—as Pamela notices when she has a chance meeting with Rhoda. A highlight of the Victor/Rhoda storyline is the New Year's Eve party that the Henrys attend. A marvelous "little moment" that I mentioned in my 1989 *Lone Star Shadows* article is "Rhoda Henry, alone and forlorn, listening to a scratchy 78 RPM recording of 'Three O'Clock in the Morning.'"[22]

Worlds away from Washington, the widowed Janice Henry (Sharon Stone) begins an affair with "Lady" Aster, who now commands the *Moray* submarine on which Byron serves. Natalie and Aaron's odyssey continues as they and Louis move from France to Nazi Germany and back to France—with the loathsome Werner Beck on their trail.

Victor finds himself back in Russia at President Roosevelt's request. Charles Lane (*The Lucy Show*) returns as his *Winds of War* character Admiral William Standley, who is stationed in Russia.

Despite the involvement of the Henrys and the Jastrows in the story, the "star" of *War and Remembrance* is actually World War II itself. The global pandemonium is much bigger than any of them. Dan Curtis, Earl Wallace, and Herman Wouk succeed in conveying the enormous scale of the war all over the world and its lasting effect on everyone. According to *TV Guide*, "*War and Remembrance* is not only the absorbing private story of the extended Henry family but also a classy retelling of the public history of the Second World War."[23] Episode #6 received a 17.5 rating and a 26 share.

War and Remembrance, **episode #7,** written by Dan Curtis, Earl Wallace, and Herman Wouk and directed by Curtis, premiered on ABC-TV on Wednesday 23 November 1988 in a two-and-one-half-hour timeslot (the actual running time is 1 hour, 57 minutes) following *Growing Pains.* The setting of show #7 is Paris, France; Kursk and Moscow, Russia; the New Hebrides; Pearl Harbor, Hawaii; Ternopol, Ukraine; Berlin, Germany; Bohusovice, Czechoslovakia; et al. from 3 April 1943 to 25 July 1943. There is also a flashback to Babi Yar, outside Kiev, Ukraine, on 29-30 September 1941, when 33,771 Jewish men, women, and children were massacred. Dan Curtis insisted that ABC air these brutal scenes uncensored.

MPI Home Video DVD liner notes: "Kommandant Blobel [Kenneth Colley] recalls the murder of some 30,000 Jews at Babi Yar outside Kiev. Aaron, Natalie, and Louis are sent to Theresienstadt, the 'paradise ghetto.' Byron is back in the Pacific aboard the submarine U.S.S. *Moray*. After major losses in Stalingrad, Field Marshall Rommel [Hardy Kruger] urges Hitler to end the war. Patton [Larry Dobkin] leads his tanks to victory in Sicily, and Mussolini falls."

This episode features outstanding sea-battle footage as Captain "Lady" Aster's submarine *Moray* sinks several Japanese ships. However, to the dismay of Byron Henry and the rest of the crew, the bloodthirsty Aster goes too far by ordering the slaughter of hundreds of Japanese soldiers floating helplessly in the water. In his private life, "Lady" continues his affair with Janice Henry. *General Hospital* star Kin Shriner plays submariner "Horseshoes" Mullen.

In Paris, Natalie's forced outing to the opera with Werner Beck is only the beginning of the new horrors facing her, Aaron, and Louis. The three of them are sent to Theresienstadt, which German propaganda paints as a luxury resort, but they soon realize that there is no "paradise" in this ghetto of sick, dying, and dead Jews. "Oh, my God," Natalie exclaims as TO BE CONTINUED flashes across the screen. Viewers must wait 23½ weeks—until May 1989—to see the rest of the story. Episode #7 received a 16.9 rating and a 25 share.

In January 1989, the first half of *War and Remembrance* won three Golden Globe Awards. John Gielgud and Barry Bostwick, both of whose roles had been played by other actors in *The Winds of War*, tied for Best Supporting Actor in a TV Miniseries. In his acceptance speech, Bostwick (whom *TV Guide* called "memorable" in his role) said,

> I accept this award not only for myself but also for the 357 other supporting players on *War and Remembrance*. We were supporting a dream—Dan Curtis's dream—of bringing to television 29 of its finest hours, a depiction of World War II so accurate and so moving that many of its images would be forever burned into our collective consciousness. I think he's done that. I thank Dan Curtis for allowing me to color in just a very small corner of his masterpiece.[24]

Although Curtis himself did not win a Golden Globe for his direction, his masterpiece won the award for Best TV Miniseries. In his acceptance speech, Curtis said, "A whole lot of people went to war about five years ago, and we're lucky to be standing up here right now. It's just a great joy to have it all appreciated and to mean something. Thank you from the bottom of my heart."[25] Two months later, *War and Remembrance* won the People's Choice Award for best miniseries. Two months after that, the miniseries finally continued.

War and Remembrance: The Final Chapter, **episode #8,** written by Dan Curtis, Earl Wallace, and Herman Wouk and directed by Curtis, premiered on ABC-TV on Sunday 7 May 1989 in a three-hour timeslot (the actual running time is 2 hours, 27 minutes) following the special, *SST: Screen, Stage, Television*. The setting of show #8 is Theresienstadt, Czechoslovakia; the Carpathian Mountains; Moscow, Russia; Tehran, Iran; Honolulu, Hawaii; Washington, DC; New Delhi, India; the Sea of Japan; Oak Ridge, Tennessee; et al. from 25 November 1943 to 16 May 1944.

MPI Home Video DVD liner notes: "Aaron, Natalie, and Natalie's young son Louis are held in the Theresienstadt 'paradise ghetto.' Berel Jastrow [Chaim Topol] escapes from the Germans. Aaron bribes the sadistic commandant Rahm [Robert Stephens] to prevent Natalie's deportation to death camps in the east."

Everything changes in this eventful and superb episode. Madeline Henry (now played by Leslie Hope) becomes engaged to naval officer Simon Anderson (William R. Moses of *Falcon Crest*). Victor and Rhoda talk about "Hack" Peters and a divorce. Victor and Pamela exchange important letters. "Lady" tells Byron about his affair with Janice—and then disaster strikes the *Moray* sub. In one of many highlights of this episode, Byron and Leslie have an urgent, emotional telephone conversation about Natalie. In another great moment, "Pug" and "Hack" have an awkward conversation about Rhoda as they share a train car on their way back to Washington from Oak Ridge.

In Theresienstadt, Aaron is literally browbeaten into accepting the position of Elder in Charge of Culture, mere "window dressing" (in his words) to make the "paradise ghetto" look livable and pleasurable to the outside world. As more and more of the Jewish residents are sent away by train "to the east" (and almost certain death), Aaron delivers an eloquent and moving explication of the Book of Job to a group of his fellow Jews. It is one of the finest moments of the entire miniseries and an Emmy-worthy performance by John Gielgud.

John Gielgud and Jane Seymour play Aaron Jastrow and Natalie Jastrow Henry in *War and Remembrance* (1988, 1989).

As the time for Natalie and Louis's transport draws closer, Aaron tries to reason with Kommandant Karl Rahm but to no avail. The episode ends on this note of terrible distress. Once again, Robert Cobert's music perfectly complements every scene. Episode #8 received a 13.4 rating and a 21 share.

War and Remembrance: The Final Chapter, **episode #9,** written by Dan Curtis, Earl Wallace, and Herman Wouk and directed by Curtis, premiered on ABC-TV on Monday 8 May 1989 in a two-hour timeslot (the actual running time is 1 hour, 35 minutes) following *MacGyver.* The setting of show #9 is Theresienstadt, Czechoslovakia; Altricam, Cheshire, England, and Stoneford, Gloucestershire, England; Berlin, Germany; Washington, DC; Utah Beach, Sword Beach, Juno Beach, Gold Beach, and Omaha Beach, Normandy, France; et al. from 16 May to 10 June 1944.

MPI Home Video DVD liner notes: "Natalie and Aaron undergo a terrifying physical ordeal. General Eisenhower [E.G. Marshall] prepares for D-Day. Conspirators in Germany plot to assassinate Hitler. Rahm brutalizes Natalie and her son Louis to ensure her cooperation during an upcoming Red Cross tour."

Natalie and Louis are exempted from the transfer east; later, Kommandant Rahm terrorizes the mother and child. In England, Leslie Slote runs into Pamela Tudsbury a couple of weeks before Leslie suffers terrible misfortune in the war effort. Pamela also reunites with "Pug," now Rear Admiral Henry, who tells her that Rhoda has divorced him. (He also mentions that Janice Henry has enrolled in law school.)

In what is almost another stand-alone episode, the majority of show number nine depicts the Allies' "Operation Overlord," or the D-Day invasion of France, on Tuesday 6 June 1944 (postponed from June 5). E.G. Marshall guest-stars as General Eisenhower, who leads the invasion. Once again, actual World War II newsreel footage and William Woodson's explanatory narration augment Curtis's new scenes. Episode #9 received a 14.4 rating and a 22 share.

War and Remembrance: The Final Chapter, **episode #10,** written by Dan Curtis, Earl Wallace, and Herman Wouk and directed by Curtis, premiered on ABC-TV on Tuesday 9 May 1989 in a two-hour timeslot (the actual running time is 1 hour, 35 minutes) following *Who's the Boss?* and *The Wonder Years.* The setting of show #10 is Theresienstadt, Czechoslovakia; Vimoutiers, Normandy, France; Berlin and Herrlingen, Germany; "Wolf's Lair," East Prussia; Chicago, Illinois; San Diego, California; Pearl Harbor, Hawaii; Stoneford, Gloucestershire, England, et al. from 22 June to 28 October 1944.

MPI Home Video DVD liner notes: "Louis is stricken with a high fever. The assassination plot against Hitler fails. As the Allies advance on the western and eastern fronts, the Germans begin to pull out of a crumbling Theresienstadt. Natalie and Aaron begin a horrifying train journey to the death camp at Auschwitz."

Much of this fine episode dramatizes the July 20 attempt to assassinate Hitler, with a briefcase bomb, at the *Wolfsschanze* or "Wolf's Lair." The operation fails: Hitler lives and summarily executes the perpetrators and 5000 more of his German enemies.

At Theresienstadt, the Red Cross officials visit the miraculously beautified camp. The ploy seemingly goes over so well that the camp officials decide to make a propaganda film, *The Fuhrer Gives Jews a Town*, at the sham "paradise." Meanwhile, Aaron's cousin Berel Jastrow hatches a plot to smuggle Louis out of the camp. The boy feigns a "high fever," his death is faked, and he is spirited away. Natalie is now without her son, but she derives comfort from believing that Louis is safe on the outside. She tells Aaron, "No matter what happens, I'm going to survive—and I'm going to find Louis." Natalie and Aaron board the train to Auschwitz.

As the European and Pacific wars turn in favor of the Allies, Victor captains the U.S.S. *Iowa*, and Byron commands the submarine *Barracuda*. A highlight of the episode is the strained father/son dinner aboard the *Iowa* when Byron quarrels with "Pug" over Pamela and his parents' divorce. Ironically, the U.S.S. *Iowa* had been in the news just one month before this episode aired when an *Iowa* crew member, possibly lovesick and/or suicidal, caused an explosion aboard the ship. Episode #10 of *War and Remembrance* received a 15.1 rating and a 24 share.

War and Remembrance: The Final Chapter, **episode #11,** written by Dan Curtis, Earl Wallace, and Herman Wouk and directed by Curtis, premiered on ABC-TV on Wednesday 10 May 1989 in a two-hour timeslot (the actual running time is 1 hour, 35 minutes) following *Growing Pains* and *Head of the Class*. The setting of show #11 is the K.L. Auschwitz camp; the Philippine Sea; Yalta, on the Crimean peninsula; Rheims, France; Berlin, Germany; Prague, Czechoslovakia; et al. from 28 October 1944 to 18 March 1945.

MPI Home Video DVD liner notes: "Natalie and Aaron arrive at Auschwitz. In the Pacific, Byron leads his submarine into battle. In Europe, the Allies deal the Germans a fatal blow at the Battle of the Bulge. Berel and Louis are rounded up during the Nazis' 'scorched-earth' retreat."

This unbearably grim episode is the hardest part of the miniseries to watch. The initial 45 minutes is one long, agonizing scene that depicts Aaron, Natalie, and countless other Jewish people on their three-day-long train ride through Czechoslovakia and Poland to their final destination, Auschwitz. This is true *horror* as we see the women, children, and men brutalized; stripped naked; shorn of their hair; and herded into the huge "shower rooms" that are actually their gas-filled tombs. Robert Cobert's Emmy-nominated music adds to the painfully sad mood of this horrific scenario. William Woodson's mournful narration marks the gassing, death, and cremation of a major character. By the end of this episode, another character will have met a terrible death.

The next 20 minutes of this episode is one long battle scene as Captain Byron Henry's submarine *Barracuda* sustains damage from a Japanese ship but then fights back, against the odds. *Beauty and the Beast* actor Jay Acovone plays Quartermaster Maselli.

Meanwhile, the Battle of the Bulge propels the Allies closer to the victory, and Hitler and his generals move underground for the remainder of the war. Because of the two aforementioned long scenes and the otherwise emphasis on historical scenes, "Pug," Rhoda, Pamela, and other characters do not appear. Episode #11 received a 15.7 rating and a 25 share.

Fiddler on the Roof star Chaim Topol plays Berel Jastrow in both of Dan Curtis's *War* miniseries.

War and Remembrance: The Final Chapter, **episode #12,** written by Dan Curtis, Earl Wallace, and Herman Wouk and directed by Curtis, premiered on ABC-TV on Sunday 14 May 1989 in a two-hour-and-twenty-minute timeslot (the actual running time is 1 hour, 51 minutes) following *Incredible Sunday* and the final episode of *Moonlighting*. The setting of show #12 is Washington, DC; Berlin and Weimar, Germany; Guam; Annapolis, Maryland; Pearl Harbor, Hawaii; Los Alamos, New Mexico; Paris, France; Geneva, Switzerland; Prague, Czechoslovakia; Essex and Surrey, England; et al. from 12 April to 7 August 1945.

MPI Home Video DVD liner notes: "The world grieves following the news of FDR's tragic death. In Germany, Hitler commits suicide as the Third Reich collapses. World War II ends in triumph for the Allies. Byron searches desperately through the legions of Europe's dispossessed children in hopes of finding his son Louis."

The miniseries concludes with this excellent episode, which opens on the sad day of the death of Franklin Delano Roosevelt. Madeline and Simon, as well as Rhoda and "Hack," have married off-camera, but the episode shows the wedding of Pamela and

Victor at the Naval Academy in Annapolis. Immediately after his wedding, "Pug" becomes the hand-picked Naval Aide to President Harry Truman (Richard Dysart).

Another long, grim interlude depicts the final hours of the Third Reich and its deranged leader. As the Allies relentlessly bomb Berlin, Adolf Hitler, sequestered underground, marries Eva Braun (Kirstie Pooley), dictates his rambling last will and testament, and simultaneously takes poison and shoots himself. Narrator William Woodson remarks that the exact whereabouts of Hitler and Braun's remains, believed to have been burned, are unknown.

A highlight of the episode is a sequence in Los Alamos, New Mexico, where both Simon Anderson and "Hack" Peters are stationed to help develop the atomic bomb. An uncredited Nicholas Pryor portrays Dr. Robert Oppenheimer.

At the heart of the episode is the love story of Byron and Natalie, who reunite in Paris where Auschwitz survivor Natalie is recuperating in a convalescent home. Natalie is suffering physically and mentally after her unspeakable ordeals at Theresienstadt and Auschwitz—especially because she does not know the whereabouts of her son Louis. In the final half-hour of the episode, Byron searches France, Switzerland, Czechoslovakia, and England for Louis (Hunter Schlesinger). The miniseries ends as "happily" as it can after so much devastation and suffering. Episode #12 received a 15.9 rating and a 26 share. Each of the May 1989 episodes received a rating and share higher than those of the previous episode—a considerable victory.

In September 1989, *War and Remembrance* won another victory—on Emmy night. The miniseries was nominated for 15 Emmy Awards in various Outstanding-Miniseries categories: best miniseries, director (Dan Curtis), lead actor (John Gielgud), lead actress (Jane Seymour), supporting actress (Polly Bergen), cinematography, special visual effects, film editing, sound editing, film-sound mixing, art direction, music composition (Robert Cobert), costumes, makeup, and hairstyling. Gielgud lost to James Woods for *My Name is Bill W.*, Seymour lost to Holly Hunter for *Roe vs. Wade*, and Bergen lost to Colleen Dewhurst for *Those She Left Behind*.

The miniseries's most formidable competition was *Lonesome Dove* (CBS, February 5-6-7-8 of 1989), the highest-rated TV miniseries in four years and, like *War and Remembrance*, itself one of the finest programs in the history of American television. *Lonesome Dove* won seven Emmys, including awards for its director Simon Wincer and its composer Basil Poledouris, who at that time were both big names from the world of theatrical films. Wincer had directed *The Man from Snowy River* in 1982 and *Phar Lap* in 1983; Poledouris had scored *The Blue Lagoon* in 1980 and *Conan the Barbarian* in 1982. *Lonesome Dove* was considered to be the front-runner for Outstanding Miniseries, but in an upset equaling *Nicholas Nickleby*'s victory over *The Winds of War*, it was *War and Remembrance*, not *Lonesome Dove*, that was named the best miniseries of 1988-1989. In his acceptance speech, Dan Curtis admitted that the victory was "a major shock," and he thanked ABC "for having the guts to pony up the dough" to make *War and Remembrance*.[26] Ultimately, *War and Remembrance* won only three Emmys, for editing (Peter Zinner, John Burnett), special visual effects (William Schirmer et al.), and Outstanding Miniseries.

Zinner and Burnett won the Eddie Award from the American Cinema Editors, and cinematographer Dietrich Lohmann won the A.S.C. Award. The U.S. TV Fan Association gave *War and Remembrance* awards for best miniseries, best director (Curtis), and best music score (Cobert). BMI (Broadcast Music, Incorporated) awarded Robert Cobert a certificate for writing the longest film score in history. (Two months earlier, BMI had given Cobert a certificate marking the one-millionth radio performance of "Quentin's Theme" from *Dark Shadows*.) Curtis won the Distinguished Service Award from the Simon Wiesenthal Center, and he was nominated for the Directors Guild Award in both 1989 and 1990. Curtis won the prestigious DGA Award in 1990, and eight years later he won the Golden Laurel Award from the Producers Guild of America. Curtis had gone from filming PGA golfers at the beginning of his career to being honored by a very different PGA near the end of his career.

Dan Curtis directs a battalion of extras for a scene in *War and Remembrance* (ABC, 1988, 1989).

In May 1989, Curtis told the Associated Press, "I'm vastly relieved that I'm done with *War and Remembrance*, yet my heart is breaking. I'm so ambivalent I want to cry. I feel my mission is accomplished. I pray that the memory and impact of it will be there with us for a long time. I pray that it will make a difference."[27] He told the *Los Angeles Times*, "I feel so good about this show because I know we've accomplished something that won't be accomplished again."[28] Of course, films such as *Schindler's List* (1993), *Saving Private Ryan* (1998), and *Flags of Our Fathers* (2006) and TV miniseries such as *When Lions Roared* (1994), *Band of Brothers* (2001) and *Hitler: The Rise of Evil* (2003) have come along in the wake of *War and Remembrance*, but nothing has matched the epic, global scope of Curtis's work. Many other filmmakers have made movies about Roosevelt, Hitler, Pearl Harbor, Midway, assassination plots, wartime romances, D-Day, the Battle of the Bulge, Hiroshima, or the Holocaust, but Dan Curtis made an enormous movie about *all* of those subjects—and did justice to all of them, especially the Holocaust. As Robert Cobert bluntly put it, "We make *Schindler's List* look sick! Of course, they had only three hours, and we had 30 hours."[29]

Curtis himself stated the case more diplomatically, but just as firmly, in the Saturday 15 March 1997 edition of the *Los Angeles Times*. The director responded to a Wednesday 26 February article about the NBC telecast of *Schindler's List*. Curtis's letter to the editor stated,

> As the executive producer/director of the 30-hour ABC-TV miniseries *War and Remembrance*, I think it important to demur to some points made by Howard Rosenberg in his February 26 column "NBC Can't Just Rest on Laurels." When he writes that NBC's airing of *Schindler's List* intact "marks a maturation high for network television" and "never within memory has one of the major networks shown such nudity or depicted so much violence so graphically," I feel compelled to comment.
>
> The dehumanizing of victims, on arrival at their destination of doom, by forcing them to disrobe, was central to scenes in the miniseries. We received widespread commendation for those scenes, and ABC deserves much credit for taking a pioneering risk in first allowing me to film them and then broadcasting them without cutting a single frame.
>
> Rosenberg himself wrote on November 23, 1988, "Never before in an American TV drama has the Holocaust been so graphically, uncompromisingly, and profoundly depicted. Tonight's scenes of rotting corpses at Auschwitz and the Nazi massacre of Jews at Babi Yar in the Soviet Union are excruciatingly and revoltingly real. This is important, landmark TV—hard to take, but even harder to ignore." The Babi Yar sequence involving the slaughter of hordes of naked Jews, which was a terrible task to film, did however evoke a protest from Nobel Laureate Elie Wiesel, who thought it unendurably graphic—an opinion I respect, but to my best ability I depicted the historic truth, nothing more.
>
> *War and Remembrance*, which won the Emmy as best mini-series of 1988-1989, represents several years of my hardest work as a filmmaker. If I am proud of it, perhaps it is a pardonable pride. Certainly, no one is looking for bragging rights to graphic violence and nudity, but with regard to the memory of the horrors of the Holocaust, where we pioneered, I want the record to show it.
>
> Signed, DAN CURTIS [30]

War and Remembrance (ABC, 13, 15-17, 20, & 22-23 November 1988; 7-10 & 14 May 1989). Executive producer: Dan Curtis. Producer: Barbara Steele. Associate producer: Branko Lustig. Director: Dan Curtis. First assistant director: Branko Lustig. Teleplay: Herman Wouk (based on his novel), Earl Wallace, Dan Curtis. Music: Robert Cobert. Director of photography: Dietrich Lohmann. Production designer: Guy Comtois. Art directors: William Cruise, Norm Baron, Veronica Hadfield, Hertha Pischinger, Jean-Michel Hurgon, Francesco Chianese. Makeup: Wes Dawn, Jim Kail, Magdalen Gaffney, Janis Clark, Dino Ganziano. Costumers: John Perry, Bill Flores, Llandys Williams, Barbara Lane, James Balker, Robert Stewart, John Napolitano, Marty Burke, Karen Lawson, Karin Schmatz.

Cast: Robert Mitchum (Victor "Pug" Henry), Polly Bergen (Rhoda Henry), Hart Bochner (Byron Henry), Jane Seymour (Natalie Jastrow Henry), John Gielgud (Aaron Jastrow), Victoria Tennant (Pamela Tudsbury), David Dukes (Leslie Slote), Michael Woods (Warren Henry), Sharon Stone (Janice Henry), Leslie Hope (Madeline Henry), Peter Graves (Palmer Kirby), Jeremy Kemp (Armin Von Roon), Topol (Berel Jastrow), Ian McShane (Philip Rule), Ralph Bellamy (Franklin D. Roosevelt). 1349 minutes. Available on VHS and DVD.

Dan Curtis Significa: Past and future *Dark Shadows* actors who appear in *The Winds of War* (1983) include Stefan Gierasch, John Harkins, John Karlen, Charles Lane, Michael McGuire, and Barbara Steele. *Dark Shadows* and *Winds of War* composer Robert Cobert makes a cameo appearance in episode number three.

Past and future *Dark Shadows* actors who appear in *War and Remembrance* (1988, 1989) include Charles Lane, Michael McGuire, Dennis Patrick, Addison Powell, and Barbara Steele. Robert Cobert, of course, composes the music. Cobert turns 95 years old on 26 October 2019.

Dan Curtis Significa: In his foreword to Jim Pierson's book *Produced and Directed by Dan Curtis* (Pomegranate Press, 2004), Herman Wouk (1915-2019) writes of his experiences "as a writer of the teleplays" of *The Winds of War* and *War and Remembrance*. "Film is not my medium," Wouk confesses, "but, guided by Dan Curtis, I tried to do a workmanlike job, and he was always the man in charge, start to finish, on the script as well as in the colossal task of shooting the movies. Once, my New York literary editor aptly compared Dan Curtis to a battlefield general. Dan likes to call me 'the Professor,' I suppose, because of the way I insisted on the historical accuracy of the films. Well, the general and the professor emerged from the great task as lifelong friends. I salute Dan and congratulate him on this well-deserved tribute to his colorful career of making movies, from Gothic mysteries and bang-up Westerns to the Battle of Midway and the Holocaust."[31]

Chapter VI: *War and Remembrance* 231

Live and Let Die star Jane Seymour performs a scene in *War and Remembrance* (ABC, 1988, 1989).

Intruders (CBS, 1992): Between *Close Encounters of the Third Kind* and *Signs,* there is Dan Curtis's UFO "mystery with horror aspects."

CHAPTER VII

Intruders: They Are Among Us

In 1992, after 25 years of exploring supernatural mysteries on TV and film, Dan Curtis turned to another one of life's greatest mysteries—unidentified flying objects—and executive-produced and directed **Intruders: They Are Among Us**, a four-hour miniseries seen on CBS-TV on Sunday, May 17, and Tuesday, May 19. *Intruders* was Curtis's follow-up to his two massive *War* miniseries of the 1980s and his 1991 remake of *Dark Shadows*, the first four hours of which had run as a two-night miniseries. CBS proudly scheduled *Intruders* during the crucial May-sweeps ratings period opposite the NBC miniseries *Cruel Doubt*.

Intruders is based on a non-fiction book of the same name by the noted ufologist (UFO expert) Budd Hopkins, who studied more than 700 cases of alien abductions. In 1964, when he was 33 years old, Hopkins saw a UFO in broad daylight, and his lifelong interest in UFOs began. A dozen years later, he began writing about UFOs, and a dozen years after that, he was one of the world's leading experts in the field of ufology and especially alien abductions. Finally, Hopkins, who was also a painter and a sculptor, headed the Intruders Foundation, which documented cases of humans abducted by aliens. He died on 21 August 2011. In his 1987 Random House book *Intruders: The Incredible Visitations at Copley Woods*, Budd Hopkins wrote,

> No aspect of this [UFO] phenomenon is as controversial—or as dramatic—as a so-called "abduction report" of the type I shall deal with in this book. Over the years, hundreds of otherwise credible people have described being somehow immobilized in their cars or homes or wherever and then taken by UFO occupants into landed UFOs for what appears to be a kind of physical examination conducted while the abductee is stretched out upon a table. What seems to be externally imposed amnesia usually prevents the abductee from recalling the full scenario of his or her experience, which generally lasts an hour or two. (Hypnosis has been the most useful method that investigators have employed to aid the victim's recollection.) Now, we would willingly dismiss any *one* of these accounts, taken alone, as nothing more than an intrinsically unbelievable aberration. But as we shall see, the overall patterns in these cases are so remarkably consistent, often down to tiny details, and the people reporting these experiences are often so inherently credible, that the phenomenon simply cannot be dismissed. However one wishes to theorize about these accounts—that they represent some strange new mass-psychological delusion or that they represent descriptions of real, physical experiences—something important is going on, something which demands open-minded, scientific investigation.[1]

Five years later, Dan Curtis co-executive-produced the film version of *Intruders* along with Robert O'Connor (*Frank Nitti: The Enforcer, Jack the Ripper*) and Michael

Apted (*21 Up, Coal Miner's Daughter*). His writers were *Medical Center* scribe Barry Oringer, who had written for *The Invaders* (1967-1968) and *Planet of the Apes* (1974), and future *Sliders* writer Tracy Torme, who had investigated several abduction cases alongside Budd Hopkins and who had written for *Star Trek: The Next Generation* (1987-1994). Both Oringer and Torme were well suited for this alien fare, which Curtis directed with earnestness and restraint, docudrama-style, but with numerous scary jolts, accentuated by Robert Cobert's staccato brass and eerie synthesizer effects, similar to his music for the 1991 *Dark Shadows* series.

Intruders (1992): The title characters go about their otherworldly work in this atmospheric shot from Dan Curtis's UFO miniseries.

Psychiatrist Dr. Neil Chase (Richard Crenna) suddenly finds himself treating two new patients, Lesley Hahn (Daphne Ashbrook) in California and Mary Wilkes (Mare Winningham) in Nebraska, and noticing startling similarities in their hazy, traumatic memories of abduction and invasive examination by "little gray men" with "burning, black eyes." The fact that these phrases can be spoken by the actors in utter seriousness and without camp or unintentional humor is a testament to the verisimilitude that director Curtis brings to *Intruders*. The *Pennsylvania Patriot-News* noted that the production is "nicely, if sedately, acted" and is "an attempt to bring respectability to the kind of tale usually reserved for the tabloids."[2] Because the acting *is* so low-key, Curtis avoids turning *Intruders* into an overwrought melodrama or a typical invasion-from-outer-space thriller. It comes across just as rational and clinical as Dr. Chase himself, who goes from skepticism to belief as he works with Lesley and Mary.

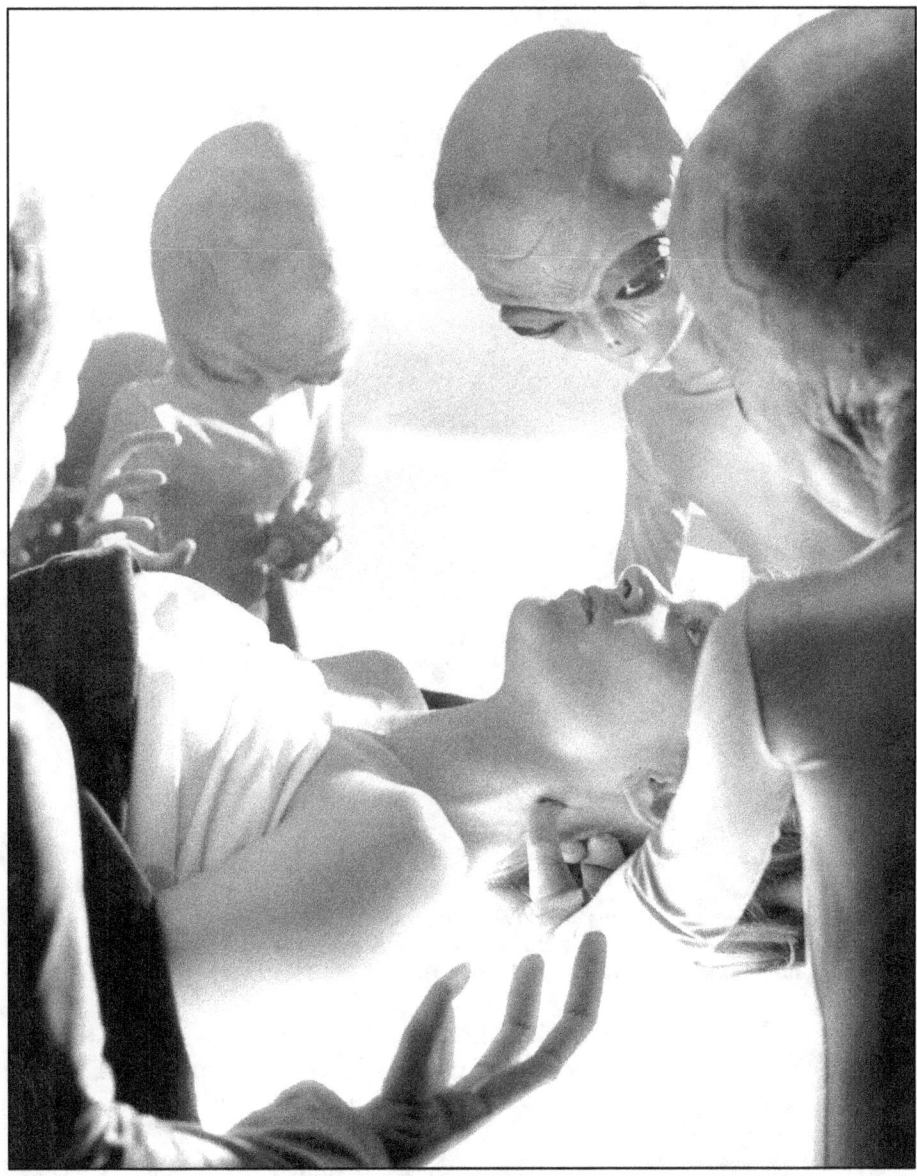

Intruders (1992): The aliens examine Daphne Ashbrook (as Lesley Hahn). In 2006, Ashbrook is a voice artist in Big Finish Productions' *Dark Shadows* CD audio drama *The Book of Temptation,* co-starring John Karlen and Kathryn Leigh Scott.

In *Intruders: They Are Among Us* (1992), alien beings affect the lives of the characters played by Mare Winningham (left, as Mary Wilkes), Joseph Cousins (as Timmy Wilkes), and Susan Blakely (as Leigh Holland).

As the stories of Lesley Hahn and her boyfriend Ray Brooks (Jason Beghe) and Mary Wilkes and her husband Joe (Alan Autry), son Timmy (Christopher and Joseph Cousins), and sister Leigh Holland (Susan Blakely) unfold, a third case study seems to corroborate the women's stories. Dr. Chase interviews mental patient Gene Randall (Ben Vereen), a former Air Force officer who is haunted by an experience in New Mexico in 1973. In a stunning flashback sequence that is one of the highlights of *Intruders*, Randall witnesses the crash of a UFO and has very brief contact with the dying alien crew members before he is whisked away, pressured into signing a statement saying that he was "on something" hallucinogenic, and relegated to a mental hospital. Ben Vereen's powerful performance earned him an Emmy Award nomination for Best Supporting Actor in a Miniseries.

Chapter VII: *Intruders: They Are Among Us* 237

Intruders (1992): Ben Vereen, as mental patient Gene Randall, is nominated for an Emmy Award for Best Supporting Actor in a Miniseries.

As Neil Chase immerses himself in the cases of Lesley and Mary—and falls in love with Mary's sister Leigh—he comes to realize that this is no "terrestrial mystery" as he first believed but an ongoing cosmic event of immense importance. Through regressive hypnosis of the women, Chase learns that they have been visited many times by the intruders, and their lives (especially Mary's and her whole family's) are strongly intertwined with those of the visitors. When one of the women mysteriously becomes pregnant and then is robbed of her fetus, Dr. Chase realizes the extent to which the intruders are involved with the women of Earth.

Torme and Oringer's script does an excellent job of expressing the disparate views of science, religion, business, and government toward the idea of alien abductions. While, in another script, the psychiatrist (Crenna), the priest (John Snyder), the hospital administrator (Robert Mandan), and the Army general (G.D. Spradlin) would be mere stock characters, this script fleshes them out and gives them thought-provoking points to make. Spradlin is especially good—as are Crenna, Vereen, and Winningham—and Steven Berkoff of *War and Remembrance* has a couple of memorable scenes as a persuasive ufologist. The characters are so rich that a four-hour miniseries is not quite enough to give all of them ample screen time. *Intruders* could have succeeded as a five- or six-hour production.

In addition to Gene Randall's "origin story" and the women's hypnosis scenes, a highlight of *Intruders* is Dr. Neil Chase's and other characters' attendance at a meeting of ufologist Addison Leach's support group for women and men who have been abducted. Here again, a lesser script and a lesser director would have made such a scenario laughable, but *Intruders* approaches the subject matter with complete seriousness and compassion. A group member's lament, "They took *my* baby, too," is heartbreaking. Dr. Chase's feelings about alien abductions change so drastically that he commits "professional suicide" by speaking out about the phenomenon at a meeting of the State Psychiatric Association.

Richard Crenna's own attitudes underwent a change as he portrayed Dr. Neil Chase. In a May 1992 interview, Crenna spoke about his own "healthy curiosity and interest" in UFOs. He said,

> People who are very skeptical are not going to change their minds as a result of this film—and that's not the intention. But it does pose enough questions that if you're an inquisitive person at all, you're going to be tempted to probe beyond what you hear on this show. [. . .] I think it's rather presumptuous on our part to assume, in this galaxy of millions and millions of stars and planets, and in the extended universe of millions and millions of galaxies, that we are the only living beings of any sort. [. . .] I'm not absolutely convinced at this point except that I'm very open-minded to the whole idea of extraterrestrial beings. [. . .] The purpose of the movie is pure entertainment, but I think in the course of that entertainment, people are going to be turned on to these various possibilities.[3]

Mare Winningham was much more emphatic when she told *TV Host* magazine that, after playing the traumatized Nebraska housewife Mary Wilkes, "it's impossible for me *not* to believe!"[4] Her personal dedication contributed to her (in the words of *TV Guide*) "winning performance"[5] which should have been nominated for an Emmy Award alongside Ben Vereen's.

Mare Winningham is surrounded by the alien beings of *Intruders: They Are Among Us* (CBS, 1992). The miniseries is nominated for Emmy, Saturn, and American Society of Cinematographers awards.

Once again, a Dan Curtis production generated positive reviews. *TV Guide* complimented all of the "stellar talent" in *Intruders*,[6] and *People* magazine called the miniseries "well acted [with a] strong supporting cast" and "absorbing whether you regard UFO stories as hogwash or gospel."[7] The *Washington Post* insisted, "It won't matter if you believe or not. You'll still be wowed."[8]

Variety declared, "Scaremaster Dan Curtis applies his directorial skills to a two-part sci-fi adventure, and the first two hours are whizbang stuff ending with a surefire cliffhanger"[9] (an alien visitation to the Wilkeses' home). *Tune in Tonight* added, "*Intruders* is a likely favorite with viewers because of its tabloid-style subject matter—abduction by alien beings—and its classy treatment by a producer-director with a known talent for creating credible drama from essentially unbelievable material. [. . .] The [alien] beings are even better than those in the now-classic *Close Encounters of the Third Kind*" [1977]. The special effects are remarkable, and the story may even convince a few skeptics."[10]

Of course, one of the greatest assets of *Intruders* is its weird, unnerving alien creatures, the "little gray men" who exude both menace and a strange comfort. Even more striking are the half-human, half-alien beings that are the product of extraterrestrial impregnation of earth women. The special effects (Robert Short), visual effects (Mitch Suskin), makeup (Jim Kail), and otherworldly costuming (Deborah Lancaster) in *Intruders* are equal to the science-fiction feature films of the day. *USA Today* called this "mystery with horror aspects" (*Intruders*) "a cross of *Close Encounters, Rosemary's Baby, Mars Needs Women,* and any number of government-conspiracy flicks."[11]

Just as Dan Curtis's horror productions were in tune with their times (e.g. *The Norliss Tapes, Dead of Night*), or ahead of their time (e.g. *The Night Stalker, The Night Strangler*), the Saturn Award-nominated *Intruders* was at the forefront of the wave of the public's 1990s/2000s fascination with aliens. *Intruders* appeared ten years before M. Night Shyamalan's film *Signs,* six years before Melinda Metz's *Roswell High* novel series, five years before Barry Sonnenfeld's film *Men in Black,* three years before Paul Shapiro's *Invaders* TV miniseries with Roy Thinnes and Scott Bakula, and one year before Fox TV's smash-hit series *The X-Files* (1993-2002), which creator Chris Carter has often said was inspired by *The Night Stalker* (1972) and *The Night Strangler* (1973).[12] Just as the *Boston Globe* called *Night of Dark Shadows* (1971) "a horror film for people who don't really like horror films,"[13] *Intruders* is a movie for people who don't necessarily like movies about UFOs, aliens, and science fiction. At its heart, it is a human drama (like *Shadow of Fear* and *The Invasion of Carol Enders*) and a family drama (like *Burnt Offerings* and *Curse of the Black Widow*) about people caught up in a horrifying, fantastical mystery. Those who *do* love sci-fi and UFO dramas will scarcely find a better one than the understated, disturbing, and thought-provoking *Intruders*.

Intruders: They Are Among Us (CBS, 17 & 19 May 1992; rerun 30-31 May 1995). Executive producers: Dan Curtis, Michael Apted, Robert O'Connor. Producer: Branko Lustig. Director: Dan Curtis. First assistant director: Branko Lustig. Teleplay: Barry Oringer, Tracy Torme (based on the book by Budd Hopkins, co-producer). Music: Robert Cobert. Director of photography: Tom Priestley. Art director: Bryan Ryman. Makeup: Jim Kail, Jeff Dawn. Costumers: Deborah Lancaster, Joseph Williams, Sybil Gray.

Cast: Richard Crenna (Dr. Neil Chase), Mare Winningham (Mary Wilkes), Susan Blakely (Leigh Holland), Alan Autry (Joe Wilkes), Christopher & Joseph Cousins (Timmy Wilkes), Daphne Ashbrook (Lesley Hahn), Jason Beghe (Ray Brooks), Ben Vereen (Gene Randall), G.D. Spradlin (General Hanley), Robert Mandan (Dr. Stanley Epstein), Steven Berkoff (Addison Leach), Warren Frost (Dr. Holtan), John Rubinow (Dr. Lustig), John Snyder (Fr. Kenmar), Romy Rosemont (Lara Chase), Mills Watson (Sheriff Ken Pears). 162 minutes. Available on VHS and DVD.

Dan Curtis Significa: When Mary and Joe Wilkes dine out in a restaurant, the background music is a new solo-piano arrangement of Robert Cobert's "Quentin's Theme." In Gene Randall's 1973 flashback sequence, Randall watches *The Carol Burnett Show* on a portable television set.

Several people in the alien-abduction support group are named after Dan Curtis Productions personnel, including producer Daniel Blatt, production assistant Margaret Hussey, and Curtis's long-time executive assistant Ruth Kennedy. In another scene, "Dr. Lustig" is named after Branko Lustig, who was the associate producer and assistant director of *War and Remembrance* (1988, 1989), the producer and assistant director of *Intruders* (1992), and one of the seven producers of Steven Spielberg's *Schindler's List* (1993).[14]

Dan Curtis Significa: In *Intruders*, the exterior and interior of the scene taking place at General Hanley's house was filmed at Greystone mansion in Beverly Hills. The 55-room Tudor Revival mansion on 18 acres of land was built in 1928 by the oil millionaire Edward Doheny, who earlier in the 1920s had played a role in the Teapot Dome scandal. Doheny gave the mansion to his son Ned and daughter-in-law Lucy. Ned was murdered in the house in 1929; Lucy lived there until 1955. The city of Beverly Hills assumed ownership of Greystone in 1965, and since 1971 it has opened the grounds (but not the house) as a public park.

Since 1963, Greystone has been seen in countless movies and TV shows, including *Alias, All of Me, Arrow, Bare Essence, Batman and Robin, The Big Lebowski, The Bodyguard, The Bold and the Beautiful, Dark Mansions, The Day Mars Invaded Earth, Dead Ringer, The Disorderly Orderly, The Flash, General Hospital, Gilmore Girls, Hart to Hart, The Immortal, The Loved One, Mannix, The Mentalist, Mission: Impossible, Murder She Wrote, NCIS, The Phantom, Picture Mommy Dead, The Prestige, Revenge, The Social Network, Spider-Man, There Will Be Blood, The Trouble with Angels, War and Remembrance, The Winds of War,* and *The Young and the Restless*. Dan Curtis also used Greystone as Collinwood both in the 1991 *Dark Shadows* series and in the never-aired 2004 *Dark Shadows* pilot for the WB television network.[15]

Dark Shadows (1991): Joanna Going plays the governess Victoria Winters.

CONCLUSION

Dan Curtis and Television Horror and Drama

It was inevitable that some of the young people who grew up watching *Dark Shadows, The Night Stalker,* and *Trilogy of Terror* (or later *The Winds of War, War and Remembrance,* and *Dark Shadows* '91) would remember the work of Dan Curtis when they too became writers, producers, and directors. Throughout the 1990s, Chris Carter, creator of *The X-Files* (1993-2002) acknowledged in interviews that *The Night Stalker* had inspired him to create his landmark paranormal drama series.[1] Critic Mark Dawidziak heard Carter say so as early as July 1993, two months before *The X-Files* premiered.[2] Later, in 1997, Carter told *Emmy* magazine that when he was young, he "loved" *The Night Stalker* and its follow-ups, so when he grew up, he "knew what I wanted to do. That was it. I wanted to scare people!"[3] Carter's creation began scaring viewers again on 24 January 2016 when *The X-Files* returned to television. In the February 1 episode, Rhys Darby (*Flight of the Conchords*) played "Guy Mann," a Carl Kolchak lookalike. The original series had cast Darren McGavin himself as "Arthur Dales" and Raymond J. Barry (*The Oldest Rookie*) as "Senator Richard Matheson."

Mad Men (2007-2015) creator Matthew Weiner and his writers obviously were *Dark Shadows* fans because in two fifth-season (2012) episodes, soap-opera actress "Megan Draper" (Jessica Pare) name-checked "Burke Devlin" and "Collinsport" and then called *Dark Shadows* by name.[4] David Selby (*Dark Shadows, Falcon Crest*) appeared in one 2009 episode, and Joanna Going (*Dark Shadows, House of Cards*) appeared in two *Mad Men* episodes in 2013.

Characters in *Frankenstein and Me* (1996), *Running with Scissors* (2006), and *Outlander* (on Starz since 2014) watch *Dark Shadows* on television, and the TV show's 1970 Parallel Time storyline is discussed in Thomas Pynchon's 2009 novel *Inherent Vice,* which takes place in 1970. In the third episode (21 June 2018) of the Paramount Network's *American Woman,* Alicia Silverstone's character calls an odd, black-clad twosome "a couple from *Dark Shadows.*" The October-November 2018 episodes of the Independent Film Channel's *Stan Against Evil* feature characters who look suspiciously like the Leviathan Oberon from *Dark Shadows,* the vampiress Carolyn Stoddard from *House of Dark Shadows,* and the reporter Carl Kolchak from *The Night Stalker. Stan Against Evil* creator/writer/actor Dana Gould (*The Simpsons*) is an admitted Dan Curtis fan. In July-August 2019, eagle-eyed viewers of Quentin Tarantino's *Once Upon a Time…in Hollywood,* which takes place in 1969, may have spied a Hollywood Boulevard bench with an advertisement for *Dark Shadows* painted on it.

Harry Benshoff's *TV Milestone Series* book *Dark Shadows* (Wayne State UP, 2011) calls the 1966-1971 series a "cult media text" (because of its vampires and its staying power) and a pioneer of "televisuality" (the excessive style of color, fashion, lighting, and camerawork that characterized late-1960s/early-1970s television and afterwards).[5]

On Halloween of 2012, *A.V. Club* columnist Farihah Zaiman wrote,

> *Dark Shadows* has direct descendants in daytime TV, like the charmingly batty *Passions* or even *Days of Our Lives*, which featured a storyline in which a prominent character was possessed by the devil. But the series's influence goes far beyond the purview of *Soap Opera Digest*. *Dark Shadows* helped solidify, if not invent, many of the ways in which TV viewers conceive of the supernatural—including the vampire tortured by conscience or love that lasts beyond the grave—and it paved the way for the confluence of science fiction/fantasy and drama. (These ideas weren't invented by *Dark Shadows*, but the series was the first to bring them to television in a serious fashion.) *Being Human*, *The Vampire Diaries*, *Twin Peaks*, *Buffy the Vampire Slayer*, *Angel*, and dozens of other shows owe much to *Dark Shadows*. All employ a supernatural concept on which to hang more universal explorations of love, loyalty, family, and—perhaps more effectively than in programs grounded entirely in reality—death.[6]

On Valentine's Day of 2014, *A.V. Club* writer Phil Dyess-Nugent made a similar case for the influential effect that *The Night Stalker*, *The Night Strangler*, and Cy Chermak's *Kolchak: The Night Stalker* have had on *American Horror Story*, *Buffy the Vampire Slayer*, *Grimm*, *Hannibal*, *Sleepy Hollow*, *Supernatural*, *Teen Wolf*, *True Blood*, *Twin Peaks*, *The Vampire Diaries*, *The Walking Dead*, and *The X-Files*.[7] *Dark Shadows*, *The Night Stalker*, and other productions of Dan Curtis have made a lasting impression upon popular culture—especially in the era of *Twilight*, *The Vampire Diaries*, *The Lair*, and *True Blood*. The emotional, reluctant vampires of the 21st century are nothing new.

Just as Dan Curtis wrote a 1997 letter to the *Los Angeles Times* reminding the public of his trail-blazing *War and Remembrance*, Jim Pierson of Dan Curtis Productions wrote the following letter, which was published in the *L.A. Times* on Sunday 14 June 2009:

> I read your article on the hit HBO series *True Blood* with a slight sense of not-quite-supernatural *déjà vu*. The attraction of that program's blend of Gothic romance with vampires in a serialized format that commands a large and loyal audience—particularly female—is nothing new. It all happened before—back in the 1960s when the late television producer-director Dan Curtis created the spooky ABC-TV daytime drama *Dark Shadows*, a pop-culture phenomenon that remains undead decades later on DVD and in an upcomingfeature-film revival starring Johnny Depp.
>
> Signed, JIM PIERSON [8]

The vampire Barnabas Collins of *Dark Shadows* has been played on screen by Jonathan Frid (pictured), Ben Cross, Alec Newman, and Johnny Depp.

In addition to his influencing subsequent productions such as *The X-Files, Moonlight, True Blood,* and *Sleepy Hollow,* one of Dan Curtis's most impressive feats is that *Dark Shadows* and his adaptations of *Frankenstein, The Strange Case of Dr. Jekyll and Mr. Hyde, The Picture of Dorian Gray, Dracula,* and *The Turn of the Screw* served as a bridge from classic film horror to modern film horror in the United States (just as the films of the Hammer Studio were doing in England). Dan Curtis was producing *Dark Shadows,* the two *Dark Shadows* movies, *Dead of Night: A Darkness at Blaisedon,* the five adaptations of the classics, the two *Night Stalker* movies, *The Norliss Tapes,* the seven *Wide World Mystery* episodes, and *Trilogy of Terror* at a time (1966-1975) when cinematic horror was becoming more brutally terrifying and realistic. As movie horror was evolving from *The Reptile, The Witches,* and *Island of Terror* (all 1966) to *The Stepford Wives, Shivers,* and *Jaws* (all 1975), Curtis was mixing elements from two different horror styles—haunted-house settings, classic monsters, and less-is-more suggestion of horror, blended with urban settings, increased bloodletting, and an innovative mixture of horror, humor, and *film noir.* Curtis characterized *The Night Stalker* as "a great story—so traditional yet so modern—and it had a sense of humor!"[9]

Curtis's work reflected the worlds of both classic horror (e.g. *Dark Shadows, The Picture of Dorian Gray, Dracula, The Turn of the Screw*) and modern horror (e.g. *House of Dark Shadows, The Night Strangler, The Norliss Tapes, Trilogy of Terror*). *Curse of the Black Widow,* the finale to Curtis's 1966-1977 horror cycle, was an extremely effective amalgam of classic and modern horror. The 1991 *Dark Shadows* and the 1996 *Trilogy of Terror II* were even more skillful modernizations of classic themes. Author David Deal remembered Curtis as "one of the most influential names in television horror."[10]

Chapter one of this book detailed Dan Curtis's funeral and memorial service. On Sunday 27 August 2006, Curtis's work and memory were honored (briefly) on NBC. During the 58th Prime-Time Emmy Awards telecast, Dan Curtis was included in the "In Memoriam" segment along with Darren McGavin (seen as Kolchak in a clip), Gloria Monty, Anthony Franciosa, Maureen Stapleton, Don Knotts, and other television luminaries who had died in 2005-2006. Curtis was seen directing Ali MacGraw as the logos of *Dark Shadows* and *The Winds of War* flashed across the screen.

No few seconds or few hours can sum up the impact on television and popular culture that Dan Curtis wielded in the 1960s with *Dark Shadows* and *The Strange Case of Dr. Jekyll and Mr. Hyde,* in the 1970s with his numerous horror classics and his one Western, in the 1980s with his unsurpassed World War II epics, or in the 1990s with *Dark Shadows* and *Intruders.* In the 2000s, as his output was slowing down, he finally was gaining a richly deserved reputation as an elder statesman of television horror and drama. At the end of his career, *Our Fathers,* one of his finest dramas, became his swan song before his rapid decline and death, just 20 days after the passing of his beloved wife Norma.

Joseph Stern, the future *Law & Order* and *Judging Amy* executive producer who worked with Dan Curtis in the late 1970s and early 1980s, remembered Curtis as "a real original" with "a big heart." According to Stern, "Dan always said, 'Basically, I work alone,'" but at the same time, Curtis valued his "stock company" of actors whom he hired again and again. "He and I became very close friends near the end of his life," Joe Stern revealed to me in a 1 August 2018 telephone conversation.[11] In the early

2000s, Curtis's daughter Tracy worked as the film editor on 32 of Stern's *Judging Amy* episodes.

William F. Nolan, who wrote 15 scripts for Curtis, including the two Melvin Purvis films and *The Turn of the Screw*, observed, "Horror does not work until you have the mood and the atmosphere to go with it. The material is one thing, but it's how you treat the material, and Dan has always done that very well. *The Norliss Tapes* was great—he kept it raining all through the movie."[12] Nolan continued,

> I've been on hand for several location shoots with Dan relating to my scripts. The one I remember best was in Sacramento for *Melvin Purvis, G-Man*, for the big shoot-out scene at the roadhouse. Dan knew I was itching to fire a Thompson submachine gun. "Okay, give Nolan a Tommy," he told the prop man. "He can die on the roof with the rest of the gang." So I happily fired my Thompson down at Purvis and his G-men and fell dead at the proper moment.
>
> Finally, when I thought the scene was over, [and I was] peering toward the camera, Dan, still shooting, yelled, "Nolan, for Christ's sake, get out of the shot! You're supposed to be dead!" [. . .] That's what made Dan so much fun to work with—his sense of humor. He can be stern and tough, but most people don't realize just how much Dan loves to laugh. We shared a lot of laughs together.[13]

In a 17 January 2010 letter to me, Bill Nolan wrote, "What a dynamic man he was! What energy! [. . .] We were good pals. I recall the last time I saw him at his office; he threw an arm around my shoulder and said to a production man who was there: 'Nolan and I have been through a helluva lot together.' He said it with genuine affection. I was touched."[14]

On 12 August 2015, what would have been Curtis's 88th birthday, Nolan wrote on Facebook, "In all, I have had some 20 TV or film projects produced, but *Burnt Offerings* remains at the top of the list. It holds up. I am proud of the screenplay. [. . .] At 87, I ain't slowing down! With much ahead. And *Logan* still runs!"

On the same day, filmmaker Ansel H. Faraj wrote on Facebook, "Happy birthday to a man who taught me so much, without my ever meeting him—Dan Curtis." Faraj is an *auteur* writer-producer-director who often casts *Dark Shadows* stars in his atmospheric thrillers, such as *Doctor Mabuse* (2013), *Doctor Mabuse: Etiopomar* (2014), *The Last Case of August T. Harrison* (2015), *The Job Interview* (2016), *The Night-Time Winds* (2017), *Will & Liz* (2018), and *Loon Lake* (2019).

Those selfsame *Dark Shadows* stars remembered Dan Curtis on the tenth anniversary of his death and the 50th anniversary of their show when they gathered in Tarrytown, New York, for the Dark Shadows Festival on June 24-25-26 of 2016. Curtis's *Dark Shadows* TV shows and movies, his *Night Stalker* movies, and all of his productions continue to fascinate long-time devotees and create new generations of fans. In one of his final interviews, Curtis again said,

> I'll probably be remembered for *Dark Shadows* instead of the things that I really cared about, which were the great epics that I made. *Dark Shadows* will be the thing that'll be on my gravestone—but *I love Dark Shadows*. I

guess it's terrific to have somehow created something that will live forever. It *will* live forever.[15]

Burnt Offerings collaborators and friends William F. Nolan (left) and Dan Curtis smile for the camera at the Museum of Television and Radio in Los Angeles on 22 April 2004. In *Master of Dark Shadows* (2019), Nolan calls Curtis "creative" and "dedicated."

Afterword
Ansel Faraj

I never got to meet Dan Curtis, but his influence on me was a singular one. From the time I first watched *House of Dark Shadows* on a VHS tape rented from Hollywood Video, I was drawn in by the heavy atmosphere, the camera constantly on the prowl – sometimes a shaky, hand-held camera – most of the shots aimed low, looking up at the actors. I was scared and captivated. Carolyn got staked, and I couldn't handle the experience any more, so I stopped the tape myself. I was six years old and overwhelmed by the frenetic energy Dan created with his camera and quick editing, and Bob Cobert's music blasting away in the background. I never saw the ending (and what a shocker of an ending it was) 'til I think a year-and-a-half later – the film so bothered me that I would rewatch only the first 38 minutes or so, then stop, too unnerved to continue, and rewind to the beginning to eventually watch again. I couldn't get enough.

As I grew older and became much more immersed in the *Dark Shadows* universe, I became much more familiar with Dan's work. *Burnt Offerings*, *The Night Strangler*, and his TV adaptation of *The Turn of the Screw* quickly became favorites. *Night of Dark Shadows* became an obsession of mine, particularly the deleted footage. In 2005, when I was 14, I "remade" NODS, deleted scenes and all, as *The Taking of Samantha Brennan* and used Greystone Mansion, 1991's Collinwood, as "the haunted house." And as I kept rewatching this body of work, and hearing Bob Cobert's familiar cues, I began to take notice of the similarities of style in camera work, art direction, and palpable sense of atmosphere – and I began to try to emulate it, to see if I could recapture that same feeling and tone that Dan created each time for me as a viewer. He said he never storyboarded (except on the battle scenes in *War and Remembrance*), that he liked to have actors "play the scene" and work out his shots from their staging, to see what the actors would come up with and then adjust the actor and the shot accordingly, which was a trait I picked up. I learned how to write screenplays from *The Dark Shadows Movie Book*, which reproduced Dan's original scripts for *House of Dark Shadows* and *Night of Dark Shadows*, and I learned how to work out and block shots from Dan's scribbled notes in the margins.

Along the way, I grew (and am still growing) as a filmmaker, and I began to develop my own sense of style. I've been influenced by a cruise ship full of other directors and filmmakers – but when I made *Doctor Mabuse* (2013) with Jerry Lacy, Kathryn Leigh Scott, and Lara Parker – I was setting up a shot of Lara as Madame Carrozza, and as she was watching me, she remarked, "You're shooting up our noses like Dan." I hadn't even thought of that; I was simply setting up a shot which came so natural to me.

A year ago, I rewatched my DVD of *Burnt Offerings* with the commentary by Dan and the late great Karen Black and William F. Nolan playing, and Dan said something to the effect of "I like low angles and seeing the ceilings of the room; it's more involving; you're looking up at it; you feel involved; I was always known as Mr. Low Angle."

I laughed.

Rondo Award-nominated *auteur* filmmaker **Ansel H. Faraj** has been making movies since he was six years old. He is the writer-producer-director of *The Rising Light* (2013), *Whatever Happened to Detective Adam Sera?* (2015), *The Night-Time Winds* (2017), and *Todd Tarantula* (2019). His 2012 film *Brother Drop Dead* won an award for comedic writing at the Buffalo Niagara Film Festival. Ansel Faraj lives in Los Angeles, and his official Internet website is **www.hollinsworthproductions.com**.

Dan Curtis (right) converses with cinematographer Jacques Marquette during the filming of *Melvin Purvis, G-Man* (1974). Marquette later works on Curtis's *Burnt Offerings* (1976).

Chapter Notes

Introduction: Dan Curtis as *Auteur* and Influence

1. qtd. in Pierson, *Produced* 206
2. Benshoff 8, 99
3. Melton, *Vampire Book,* 1st ed., 150
4. King 223
5. MacKenzie 15
6. "Sunday" A-45
7. qtd. in Robin, 61:15
8. qtd. in Thompson, *Television Horrors* 2, 52

Chapter I. The Career of Dan Curtis: An Overview

1. Thompson, *Television Horrors* 19; Thompson, *House of Dan Curtis* 14
2. qtd. in *Stalker Interview*
3. Ibid.
4. Graham, e-mail 26 April 2010
5. qtd. in *Behind*
6. Ibid.
7. qtd. in *A Novel*
8. Thompson, *Television Horrors* 56-57
9. qtd. in *Collection* 11
10. Scott and Pierson, *Almanac,* Millennium ed., 104
11. qtd. in *Collection* 11
12. Scott and Pierson, *Almanac,* Millennium ed., 104
13. qtd. in *Inside*
14. Ibid.
15. qtd. in *Behind*
16. qtd. in Pierson, *Produced* 205
17. qtd. in Pierson, *Produced* 14
18. qtd. in Pierson, *Produced* 205
19. qtd. in Stewart 11
20. qtd. in *Behind*
21. Jenkins 137
22. qtd. in "Director/Co-Producer" 11
23. Ibid.
24. qtd. in Pierson, *Produced* 21
25. Showalter 197
26. Stevenson 79
27. Stevenson 77
28. Stevenson 55
29. qtd. in Pierson, *Produced* 16
30. qtd. in Pierson, *Produced* 43
31. qtd. in Pierson, *Produced* 44
32. Ibid.
33. qtd. in Burlingame
34. qtd. in Pierson, *Produced* 11
35. O'Neil 124-128
36. Scott, letter
37. Burlingame
38. Pierson, e-mail 20 June 2009
39. Scott and Pierson, *Movie Book* 19
40. qtd. in Scott and Pierson, *Movie Book* 20
41. qtd. in *Inside*
42. qtd. in Scott and Pierson, *Movie Book* 22
43. qtd. in Pierson, *Produced* 52
44. Glut 305
45. Thompson, *Television Horrors* 6
46. qtd. in *Collection* 16
47. Ibid.
48. Benshoff 96
49. qtd. in Pierson, *Produced* 57
50. Lucas, "*House of Dark Shadows* and *Night of Dark Shadows*" 67
51. qtd. in Scott and Pierson, *Movie Book* 26
52. Weiler
53. qtd. in Pierson, *Produced* 57
54. Ibid.
55. Ebert, "*Night*"
56. Scott and Pierson, *Almanac,* Millennium ed., 162
57. qtd. in Thompson, *Television Horrors* 86
58. King 224
59. qtd. in Robin, 81:11
60. Ibid.
61. qtd. in Dawidziak, *Stalker* 21
62. qtd. in Burlingame
63. qtd. in Dawidziak, *Stalker* 63
64. Pierson, e-mail 7 May 2009

65 qtd. in Burlingame
66 qtd. in Pierson, *Produced* 66
67 Ibid.
68 Ibid.
69 qtd. in Dawidziak, *Stalker* 83
70 qtd. in Pierson, *Produced* 19
71 qtd. in Pierson, *Produced* 69
72 Ibid.
73 Florescu 198
74 qtd. in McCarty, "Nolan Looks"
75 Knowles
76 qtd. in Pierson, *Produced* 73
77 Ibid.
78 Ibid.
79 qtd. in Pierson, *Produced* 208
80 qtd. in McCarty, "Curtis Continues"
81 Nolan, personal interview 28 Feb. 2010
82 qtd. in Pierson, *Produced* 75
83 qtd. in Shinnick 51
84 qtd. in Shinnick 50
85 qtd. in Pierson, *Produced* 75
86 Deal 48
87 qtd. in Burlingame
88 Thompson, *Television Horrors* 112
89 qtd. in *Collection* 8
90 qtd. in McCarty, "Nolan Looks"
91 qtd. in *Macabre*
92 Ibid.
93 qtd. in McCarty, "Nolan Looks"
94 qtd. in *Macabre*
95 qtd. in Pierson, *Produced* 99
96 Ibid.
97 Thompson, *House of Dan Curtis* 127
98 Ibid.
99 Thompson, *House of Dan Curtis* 134-135
100 qtd. in *Stalker Interview*
101 qtd. in Pierson, *Produced* 107
102 Ibid.
103 Thompson, *House of Dan Curtis* 136
104 qtd. in Pierson, *Produced* 205
105 qtd. in Bosco
106 Ibid.
107 qtd. in Pierson, *Produced* 22-23
108 qtd. in Burlingame
109 qtd. in *Trilogy* DVD commentary
110 qtd. in *Three Colors Black*
111 qtd. in Pierson, *Produced* 109
112 qtd. in Pierson, Produced 114
113 Thompson, *Television Horrors* 154
114 Thompson, *House of Dan Curtis* 42
115 Thompson, "Burnt"
116 qtd. in *Burnt* DVD commentary
117 Marasco 55
118 Marasco 226, 190, 214
119 "Not So Very" 6-D
120 qtd. in Pierson, *Produced* 120
121 Ibid.
122 "Outstanding Terror"
123 qtd. in Pierson, *Produced* 120
124 qtd. in *Burnt* DVD commentary
125 Ibid.
126 "Outstanding Terror"
127 qtd. in Pierson, *Produced* 120
128 Ibid.
129 qtd. in McCarty, "Nolan Looks"
130 LaVoo 7
131 qtd. in LaVoo 10
132 qtd. in *Burnt* DVD commentary
133 qtd. in *Trilogy* DVD commentary
134 qtd. in Thompson, *Television Horrors* 6
135 qtd. in Pierson, *Produced* 126
136 Deal 27
137 qtd. in Pierson, *Produced* 24
138 qtd. in Pierson, *Produced* 132
139 Ibid.
140 Pierson, *Produced* 24
141 Pierson, *Produced* 131
142 Pierson, e-mail 22 Oct. 2007
143 qtd. in Pierson, *Produced* 25
144 Pierson, e-mail 22 Oct. 2007
145 qtd. in Robin, 107:22
146 qtd. in Pierson, *Produced* 145-146
147 qtd. in Pierson, *Produced* 146
148 Thompson, *House of Dan Curtis* 54
149 O'Neil 275
150 Pierson, e-mail 23 August 2009
151 qtd. in Pierson, *Produced* 151
152 Thompson, *Television Horrors* 89
153 Durbani 34
154 qtd. in Robin, 54/55: 15
155 Benshoff 99
156 Muir, *Terror Television* 296
157 qtd. in Pierson, *Produced* 180
158 Ibid.
159 Ibid.
160 Ibid.
161 Pierson, *Resurrected* 9
162 Pierson, e-mail 7 May 2009
163 qtd. in "Director/Co-Producer" 10-11
164 qtd. in Robin, 67:15
165 Ibid.
166 Ibid.
167 Ibid.
168 Ibid.
169 qtd. in McCarty, "Nolan Looks"
170 qtd. in Robin, 78:10
171 qtd. in Pierson, *Produced* 198; Robin, 78:10
172 qtd. in Robin, 78:10
173 qtd. in Robin, 79:9
174 Robin, 79:9
175 qtd. in McCarty, "Nolan Looks"
176 Dawidziak, *Stalker* 194

177 qtd. in Robin, 82:10
178 Ibid.
179 Ibid.
180 qtd. in Pierson, *Produced* 202
181 Ibid.
182 qtd. in Pierson, *Produced* 206
183 Wiater, Bradley, and Stuve 196
184 qtd. in *Reunion*
185 Gross, "Staked!" 64
186 qtd. in Gross, "Staked!" 64
187 Ibid.
188 qtd. in Gross, "Staked!" 65
189 Ibid.
190 qtd. in Gross, "Staked!" 82
191 Pierson, e-mail 12 July 2009
192 qtd. in Robin, 82:10
193 qtd. in Robin, 104:11
194 qtd. in Pierson, *Produced* 213
195 Ibid.
196 Stewart 57
197 qtd. in Robin, 106:9
198 Ibid.
199 qtd. in Pierson, *Produced* 216
200 qtd. in Robin, 106:9
201 Ibid.
202 Ibid.
203 Ibid.
204 qtd. in Robin, 107:13
205 Scott, letter
206 Robin, 107:13
207 all qtd. in Robin, 108:8
208 qtd. in Pierson, *Produced* 206
209 qtd. in Robin, 108:8
210 Scott, letter
211 qtd. in Robin, 108:8
212 qtd. in Del Valle
213 Ibid.
214 qtd. in Dawidziak, *Stalker* 95; Pierson, *Produced* 29
215 Burr
216 Chang
217 Burr
218 "Vampire, Thirsty"
219 Chang
220 Burr
221 Logan, "Vamp Camp"
222 Stone D-1
223 Kennedy 7-A
224 Robin, 122/123: 33-34
225 qtd. in Robin, 122/123:334-34
226 Ibid.
227 all quotations from *Master of Dark Shadows*
228 Thompson, *Television Horrors*, 2nd ed., 232

Chapter II. *Dracula*
1 qtd. in Pierson, *Produced* 21
2 Stoker 320
3 qtd. in *Macabre*
4 Benshoff 101
5 qtd. in *Macabre*
6 qtd. in Pierson, *Produced* 85
7 Ibid.
8 qtd. in *Macabre*
9 Glut 293
10 Melton, *Vampire Book,* 2nd ed., 758-764
11 Stoker 29
12 Stoker 30
13 Stoker 30-31
14 Stoker 241-242
15 Melton, *Vampire Book,* 2nd ed., 702-703
16 Melton, *Vampire Book,* 2nd ed., 603-604
17 Melton, *Vampire Book,* 1st ed., 669
18 Stoker 303-304
19 Thompson, *Dracula* liner notes
20 qtd. in Burlingame
21 Thompson, *Dracula* liner notes
22 Ibid.
23 Ibid.
24 McNally and Florescu 273
25 Melton, *Vampire Book,* 1st ed., 670
26 qtd. in *Macabre*
27 qtd. in Pierson, *Produced* 86
28 Pierson, e-mail 30 July 2015
29 Dawidziak, *Matheson's* 5
30 Dawidziak, *Matheson's* 71 (script p. 13)
31 Dawidziak, *Matheson's* 102 (script p. 46)
32 Dawidziak, *Matheson's* 88 (script p. 29)
33 Dawidziak, *Matheson's* 89 (script p. 30)
34 Dawidziak, *Matheson's* 90-91 (script pp. 31-32)
35 Dawidziak, *Matheson's* 107 (script p. 52)
36 Dawidziak, *Matheson's* 121 (script p. 65A)
37 Ibid.
38 Dawidziak, *Matheson's* 195 (script p. 134)
39 Ibid.
40 qtd. in Dawidziak, *Matheson's* 34
41 qtd. in Dawidziak, *Matheson's* 41
42 qtd. in Dawidziak, *Matheson's* 43
43 qtd. in Dawidziak, *Matheson's* 22
44 Dawidziak, *Matheson's* 22-23
45 qtd. in Dawidziak, *Matheson's* 22
46 qtd. in Thompson, *Television Horrors* 151; Thompson, *House of Dan Curtis* 173
47 Newman xiii
48 Ibid.
49 Thompson, *House of Dan Curtis* 97

Chapter III. *Melvin Purvis, G-Man; The Kansas City Massacre;* and More

1. *Dillinger* DVD liner notes
2. Ibid.
3. Kirchner 228
4. Purvis 338
5. Purvis 4
6. Marill, *Movies 1964-2004,* vol. 1, 147
7. qtd. in Pierson, *Produced* 94
8. qtd. in Pierson, *Produced* 93
9. Ibid.
10. qtd. in Pierson, *Produced* 94
11. qtd. in *Directing the Night*
12. qtd. in Pierson, *Produced* 208
13. qtd. in Pierson, *Produced* 114
14. Ibid.
15. Ibid.
16. Sragow
17. Zacharek
18. qtd. in Markovitz
19. qtd. in Parks
20. qtd. in "Thayer David Quotes"
21. Thompson, *Nights of Dan Curtis*, 1st ed., 205-211

Chapter IV. *The Last Ride of the Dalton Gang*

1. qtd. in *Daltons*
2. Ibid.
3. Ibid.
4. "Dalton Gang Raid"
5. Ibid.
6. Ibid.
7. Kirchner 225
8. qtd. in *Daltons*
9. Ibid.
10. Crist A8-A9
11. qtd. in *Daltons*
12. Ibid.
13. various pages of Earl Wallace's unpublished script *Raid on Coffeyville*, 10 April 1978
14. Wallace, *Raid on Coffeyville*, pp. 83-84, revised 4 May 1978
15. various pages of Earl Wallace's unpublished script *Raid on Coffeyville*, 10 April 1978
16. Wallace, *Raid on Coffeyville*, pp. 155-157A, revised 10 May 1978
17. Wilcox, e-mail 6 Feb. 2016
18. Thompson, *House of Dan Curtis* 137, 146
19. Thompson, *House of Dan Curtis* 146-147

Chapter V. *The Winds of War*

1. Muir, *Terror Television* 65
2. qtd. in *A Novel*
3. qtd. in "Director/Co-Producer" 11
4. qtd. in *Making the Winds*
5. qtd. in Pierson, *Produced* 208
6. qtd. in Thompson, "*Winds*" 52
7. qtd. in Seymore 74
8. qtd. in Thompson, "*Winds*" 52
9. qtd. in Pierson, *Produced* 205
10. qtd. in *Making the Winds*
11. Ibid.
12. qtd. in Pierson, *Produced* 156
13. Ibid.
14. Ibid.
15. MacKenzie 15
16. qtd. in Pierson, *Produced* 156
17. Thompson, "*Winds*" 52
18. MacKenzie 15
19. qtd. in *Daltons*
20. MacGraw 138
21. "Screening" A-3
22. qtd. in Thompson, *Television Horrors* 123; Thompson, *House of Dan Curtis* 106
23. qtd. in Thompson, "*Winds*" 53
24. various writers
25. O'Neil 299-300, 303-307
26. qtd. in Thompson, "*Winds*" 52
27. Thompson, *House of Dan Curtis* 54, 130
28. Gerani 26
29. Gerani 28
30. Ibid.
31. Gerani 24
32. Ibid.

Chapter VI. *War and Remembrance*

1. qtd. in *Making of War*
2. qtd. in Gendel 10-F
3. Robin, 47:4
4. qtd. in Gendel 10-F
5. qtd. in *Making of War*
6. qtd. in DuBrow 4-F
7. qtd. in Pierson, *Produced* 208
8. qtd. in Pierson, *Produced* 205
9. qtd. in Pierson, *Produced* 206
10. qtd. in Stewart 13
11. qtd. in *Making of War*; Stewart 13
12. qtd. in Stewart 13
13. qtd. in Pierson, *Produced* 169
14. Ibid.
15. Ibid.
16. Ibid.
17. Ibid.

18	Ibid.	10	qtd. in Robin, 61:15
19	qtd. in Pierson, *Produced* 168	11	Ibid.
20	Thompson, "Miniseries to Remember" 8	12	Dawidziak 13-18; Karol 5; Robin, 82:10; Robin, 108:8
21	Ibid.	13	qtd. in Pierson, *Produced* 57
22	Ibid.	14	Thompson, *House of Dan Curtis* 156
23	"Tuesday" A-91	15	Ibid.
24	qtd. in Robin, 46:9		
25	Ibid.		
26	qtd. in O'Neil 396		
27	qtd. in Robin, 47:7		
28	Ibid.		
29	qtd. in *Making of War*		
30	Curtis, "Remember"		
31	qtd. in Pierson, *Produced* 9		

Chapter VII. *Intruders: They Are Among Us*

Conclusion: Dan Curtis and Television Horror and Drama

1	Hopkins 4-5	1	Karol 5; Robin, 108:8; et al.
2	qtd. in Robin, 61:15	2	Dawidziak, *Stalker* 13-18
3	Ibid.	3	qtd. in Robin, 82:10
4	Ibid.	4	Thompson, "Fandom" 33
5	Ibid.	5	Benshoff 3, 13
6	Ibid.	6	Zaiman
7	Ibid.	7	Dyess-Nugent
8	qtd. in Pierson, *Produced* 188	8	Pierson, "Blood Lust Goes Way Back"
9	Ibid.	9	qtd. in Pierson, *Produced* 17
		10	Deal 26
		11	Stern, personal interview, 1 August 2018
		12	qtd. in *Burnt* DVD commentary
		13	qtd. in Pierson, *Produced* 207
		14	Nolan, letter 17 Jan. 2010
		15	qtd. in Thompson, *Television Horrors* 74

Ralph Bellamy portrays President Franklin Delano Roosevelt in *Sunrise at Campobello* (1960), *The Winds of War* (1983), and now *War and Remembrance* (1988, 1989).

Bibliography

Angie the Lieutenant. Dir. Robert Collins. Prod. Dan Curtis. Perf. Angie Dickinson, Nicholas Pryor, Jesse Dabson, Angela Bassett. RLC Productions & Dan Curtis Productions & MGM/UA Television, 1992.

Arkelian, John. "'Our Revels Now Are Ended': In Memory of Jonathan Frid." *Arts Forum*. 15 April 2012. Web. 25 April 2012.

Barton, Kristin M., and Jonathan M. Lampley, eds. *Fan Culture: Essays on Participatory Fandom in the 21st Century*. Jefferson, NC: McFarland, 2014. Print.

Beahm, Justin. "Tim Burton Steps into the Shadows." *Famous Monsters of Filmland* no. 261 (May-June 2012): 62-69.

Benshoff, Harry. *Dark Shadows*. Detroit: Wayne State UP, 2011.

Big Easy. Dir. Jud Taylor. Prod. Dan Curtis. Perf. William Devane, Mary Crosby, Ja'net Dubois, Barbara Babcock. Dan Curtis Productions & Paramount Television, 1982.

Birnes, William. *The UFO Magazine UFO Encyclopedia*. New York: Pocket Books, 2004. Print.

Black, Karen. DVD interview. *Three Colors Black*. Dir. David Gregory. *Trilogy of Terror*. Dark Sky Films, 2006. DVD.

Black, Karen, and William F. Nolan. DVD commentary. *Trilogy of Terror*. Dark Sky Films, 2006. DVD.

Black, Karen; Dan Curtis; and William F. Nolan. DVD commentary. *Burnt Offerings*. MGM Home Entertainment, 2003. DVD.

Boedeker, Hal. "Dan Curtis Thought Big." *Orlando Sentinel Blog*. 28 March 2006. Web. 3 Sept. 2006.

Borzellieri, Frank. *The Physics of Dark Shadows: Time Travel, ESP, and the Laboratory*. New York: Cultural-Studies Press, 2008. Print.

Bosco, Scott. Liner notes. *Trilogy of Terror*. Anchor Bay Entertainment, 1999. Videocassette.

Breznican, Anthony. "Into the Shadows." *Entertainment Weekly* no. 1206 (11 May 2012): 30-36. Print.

Brooks, Tim, and Earle Marsh. *The Complete Directory to Prime-Time Network and Cable-TV Shows 1946-Present*. 9th ed. New York: Ballantine Books, 2007. Print.

Brosnan, John. *The Horror People*. New York: Plume Books, 1976. Print.

Burlingame, John. Liner notes. *The Night Stalker and Other Classic Thrillers*. Composed and conducted by Robert Cobert. Varese Sarabande, 2000. CD.

Burnt Offerings. Dir. Dan Curtis. Perf. Karen Black, Oliver Reed, Bette Davis, Lee Montgomery. United Artists, 1976.

"*Burnt Offerings* Is an Outstanding Terror Movie." *New York Times Online* 30 Sept. 1976. Web. 11 August 2006.

"*Burnt Offerings* Not So Very Well Done." *The* [Nashville] *Tennessean* 19 Nov. 1976: 6-D. Print.

Burr, Ty. "*Dark Shadows*." *Boston Globe* 10 May 2012. Web. 10 May 2012.

Cameron, Ian. *A Pictorial History of Crime Films*. London: Hamlyn, 1975. Print.

Capley, Vance. "Shades of Darkness: An Interview with Dr. Jeff Thompson." *Monster Magazine* no.4 (Feb. 2019): 11-16.

Carroll, David, and Kyla Ward. "The Horror Timeline." *Tabula Rasa*. 2005. Web. 22 July 2006.

Cast and Characters. Dir. Donald Beck. *The Winds of War, Part V*. Paramount DVD, 2004. DVD.

CBS Golf Classic. Dir. Frank Chirkinian. Prod. Dan Curtis. CBS-TV, 1963-1973.

Challenge Golf. Dir. various. Prod. Dan Curtis. ABC-TV, 1963.

Chang, Justin. "*Dark Shadows*." *Variety* 10 May 2012. Web. 10 May 2012.

Cobert, Robert. DVD interview. *The Music of War and Remembrance*. Dir. Donald Beck. *War and Remembrance: The Final Chapter, Parts XI-XII*. MPI Home Video, 2003. DVD.

---. Liner notes. *War and Remembrance*. Composed and conducted by Robert Cobert. MPI Music, 2003. CD.

Come Die with Me. Dir. Burt Brinckerhoff. Prod. Dan Curtis. Perf. Eileen Brennan, George Maharis, Kathryn Leigh Scott, Charles Macaulay. Dan Curtis Productions, 1974.

Crist, Judith. "This Week's Movies." *TV Guide* 17-23 Nov. 1979: A8-A9. Print.

Culhane, Michael. "Welcome to Collinwood: *Dark Shadows* 101." *Famous Monsters of Filmland* no. 261 (May-June 2012): 32-33.

Curse of the Black Widow. Dir. Dan Curtis. Perf. Anthony Franciosa, Donna Mills, Patty Duke Astin, Roz Kelly. ABC Circle Films, 1977.

Curtis, Dan. DVD commentary. *War and Remembrance: The Final Chapter, Parts XI-XII*. MPI Home Video, 2003. DVD.

---. DVD interview. *Dan Curtis and the Daltons*. Prod. Jim Pierson. *The Last Ride of the Dalton Gang*. MPI Home Video, 2005. DVD.

---. DVD interview. *Directing The Night Strangler*. Prod. & dir. Greg Carson. *The Night Stalker & The Night Strangler*. MGM Home Entertainment, 2004. DVD.

---. DVD interview. *Inside the Shadows*. Prod. Jim Pierson. *Dark Shadows Special Edition*. MPI Home Video, 1999. DVD.

---. DVD interview. *The Night Stalker: Dan Curtis Interview*. Prod. & dir. Greg Carson. *The Night Stalker & The Night Strangler*. MGM Home Entertainment, 2004. DVD.

---. DVD interview. Prod. Jim Pierson. *The Dan Curtis Macabre Collection*. MPI Home Video, 2002. DVD.

---. DVD interview. Prod. Jim Pierson. *Dark Shadows DVD Collection 2*. MPI Home Video, 2002. DVD.

---. DVD interview. Prod. Jim Pierson. *Dark Shadows DVD Collection 8*. MPI Home Video, 2003. DVD.

---. DVD interview. Prod. Jim Pierson. *Dark Shadows DVD Collection 11*. MPI Home Video, 2004. DVD.

---. DVD interview. Prod. Jim Pierson. *Dark Shadows DVD Collection 16*. MPI Home Video, 2005. DVD.

---. DVD interview. Prod. Jim Pierson. *Dark Shadows DVD Collection 24*. MPI Home Video, 2006. DVD.

---. Foreword. *Dark Shadows Resurrected*. By Jim Pierson. Los Angeles: Pomegranate Press, 1992. 9. Print.

---. "Frank Explanation of Producer's Version." Rpt. in *Shadowgram* no. 63 (Jan. 1993): 10. Print.

---. "Remember *Remembrance*." Rpt. in *Shadowgram* no. 79 (May 1997): 9. Print.

Curtis, Dan, and Lynn Redgrave. DVD interviews. Prod. Jim Pierson. *The Dan Curtis Macabre Collection*. MPI Home Video, 2002. DVD.

"Dalton Gang Raid." *Investigating History*. Prod. Bill Kurtis. Kurtis Productions, 2004. DVD.

Dark Shadows. Dir. Dan Curtis, Lela Swift, et al. Perf. Joan Bennett, Jonathan Frid, Grayson Hall, Louis Edmonds. ABC-TV, 1966-1971.

Dark Shadows. Dir. Dan Curtis, Rob Bowman, et al. Perf. Jean Simmons, Ben Cross, Barbara Steele, Roy Thinnes. NBC-TV, 1991.

Dark Shadows. Dir. P.J. Hogan. Prod. Dan Curtis. Perf. Blair Brown, Alec Newman, Kelly Hu, Martin Donovan. Filmed for the WB television network in April 2004 but never aired.

Dark Shadows. Dir. Tim Burton. Prod. David Kennedy. Perf. Michelle Pfeiffer, Johnny Depp, Helena Bonham Carter, Jonny Lee Miller. Warner Bros., 2012. DVD.

Dark Shadows Behind the Scenes. Prod. Jim Pierson. *Dark Shadows Special Edition*. MPI Home Video, 1999. DVD.

Dark Shadows Reunion: 35th Anniversary Celebration. Prod. Jim Pierson. MPI Home Video, 2003. DVD.

Dawidziak, Mark. *Blood Lines: Richard Matheson's* Dracula, I Am Legend, *and Other Vampire Stories*. Colorado Springs, CO: Gauntlet Press, 2006. Print.

---. *The Night Stalker Companion: A 25th Anniversary Tribute*. Los Angeles: Pomegranate Press, 1997. Print.

Dead of Night. Dir. Dan Curtis. Perf. Ed Begley Jr., Patrick Macnee, Joan Hackett, Lee Montgomery. Dan Curtis Productions, 1977.

Dead of Night: A Darkness at Blaisedon. Dir. Lela Swift. Prod. Dan Curtis. Perf. Kerwin Mathews, Marj Dusay, Thayer David, Louis Edmonds. Dan Curtis Productions & Donnybrook Productions, 1969.

Deal, David. *Television Fright Films of the 1970s*. Jefferson, NC: McFarland, 2007. Print.

Del Valle, David. "Memories of Dan Curtis." *Films in Review*. 28 March 2006. Web. 14 June 2006.

Dillinger. Dir. John Milius. Perf. Ben Johnson, Warren Oates, Michelle Phillips, Richard Dreyfuss. American International Pictures, 1973.

"Director/Co-Producer Dan Curtis." *Drama-Logue* 14 Oct. 1993: 10-11. Print.

Dracula. Dir. Dan Curtis. Perf. Jack Palance, Nigel Davenport, Simon Ward, Penelope Horner. Dan Curtis Productions, 1974.

DuBrow, Rick. "*Winds of War II:* The Saga Continues." *Los Angeles Herald-Examiner* 17 May 1984: 4-F. Print.

Durbano, Art. "This Week's Movies." *TV Guide* 28 July-3 Aug. 1990: 34-35. Print.

Dwyer, Jessica. "*Dark Shadows*: A *Horror Hound* Retrospective." *Horror Hound* March-April 2012: 26-33. Print.

---. "The Man Who Built Collinwood: Dan Curtis." *Horror Hound* March-April 2012: 52-53. Print.
Dyess-Nugent, Phil. "How *Kolchak: The Night Stalker* Developed an Early Model for Television Horror." *A.V. Club*. 14 Feb. 2014. Web. 22 Aug. 2015.
Ebert, Roger. "*House of Dark Shadows*." *Chicago Sun-Times Online*. 6 Oct. 1970. Web. 11 August 2006.
---. "*Night of Dark Shadows*." *Chicago Sun-Times Online*. 21 Sept. 1971. Web. 11 Aug. 2006.
Everson, William. *Classics of the Horror Film*. Secaucus: Citadel Press, 1974. Print.
Express to Terror. Dir. Dan Curtis. Prod. Rod Amateau. Perf. Robert Alda, Edward Andrews, Steve Lawrence, Don Meredith. Dan Curtis Enterprises, 1979.
"Featured Filmmaker—Dan Curtis—The Career of the Man Behind *Dark Shadows* and Kolchak." *Film Force*. 8 July 2003. Web. 27 May 2006.
Finney, Jack. "Second Chance." *The Third Level*. New York: Dell, 1959. 153-172. Print.
Fleming, Thomas. "Wartime Romance: There Was a Special Glow…and Sadness." *TV Guide* 12-18 Nov. 1988: 26-30. Print.
Florescu, Radu. *In Search of Frankenstein*. Boston: New York Graphic Society, 1975. Print.
Florescu, Radu, and Raymond McNally. *Dracula: Prince of Many Faces*. Boston: Little, Brown, and Co., 1989. Print.
Frankenstein. Dir. Glenn Jordan. Prod. Dan Curtis. Perf. Robert Foxworth, Bo Svenson, Susan Strasberg, Heidi Vaughn. Dan Curtis Productions, 1973.
Gendel, Morgan. "ABC at *War* Again with Miniseries, Maxi-Sequel." *Los Angeles Times* 6 Sept. 1986: 10-F. Print.
Gerani, Gary. "The Many Horrors of Dan Curtis." *Weird Tales of the Macabre* vol. 1, no. 1 (Jan. 1975): 24-30. Print.
"Ghoul Show." *Newsweek* 21 Aug. 1967: 60. Print.
Gibron, Bill. "Character over Carnage: Dan Curtis." *Pop Matters*. 3 April 2006. Web. 27 May 2006.
"Giddy Gothic." *TV Guide* 3-9 Dec. 1966: 12-13. Print.
Gifford, Denis. *A Pictorial History of Horror Movies*. London: Hamlyn, 1973. Print.
Glut, Donald. *Classic Movie Monsters*. Metuchen: Scarecrow, 1978. Print.
---. *The Dracula Book*. Metuchen: Scarecrow, 1975. Print.
Graham, Ed. E-mail to the author. 26 April 2010.
Great Ice Rip-Off. Dir. Dan Curtis. Perf. Gig Young, Lee J. Cobb, Grayson Hall, Robert Walden. Dan Curtis Productions & ABC Circle Films, 1974.
Gross, Darren. "Closed Rooms in the *House of Dark Shadows*." *Video Watchdog* no. 40 (1997): 26-31. Print.
---. "*Dark Shadows* Staked!" *Fangoria* no. 239 (Jan. 2005): 62 +. Print.
---. "Illuminating *Night of Dark Shadows*." *Video Watchdog* no. 40 (1997): 32-45. Print.
Gross, Edward. "Dan Curtis." *Dark Shadows Tribute*. Las Vegas: Pioneer Books, 1990. Print.
---. "Dan Curtis: His 'Dream' Started It All." *The Dark Shadows Interviews*. Las Vegas: Schuster & Schuster, 1988. Print.
Hobson, Dorothy. *Soap Opera*. Cambridge: Polity Press, 2003. Print.
Hogan, Ron. *The Stewardess Is Flying the Plane! American Films of the 1970s*. New York: Bullfinch Press, 2005. Print.
Hopkins, Budd. *Intruders: The Incredible Visitations at Copley Woods*. New York: Random House, 1987. Print.
House of Dark Shadows. Dir. Dan Curtis. Perf. Joan Bennett, Jonathan Frid, Grayson Hall, Louis Edmonds. MGM, 1970.
"*House of Dark Shadows* Stresses the Sinister." *New York Times Online*. 29 Oct. 1970. Web. 31 May 2006.
Howard, Malia. *Jonathan Frid: An Actor's Curious Journey*. Fort Worth: Howard Books, 2001. Print.
Intruders: They Are Among Us. Dir. Dan Curtis. Perf. Richard Crenna, Mare Winningnam, Ben Vereen, Daphne Ashbrook. Osiris Films, CBS Entertainment Productions, and Dan Curtis Productions, 1992.
Invasion of Carol Enders. Dir. Burt Brinckerhoff. Prod. Dan Curtis. Perf. Charles Aidman, Meredith Baxter, Christopher Connelly, John Karlen. Dan Curtis Productions, 1974.
I Think I'm Having a Baby. Dir. Arthur Allan Seidelman. Prod. Joseph Stern. Perf. Jennifer Jason Leigh, David Birney, Shawn Stevens, Helen Hunt. Dan Curtis Associates, 1981.
Javna, John. *Cult TV*. New York: St. Martin's Press, 1985. Print.
James, Henry. *The Turn of the Screw*. New York: Dover, 1991. Print.
Jamison, R.J. "*Dark Shadows* Resurrected." *Screem* no. 24 (2012): 2-5. Print.
---. *Grayson Hall: A Hard Act to Follow*. New York: iUniverse, 2006. Print.

Jenkins, Henry. *Convergence Culture: Where Old and New Media Collide.* New York: New York UP, 2006. Print.

---. *Textual Poachers: Television Fans and Participatory Culture.* New York: Routledge, 1992. Print.

***Johnny Ryan.* Dir. Robert Collins. Prod. Dan Curtis. Perf. Clancy Brown, Bruce Abbott, Teri Austin, Christine Moore. Dan Curtis Productions & MGM/UA Television & NBC Productions, 1990.**

Joslin, Lyndon. *Count Dracula Goes to the Movies: Stoker's Novel Adapted, 1922-1995.* Jefferson, NC: McFarland, 1999. Print.

Just, Ward. "Images of War: How America Re-creates the 'Blood and Darkness.'" *TV Guide* 29 Jan.-4 Feb. 1983: 2-4. Print.

Kane, Tim. *The Changing Vampire of Film and Television: A Critical Study of the Growth of a Genre.* Jefferson, NC: McFarland, 2006. Print.

***Kansas City Massacre.* Dir. Dan Curtis. Perf. Dale Robertson, Bo Hopkins, John Karlen, Sally Kirkland. Dan Curtis Productions & ABC Circle Films, 1975.**

Karol, Michael. *The ABC Movie of the Week: A Loving Tribute to the Classic Series.* New York: iUniverse, 2005. Print.

Katz, Ephraim. *The Film Encyclopedia.* 6th ed. New York: Harper Collins, 2008. Print.

Kawin, Bruce. "Children of the Light." *Film Genre Reader II.* Ed. Barry Keith Grant. Austin: U of Texas Press, 1995. 308-329. Print.

Kennedy, Lisa. "Burton and Depp's *Dark Shadows* Casts Its Comedic Lot Amid the Details." *Denver Post* 11 May 2012: 7-A. Print.

Kersey, Nancy, and Helen Samaras, eds. *Remembering Jonathan Frid.* West Hempstead, NY: Evil Twin Publications, 2014. Print.

King, Stephen. *Stephen King's Danse Macabre.* New York: Berkley Books, 1981. Print.

Kirchner, L.R. *Robbing Banks: An American History, 1831-1999.* Edison, NJ: Castle Books, 2003. Print.

Knowles, Christopher. "The Norliss Tapes." *Weekend Matinee* 7 Oct. 2012. Web. 24 Oct. 2012.

Kuttner, Henry. "The Graveyard Rats." *Dying of Fright.* Ed. Les Daniels. New York: Scribner's, 1976. 189-195. Print.

Labbe, Rod. "Directing in the Shadows." *Fangoria* no. 313 (May 2012): 45-46. Print.

---. "From Bruce to Barnabas." *Fangoria* no. 313 (May 2012): 46-47. Print.

Lampley, Jonathan. *Women in the Horror Films of Vincent Price.* Jefferson, NC: McFarland, 2011. Print.

Lampley, Jonathan; Ken Beck; and Jim Clark. *The Amazing, Colossal Book of Horror Trivia.* Nashville, Cumberland House, 1999. Print.

***Last Ride of the Dalton Gang.* Dir. Dan Curtis. Perf. Jack Palance, Cliff Potts, Randy Quaid, Larry Wilcox. Dan Curtis Enterprises & NBC Productions, 1979.**

LaVoo, George. "*Burnt Offerings* Filmbook." *The Old, Dark House* no. 1 (winter 1976-1977): 4-13. Print.

Lemire, Christy. "Visuals Shine, But Story Hides in *Dark Shadows.*" *The* [Nashville] *Tennessean* 11 May 2012: D-3. Print.

Loban, Leila, and Richard Valley. "The Pictures of Dorian Gray." *Scarlet Street* no. 41 (2001): 36 +. Print.

---. "The Pictures of Dorian Gray, Part II." *Scarlet Street* no. 42 (2001): 52 +. Print.

---. "The Pictures of Dorian Gray, Part III." *Scarlet Street* no. 43 (2001): 48 +. Print.

Logan, Michael. "*Children* on the Move." *TV Guide* 24-Aug.-6 Sept. 2009: 78. Print.

---. "Vamp Camp." *TV Guide* 7-20 May 2012: 42-43. Print.

***Long Days of Summer.* Dir. Dan Curtis. Perf. Dean Jones, Joan Hackett, Ronnie Scribner, Louanne Sirota. Dan Curtis Associates, 1980.**

***Love Letter.* Dir. Dan Curtis. Perf. Campbell Scott, Jennifer Jason Leigh, David Dukes, Estelle Parsons. Hallmark Hall of Fame Productions, 1998.**

Lucas, Tim. "*Dracula.*" *Video Watchdog* no. 15 (Jan.-Feb. 1993): 11-12. Print.

---. "*House of Dark Shadows* and *Night of Dark Shadows.*" *Video Watchdog* no. 22 (March-April 1994): 65-67. Print.

MacGraw Ali. *Moving Pictures.* New York: Bantam Books, 1991. Print.

MacKenzie, Robert. "Review: *The Winds of War.*" TV Guide 29 Jan.-4 Feb. 1983: 15. Print.

Making of War and Remembrance. Dir. Donald Beck. *War and Remembrance: The Final Chapter, Parts V-VII.* MPI Home Video, 2003. DVD.

Making The Winds of War. Dir. Donald Beck. *The Winds of War, Part V.* Paramount DVD, 2004. DVD.

Maltin, Leonard, ed. *Leonard Maltin's 2015 Movie Guide.* New York: Signet, 2014. Print.

Manning, Stuart. "Remembering Dan Curtis." *Dark Shadows Journal.* 28 March 2006. Web. 20 May 2006.

Marano, Michael. "Family Values." *Sci-Fi* June 2012: 36-39. Print.
Marasco, Robert. *Burnt Offerings.* New York: Delacorte Press, 1973. Print.
Marill, Alvin. *Movies Made for Television 1964-1979.* Westport, CT: Arlington House, 1980. Print.
---. *Movies Made for Television 1964-1984.* New York: New York Zoetrope, 1984. Print.
---. *Movies Made for Television 1964-2004.* 5 vols. Lanham, MD: Scarecrow Press, 2005. Print.
Markovitz, Adam. "Johnny Depp, Tim Burton on Board for *Dark Shadows*." *EW.com.* 25 June 2009. Web. 26 June 2009.
Matheson, Richard. DVD interview. *Richard Matheson: Terror Scribe.* Dir. David Gregory. *Trilogy of Terror.* Dark Sky Films, 2006. DVD.
---. *I Am Legend.* Garden City, NY: Nelson Doubleday, 1954. Print.
---. *Journal of the Gun Years.* New York: Berkley Books, 1992. Print.
---. "Likeness of Julie." *Shock II.* New York: Dell, 1964. 79-90. Print.
---. "Needle in the Heart," a.k.a. "Therese." *Shock Waves.* New York: Dell, 1970. 109-111. Print.
---. "No Such Thing as a Vampire." *Shock II.* New York: Dell, 1964. 27-38. Print.
---. "Prey." *Shock Waves.* New York: Dell, 1970. 119-131. Print.
---. *Shock!* New York: Dell, 1961. Print.
---. *Shock III.* New York: Dell, 1966. Print.
McCarty, Michael. "Dan Curtis Continues to Thrive in the *Dark Shadows*." *Sci-Fi.* 2002. Web. 14 June 2006.
---. "William F. Nolan Looks Back at the Legacy of *Logan's Run* and Looks Forward to Bryan Singer's Remake." *Sci-Fi.* 2005. Web. 21 July 2006.
McNally, Raymond, and Radu Florescu. *In Search of Dracula.* New ed. Boston: Houghton Mifflin, 1994. Print.
McNeil, Alex. *Total Television.* 4th ed. New York: Penguin Books, 1996. Print.
Me and the Kid. Dir. Dan Curtis. Perf. Danny Aiello, Alex Zuckerman, Cathy Moriarty, David Dukes. Dan Curtis Productions, 1993.
Meikle, Denis. *A History of Horrors: The Rise and Fall of the House of Hammer.* Lanham, MD: Scarecrow Press, 1996. Print.
Melton, J.Gordon. *The Vampire Book: The Encyclopedia of the Undead.* Detroit: Visible Ink Press, 1994. Print.
---. *The Vampire Book: The Encyclopedia of the Undead.* 2nd ed. Detroit: Visible Ink Press, 1999. Print.
---. *Vampires on Video.* Detroit: Visible Ink Press, 1997. Print.
Melvin Purvis, G-Man. Dir. Dan Curtis. Perf. Dale Robertson, Harris Yulin, John Karlen, Steve Kanaly. American International & Dan Curtis Productions, 1974.
Modleski, Tania. *Loving with a Vengeance.* Hamden, CT: Archon Books, 1982. Print.
"Monster Revival." *Newsweek* 7 Jan. 1991: 58-59. Print.
Mrs. R's Daughter. Dir. Dan Curtis. Perf. Cloris Leachman, Season Hubley, Donald Moffat, Stephen Elliott. Dan Curtis Enterprises & NBC Productions, 1979.
Muir, John Kenneth. *Horror Films of the 1970s.* 2 vols. Jefferson, NC: McFarland, 2002. Print.
---. *Terror Television: American Series, 1970-1999.* 2 vols. Jefferson, NC: McFarland, 2001. Print.
Nahmod, David-Elijah. "Ladies of the Shadows." *Famous Monsters of Filmland* no. 261 (May-June 2012): 56-61. Print.
Nance, Scott. *Bloodsuckers: Vampires at the Movies.* Las Vegas: Pioneer Books, 1992. Print.
Newman, Kim. Foreword. *The Vampire Archives: The Most Complete Volume of Vampire Tales Ever Published.* Ed. Otto Penzler. New York: Vintage Books, 2009. xi-xiv. Print.
Nightmare at 43 Hillcrest. Dir. Lela Swift. Prod. Dan Curtis. Perf. Peter Mark Richman, Jim Hutton, Mariette Hartley, John Karlen. Dan Curtis Productions, 1974.
Night of Dark Shadows. Dir. Dan Curtis. Prod. Dan Curtis. Perf. David Selby, Kate Jackson, John Karlen, Grayson Hall. MGM, 1971.
Night Stalker. Dir. John Llewellyn Moxey. Prod. Dan Curtis. Perf. Darren McGavin, Simon Oakland, Carol Lynley, Barry Atwater. ABC Circle Films, 1972.
Night Strangler. Dir. Dan Curtis. Prod. Dan Curtis. Perf. Darren McGavin, SimonOakland, Jo Ann Pflug, Richard Anderson. ABC Circle Films, 1973.
Nolan, William F. *Impact 20.* New York: Paperback Library, 1963. Print.
---. Letter to the author. 17. Jan. 2010.
---. *Logan's Search.* New York: Bantam Books, 1980. Print.
---. *Logan's World.* New York: Bantam Books, 1977. Print.
---. Personal interview. 28 Feb. 2010.

Nolan, William F., and George Clayton Johnson. *Logan's Run*. New York: Dial Press, 1967. Print.

Norliss Tapes. Dir. Dan Curtis. Perf. Roy Thinnes, Don Porter, Angie Dickinson, Nick Dimitri. Dan Curtis Productions & Metromedia, 1973.

Novel for Television. Dir. Donald Beck. *The Winds of War, Part V*. Paramount DVD, 2004. DVD.

O'Flinn, Paul. "Production and Reproduction: The Case of *Frankenstein*." *The Horror Reader*. Ed. Ken Gelder. London: Routledge, 2000. 114-127. Print.

O'Hallaren, Bill. "He's the Only Gary Cooper Still Alive." *TV Guide* 29 Jan.-4 Feb. 1983: 8-11. Print.

O'Neil, Thomas. *The Emmys*. 3rd ed. New York: Berkley, 1998. Print.

On Location. Dir. Donald Beck. *The Winds of War, Part V*. Paramount DVD, 2004. DVD.

Our Fathers. Dir. Dan Curtis. Perf. Ted Danson, Christopher Plummer, Brian Dennehy, Ellen Burstyn. Dan Curtis Productions, Peach Arch Entertainment Group, and Showtime, 2005.

Palance, Jack. DVD interview. Prod. Jim Pierson. *The Dan Curtis Macabre Collection*. MPI Home Video, 2002. DVD.

Panitt, Merrill. "Review: *War and Remembrance*." *TV Guide* 12-18 Nov. 1988: 40. Print.

Parks, Tim. "Burton: *Dark Shadows* Will Be a Challenge." *Digital Spy*. 22 July 2009. Web. 26 July 2009.

Pattison, Barrie. *The Seal of Dracula*. New York: Bounty Books, 1975. Print.

Peer, Kurt. *TV Tie-Ins: A Bibliography of American TV Tie-In Paperbacks*. Tucson, AZ: Neptune Publishing, 1997. Print.

Picture of Dorian Gray. Dir. Glenn Jordan. Prod. Dan Curtis. Perf. Shane Briant, Nigel Davenport, Charles Aidman, Linda Kelsey. Dan Curtis Productions, 1973.

Pierson, Jim. "The Blood Lust Goes Way Back." *Los Angeles Time On-Line*. 14 June 2009. Web. 19 June 2009.

---. *Dark Shadows Festival Memory Book 1983-1993*. Maplewood, NJ: Dark Shadows Festival, 1994. Print.

---. *Dark Shadows Resurrected*. Los Angeles: Pomegranate Press, 1992. Print.

---. E-mail to the author. 30 July 2006.

---. E-mail to the author. 22 Oct. 2007.

---. E-mail to the author. 27 June 2008.

---. E-mail to the author. 7 May 2009.

---. E-mail to the author. 20 June 2009.

---. E-mail to the author. 12 July 2009.

---. E-mail to the author. 25 July 2009.

---. E-mail to the author. 23 Aug. 2009.

---. E-mail to the author. 13 Sept. 2009.

---. E-mail to the author. 12 Nov. 2009.

---. E-mail to the author. 16 July 2015.

---. E-mail to the author. 30 July 2015.

---. E-mail to the author. 4 Aug. 2015.

---. E-mail to the author. 7 Sept. 2015.

---. Liner notes. *Dark Shadows: The 30th Anniversary Collection*. Composed by Robert Cobert. Varese Sarabande, 1996. CD.

---. Liner notes. *House of Dark Shadows and Night of Dark Shadows*. Composed and conducted by Robert Cobert. Turner Classic Movies Music, 1996. CD.

---. *Produced and Directed by Dan Curtis*. Los Angeles: Pomegranate Press, 2004. Print.

Purvis, Alston, and Alex Tresniowski. *The Vendetta: Special Agent Melvin Purvis, John Dillinger, and Hoover's FBI in the Age of Gangsters*. New York: Public Affairs, 2005. Print.

Rathbun, Mark, and Graeme Flanagan. *Richard Matheson: He Is Legend*. Chico, CA: Rio Lindo, 1984. Print.

Raw, Laurence. *Adapting Henry James to the Screen: Gender, Fiction, and Film*. Lanham, MD: Scarecrow, 2006. Print.

Real Untouchables: Melvin Purvis. Prod. Anthony Geffen. Dir. James Fothergill. Atlantic Productions, 2001. Videocassette.

Redgrave, Lynn. DVD interview. Prod. Jim Pierson. *The Dan Curtis Macabre Collection*. MPI Home Video, 2002. DVD.

"Reel World." *Enigma* 10 May 2012: 16. Print.

Resch, Kathleen, and Marcy Robin. *Dark Shadows in the Afternoon*. New York: Image Publishing, 1991. Print.

Rice, Jeff. *The Night Stalker*. New York: Pocket Books, 1973. Print.

---. *The Night Strangler*. New York: Pocket Books, 1974. Print.

Robin, Marcy, ed. "Dan Curtis News." *Shadowgram* no. 41 (Feb. 1988): 5. Print.

---. "Dan Curtis News." *Shadowgram* no. 46 (April 1989): 9. Print.
---. "Dan Curtis News." *Shadowgram* no. 47 (August 1989): 7. Print.
---. "Dan Curtis News." Shadowgram no. 54/55 (Jan. 1991): 2. Print.
---. "Dan Curtis News." *Shadowgram* no. 61 (August 1992): 15. Print.
---. "Dan Curtis News." *Shadowgram* no. 67 (Jan. 1994): 15. Print.
---. "Dan Curtis News." *Shadowgram* no. 78 (Feb. 1997): 10-11. Print.
---. "Dan Curtis News." *Shadowgram* no. 79 (May 1997): 9. Print.
---. "Dan Curtis News." *Shadowgram* no. 81 (Nov. 1997): 11. Print.
---. "Dan Curtis News." *Shadowgram* no. 82 (Feb. 1998): 10. Print.
---. "Dan Curtis News." *Shadowgram* no. 87 (Nov. 1999): 10. Print.
---. "Dan Curtis News." *Shadowgram* no. 94 (Nov. 2001): 10. Print.
---. "Dan Curtis News." *Shadowgram* no. 96 (June 2002): 9. Print.
---. "Dan Curtis News." *Shadowgram* no. 97 (Oct. 2002): 10. Print.
---. "Dan Curtis News." *Shadowgram* no. 104 (April 2005): 11. Print.
---. "Dan Curtis News." *Shadowgram* no. 106 (Oct. 2005): 8-9. Print.
---. "Dan Curtis News." *Shadowgram* no. 107 (April 2006): 12-13, 22-23. Print.
---. "Dan Curtis News." *Shadowgram* no. 108 (June 2006): 8-10. Print.
---. "*Dark Shadows* News." *Shadowgram* no. 54/55 (Jan. 1991): 15-16. Print.
---. "*Dark Shadows*: the 2012 Movie." *Shadowgram* no. 122/123 (Jan. 2014): 7-10. Print.
---. "Robert Cobert News." *Shadowgram* no. 49 (Jan. 1990): 9. Print.
Ross, Marilyn. *Barnabas, Quentin, and the Mummy's Curse.* New York: Paperback Library, 1970. Print.
Rossen, Jake. "14 *Dark Shadows* Facts with Bite." *Mental Floss.* 15 Oct. 2015. Web. 17 Oct. 2015.
Samaras, Helen, ed. *Fangs for the Memories: Memoirs of Dark Shadows Fans and Cast Members.* West Hempstead, NY: Evil Twin Publications, 1996. Print.
Saving Milly. Dir. Dan Curtis. Perf. Madeleine Stowe, Bruce Greenwood, Robert Wisden, Claudia Ferri. 2 Dans Productions, 2005.
Schow, David and Jeffrey Frentzen. *The Outer Limits: The Official Companion.* New York: Ace Science-Fiction Books, 1986. Print.
Scott, Kathryn Leigh. *The Dark Shadows Companion.* Los Angeles: Pomegranate Press, 1990. Print.
---. *Dark Shadows Memories.* Los Angeles: Pomegranate Press, 2001. Print.
---. Letter to the author. 15 June 2006.
---. *My Scrapbook Memories of Dark Shadows.* Los Angeles: Pomegranate Press, 1986. Print.
Scott, Kathryn Leigh, and Jim Pierson, eds. *Dark Shadows Almanac.* Los Angeles: Pomegranate Press, 1995. Print.
---. *Dark Shadows Almanac.* Millennium ed. Los Angeles: Pomegranate Press, 2000. Print.
---. *Dark Shadows Movie Book.* Los Angeles: Pomegranate Press, 1998. Print.
---. *Dark Shadows: Return to Collinwood.* Los Angeles: Pomegranate Press, 2012. Print.
Scott, Lesley. "The Vamp in the Mirror: How Popular Culture's Obsession with the Undead Reveals What We're Really Afraid Of." *Stitch* vol. 1, no. 4 (Dec. 2003): 104-109. Print.
Scream of the Wolf. Dir. Dan Curtis. Perf. Peter Graves, Clint Walker, Jo Ann Pflug, Philip Carey. Dan Curtis Productions & Metromedia, 1974.
"Screening Room." *TV Guide* 5-11 Feb. 1983: A-3. Print.
Selby, David. *In and Out of the Shadows.* New York: Locust Grove Press, 1999. Print.
Seymore, James. "Rough, Tough, and Rowdy: Robert Mitchum." *People Weekly* 14 Feb. 1983: 72 +. Print.
Shadow of Fear. Dir. Herbert Kenwith. Prod. Dan Curtis. Perf. Claude Akins, Anjanatte Comer, Jason Evers, Philip Carey. Dan Curtis Productions, 1974.
Shelley, Mary. *Frankenstein, or The Modern Prometheus.* London: Penguin, 1992. Print.
Shinnick, Kevin. "Come Back, Shane Briant." *Scarlet Street* no. 42 (2001): 46 +. Print.
"Ship of Ghouls." *Time* 20 Aug. 1968: 66. Print.
Showalter, Elaine. "Dr. Jekyll's Closet." *The Horror Reader.* Ed. Ken Gelder. London: Routledge, 2000. 190-197. Print.
Silver, Alain, and James Ursini. *The Vampire Film.* 2nd ed. New York: Limelight Editions, 1993. Print.
Simpson, Robert. "Collinwood Calling: The Life of *Dark Shadows*." *Diabolique* no. 11 (July-August 2012): 20-27. Print.
Skal, David. *The Monster Show: A Cultural History of Horror.* 2nd ed. New York: Faber and Faber, 2001. Print.
Smith, Robert Barr. *Daltons! The Raid on Coffeyville, Kansas.* Norman, OK: Oklahoma UP, 1996. Print.

Sosnowski, Matthew. "Stevenson and Curtis: Masters of the Macabre." Paper. University of Hartford, 2011. Print.

Stevenson, Robert Louis. *The Strange Case of Dr. Jekyll and Mr. Hyde*. New York: Books, Inc., n.d. Print.

Stewart, Susan. "Hits and Misses." *TV Guide* 13-19 March 2005: 57. Print.

Stewart, Zan. "Bob Cobert Scores His Own Victory in *War and Remembrance*." Rpt. in *Shadowgram* no. 45 (Jan. 1989): 13. Print.

St. John in Exile. Dir. Dan Curtis. Perf. Dean Jones. DJ Productions, 1986.

Stoker, Bram. *Dracula*. New York: Signet Classic, 1992. Print.

Stone, Jay. "*Dark Shadows* Stylish But Tedious." *The* [St. John, New Brunswick] *Telegraph-Journal* 11 May 2012: D-1—D-2. Print.

Strange Case of Dr. Jekyll and Mr. Hyde. Dir. Charles Jarrott. Prod. Dan Curtis. Perf. Jack Palance, Denholm Elliott, Billie Whitelaw, Tessie O'Shea. Dan Curtis Productions & CBC-TV, 1968.

"Sunday Previews." *TV Guide* 12-18 Nov. 1988: A-45. Print.

Supertrain. Dir. Dan Curtis, Barry Crane, et al. Perf. Dick Van Dyke, Roy Thinnes, Scott Brady, Sylvia Sidney. NBC-TV, 1979.

Swaim-Robb, Connie. "Vampires Becoming More Romantic Through the Years." *Antique Week* vol. 44, no. 2256 (29 Oct. 2012): 1, 25. Print.

"Terror on TV: 1969-1983." *The Terror Trap*. 1998. Web. 22 July 2006.

"Thayer David Quotes." *Brainy Quotes*. 2006. Web. 14 June 2006.

Thompson, Jeff. "Barnabas, Quentin, and the Prolific Author: The *Dark Shadows* Novels of Dan 'Marilyn' Ross." *Paperback Parade* no. 43 (August 1995): 80-91. Print.

---. "Breathing Down Our Necks: The 1970 Leviathan Storyline." *The Music Box* no. 9 (summer 1993): 21-23. Print.

---. "*Burnt Offerings*." *Movie Club* no. 12 (autumn 1997): 14-15. Print.

---. "*Burnt Offerings*." *You're Next! Loss of Identity in the Horror Film*. Ed. Anthony Ambrogio. Baltimore: Midnight Marquee Press, 2008. Print.

---. "Dark Dreamer: Dan Curtis and Television Horror." Diss. Middle Tennessee State U, 2007. Print.

---. *Dark Shadows Comic Books*. Los Angeles: Joseph Collins Publications, 1984. 2nd ed. 1988. Print.

---. "*Dark Shadows* Episode 1,245." *Television Finales: From* Howdy Doody *to* Girls. Eds. Douglas Howard and David Bianculli. Syracuse: Syracuse UP, 218. 78-83.

---. "*Dark Shadows* Fandom, Then and Now (1966-2013)." *Fan Culture: Essays on Participatory Fandom in the 21st Century*. Eds. Kristin M. Barton and Jonathan M. Lampley. Jefferson, NC: McFarland, 2014. Print.

---. "*Dark Shadows* in the 1970s: Best Episodes." *Shadows of the Night*. 20 Jan. 2006. Web. 20 July 2006.

---. *Dark Shadows Memorabilia Slide Show*. Slide program. 1985-1992.

---. "*Death at Love House*." *You're Next! Loss of Identity in the Horror Film*. Ed. Anthony Ambrogio. Baltimore: Midnight Marquee Press, 2008. Print.

---. "*Die! Die! My Darling!*" *Midnight Marquee* no. 57 (summer 1998): 13. Print.

---. "Effective Use of Actual Persons and Events in the Historical Novels of Dan Ross." Thesis. Tennessee State U, 1991. Print.

---. "Films of Barbara Steele." *Movie Club* no. 7 (summer 1996): 40-41. Print.

---. "Four-Color Shadows: The *Dark Shadows* Comic Books and Newspaper Comic Strip." Part 1. *Southern Fandom Update* no. 6 (June 2009): 9-15. Web. 10 June 2009.

---. "Four-Color Shadows: The *Dark Shadows* Comic Books and Newspaper Comic Strip." Part 2. *Southern Fandom Update* no. 8 (August 2009): 7-13. Web. 1 Aug. 2009.

---. "Four-Colour Shadows: The Gold Key Comics." *Dark Shadows Journal*. 19 March 2006. Web. 20 March 2006.

---. "History of the East Coast Dark Shadows Festivals, 1983-1993." *Dark Shadows Festival Memory Book, 1983-1993*. Ed. Jim Pierson. Maplewood, NJ: Dark Shadows Festival, 1994. 93-99. Print.

---. *House of Dan Curtis: The Television Mysteries of the Dark Shadows Auteur*. Nashville: Westview, 2010. Print.

---. "*House of Dark Shadows*." *You're Next! Loss of Identity in the Horror Film*. Ed. Anthony Ambrogio. Baltimore: Midnight Marquee Press, 2008. Print.

---. "In Memoriam: Dan Curtis." *Scoop*. 2002. Web. 31 March 2006.

---. "Introduction: *Dark Shadows*: A Final Look at the Comics." *Dark Shadows: The Complete Original Series*. Vol. 5. Ed Daniel Herman. Neshannock, PA: Hermes Press, 2012.

---. "Introduction: *Dark Shadows*: A Look at the Comics." *Dark Shadows: The Complete Original Series*. Vol. 2. Ed Daniel Herman. Neshannock, PA: Hermes Press, 2011.

---. "Introduction: *Dark Shadows*: A Look at the Comics." *Dark Shadows: The Complete Original Series*. Vol. 3. Ed Daniel Herman. Neshannock, PA: Hermes Press, 2011.

---. "Introduction: *Dark Shadows*: A Look at the Comics." *Dark Shadows: The Complete Original Series*. Vol. 4. Ed Daniel Herman. Neshannock, PA: Hermes Press, 2012.

---. "Introduction: *Dark Shadows* and the Comics." *Dark Shadows: The Complete Original Series*. Vol. 1. Ed Daniel Herman. Neshannock, PA: Hermes Press, 2010.

---. "Introduction: The Best of *Dark Shadows*." *Dark Shadows: The Best of the Original Series*. Ed Daniel Herman. Neshannock, PA: Hermes Press, 2011.

---. "Introduction: *Dark Shadows*: The Story Digest." *Dark Shadows: The Original Series Story Digest*. Ed Daniel Herman. Neshannock, PA: Hermes Press, 2011.

---. "Life from a Coffin: How *Dark Shadows* Has Affected My Life." *Fangs for the Memories: Memoirs of Dark Shadows Fans and Cast Members*. Ed. Helen Samaras. West Hempstead, NY: Evil Twin Publications, 1996. 61-64. Print.

---. Liner notes. *Burnt Offerings*. Composed by Robert Cobert. Counterpoint, 2011. CD.

---. Liner notes. *Dracula*. Composed by Robert Cobert. Varese Sarabande, 2014. CD.

---. "Matinee." *Science-Fiction Invasions*. Ed. Don Dohler. Baltimore: Movie Club, 1998. 29-30. Print.

---. "Night of Dark Shadows." *You're Next! Loss of Identity in the Horror Film*. Ed. Anthony Ambrogio. Baltimore: Midnight Marquee Press, 2008. Print.

---. "Overview of *Dark Shadows* Fandom." *Southern Fandom Bulletin* no. 8 (January 1991): 18-21. Print.

---. "Remembering Forrest J Ackerman." *Chattanooga Airwaves* vol. 16, no. 4 (July/Aug. 2009): 8-10. Print.

---. "Soap and Sorcery: Lara Parker." *Femme Fatales* vol. 4, no. 1 (summer 1995): 28-31 ff. Print.

---. "Somewhere in Class." *INSITE* vol. 25, no. 3 (mid-2014): 12-14. Print.

---. "Strange Possession of Mrs. Oliver." *You're Next! Loss of Identity in the Horror Film*. Ed. Anthony Ambrogio. Baltimore: Midnight Marquee Press, 2008. Print.

---. *Television Horrors of Dan Curtis:* Dark Shadows, The Night Stalker, *and Other Productions, 1966-2006*. Jefferson, NC: McFarland, 2009. Print.

---. "Timeless Loves: *Titanic* and *Somewhere in Time*." *Scarlet Street* no. 28 (mid-1998): 29-31. Print.

---. "Trilogy of Terror." *You're Next! Loss of Identity in the Horror Film*. Ed. Anthony Ambrogio. Baltimore: Midnight Marquee Press, 2008. Print.

---. "Trilogy of Terror II." *You're Next! Loss of Identity in the Horror Film*. Ed. Anthony Ambrogio. Baltimore: Midnight Marquee Press, 2008. Print.

---. "Visit with Marilyn and Dan Ross." *Dark Shadows Lives!* Ed. James Van Hise. Las Vegas: Schuster & Schuster, 1988. 57-67. Print.

---. "War and Remembrance: A Miniseries to Remember." *Lone Star Shadows* vol. 2, no. 7/8 (summer/fall 1989): 8. Print.

---. "Warm Acquaintance." *Remembering Jonathan Frid*. Eds. Nancy Kersey and Helen Samaras. West Hempstead, NY: Evil Twin Publications, 2014. Print.

---. "Winds of War." *The World of Dark Shadows* no. 36 (Dec. 1983): 52-53. Print.

Toland, John. *Adolf Hitler*. New York: Doubleday & Company, 1976. Print.

Trilogy of Terror. Dir. Dan Curtis. Perf. Karen Black, Robert Burton, John Karlen, George Gaynes. Dan Curtis Productions & ABC Circle Films, 1975.

Trilogy of Terror II. Dir. Dan Curtis. Perf. Lysette Anthony, Geraint Wyn Davies, Matt Clark, Geoffrey Lewis. Dan Curtis, Power Pictures, and Wilshire Court Productions, 1996.

"Tuesday Previews." *TV Guide* (19-25 Nov. 1988): A-91. Print.

Tulloch, John, and Henry Jenkins. *Science-Fiction Audiences: Watching* Doctor Who *and* Star Trek. London: Routledge, 1995. Print.

Turan, Kenneth. "The Fallen Star Battles Back." *TV Guide* 29 Jan.-4 Feb. 1983: 12-14. Print.

"Turned-On Vampire." *Newsweek* 20 April 1970: 107. Print.

Turn of the Screw. Dir. Dan Curtis. Perf. Lynn Redgrave, Megs Jenkins, Jasper Jacob, Eva Griffith. Dan Curtis Productions, 1974.

"TV Terror: Dan Curtis." *The Terror Trap*. 1998. Web. 27 May 2006.

"Vampire, Thirsty and Bewildered." *New York Times* 10 May 2012. Web. 10 May 2012.

Wallace, Earl. *The Raid on Coffeyville*. Unpublished script. 10 April 1978. Print.

Wallace, Marie. *On Stage and in Shadows*. New York: iUniverse, 2005. Print.

Waller, Gregory. "Introduction to *American Horrors*." *The Horror Reader*. Ed. Ken Gelder. London: Routledge, 2000. 256-264. Print.

War and Remembrance. **Dir. Dan Curtis. Perf. Robert Mitchum, Polly Bergen, Hart Bochner, Jane Seymour. Dan Curtis Productions & ABC Circle Films, 1988, 1989.**
War and Remembrance: Behind the Scenes. Exec. Prod. Jim Pierson. *War and Remembrance: The Final Chapter, Parts XI-XII.* MPI Home Video, 2003. DVD.
Warren, Elaine. "Replacements Rushed to the Front Lines." *TV Guide* 12-18 Nov. 1988: 33-38. Print.
Weiler, A.H. "*Night of Dark Shadows* Arrives." *New York Times Online.* 14 Oct. 1971. Web. 31 May 2006.
Wells, Paul. *The Horror Genre: From Beelzebub to Blair Witch.* London: Wallflower, 2000. Print.
"What a Doll!" *TV Guide* 1 March 1975: 12-13. Print.
Wheatley, Helen. *Gothic Television.* Manchester: Manchester UP, 2006. Print.
When Every Day Was the Fourth of July. **Dir. Dan Curtis. Perf. Dean Jones, Louise Sorel, Chris Peterson, Katy Kurtzman. Dan Curtis Productions, 1978.**
Wiater, Stanley; Matthew Bradley; and Paul Stuve, eds. *The Richard Matheson Companion.* Colorado Springs: Gauntlet Press, 2008. Print.
---, eds. *The Twilight and Other Zones: The Dark Moods of Richard Matheson.* New York: Citadel Press, 2009. Print.
Wilcox, Larry. E-mail to the author. 28 Sept. 2015.
---. E-mail to the author. 2 Nov. 2016.
---. E-mail to the author. 6 Feb. 2016.
Wilde, Oscar. *The Picture of Dorian Gray.* New York: Modern Library, 2004. Print.
Wilson, Edmund. "The Ambiguity of Henry James." *Hound and Horn* VII (April-June 1934): 385-406. Print.
Windolf, Jim. "The Young and the Lifeless." *Vanity Fair* April 2012: 156-157. Print.
Winds of War. **Dir. Dan Curtis. Perf. Robert Mitchum, Polly Bergen, Jan-Michael Vincent, Ali McGraw. Dan Curtis Productions & Paramount Television, 1983.**
Winkle, Michael. "The Measure of Success." *Geocities.* 1999. Web. 21 July 2006.
Wolcott, James. "The Undead Don't Like to Leave Anything Undone." *Vanity Fair.* 24 Oct. 2012. Web. 24 Oct. 2012.
Wood, Robin. "The American Nightmare: Horror in the 1970s." *Horror, the Film Reader.* Ed. Mark Jancovich. London: Routledge, 2002. 25-32. Print.
Wouk, Herman. *War and Remembrance.* Boston: Little, Brown, and Co., 1978. Print.
---. *The Winds of War.* Boston: Little, Brown, and Co., 1971. Print.
Zacharek, Stephanie. "*Public Enemies.*" *Salon Arts & Entertainment.* 1 July 2009. Web. 2 July 2009.
Zahl, Paul. "A Sad but Important Week." *Trinity Episcopal School for Ministry.* 3 April 2006. Web. 21 July 2006.
Zaiman, Farihah. "How *Dark Shadows* Brought the Supernatural to Television Drama." *A.V. Club.* 31 Oct. 2012. Web. 22 Aug. 2015.
Zicree, Marc Scott. *The Twilight Zone Companion.* New York: Bantam Books, 1982. Print.

Index

A&E 144
Abascal, Silvia 203
Abbott, Bruce **93**
Abbott, Maggie 192
ABC (American Broadcasting Company) 2, 3, 5, 6, 7, 13, 14, 15, 16, 17, 19, 27, 30, 31, 32, 34, 38, 42, 43, 45, 46, 47, 49, 50, 54, 55, 57, 59, 61, 62, 64, 65, 67, 69, 79, 83, 85, 88, 90, 91, 92, 99, 100, 101, 106, 117, 119, 124, 126, 127, 131, 144, 156, 157, 158, 160, 165, 167, 168, 171, 179, 189, 190, 193, 194, 195, 196, 197, 199, 201, 202, 203, 207, 208-209, 210, 211, 212, 213, 214, 216, 218, 219, 220, 221, 222, 224, 225, 226, 227, 229, 230, 231, 244
ABC Friday Night Movie 165
ABC Movie of the Week 43, 46, 156
Abominable Dr. Phibes 153
Academy Awards 10, 29, 31, 79, 117, 128, 139, 143, 150, 151, 180, 192, 215
Ace-High Western Stories 172
Acovone, Jay 225
Adam-12 101
Adventures in Paradise 26
Adventures of Robin Hood 28
Afternoon Playhouse 90
Against the Mob 92
Agnew, Spiro 59
Aidman, Charles 54, 59, 83, 89, 161
Aiello, Danny 102, **103**
Aiello, Rick 102
AIP (American International Pictures) 10, 61, 153, 156, 157, 159
Akins, Claude 52, 56, 57
Albert, Eddie 210
Albertson, Frank 176
Alda, Robert 86, 198
Alexander, Geoffrey 30
Alias 196, 241
Alias Smith and Jones 69
Alice in Wonderland 124, 167
Allen, Woody 6, 161, 198

All My Children 27
All of Me 241
Allyson, June 79, 81, 83
Altman, Robert 6, 161, 198
Alzheimer's Association PSA 19, 115, 129
Amadeus 29, 151
Amanda's 199
Ambrogio, Anthony 8, 11
"Amelia" 12, 68-**70**, 105
American Gangster 212
American Horror Story 244
American Society of Cinematographers 228, 239
American Woman 243
Amoaku, Kwame 168
Ancier, Garth 113
"And a Cup of Kindness, Too" 86
Anderson, Barbara 32
Anderson, Judith 32
Anderson, Richard 46, **48**
Anderson, Paul Thomas 150
Andrews, Edward **87**
Angel 244
Angel for Satan 192
Angie 171,
Angie the Lieutenant 6, 8, 19, 99, **100**, 101, 129, 144
Ann-Margret 202
Anno Dracula 150
Another World 17, 33
Anthony, Lysette 96, **104**-105, 106
Anthony, Ray 214
Anti-Defamation League 202
Antwerp Film Festival 76
AP (Associated Press) 213, 228
Apted, Michael 233-234, 240
Arch, Jeff 115
Argento, Dario 111, 126
Argo, Victor 92
Arizona Republic 92

Arkoff, Samuel Z. 153, 167
Armchair Theatre 27
Armstrong Circle Theatre 26
Arneson, Donald J. 32
Around the World in 80 Days 192
Arrow 241
Arthur, Beatrice 199
Ashbrook, Daphne 106, 234, **235**, 240
Asner, Edward 198
Assassination Bureau 71
As the World Turns 17, 33
Astin, Mackenzie 83
Astin, Patty Duke 79, 81, 83
Astin, Sean 83
Astredo, Humbert Allen 20, 21
Atkins, Damien 116
Atlas/Seaboard Comics 203
Atwater, Barry 43, 44
Atwood, Colleen 168
Aubrey, James 3, 15, 40, 42
August, John 121
Austin, Teri **93**
Autry, Alan 236, 240
A.V. Club 244
Avengers 76
Avon Books 7
Azevedo, Lex de 214

Babcock, Barbara 91
Baby Face Nelson 169
Back Door to Hell 163
Back to the Future 116
Badman's Territory 176
Bad News Bears movies 139
Bad Ronald 65
Bad Seed 79
Bain, Conrad 16
Bakula, Scott 240
Baldwin, Daniel 116
Bale, Christian 153, 165-166, 168
Balker, James 230
Baltimore Sun 31, 166
Band of Brothers 228
Bank Shot 6, 67
Barbarians at the Gate 47
Bare Essence 241

Barker, Doc 156, 160, 164, 168
Barker, Fred 156, 160,164
Barnabas, Quentin, and the Mummy's Curse 32
Barnaby Jones 165
Baron, David 89
Baron, Norm 230
Barovic, Dick 15
Barrett, Nancy 16, 19, 21, 26, 31, 35, 40, 109, 127, 128
Barrow, Blanche 163-164
Barrow, Buck 163-164
Barrow, Clyde 154, 156, 163-164
Barry, Raymond J. 243
Barzman, Paolo 30
Bass, Emory 22
Bassett, Angela 101
Bates Motel 72, 121
Batman 3, 15, 64, 160
Batman and Robin 176, 241
Batman Forever 105
Batman Returns 121
Batman vs. Dracula 133
Battle Creek 120-121
Bauer, Chris 116
Baxter, Meredith 59, **60**
Bay, Michael 192
BBC (British Broadcasting Corporation) 27, 131
Beaumont, Charles 38
Beauty and the Beast 94-95, 115, 225
Beefsteak Room 136
Beethoven, Ludwig 211
Beghe, Jason 93, 236, 240
Begley Jr., Ed 76, **77**
Being Human 244
Bellamy, Ralph 190, 192, 196, 202, 203, 210, 214, **217**, 230, **256**
Bellis, Richard 94
Beltway Boys 115
Bennett, Joan 16, 19, 20, 21, 111
Bennett, Ronan 168
Benny, Jack 92, 164
Benshoff, Harry 11, 243-244
Bentt, Michael 168
Bergen, Polly **189**, 190, 192, 194, **200**, 202, 203, 210, 212, 214, 227, 230
Berkoff, Steven **210**, 214, 238, 240
Berneau, Christopher 22

Index 269

Bernstein, Leonard 213
Bernt, Eric 110
Berrigan, Don 92
Best, Wayne 116
Better Call Saul 120
Bewitched 202
Beyond the Law 176
Biderman, Ann 168
Big Easy 8, 19, 90, **91**, 129
Big Event 83
Big Finish Productions 11, 112, 125, 235
Big Fish 121
Big Lebowski 241
Big Wednesday 153
Billboard magazine 19
Binney, Geoffrey 153
Biograph Theatre 154, 163, 164, 166,
Birney, David 90
Black, Karen 57, 67, 68, 69, **70**, **71**, 72, **75**, 76, 104, 109, 118, 126, 249
Blackburn, Clarice 20
Black Hawk Down 212
Black Lightning 121
Black Scorpion 79
Black Sunday 192
Blacula 64, 156
Blakely, Susan **236**, 240
Blake's 7 62
Blatt, Daniel 118, 119, 240
Blees, Robert 79
Blessed, Brian 210
Bloch, Robert 11
Bloodlines: Matheson's Dracula 144-147, 149
"Blood Son" 131
B.L. Stryker 95
Blue Lagoon 227
Blumgarten, James 64
Blunden, Bill 108
Blye, Margaret 156, 167, 169
BMI (Broadcast Music, Incorporated) 228
Boardman, Chris 94
"Bobby" (1977) 79, **80**, 105, 106
"Bobby" (1996) **104**, 105, 106
Bochner, Hart 118, 210, **211**, **212**, 214, 230
Bodyguard 241
Bold and the Beautiful 241
Bold Ones 47, 57

Bonanza: The Next Generation 180
Bonnie and Clyde 153, 164, 172
Book of Temptation 235
Boorstin, Jon 95
Boston Globe 31, 38, 41, 122, 124, 240
Boston Herald 117
Bostwick, Barry 118, 210, **212**, 215, 222
Bourneuf, Philip 47
Bowman, Rob 94, 110, 111, 113
Bracken's World 163
Bradbury, Ray 76
Bradley, Edson 186
Brady, Scott 84, 86, **160**, 185, 187, 198, 202
Bram Stoker's Dracula 133, 135, 140, 144, 147
Brando, Marlon 126
Bratt, Benjamin 219
Braun, Eva 227
Brave New World 59
Break in the Ice 66
Breaking Bad 120
Brennan, Eileen **64**
Brenner, Jules 167
Brenon, Trudi 172
Brian Keith Show 131
Briant, Shane **54**, 55
Bright Promise 57
Brinckerhoff, Burt 42, 59, 64
Briscoe, Don 20
Broadwell, Dick 173, 174, 175, 176, 185
Brody, Larry 57
Brockman, Michael 127
Bronk 146
Bronte, Charlotte 3, 15, 18
Bronte, Emily 18, 26, 150, 169
Brother Drop Dead 249
Bronze Wrangler Awards 172, 180
Brood 79
Brooke, Walter 65
Brooklyn Horror-Film Festival 128
Brooks, Hindi 89
Brooks, Scott 153
Brotherhood of Satan 38
Brown, Blair 111
Brown, Clancy 92, **93**
Brown, G. Mac 168
Brown, Mary Jane 198
Brown, Murray 131, **132**, **148**, 150

Brown, Pamela 131, 150
Bruce, Ed 168
Bruns, Philip 162
Bryant, Charlie 173, 185
Bucholz, Horst **5**, 76
Buff, Warren 7
Buffalo Niagara Film Festival 249
Buffy the Vampire Slayer 244
Bureau of Investigation 10, 61, 150, 153, 154, 155, 159, 163, 164, 166
Burke, Marty 230
Burlingame, Jon 11, 32
Burnett, John 227-228
Burnt Offerings (Marasco) 69, 70-76
Burnt Offerings (1976) 7, 8, 69, **70**, 71-**73**, 74, **75**, 76, 79, 88, 101, 118, 119, 129, 140, 149, 179, 180, 240, 246, 248, 249, 250
Burr, Ty 122, 124
Burrough, Bryan 168
Burstyn, Ellen 116
Burton, Robert "Skip" 67, 81
Burton, Tim 5, 10, 19, 121, 122, 123, 124, 125, 167
Bushman, David 128
Butler, Josephine 121

Caesar, Sid 79, 81
Caine Mutiny 190
Caldwell, Joe 26, 127
California ship 201
Calomee, Gloria 89
Cameron, James 139
camp 59, 111, 124, 234
Camp, Bill 168
Campanelli, Linda 95
Campbell, J. Kenneth 92, 93
Campbell, Julia 93
Canary, David 157, 168
Cannon, Orin 79, 161, 185
Capone, Al 163
Captains and the Kings 111, 214
Carey, Denise 186
Carey, MacDonald 16, 198
Carey, Philip 56, 57
Cariou, Len 117
Carol Burnett Show 240

Carpenter, Karen 121
Carpenter, Richard 121
Carradine, John 46
Carrie 79
Carrington, Robert 169
Carroll, Bryan 168
Carson, Sarah 101
Carter, Chris 240, 243
Carter, Helena Bonham 121
Cartwright, John 203
Casablanca 92
Case, David 55
"Case of Charles Dexter Ward" 38
Casino Royale (2008) 112
Castellari, Enzo 196
Castle, William 176
Cattle Annie and Little Britches 176
CBC (Canadian Broadcasting Corporation) 30, 31
CBS (Columbia Broadcasting System) 2, 3, 13, 14-15, 17, 26, 40, 59, 90, 101, 102, 106, 109, 115, 130, 131, 133, 144, 150, 157, 165, 171, 200, 202, 227, 233, 240
CBS Golf Classic 3, 10, 13, 14-15, 127, 129
CBS Late Movie 186
Chaguanian, Anatoly 201
Challenge Golf 10, 14, 114, 129
Champ 102
Chaney Jr., Lon 38, 176
Chang, Justin 122, 124
Changeling 95
Charlie and the Chocolate Factory 124, 167
Charlie's Angels 162
Chastain, Jessica 111
Cherkoss, Daniel *see* Curtis, Dan
Cherkoss, Edward 14
Cherkoss, Mildred 14
Chermak, Cy 44, 47, 244
Chianese, Francesco 230
Chicago Bears 154
Chicago Sun-Times 42, 98,
Children Nobody Wanted 84
Children of Rage 90
Chiller TV 99
China Shadow 7
Chinatown 80
CHiPs 2, 91, 172, 173, 182, 184
Chirkinian, Frank 15

Index

Christian Science Monitor 108
Christie, Agatha 67
Christmas Carol 109
Chulack, Christopher 92
Churchill, Winston 192, 197, 198, 200, 214, 217, 221
Cimarron Kid 176
Cinefantastique 37, 105
cinema verite 43
Clark, Eugene **93**
Clark, Matt 66, 105, 157, 158, 160, 161, 167, **171**, 173, **185**, 202, 218, 220
Clarke, Frederick S. 37
Clark, Janis 230
Clarke, Stanley 101
classic horror 43, 44-45, 47, 128, 246
Classic Mystery Ghost Stories 46
Claxton, William 180
Clayton, Jack 61
Cleveland Plain Dealer 31-32
Clique Publishing 7
Cloning of Clifford Swimmer 178
Close Encounters of the Third Kind 232, 239, 240
Clothes of Sand 112
Coal Miner's Daughter 234
Cobb, Lee J. 65, **66**, 67
Cobert, Robert 11, 12, 18-19, 31, 32, 36, 42, 45-47, 50, 55, 57, 59, 60, 62, 65, 67, 69, 74, 79, 83, 86, 88, 94, 102, 105, 106, 109, 110, 111, 117, 118, 120, 121, 122, 125, 127, 140, 147, 150, 156, 162, 167, 168, 172, 177, 180, 185, 194, 203, 213, 214, **218**, 220, 224, 225, 227, 228, 229, 230, 234, 240, 249
Coburn, James 198
Cody, Kathleen 25
Cody, William 177
Cohen, Stanley 102
Colan, Gene 150
Collateral 165
Colley, Kenneth 221
Collier, Don 172, 185
Collins, Robert 92, 94, 99-100, 101
Collinwood Revisited 7
Colman, Ronald 164
Come Die with Me 8, 42, **64**-65, 129, 140
Comer, Anjanette **5**, 57, **58**, 76, **78**
comic books 3, 6, 7, 15, 32, 64, 99, 105, 121, 125, 133, 160, 167, 176, 203, 241

Command Performance 169
Comtois, Guy 230
Conan the Barbarian 227
Concentration 17
Condemned 169
Condo 199
Connell, Richard 56
Connelly, Charles 175, 176
Connelly, Christopher 59, **60**
Connors, Mike 211, 219
Cook Jr., Elisha 169
Cooper, Abraham 118
Cooper, Alice 122, **123**
Cooper, Mary 26
Coopers 90, 203
Coppola, Francis Ford 133, 135, 140, 144, 147
Corey, Jeff 79, 81
Corman, Roger 38, 153
Corpse Bride 121
Correll, Charles 5, 91, 202, 203
Cortese, Dan 153
Costello, Frank 92
Costner, Kevin 102-103
Cotillard, Marian 166, 168
Count Dracula 149
Cousins, Christopher 236, 240
Cousins, Joseph **236**, 240
Cowley, Samuel 154, 156, 158, 160, 162, 163, 164, 165, 167, 168
Cox, Wally 46
Crawford, Terrayne 20
Crenna, Richard 234, 238, 240
Crist, Judith 179-180
Crittenden, James **171**, 173, **185**
Crosby, Mary 91
Cross, Ben 96, **97**, 98, 111, 127, 245
Cross of Iron 196
Crothers, Joel 16, 19, 20
Crowley, Nathan 168
Crudup, Billy 165, 168
Cruel Doubt 233
Cruise, William 230
CSI: 117
C-Span 200
Cujo 119
Cummings, Jeffrey 118
Cumpanas, Ana 154, 167, 168

Curse of Dark Shadows 40
Curse of the Black Widow 8, 79, 81, **82**, 83, 129, 179, 189, 190, 240, 246
Curtis, Cathy 14, 17, 43, 118, 121, 126
Curtis, Dan
 auteur 5-6, 94, 127, 153, 161, 171, 179, 190, 194, 198, 201
 birth 14
 death 14, 118, 121, 246
 funeral 118, 246
 illness 118, 246
 live-theatre effect in his productions 65, 196, 199, 200
 low camera angles in his films 1, 43, 57, 61, 65, 68, 74, 79, 88, 105, 143, 156, 159, 203, 249
 memorial service 56, 89, 118-120, 246
 personal life 14, 43, 65, 110, 118, 119, 126, 127
 photographs 4, **13**, **86**, **103**, **114**, **116**, **130**, **152**, **159**, **170**, **188**, **193**, **195**, **197**, **200**, **201**, **204**, **205**, **208**, **218**, **220**, **228**, **248**, **250**
 sense of place in his films 46, 47, 56, 65
 stock company of actors in his films 1, 6, 61, 109, 119-120, 160-161, 169, 198, 202, 215, 218, 220, 246
 sympathy for the monster in his films 49, 133
Curtis, Linda 14, 17, 43, 65
Curtis, Norma Mae Klein 14, 15, 43, 66, 110, 118, 119, 126, 190, 207, 246
Curtis, Tracy 14, 17, 43, 76, 79, 81, 102, 118, 121, 126, 247
Cuse, Carlton 121
CW television network 133
Czuchry, Matt 110

Dabson, Jesse **100**,
Dallas 110-111, 158, 220
Dallas Cowboys Cheerleaders II 182
Dalton, Adeline 172
Dalton, Bill 172, 176, 180, 181, 183, 185
Dalton, Bob 172, 173, 174, 175, 176, 177, 179, 180, 181-182, 184, 185
Dalton, Emmett 172, 173-174, 175, 176, 177, 180, 181-184, 185
Dalton, Frank 172, 180, 182, 183, 185
Dalton, Gratton 172, 174, 175, 176, 177, 179, 180, 181, 182, 185

Dalton, Julia 176, 181-184, 185
Dalton, Leona 172
Dalton, Lewis 172, 185
Dalton Gang 176
Dalton Girls 176
Daltons Ride Again 176
Damien—Omen II 72
Dan Curtis Associates 14, 90
Dan Curtis Holdings 11
Dan Curtis Legacy Award 120-121
Dan Curtis Productions 3, 11, 14, 55, 119, 125, 156, 157, 240, 244
Daniels, Dorothy 17
Dano, Royal 172, 185
Danson, Ted 116
Dante, Joe 47, 161, 198
Darby, Rhys 243
Daredevil 180
Dark Crystal 143
Dark Destroyer 79
Dark Mansions 241
"Darkness at Blaisedon" 8, **9**, 26, 32, **33**, 34, 62, 129, 246
Dark Secret of Harvest Home 91
Dark Shadows (1966-1971) 3, 5, 6, 7, 8, 11, 12, 13, 14, 15-**16**, 17-**21**, **22**-23, **24**-27, 31, 32, 34, 35, 36, 38, 42, 45, 47, 49, 55, 59, 61, 62, 64, 65, 67, 74, 83, 89, 94, 98, 99, 103-104, 108, 109, 110, 111, 112, 113, 117, 118, 119-120, 121, 122, 124, **126**, 127, 128, 129, 133, 140, 147, 156, 161, 162, 167, 169, 186, 194, 196, 198, 202, 214, 217, 218, 220, 228, 230, 235, 243-244, **245**, 246, 247, 249
Dark Shadows (1991) 6, 8, 12, 13, 52, 94, **95**, 96, **97**, **98**, 99, 104, 110, 111, 113, 120, 121, 122, 127, 129, 140, 161, 192, 195, 197, 215, 233, 234, 241, 242, 243, 246, 247
Dark Shadows (2004) 6, 8, 97, 104, 110-111, **112**, 113, **114**, 121, 127, 129, 215, 241, 247
Dark Shadows (2012) 6, 10, 121-122, **123**, 124-125, 127, 167, 168
 Dark Shadows Collector's Guide 7
Dark Shadows Festival 11, 12, 14, 34, 42, 109, 111, 113, 118, 161, 247
Dark Shadows Journal 7
Dark Shadows Movie Book 249
Dark Shadows Resurrected 99
Dark Shadows Story Digest Magazine 7
Dark Shadows: The Comic-Strip Book 7

Darrow, Clarence 92
Das Boot 213
Dating Game 17
Davenport, Nigel 54, 131, **136**, **141**, **143**, 150
David, Thayer 16, 19, 20, 21, 32, 35, **37**, **41**, 161, 169
Davies, Geraint Wyn 105
Davis, Alexander J. 186-187
Davis, Bette 69, 72, 76
Davis, Roger 20, 21, 36, 109, 118, 127
Davis Jr., Sammy 3, 15
Dawidziak, Mark 11, 31-32, 111, 144-147, 149, 243
Dawn, Jeff 240
Dawn, Wes 203, 230
Day-Lewis, Daniel 150
Day Mars Invaded Earth 241
Day of the Locust 71
Days of Our Lives 16, 244
DC Comics 3, 15
Dead of Night: A Darkness at Blaisedon (1969) 8, **9**, 26, 32, **33**, 34, 62, 129, 246
Dead of Night (1977) **5**, 6, 8, 76, **77**, **78**, 79, **80**, 83, 104, 105, 108-109, 129, 169, 180, 189, 240
Dead Ringer 241
Deadwood 125
Deal, David 57, 83, 246
Dean Martin Show 131
Death at Love House 7, 203
Death Becomes Her 122
Deathwork 169
Decades network 128
Dee, Deborah 168
Deep Red 111
Defenders 28
Deford, Frank 110, 169
Dehner, John 211
Del Valle, David 11, 120
Demon 150
Demons of the Mind 132
De Niro, Robert 168
Dennehy, Brian 115
Denver Post 124
Depp, Johnny 121, 124, 165-166, 167, 168, 244, 245
De Ravin, Emilie 168
Desert Fury 90, 91

DeSouza, Steven 110
Desperate Housewives 113
"detective jazz" 45, 46-47, 83
Detroit News 193-194
Devane, William 90, **91**
Devil's Daughter 108
DeVol, Larry 160, 164
DeVorzon, Barry 154, 167
Dewan Tatum, Jenna 113
Dewhurst, Colleen 227
DGA (Directors Guild of America) 118, 120, 228
Dial M for Murder 90
Diary of a Gunfighter 169
Diary of Anne Frank 109
DiCenzo, George 59
Dick, Philip K. 105-106
Dickens, Charles 109, 202
Dickinson, Angie 52, 99, **100**, 101
Diffring, Anton 190
Diller, Barry 189,
Dillinger, John 10, 61, 153-154, 160, 163, 164, 165-166, 167, 168, 169
Dillinger (1973) 10, 61, 84, 153-154, 155, 156, 158, 159, 162, 167
Dillon, Hugh 116
Dimitri, Nick 52, **53**
Dirty Sally 131
Discovery 186
Disorderly Orderly 97, 241
Distinguished Service Awards 228
Dobkin, Larry 221
Doctor Mabuse 247, 249
Doctor Mabuse: Etiopomar 247
Doctors 18
Doctor Who 62
Doheny, Edward 96, 241
Doheny, Lucy 241
Doheny, Ned 241
Donnelly, Thomas Michael 117
Donovan 121
Donovan, Martin 110-111,
Doolin, Bill 173, 176, 183, 185
Doolins of Oklahoma 176
Dorff, Stephen 168
Douglas Fairbanks Presents 14
Douglas, Gordon 176
Douglas, Kirk 198

Douglas, Sarah 131, 150
Downey, Roy 202
Dracula (Stoker) 6, 10, 17, 128, 131-150
Dracula (1931) 44
Dracula (1974) 6, 7, 8, 10, 34, 49, 59, 65, 74, 119, 129, 130-**132**, 133-**134**, 135-**136**, 137-**138**, **139**, 140-**141**, **142**, **143**, 144-**146**, 147-**148**, 149-150, 151, 152, 177, 179, 189, 246, 247
Dracula (2007) 136
Dracula: A Biography of Vlad the Impaler 135
Dracula Book 37, 133
Dracula in Istanbul 135
Dracula's Daughter 18
Dracula Sucks 150
Dragnet 14
Dr. Christian 28
Dr. Cyclops 105
Dreamer of Oz 115
Dream Lover 95
Dress Gray 47
Dreyfuss, Richard 154, 167
Dr. Jekyll and Mr. Hyde (1931) 186
Drop Dead Diva 59
Dr. Phibes Rises Again 79, 146
Dubbins, Don 65
DuBois, Ja'net 90, **91**
Duel 10, 105
Duff, Howard 211
Duggan, Andrew 89, 190, 202
Duke, Patty 79, 81, 83
Dukes, David 102, 106, 108, 190, 194, **195**, 203, 210, 216, 230
Du Maurier, Daphne 38, 122
Dune 113
Dunsmuir House 73
Durbano, Art 92
Durkin, Betsy 20
Dusay, Marj **9**, 33
Dusty and Sweets McGee 38
Dyess-Nugent, Phil 244
Dynamite Entertainment
Dynasty 94
Dysart, Richard 227

Eastwood, Clint 102-103
Ebert, Roger 42
Eddie Awards 228
Eddie Macon's Run
Edgar Awards 30, 43, 84
Edge of Night 17, 27
Edmiston, Walker 69
Edmonds, Louis 16, 19, 20, 21, 26, 32, 35, 161
Edward Scissorhands 105
Edwards, Blake 40
8½ 192
Eichmann, Adolf 216
Eilbacher, Lisa 118, **189**, 200, 203
Eis, Elizabeth 23,
Eischied 92
Eisenhower, Dwight D. 224
Eisenmann, Ike 158
Elektra 111
Elfman, Blossom 90
Elfman, Danny 19, 121
Elizabeth R 214
Elizabeth the Queen 32
Ellen 124
Ellingwood, Tom 167
Elliott, Denholm 30
Ellis, Ralph 26
Emmy Awards 3, 5, 13, 14-15, 18, 27, 32, 90, 91, 94, 99, 105, 115, 119, 120, 180, 192, 202, 214, 217, 218, 220, 223, 225, 227, 229, 236, 237, 238, 239, 246
Emmy magazine 243
Empire Strikes Back 99
Encore Western channel 185
Enterprise ship 217
Entertainment Tonight 119, 192
Entertainment Weekly 108, 117, 124-125
ER 92, 110
Erman, John 202
Evers, Jason 57
Every Little Crook and Nanny 38
Exorcist movies 29, 79
"Express to Terror" **4**, **85**, **86**, **87**, 170
Eyes of Charles Sand 178

Facebook 84, 247
Fairman, Michael 92
Falcon Crest 223, 243
Falk, Peter 115

Fall Guy 197
Family 88, 89, 171
Family Plot 71
Family Ties 115
Fan Culture 8
Fantasy Island 87
fanzines 7, 119, 124-125, 167, 194, 214, 216, 221
Faraj, Ansel H. 10, 11, 247, 249
Farrell, Sharon **171**, 177, **178**, **185**
Fatal Attraction 125
"Father-Thing" 105-106
FBI vs. Alvin Karpis 157, 158
Feke, Steve 95
Fein, Rita 126
Feitshans, Buzz 167
Felony Squad 101
feminism 156
Fengriffin 55
Fenwick, Gillie 30
Fiddler on the Roof 10, 143, **226**
Fifteen Western Tales 172
film noir 6, 43, 45, 80, 90, 94, 105, 160, 198, 246
Films in Review 74
Fimple, Dennis **171**, 173, **185**
Findley, Timothy 169
Finney, Jack 76, 77, 106, 108-109, 169
Fischer, Vicki 168
Fitzpatrick, John 87, **171**, 173, **185**
Five Heartbeats 101
Flags of Our Fathers 228
Flame in the Wind 26
Flanagan, Fionnula 55
Flash 241
Fleming, Al 75
Flesh and the Fiends 30
Fletch movies 139
Flight of the Conchords 243
Flores, Bill 230
Florescu, Radu 10, 50, 135, 140, 150
Floyd, "Pretty Boy" 154, 158, 160, 161, 162, 167, 168
Foch, Nina 211
Fonda, Henry 92
Fontane, Char **86**,
Ford, David 19, 20,
Forsyte Saga 214
Fort Worth Star-Telegram 74, 98

Foster, Penelope 185, 203
Four Freedoms 110
Fowkes, Conard 16
Fox television network 110, 240
Fox, Colin 116
Fox, Michael J. 115, **116**
Foxworth, Robert 47, **49**, 50, 65
France, David 116
Franciosa, Anthony 79, 81, **82**, 246
Frank Nitti: The Enforcer 233
Frankenstein (Shelley) 20, 47, 49-50
Frankenstein (1931) 3
Frankenstein (1973) 7, 8, 31, 47, **49**-50, 54, 55, 62, 65, 129, 246
Frankenstein (2004) 113
Frankenstein and Me (1996) 243
Franklin, Hugh 16
Frechette, Billie 154, 156, 164, 166, 167, 168
Frees, Paul 126
Freund, Karl 186
Frey, Sami 214
Frid, Jonathan 14, 17-18, 19, **21**, **22**, 23, **24**, 26, 27, 34, **35**-36, 38, 96, 111, 122, **123**, 124, 127, **128**, **245**
Fringe 121
Frogs 79, 153
From Time to Time (Finney) 76, 169
Frost, Warren 240
Fugitive 157, 180, 197, 215
Fujikawa, Jerry 190, 202
Fuller, Bryan 121
"Funeral" 131
Fyfe, Jim 96

Gable, Clark 166
Gaffney, Magdalen 230
Gail, Max 79, 80
game shows 17, 18
Ganziano, Dino 230
Garabedian, Mitchell 116, 117
Garfunkel, Art 121
Gauntlet books 108-109, 147
Gaynes, George 68
gender 65, 79, 100, 156
General Foods 14
General Hospital 97, 222, 241

General Service Studios 57
Genesis II 43
Genn, Leo 30
Gentry, Robert 47
Geoghan, John 116
George, Anthony 20
George, James 167, 185
Gerard, Merwin 59
Gerani, Gary 203
Ghost in Monte Carlo 96
Ghost Watcher 112
Ghost Whisperer 113
Gideon's Trumpet 92
Gielgud, John 120, **205**, 210, 214, **215**, 222, **223**, 227, 230
Gierasch, Stefan 96, 195, 230
Gilligan, Vince 120-121
Gillin, Hugh 91, 202
Gillis, Jamie 150
Gilmore Girls 241
Girls of Huntington House 90
Girl with Something Extra 131
Gladiator 212
Gloria 187
Glut, Donald F. 37, 133
Godfather movies 29
"Goin' to Mexico" 102
Going, Joanna 96, **98**, **242**, 243
Gold, Tracey 90
Goldberg, Harry
Goldberg, Leonard 16, 127
Goldberg, Whoopi 128
Golden Globe Awards 202, 222
Golden Halo Awards 85, 90
Golden Laurel Awards 109, 228
Goldenthal, Elliot 166, 168
Gold Key Comics 7, 32
Gone with the Wind 55
Goodman, Benny 166
Good Times 91, 131
Good Year 212
Goodyear TV Playhouse 26
Gordon, George, Lord Byron 18, 150
Gordon, Leo 169
Gordon-Levitt, Joseph 96, **98**
Gould, Alexander 111
Gould, Anna 187

Gould, Dana 243
Gould, Helen 187
Gould, Jay 185, 187
Graham, Ed 3, 11, 14, 15
Graham, Gerrit 106
Graham, Stephen 168
Grahame-Smith, Seth 121, 124
Grammy Awards 31
Graves, Peter **56**, 118, 190, 194, **200**, 203, 210, 214, 230
"Graveyard Rats" 12, 105, 106
Gray, Sybil 240
Gray, William 95, 120
Great Ice Rip-Off 6, 8, 65, **66**, 67, 84, 102, 127, 129, 139, 158
Green, Eva 112, 121
Green Hornet 65
Greenley, Howard 186
Greenwood, Bruce 115, 118
Gregory, David 10, 125-126, 127
Gremlins 47
Greystone mansion 96-97, 110-111, 215, 241, 249
Griffith, Eva 61
Grimm 244
Grooms, W.J. 159
Gross, Darren 11, 42
Growing Pains 216, 221, 225
Guiding Light 90
Guttman, Richard 163-164

Hacker, Joseph 210
Hackett, Joan 79, **80**, **89**, 105
Hadfield, Veronica 230
Haggerty, H.B. 81
"Hail to the Chief" 86
Hale, Billy 169
Haley, Jackie Earle 121
Hall, Grayson 18, 19, 20, **21**, 34, **37**, 38, **39**, 65, **66**, 67, 127, 161
Hall, Matthew 94
Hall, Sam 7, 26, 32, 33, 34, 37, 38, 42, 47, 49, 94, 169
Hallmark Channel 113
Hallmark Hall of Fame 32, 106, **107**, 108-109
Halloween 79
Halpen, Ellen 168

Hamilton, Margaret 46
Hamilton, Polly 167, 168
Hamlet 119
Hamlisch, Marvin 115
Hammer, Ben 196
Hammer films 246
Hamrick, Craig 7
Hannibal 212, 244
Happy Days 82, 156, 171, 196
Hardester, Crofton 91
Hardman, Richard 69, 159, 162, 168
Hard Times of R.J. Berger 121
Hardy, Robert 214
Harkins, John 23, 198, 230
Harrad Experiment 156
Harris, Richard A. 139
Harrison, Gregory 67
Hartley, Mariette 65
Hart to Hart 241
Hatfield, Hurd 55
Hatosy, Shawn 168
Haunted 27
Haunted Palace 38
Hawaii Five-O 165
HBO (Home Box Office) 244
Head of the Class 225
Heat 165
Heathcote, Bella 121
Heckart, Eileen 69, 72
Heiress 18
Henerson, James 106, 108–109, 169
Henesy, David 16, 19, 21, **22**, 25
Hennick House 61
Henry, Emmaline 65
Herman, Daniel 7
Hermanson, Frank 159
Hermes Press 7
Herrmann, Bernard 19
Hessler, Gordon 7–8
Heston, Charlton 32, 198
"He Who Kills" 105
High Anxiety 83
Highlander: Endgame 110
Highlander: The Search for Vengeance 133
Hijacking of the Achille Lauro 94
Hill, Jim 158, 161, 168
Hill, Julie 176, 182, **185**

Hill, Nathan 30
Hill, Steven 153
Hingle, Pat 211
Hitchcock, Alfred 5, 19, 71, 72
Hitler, Adolf 194, 196, 197, 198, 199, 210, 214, 216, 219, 221, 224, 225, 227, 229
Hitler: The Rise of Evil 228
Hoffman, Dustin 36
Hoffman, Elizabeth 198, 214
Hogan, Frank S. 92, 93
Hogan, P.J. 111, 113
Holbrook, Hal 92
Holdridge, Lee 115
Holiday, Billie 166
Holliman, Earl 100
Hollinsworth Productions 249
Holly, Lillian 164, 168
Hollywood Reporter 32, 47, 52, 54, 67, 76, 98, 106, 115
Holmes, Rupert 110
Holocaust 213-214
Home Alone 102
Homefront 92
homosexuality 28, 30, 51
Honath, Norman 161
Hoodlum Priest 15
Hoods 169
Hoover, J. Edgar 158, 165, 168
Hopalong Cassidy 3, 14
Hope, Bob 144
Hope, Leslie 223, 230
Hopkins, Bo 86, 160, **161**, **171**, 173, **174**, **185**
Hopkins, Budd 101, 233, 234, 240
Hopkins, Harry 217
Horizon House Institute 85
Horner, Penelope 131, 150
Horrible Dr. Hichcock 192
horror *see* classic horror; modern horror
Horror of Dracula 44, 147
Hot Rock 67
Houdini, Harry 186
Houghton Mifflin 135
Hours of Love 192
"House" 26, 127
Houseman, John 190, 194, 203, 210
House of Cards 243
House of Dan Curtis 8, 9, 10

House of Dark Shadows 6, 7, 8, 23, 31, 32, 34-**35**, 36-**37**, 38, 41, 42, 44, 46, 55, 65, 94, 96, 101, 110, 127, 129, 137, 140, 186-187, 203, 243, 246, 247, 249
House of Dracula 18
House of Frankenstein 18
House of Terror 106
House That Would Not Die 43
Howitzer, Bronson 69, 159, 162, 168
Howling 119
How to Succeed in Business without Really Trying 59
Hu, Kelly 111, 113
Hubley, Season 87, **88**
Huggins, Roy 157
Humanitas Prize 115
Human Target 87
Hungary in Ancient...Times 136
Hunt, Helen 90
Hunted Past Reason
Hunter, Holly 227
Hunter, Ian McLellan 27-28, 30, 31
"Hunter" 55, 150
Hunt for Red October 180
Hurgon, Jean-Michel 230
Hussey, Margaret 240
Hutson, Lee 84, 89, 90, 169, 203
Hutton, James 65
Hyman, Dick 90

I Am Legend 43, 105, 131, 144
Ideas into Books 8
Il Mare 108
I Love Harrisburg in the Springtime 109, 169
Imagen Awards 115
"I'm Gonna Dance for You" 31
Immortal 241
Incredible Shrinking Man 12, 43, 105
Incredible Sunday 214, 219, 226
Independent Film Channel 243
Inferno 111
Inherent Vice 243
Inner Sanctum 76
Innocents 61, 79
Innovation Comics 99
In Search of Dracula 135
In Search of Frankenstein 50

Interview with the Vampire 18, 150
Intruders: The Incredible Visitations 233
Intruders: They Are Among Us 7, 8, 10, 93, 101, 129, 144, 212, **232**, **233**, **234**, **235**, **236**, **237**-238, **239**, 240-241, 246, 247
Invaders 50, 51, 194, 234, 240
Invasion 113
Invasion of Carol Enders 8, 42, 59, **60**, 61, 64, 129, 240
Iowa ship 225
Iron Horse 155
Ironside 32, 47
Iron Will 115
Irving, Henry 143, 150
Island of Terror 246
I Think I'm Having a Baby 90, 108, 129, 180
It's Alive 79

Jack the Ripper 150, 233
Jackson, Kate 25, 38, 109, 111
Jackson, Shirley 26
Jacob, Jasper 61, **63**
James, Anthony 72
James, Brion 160
James, Frank 172
James, Henry 61-63
James, Jesse 172, 176, 185
Jane Eyre 3, 15, 18
Jarrett, Janice 154
Jarrott, Charles 27, 31
Jaws 74, 246
Jaws 2 108
Jekyll and Hyde (2008) 30
Jelliffe, Bill 173, 185
Jenkins, Henry 19
Jenkins, Megs 61, 62
Jennifer Eight 111
Jenson, Roy 154, 167
Jeremiah Johnson 153
Jesse James vs. the Daltons 176
Job 223
Job Interview 247
John, Elton 121
Johnny Ryan 8, 19, 92, **93**, 94, 101, 129
Johns, Milton 216
Johnson, Ben 61, 153, 154, 162, 167

Johnson, Chantelle 168
Johnson, J.J. 91
Jones, Dean 83, **89**, 92, 118
Jones, Jamie 8, 11
Jones, Lory Basham 92
Jones. W.D. 163-164
Jordan, Glenn 47, 49, 50, 54,
Jordon, William 160
Journal of Frankenstein 49
Journal of the Gun Years 104
Judging Amy 246-247
"Julie" 67, 69
Julliard School of Music 18

Kail, Jim 203, 230, 240
Kanaly, Steve 154, 156, **157**, 158, 162, 167
Kansas City Massacre 7, 8, 10, 61, 69, 84, 94, 129, 139, 152, 153, 155, 157, 158-**159**, **160**, **161**, 162, **165**, 168, 169, 174, 177, 179, 247
Kansas City Star 214
Kaplan, Henry 27
Karlen, John 8, 11, 19, 21, 25, 26, 35, 40, **49**, **54**, 55, 59, 65, 68, 89, 96, 102, 109, **114**, 118, 127, 156, 157, **158**, **159**, 160, 161, 167, 185, 190, 202, 218, 230
Karpis, Alvin 160, 164, 168
Katic, Branka 168
Katz, William 65
Kavanaugh, Derek 150
Kearney, Gene R. 59,
Keel, Howard 198
Kelly, Grace 14
Kelly, "Machine Gun" 61, 156, 158, 162, 163, 167
Kelly, Roz 79, 81, **82**
Kemp, Jeremy 190, 203, 210, 230
Kemp, Sally 59
Kennedy, David 118, 119, 121
Kennedy, Ruth 240
Kennedy, Lisa 124
Kenwith, Herbert 57, 58
Kernochan, James 186
Key, Steve 168
Kid 102
Kiley, Richard 202
Kill and Kill Again
Killing at Hell's Gate 89

Kilmer, Val 126
King, Burton L. 186
King, Stephen 7, 43, 150
Kingdom of Heaven 212
Kirchner, L.R. 153, 176
Kirkland, Sally 158
Kiser, Terry 172, 185
Klune, Donald C. 156, 167
Klute 111
Knightwatch 219
Knots Landing 91, 93
Knotts, Don 246
Knowles, Christopher L. 52
Kojak 59, 186
Kolchak Tapes 52, 150
Kolchak: The Night Stalker 44, 47, 100, 117-118, 244
Komine, Pike, and W.D. Baldry 169
Kondracke, Millicent M. 115
Kondracke, Mort 115
Kovacs, Mijou 216
Krall, Diana 166, 168
Kring, Tim 90, 203
Kripke, Eric 121
Kruger, Hardy 221
Kubrick, Stanley 5
Kurtzman, Katy 83, **84**
Kuttner, Henry 105, 106

Lacy, Jerry 20, 21, 25, 96, 109, 118, 127, 249
Lair 133, 244
Lake House 107, 108
Lampley, Jonathan 8, 11
Lancaster, Deborah 240
Land Beyond the Forest 137
Landau, Richard 47, 49
Lane, Charles 190, 202, 221, 230
Lane, Barbara 230
Lang, Howard 192, 197
Lang, Stephen 168
Langella, Frank 150
Lansbury, Angela 55
Lansky, Meyer 92
Larraz, José Ramon 148
Lasky, Kathleen 116
Last Case of August T. Harrison 247
Last Child 43

Last Detail 175
Last Man on Earth 105
Last of Sheila 80
Last of the Crazy People 169
Last Ride of the Dalton Gang 1-2, 7, 10, 13, 59, 79, 88, 99, 113, 119, 129, 164, 169, 170, **171**, 172-**173**, **174**, **175**-176, **177**, **178**, **179**-184, **185**, 186, 187, 190, 246, 247
Last Summer 169
Last Tenant 87, 90
Laszowska, Emily Gerard 137
Late-Night Horror 131
Laugh-In 64
Laurenson, James 61
Laverne and Shirley 196
LaVoo, George 76
Law, Bernard 115, 116, 117
Law & Order 246-247
Lawman 159
Lawrence, Steve **86**
Lawrence, Vicki 86
Lawson, Eric **171**, 173, **185**
Lawson, Karen 230
Leachman, Cloris 87, **88**, 154, 167
Lee, Christopher 121, 126, 143, 150
Legend of Johnny Dillinger 69, 164, 165
Legend of Machine Gun Kelly 61, 169
Leigh, Jennifer Jason 90, 106, **107**, 108
Leisure Books 7
Leone, Nola 128
Les Dalton 176
Les Miserables 47
Lesson Plans 8
Lester, Mark 63
Let's Make a Deal 17
Levinson, Art 168
Lewin, Albert 54, 55
Lewin, Robert 163
Lewis, Al 46
Lewis, Fiona 131, **139**, **146**, 147, 150
Lewis, Geoffrey 66, 83, **84**, 105, 154, 158, 167
Lewis, Juliette 84
Lewis, Traci 168
Lexington ship 217
Life and Times of Judge Roy Bean 153
"Likeness of Julie" 67
Lilies of the Field 192

Lincoln 98
Lindley, Barbara 131, 150
Linus! the Lion-Hearted 3, 14, 15
Little Big Man 36
Little, Brown books 209
Littlefield, Warren 99
Little Game 79
Little Orphan Annie 162
Live and Let Die 231
Locke, Rosanna 81
Lockhart, June 79, 83
Lockwood-Mathews Mansion 36
Logan, Michael 124
Logan's Run 46, 69, 247
Lohmann, Dietrich 228, 230
Lohmann, Paul 66, 83, 168
Lolita 143
Lonesome Dove 94, 227
Lone Star Shadows 7, 214, 216, 221
Long Days of Summer 5, 6, 14, 19, 76, 88, **89**, 90, 115, 118, 129, 169, 203
Long Hot Summer 50
Look at Monaco 14
Loon Lake 247
Loring, Lynn 162
Lorre, Peter 216
Los Angeles Herald-Examiner 62, 85, 90, 156
Los Angeles Times 6, 27, 47, 50, 85, 90, 103, 133, 156, 161, 208, 214, 228, 229, 244
Lost 113, 120
Lost Soul: The Doomed Journey 126
Lottery 26
Louis, Joe 89
Love Boat 85, 87
Lovecraft, H.P. 38
Loved One 5, 97, 241
"Love Letter" (Finney) 76, 106, 108-109
Love Letter 6, 76, 106, **107**, 108-109, 119, 129, 169, 216
Love Machine 40
Love of Life 26
Love on a Rooftop 106
Love Trap 83
Lowery, Robert 176
Lowery, William D. 101
Loy, Myrna 166
Lucan 91

Lucas, Donna 42
Lucas, Tim 40, 42
Lucky Luke 176
Lucy Show 221
Lugosi, Bela 128, 133, 150
Lumb, Patrick 168
Lustig, Branko 208, 212, 230, 240-241
Lye, Reg 150
Lyman, Will 116
Lynch, Paul 94, 120
Lyndhurst 34-35, 38, **39**, 40-**41**, 127, 186-187

MacArthur, Douglas 69
Macaulay, Charles **64**
MacElhanie, Bill 173, 185
MacGraw, Ali 120, **189**, 190, 192, **193**, 194, **195**, 198, 203, 210, 246
MacGyver 224
MacKelvie, Jock 162-163
MacKenzie, Robert 10, 194
Mackintosh Man 143
Mackley, Charles 154, 164, 167, 168
Macnee, Patrick 76
MacRae, Michael **100**
Mad Men 243
Magnificent Seven 5
Maharis, George **64**
Making It 169
Maltese Falcon 80
Maltin, Leonard 157
Mancini, Henry 45, 65
Mandan, Robert 238, 240
Manetti, Larry 160
Man from Beyond 186
Man from Snowy River 227
Man from U.N.C.L.E. 84
Manhattan Melodrama 166
Mann, Michael 10, 164, 165, 166, 168
Manning, Stuart 7
Mannix 97, 219, 241
Man with the Golden Gun 143
Marasco, Robert 69, 71-72, 74, 76
March, Fredric 31
Marcus Welby, M.D. 156
Marill, Alvin 156
Marin, Andrew Peter 65, 67

Marjorie Morningstar 190
Marmorstein, Malcolm 26, 127-128
Marquette, Jacques 167, **250**
Mars Attacks! 121
Marshall, E.G. 211, 224
Mars Needs Women 240
Martin, Ben 15
Martin, Ian 34
Martin, Jared 91
Martin, Quinn 157
Marvel Comics 111, 180, 210, 241
Mary Hartman, Mary Hartman 77, 162
Master of Dark Shadows 10, 92, 125-128, 248
Masterpiece Theatre 136
Mastroianni, Armand 94, 120, 127
Matheson, Richard 6, 7, 10, 11, 12, 43, 46, 47, 53, 55, 56, 57, 59, 67-68, 74, 76, 79, 104, 105, 108-109, 119, 126, 131, 132, 133, 135, 137, 141, 142, 143, 144-147, 149, 150-151, 169, 243
Mathews, Kerwin 32, **33**
Matinee 47
Maugham, William Somerset 199, 200
Mayne, Ferdy 190, 195
MCA (Music Corporation of America) 14
McCarthy, Tom 117
McDowell, Charlie 186
McElhanie, Bill 173
McFarland books 8, 57, 83, 96
McGavin, Darren 43, **44**, 46, 47, **48**, 52, 101, 117, 118, 144, 243, 246
McGrath, Gulliver 98, 121
McGuire, Michael 25, 89, 196, 217, 230
McKain, Lyle 155
McKechnie, Donna 21
McKellar, Kenneth 168
McMahon, John 118
McNally, Raymond T. 10, 135, 140, 150
McRae, Frank 154, 167
McShane, Ian 120, 125, 211, 214, 230
Me and the Kid 6, 49, 101-**103**, 129, 144, 216
Medical Center 234
Medium 59, 113
Meet-Up 12
Megowan, Don 157, 158, 161, 168
Meisner, Gunter 194, **197**, 210
Melton, J. Gordon 6, 7, 11, 140

Melvin Purvis, G-Man 6, 7, 8, 10, 61, 69, 119, 129, 139, 152, 153, **155**, 156, **157**, **158**, 159, 162, 163, 164, 167-168, 169, 177, 179, 247, **250**
Men in Black 240
Mentalist 241
Mephisto Waltz 50
Mercury News 117
Meredith, Burgess 69, 72, 76
Meredith, Don 86, **87**
Merritt, George 187
Methvin, Henry 163-164
Metromedia 76
Metz, Melinda 240
MGM (Metro-Goldwyn-Mayer) 15, 34, 35, 38, 40, 54, 55
Miami News 52
Middle Tennessee State University 8
Midnight Express 175
Midnight Marquee Press 7
Midway 213
Milicevic, Ivana 111, **112**
Milius, John 10, 61, 153, 154, 155, 156, 157, 162, 165, 166, 167
Millay, Diana 17, 19, 21, **41**
Miller, Jason 203
Miller, Jonny Lee 121
Miller, Vernon 158, 160, 162
"Millicent and Therese" 67-68, 69
Mills, Donna 79, 80
Milton, John 54
"Mimsy Were the Borogroves" 105
Minor, Mike 203
Miranda, Robert 93
Misher, Kevin 168
Miskatonic Institute 128
Mission: Impossible 89, 219, 241
Missouri ship 192, 200
"Missy" 65
Mister Rock and Roll 64
Mitchell, Julian 169
Mitchell, Thomas 116
Mitchum, Robert **189**, 190, **191**, 192, 194, 198-199, 203, **208**, 210, 214, 219, **220**, 230
Mockingbird Lane 121
modern horror 38, 43, 44-45, 47, 79, 128, 246
Moffat, Donald 87, 89
Moltke, Alexandra **16**, 19, 20, 109, **126**

Moneychangers 214
Monkees 163
Monster Club 138
Montgomery, Lee Harcourt 72, **73**, 79
Monty, Gloria 246
Moody Blues 121
Moonlight 246
Moonlighting 225
Moore, M.M. Shelley 95
Moretz, Chloe Grace 121
Morgan Creek Productions 106
Morgan, George 49
Moriarty, Cathy 102
Morley, Robert 211, 215
Morris, Anita 102
Morris, Oswald 10, 143, 150
Morrow, Vic 79, 80
Morse, Barry 190, 192, 197, 199, 203, 215, 219
Moscow Mists 7
Moses, William R. 223
"Most Dangerous Game" 56
Moulin Rouge 143
Moving Pictures 198
Moxey, John Llewellyn 43, 45
MPAA (Motion-Picture Association of America) 38
MPI Home Video 11, 125, 139, 144, 180, 214, 216, 219, 221, 222, 224, 225, 226
Mr. District Attorney 28
Mrs. R's Daughter 87, **88**, 89, 115, 129, 170, 196
M Squad 59
MTV 167
Muir, John Kenneth 96, 189
Muktar, Mehmet 135
multiculturalism 6, 100, 113
Mummy 186
Murder, She Wrote 241
Murphy, Audie 176
Murphy, Ben 120, **189**, 196, 203
Murray, Don 3, 15
Museum of Television and Radio 106, 109, 113, **114**, 248
Mussolini, Benito 196, 221
Myers, Ruth 150
My Music 3
My Name Is Bill W. 227
Mysterious Stranger 169

Naldi, Nita 186
Name of the Game 82
Napier, Alan 64
Napolitano, John 203, 230
Nash, Frank "Jelly" 158, 159, 160, 165
Nashville 83
Nashville Banner 198
Nashville State Community College 12
National Cowboy Hall of Fame 172, 180
National Periodical Publications 3, 15
NBC (National Broadcasting Company) 2, 3, 4, 6, 13, 14, 16, 17, 26, 32, 50, 76, 83, 85, 86, 87, 88, 92, 94, 98, 99, 100, 131, 164, 165, 171, 185, 202, 203, 213, 229, 233, 246
NBC Saturday Night at the Movies 73
NBC Special Treat 90
NCIS 241
"Needle in the Heart" 67-68
Nelson, "Baby Face" 154, 158, 160, 162-163, 164, 165, 167, 168, 169
Nelson, Byron 14
Neptune Publishing 7
Nero, Franco 126
Nero Wolfe 169
Ness, Eliot 163
Netflix 186
Newark Star Ledger 213
Newcomb, George 173-174, 176, 185
Newlywed Game 17
Newman, Alec 110, 111, **112**, 113, 127-128, 245
Newman, Kim 150
Newsday 193, 213
Newsweek 37, 116
New York Daily News 105, 115
New York Times 40, 45, 47, 74, 122, 153
Nicholas Nickelby 202, 227
Nickerson, Denise 20, 21
Night Before 42
Night Gallery 59
Night Killers 47
Nightlife 96
Nightmare at 43 Hillcrest 8, 65, 129
Night of Dark Shadows 7, 8, 31, 34, 38, **39**, 40, **41**, 42-43, 59, 60, 62, 65, 67, 72, 83, 99, 101, 110, 124, 125, 127, 129, 186-187, 240, 246, 247, 249
Nights of Dan Curtis 8, 10

Night Stalker 6-7, 8, 43, **44**, 45-46, 47, 50, 52, 55, 56, 80, 83, 101, 104, 106, 113, 117, 119, 129, 150, 169, 203, 240, 243, 244, 246, 247
Night Stalker (2005) 104, 106, 117-118, 129
Night Strangler 6, 7, 8, 44, 46-47, **48**, 49, 50, 52, 55, 56, 80, 83, 101, 104, 106, 113, 117, 129, 160, 189, 198, 203, 240, 243, 244, 246, 247, 249
Night-Time Winds 247, 249
Nikerk, Johannes 203
94 Feet 2
Nitti, Frank 168
Nixon, Richard 59
Nolan, William Francis 11, 46, 50, 52, 53, 61, 62, 67, 69, 72, 74, 105, 106, 109, 128, 150-151, 152, 156, 157, 159, 162, 164, 165, 167, 168, 247, **248**, 249
Nolte, Nick 106
Norman, Eric Van Haren 108
Norliss Tapes 6, 8, 50, **51**, 52, **53**, 129, 150, 155, 161, 189, 240, 246, 247
Northampton ship 202, 214, 217, 220
Nosferatu 44, 150
"No Such Thing as a Vampire" **5**, 76, **78**, 131

Oakland, Simon **44**, 46, 47
Oak Ridge 17, 223
Oates, Joyce Carol 110
Oates, Warren 61, 153, 156, 167
Odd Couple 131, 194
Odessa File 143
"Ode to Angelique" 65
Of Human Bondage 199
O'Connor, Robert 233, 240
Oklahoma Crude 134
Old Dark House magazine 76
Oldest Rookie 243
Oldman, Gary 150
O'Leary, Mary 128
Oliver! 63
Oliver, James 116
Omen 76
Once Upon a Time...in Hollywood 243
One-Eyed Jacks 90
One Life to Live 17, 26
One Step Beyond 59
Only Make-Believe 7

Opera 111
Oppenheimer, Robert 227
Orange County Register 103
Orci, Roberto 121
Oringer, Barry 234, 238, 240
Orion Pictures 101, 103
Ornitz, Arthur 37
Ortelli, Dyanna 101
O'Shea, Tessie 30, 32
Other 79
Our Family Honor 217
Our Fathers 10, 115-117, 119, 121, 129, 192, 246
Outlander 243
Outsiders 99
OuYang, Lucille 168

Paget, Debra 38
Palance, Jack 27, **29**, 31, 46, 59, 131, **132**, 133, **134**, 140, **141**, **142**, 143, 144, **146**, 150, **151**, 176, **177**, 185
Paley Center for Media 128
Palmer, Arnold 14
Pantoliano, Joe 102
Paperback Library 17, 32
Paradise Lost 54
parallel time 23, 25-26, 38, 108, 109, 162, 165, 198, 243
Parallel Times 7
Paramount Home Entertainment 194, 195, 196, 197, 199, 201
Paramount Network 243
Paramount Pictures 91, 99, 194
Pare, Jessica 243
Parents Television Council 115
Parfrey, Woodrow 168
Parker, Bonnie 154, 156, 163-164
Parker, Isaac 173, 176, 180, 185
Parker, Lara 17, 20, 26, 34, 38, 109, 118, 120, 122, **123**, 124, 127, 249
Parks, Michael 203
Parsons, Estelle 108
Parsons, Ned 185
Passions 244
Patrick, Dennis 19, 22, 211, 220, 230
Patton, George S. 221
Patton, Will 153

Paul, Adrian 99
Paulding, William 187
Paull, Morgan 160
PBS (Public Broadcasting System) 3
Pearl Harbor 192
Peckinpah, Sam 40
Pecos Kid Western 172
Peer, Kurt 7
Penn, Arthur 36, 153, 164
Pennock, Christopher 22, 23, 25, **41**, 109, 120, 127
Pennsylvania Patriot-News 234
People magazine 192, 239
People's Choice Awards 222
Perfect World 102-103
Perlman, Ron 126
Perry, John 168, 230
Persoff, Nehemiah 86
Peter Gunn 45
Peter Pan 111
Petersen, Chris 83
Petticoat Junction 202
Petty, Dee-Dee 99, 185
Petty, Jack 185
Peyton Place 26
Pfeiffer, Michelle 121
Pflug, Jo Ann 46, 47, 56
PGA (Producers Guild of America) 109, 228
PGA (Professional Golfers' Association) 228
Phantom 241
Phar Lap 227
Philadelphia Enquirer 193
Phillips, Fred 52
Phillips, Michelle 154, 156, 167
Phyllis 88
Picard, Paul 167
Picture Mommy Dead 241
Picture of Dorian Gray (Wilde) 21, 27, 54-55, 149
Picture of Dorian Gray (1945) 54, 55
Picture of Dorian Gray (1973) 8, 31, **54**-55, 62, 129, 136, 149, 246
Pierce, Charles 155, 167, 168
Pierce, Charley 173
Pierpont, Harry 154, 158, 160, 164, 167, 168
Pierson, Jim 3, 7, 8, 11, 15, 34, 42, 46, 76, 85, 87, 90, 99, 101, 115, 118, 119, 121, 127, 144, 230, 244
Pine, Phil 59

Pinewood Studios 122, 123, 211
Pischinger, Hertha 230
Plague Town 126
Planet of the Apes 234
Player, Gary 14
Playhouse 90 43
Playroom 67
Plummer, Christopher 115
Pocket Books 7
Poe, James 192
Poirot Investigates 67
Poledouris, Basil 94, 227
Police Story 92, 99-100
Police Woman 99-100, 165
Pomegranate Press 7, 99, 230
Pooley, Kirstie 227
Porter, Don 50
Post Cereals 3, 14
Postman Always Rings Twice 90
Potts, Cliff **171**, 172, **173**, 177, **179**, **185**
Pouget, Ely 96
Powell, Addison 20, 211, 214, 230
Powell, Hall 95
Powell, William 166
Power, Bill 173, 174, 175, 176, 185
Pravda, Hanna-Maria **132**
Prentice, Keith 26
Prentiss, Paula 126
Prestige 241
Preston, Robert 198
"Prey" 68-**70**, 105
Price, Vincent 38
Price Is Right 18
Price of Honor 110, 169
Priestley, Tom 240
Prime Target 94
Prince, William 211
Prince of Wales ship 192, 200
Produced and Directed by Dan Curtis 118, 230
Project U.F.O. 203
Prosky, Robert 93
Pryor, Nicholas 90, 227
Psycho 72, 121
Public Enemies 10, 164, 165-167, 168
Purvis, Alston 154-155
Purvis, Melvin 10, 61, 69, 150, 153-169
Pushing Daisies 121

Pynchon, Thomas 243

Quaid, Randy **171**, 172, **175**, **179**, **185**
Quantum Leap 94
"Queen and the Improbable Knight" 86
Queen Mary ship 207
Queen of the Damned 117
"Quentin's Theme" 12, 31, 42, 55, 67, 127, 194, 214, 228, 240
Quick, Flo 177, 178, 180, 181-182, 184, 185
Quicksilver 117
Quillan, Eddie 168

Rabiger, Paul 150
Raggedy Ann & Andy 171
Raid on 330 Park 169
Raid on Coffeyville 171, 180-184
Rampling, Charlotte 126
Ranch Romances 172
Random House 233
Rappaport, I.C. 90, 203
Rau, Sajeed 32, **33**
Raven and the Phantom 7
Rawhide 159
Ray Bradbury Theater 2
Ray, Fred Olen 133
Rebecca 38, 122
Redford, Robert 186
Redgrave, Lynn 61, 62, **63**
Redgrave, Michael 61
Reed, Oliver 69, **71**, 72, **73**, 76
Reed, Rex 74
Reeves, Keanu 147
Reiner, Carl 14
Renert, Jerry 169
Reptile 246
Resch, Kathy 7, 11, 194
Return 53, 150
Revenge 241
Reversal of Fortune 187
Revolution 121
Reward 203
Reyes, Amanda 128
RFK: Between the Gunshots 169
Rhoades, Barbara 86

Rhys-Davies, John 211, 214
Ribisi, Giovanni 168
Rice, Anne 6, 18, 150
Rice, Jeff 43, 47
Rich, Monica 38
Richard Matheson Companion 108-109
Richards, Lisa 22
Richardson, Keith 11, **293**
Richetti, Adam 160
Richman, Peter Mark 65
Rich Man, Poor Man 214
Rickman, Tom 109
Rifkin, Ron 87, 196
Ripley's Believe It or Not 194, 201
Rising Light 249
Rivas, Geoffrey **100**
Riverdale 121
Robards, Jason 27
Robbing Banks 153, 176
Roberts, Michael D. 113
Roberts, Stephen 89
Robertson, Dale 61, 153, **155**, 156, **157**, 158, **159**, **160**, 161, **165**, 167, 173, 176, 185
Robin, Marcy 11, 119, 124-125, 167
Robinson, "Sugar" Ray 92
Rockford Files 165
Rodan, Robert 20, 109, 118, 120
Rodgers, Mark 92
Roe vs. Wade 227
Rogers, Will 166
Rolike, Hank 168
Romeo and Juliet 119
Romeo Must Die 110
Rommel, Erwin 221
Rondo Awards 8, 249
Rookies 162
Rooney, Mickey 169
Roosevelt, Eleanor 198, 200, 214
Roosevelt, Franklin 89, 110, 190, 192, 196, 198, 199, 200, 203, 214, 217, 221, 225, 226, 229, 230, 256
Roots 193, 214
Rose, Reginald 43
Roseanne 221
Rosemary's Baby 79, 240
Rosemont, Romy 240
Rosenberg, Howard 214, 229

Rosenthal, Jane 168
Ross, Clarissa 7
Ross, Dan 7, 11, 17, 32
Ross, Dana 7
Ross, Diana
Ross, Duncan 200
Ross, Marilyn 7, 11, 17, 32
Rossilli, Paul 93
Roswell High 240
Roth, Peter 110,
Roulette Records 65
Roush, Matt 117
Route 66 64
Routledge books 19
Rowling, J.K. 137
Royal Shakespeare Company 202
Roysden, Tom 203
Rubes, Jan 116
Rubino, George 87
Rubinow, John 240
Running with Scissors 243
Russell, Gordon 26, 34, 37, 94
Russell, Ken 40, 126
Ryan, John 153, 167
Ryan, Mitchell 16, 19, 109, 198
Ryan's Hope 27, 32
Ryman, Bryan 240

Saberhagen, Fred 150
Sacramento Union 31
SAG (Screen Actors Guild) 115
Sage, Ana 154, 167, 168
Salem's Lot 150
Salon 166-167
Sand, Paul 86
Sanders, George 55
San Diego Comic-Con 167
Sandy, Gary 160
San Francisco Chronicle 153
San Francisco Examiner 42
Sargent, Dick 156, 168, 169
Saturday Evening Post 106
Saturn Awards 76, 99, 120-121, 218, 239, 240
Savage Harvest 92
Savile, Philip 149

Index

Saving Milly 10, 19, 110, 115, **116**, 118, 119, 120, 121, 129, 192
Saving Private Ryan 228
Savory, Gerald 149
Scarecrow books 37, 133
Scarlet Pimpernel 18
Schallert, William 211, **217**
Scharf, Walter 84, 89
Schecter, Sarah 121
Schick, Elliot 156
Schindler's List 109, 212, 228-229, 241
Schirmer, William 227
Schlesinger, Hunter 227
Schlitt, Robert 163
Schmartz, Karin 230
Schmeling, Max 89
Schofield, Frank 16, 19
Schott, Bob 52, **53**
Schreck, Max 150
Schwarzenegger, Arnold 139
Sci-Fi Channel 99, 113, 117, 128
Scorpion 121
Scott, Campbell 106, **107**, 108
Scott, Geoffrey 22
Scott, Jan 108
Scott, Kathryn Leigh 7, **16**, 18, 19, 20, 21, 25, 32, 35, 61, 64, 109, 111, 112, 118, 119-120, 122, **123**, 124, 127, 161, 218, 235, 249
Scott, Lizabeth 91
Scott, Randolph 176
Scott, Ridley 212
Scream of the Wolf 8, 55, **56**, 57, 129, 139, 150, 169, 189
Scribner, Ronnie 89
Search for Tomorrow 17
Seattle Underground 46
Seaview Terrace 16, **126**, 186, 187
"Second Chance" 76, **77**
Second Hundred Years 106
"Secret Room" 121
Secret Storm 17
Sedwick, John 27
Seidelman, Arthur A. 90, 180
Selby, David 17, 20, **22**, 31, 34, 38, **39**, 42, 109, 118, 120, 122, **123**, 124, 127, 128, 218, 243
Selleck, Tom **58**
Serling, Rod 27

Serrano, Nestor **93**
Seven-Percent Solution 10
Seventh Voyage of Sinbad 32
Severin Films 125
79 Park Avenue 216
Seymour, Jane 118, **205**, **206**, 210, 214-215, **223**, 227, 230, **231**
Shadow 162
Shadowgram 119, 124-125, 167
Shadow of Fear 8, 57, **58**, 59, 65, 129, 240
Shadows of the Night 7
Shaft's Big Score 55
Shakespeare, William 17, 61, 119
Shapiro, Paul 240
Shaw, Jason 111
Shaw, Steven 116
Sheedy, Ally 90
Shelley, Dave 89
Shelley, Mary 47, 49-50
Shell's Wonderful World of Golf 13
Shelton, Marley 110
She Waits 26
Shine on Harvest Moon 26
Shipman, Herbert 186
Shipman, Julia Bradley 186
Shirley, Ray 121
Shivers 246
Shogun 214
Short, Richard 165, 168, 239
Short, Robert
Shotgun Slade 84
Showalter, Elaine 28
Showtime 115, 117
Shriner, Kin 222
Shrinking Man 43, 105
Shyamalan, M. Night 240
Sidney, Sylvia 72
Siebert, Barbara 167
Siegal, Don 169
Signs 232, 240
Silverstone, Alicia 243
Simon, Paul 121
Simon, Ron 128
Simon Wiesenthal Center 228
Simmons, Jean **95**, 96, 111, 202
Simpsons 104, 243
Singer, Josh 117

Singer, Robert 118, 119, 150, 168
Sinutko, Shane 90
Sirota, Louanne 89
Sitges-Catalonian Film Festival 76
Six-Million-Dollar Man 131
16 magazine 128
Skinner, William 168
Sky Heist 151
Slater, Mary Jo 6
Slattery, Richard X. 190, 202
"Slaughter House" 46
Sleepless in Seattle 115
Sleepy Hollow 121, 244, 246
Sleuth 143
Small Soldiers 47
Smallville 110
Smith, Bubba 185
Smith, Cecil 50
Smith, Dick 29, 31, 36, 151
Smith, Lane 90
Smyth Lentz, Sharon 19, 20
Snyder, John 238, 240
Soap Opera Digest 244
soap operas 16, 17, 18, 26, 27, 32, 33, 36, 57, 61, 77, 90, 97, 99, 108, 110, 120, 124, 127, 128, 162, 167, 217, 222, 241, 243, 244
Sobel, Mark 94
Sobieski, Leelee 168
Social Network 241
Solie, John 55
Somewhere in Time 10, 43, 105, 107, 108, 109, 206, 215
Sonnenfeld, Barry 240
Sorel, Louise 83
Southern Fandom Update 7
Soylent Green 55
Space for Hire 50
Space: 1999 197, 199
Spagnolia, Dominic 115
Spence, Rebecca 168
Spider Lady 79
Spider-Man 241
Spielberg, Steven 98, 120, 212
Spinotti, Dante 168
Spotlight 117
Spotnitz, Frank 118
Spradlin, G.D. 217, 238, 240

Sproat, Ron 26, 127
Sragow, Michael 166
SST: Screen, Stage, Television 222
Staab, Rebecca 96
Stahl, Richard 65
Stalin, Josef 201
Stan Against Evil 243
Stanley, Frank 185
Stanley, Richard 126
Stanton, Harry Dean 154, 167
Stapleton, Maureen 246
Star Trek 57, 97
Star Trek: The Next Generation 94, 234
Star Trek (2009) 97
Star Trek: Discovery 121
Starz 243
Steambath 59
Steele, Barbara 11, 92, 96, 118, 120, 126, 127, 169, 192, 197, 202, 211, 230
Stein, Ben 102
Stepford Wives 246
Stephen King's IT 94
Steenburgen, Mary 186
Stephens, Robert 222
Stern, Joseph 11, 87, 88, 89, 90, 102, 185, 246-247
Stevens, Alex 22
Stevens, Shawn 90
Stevens, Stella 86
Stevenson, McLean 199
Stevenson, Robert Louis 27-32, 37
Stewart, Fred Mustard 50
Stewart, Robert 230
Stewart, Susan 115
Sting 67
St. John in Exile 92, 118, 129
Stoddard, Brandon 6, 16, 119, 207
Stoker, Bram 6, 10, 128, 131-150
Stolte, Christian 168
Stone, Jay 124
Stone, Sharon 210, **212**, 221, 230
Stories of the Century 176
Storm, James 11, 25, 38, 81, 109, 118, 127, 160, 161
Story of Pretty Boy Floyd 157, 158
Stowe, Madeleine 115, 120
Strain 121

Strange Case of Dr. Jekyll and Mr. Hyde (Stevenson) 23, 27-32, 37, 149

Strange Case of Dr. Jekyll and Mr. Hyde (1968) 8, 17, 27-**29**, 30-32, 36, 37, 49, 55, 83, 127, 129, 149, **151**, 169, 246

Strange Game of Hyde and Seek 30

Strange Paradise 26, 34, 57, 116

Strange Possession of Mrs. Oliver 7-8

Stranger Within 79

Strasberg, Susan 47, 50

Stratton, Rick 105

Street, Elliott 156, 157, 158, 160, 161, 168, 177

Streisand, Barbra 115

Stroka, Michael 25

Studio One 26, 43

Sullivan, Susan 111

Sunrise at Campobello 190, 256

"Sunshine's on the Way" 90

Super Friends 194

Supergirl (movie) 108, 138

Supergirl (TV) 87, 121

"Superstar" 86

Supernatural 113, 121, 244

Supertrain 4, 6, 52, 79, **85**, **86**, **87**, 95, 127, 129, 161, 174

Susann, Jacqueline 40

Suskin, Mitch 240

Suspense 32

Suspiria 111

Svehla, Gary 8, 11

Svehla, Susan 8, 11

Svenson, Bo 47, **49**, 50

Swackhamer, E.W. 7, 203

Swann, Francis 26

Swift, Lela 26-27, 32, 62, 65, 109

Sylvester, Harold **100**

Syndicated 117, 125

Syracuse University 3, 14

Szwarc, Jeannot 108

Taking Gary Feldman 102

Taking of Samantha Brennan 249

Talent for the Game 117

Tales from the Darkside 94

Tannenbaum, Richard 102

Tarantino, Quentin 243

Tartikoff, Brandon 94, 99

Tattered Web 26

Tatum, Channing 168

Taub, Bill 95

Taxi 171

Taylor, Don 72

Taylor, Jud 90

Taylor, Lili 168

Teen Wolf 244

Telegraph-Journal 124

"televisuality" 243-244

Television Fright Films of the 1970s 57, 83

Television Horrors of Dan Curtis 8, 10, 115

Tennant, Victoria 190, **191**, 194, 203, **205**, 210, **212**, 215, 218, 230

Tennessee State University 7, 12, 154

Tepes, Vlad 10, 131, 135-137, 140, 144, 149, 150

Terror Television 96, 189

Terror Train 211

Texas 217

Texas Chainsaw Massacre 36, 79

Textual Poachers 19

That Championship Summer 203

Theatre Bizarre 126

Then Came Bronson 203

There Will Be Blood 150, 241

They Shoot Horses, Don't They? 192

Thinnes, Roy 50, **51**, 52, 53, 86, **95**, 96, **98**, 161, 240

"Third Level" 76

Third Watch 92

This Is Your FBI 214

This TV 155

Thomas, Heck 173, 176, 185

Thomas, Lowell 166

Thomas, Kevin 47

Thomas, Robin 102

Thompson, E.D. 11, 12, 65

Thompson, Howard 47

Thompson, Jeff 7-12, 42, 46, 53, 103, 106, 115, 150, 164, 184, 194, 214, 216, 221, 246-247, **293**

Thompson, Sonia 11, 12, 65, 115

Thor, Cameron **93**

Thorn Birds 193, 202, 214

Thorne, Kate 156

Thorpe, Alexis 110

Those She Left Behind 227
Three Musketeers 136
Three's Company 171
Thrilling Western 172
Time magazine 37
Time After Time 83
Time and Again 76
Timecop 110
Time Killer 46
Timeless 121
Tinnell, Robert
Titanic 139, 210
T.J. Hooker 92
TNT (Turner Network Television) 99, 104
Todd Tarantula 249
Tolan, Michael 101
Tolson, Clyde 168
Toma 131
Tomashoff, Sy 16, 109, 186
Tomb of Dracula 150
Tomerlin, John 54
Tony Awards 32
Topol, Chaim 190, 203, 210, 222, **226**, 230
Torch of Liberty award 202
Torme, Mel 94
Torme, Tracy 234, 238, 240
To Tell the Truth 18
Townsend, Stuart 117
TP de Oro award 202
Trading Hearts 169
Trail of Danger 182
Trauma 111
Traveling Executioner 38
T. Rex 121
Trilogy of Terror 6, 7, 8, 57, 67-69, **70**, 76, 79, 104, 105, 106, 109, 118, 119, 129, 150, 158, 189, 243, 246
Trilogy of Terror II 7, 8, 68, **104**-106, 129, 246
Trouble with Angels 241
True Blood 244, 246
Truman, Harry S. 227
Tucci, Stanley 117
Tuckahoe historic home 108
Tune In Tonight 239
Turn of the Screw (James) 27, 61-63
Turn of the Screw (1974) 8, 61-62, **63**, 64, 129, 156, 189, 246, 247, 249

Turquand, Todd 72
TV Guide 10, 87, 88, 92, 94, 115, 117, 124, 162, 179-180, 193, 194, 198, 213, 221, 222, 238, 239
TV Host 238
TV Milestone Series: Dark Shadows 243-244
TV Tie-Ins 7
Twain, Mark 92
21 Up 234
Twilight 244
Twilight Zone 43, 54, 94
Twin Peaks 244
"Twonky" 105

UFOs 10, 232-241
Under a Shroud of Smoke: A Detective Adam Sera Tale 249
Underhill, Wilbur 160, 164, 165
Under Siege 180
Unholy 97
Union Pacific 14
United Artists 71
Universal movies 3, 10, 18, 150, 165, 168
UPI (United Press International) 74
Upstairs, Downstairs 62, 214
Urschel, Charles 156
USA Network 104
USA Today 105, 108, 115, 117, 240
U.S. TV Fan Association 228

Vacca, Vicki 168
Vachon, Paul 203
Vambery, Arminius 135-137
Vampire Archives 150
Vampire Book 6, 7, 140
Vampire Diaries 133, 244
Vampire Lestat 150
Vampyres 148
Van Dyke, Dick 86
Van Dyke, W.S. 166
Van Gelder, Lawrence 74
Van Meter, Homer 154, 160, 164, 167, 168, 169
Variety 50, 52, 55, 62, 67, 69, 91, 98, 103, 108, 117, 122, 124, 143, 157, 161, 167, 193, 239
Vaughan, Peter 219

Index

Vaughn, Heidi 47
Vendetta 155
Vendettas 121
Venturi, Ken 14
Vereen, Ben 236, **237**, 238, 240
Verheiden, Mark 110, 111, 127
Vestoff, Virginia 25
Viacom 46
Victory at Sea 14
Video Watchdog 40, 42
Vigoda, Abe 102
Village of the Damned 79
Vincent, Jan-Michael **189**, 190, 194, 198, 203, 210
Vintage Books 150
Virginian 47
Virkler, Dennis 180
Visible Ink Press 7, 140
Vista Theatre 127, 144
Vogue 74
Von Buelow, Erick 68
Von Leer, Hunter 160

Wager, Walter
Wagner, Bob 168
Wait Until Dark 169
Walden, Robert 66, 160, 161
Walker, Clint **56**
Walking Dead 244
Wallace, Art 26, 122, 127
Wallace, Earl W. 10, 53, 79, 150-151, 164, 169, 172, 173, 179, 180-184, 185, 190, 203, 207, 210, 214, 217, 218, 219, 220, 221, 222, 224, 225, 226, 230
Wallace, Marie 11, 20, 21, 22, 111, 127
Wallis, Bill 214, 216
Walnum, Sven **73**
Waltons 90, 203
WAMB radio 12, 214
Wandrey, Donna 23, **24**
War and Remembrance 3, 6, 7, 10, 13, 14, 59, 69, 79, 89, 92, 94, 102, 104, 108, 109, 113, 118, 119, 120, 125, 127, 129, 169, 179, 180, 188, 189, 192, 196, 198, 201, **204**, **205**, **206**, 207-**208**, **209**, **210**, **211**, **212**-214, **215**-216, **217**, **218**-219, **220**-222, **223**-225, **226**-227, **228**-230, **231**, 233, 238, 241, 243, 244, 246, 247, 249, **256**

Ward, Simon 131, **136**, **138**, **141**, **143**, 150
Warner Brothers 42, 110, 113, 125
Washington Post 213, 239
Watkins College of Art, Design, & Film 12
Watson, Mills 86, 158, 160, 161, 172, 185, 215, 218, 240
Waxman. Michael 168
Wayne, John 1
Wayne State University Press 243-244
"Way We Were" 115
WB television network 104, 110, 111, 112, 113, 127
Web 26, 32
Wednesday Play 27
Weekend Matinee 52
Weiler, A.H. 40
Weiner, Matthew 243
Weir, Peter 79
Weird Tales 105
Weird Tales of the Macabre 203
Weiss, Michael 96
Weissman, "Solly" 159
Welch, Raquel 126
Welles, Orson 161, 198
Welles, Sumner 196
Welles, Violet 26
Wells, John 110, 111, 113
Welsh, Kenneth 116
Welsh, Tommy 202, 203
Wenham, David 168
Westmore, Mike 168
Westview Publishing 8, 9
West Wing 110
Wetherell Bates, Virginia 131, **132**, 150
WGA (Writers Guild of America) 106, 117
What Dreams May Come 151
Whatever Happened to Detective Adam Sera? 249
Wheeler, Ellen 96
When a Stranger Calls 95
When Every Day Was the Fourth of July 6, 14, 19, 45, 76, 83, **84**, 85, 89, 90, 115, 118, 119, 129, 169, 180, 203
When Lions Roared 228
When the Daltons Rode 176
When the Storm God Rides 176
White, Barry 122
Whitelaw, Billie 30, 31

Whitney, Phyllis A. 17
Who's the Boss? 221, 224
Who Will Love My Children? 202
Wicker Man 79
Wide World Mystery 8, 26-27, 42, 47, **49**-50, **54**-55, 57, **58**, 59, **60**, 61-62, **63**, **64**, 65, 155, 196, 246
Wide World of Sports 13
Wiesel, Elie 229
Wiesenthal, Simon 228
Wilcox, Derek 1, 185-186
Wilcox, Larry 1-2, 12, 88, **171**, 172, **173**, 180, 182, 184, **185**
Wild Bunch 172
Wilde, Oscar 54-55
Wilhelm, Jeff 169
Will & Liz 247
Williams, Chandler 168
Williams, John 213
Williams, Joseph 240
Williams, Llandys 230
Williams, Trevor 32, 150, 155, 167, 168
Wilson, Demond 102
Willy Wonka and the Chocolate Factory 124, 167
Wincer, Simon 227
Wind and the Lion 153
Winds of War 3, 5, 7, 10, 12, 13, 14, 67, 79, 89, 91, 92, 101, 104, 113, 118, 119, 120, 127, 129, 169, 179, 180, 188, **189**-190, **191**, 192-**193**, 194-**195**, 196-**197**, 198-**200**, **201**, 202-203, 207, 209, 210, 211, 212, 213, 214, 215, 221, 222, 227, 230, 233, 241, 243, 246, 247, 256
Winkler, Gus 154-155
Winningham, Mare 234, **236**, 238, **239**, 240
Winstead, Charles 168
Winston, Daoma 17
Winters, Deborah **189**, 196, 203, 210
Winter's Tale 187
Wire 103, 116
Witches 246
Witness 10, 79, 150, 172
Wolf Man 180
WOLS radio 154
woman-in-jeopardy subgenre 17, 57, 79

Wonderful World of Disney 203
Wonder Years 224
Woodrow Wilson Dime 76
Woods, James 227
Woods, Michael **212**, 217, 230
Woodson, William T. 194, 214, 216, 217, 224, 225, 227
World of Dark Shadows 7, 194
Worst Witch 187
Wouk, Herman 10, 79, 104, 118, 189-190, 194, 195, 196, 197, 199, 201, 203, **205**, 207, 208, **209**, 210, 214, 216, 217, 218, 219, 220, 221, 222, 224, 225, 226, 230
Wujek, Heidi 203
Wuthering Heights 18, 26, 150, 169
Wuthering Heights (1970) 153
Wynant, H.M. 185
Wynn, Keenan **87**

Xanadu 180
X-Files 117, 118, 240, 243, 244, 246

You Are There 176
Young, Gig 65, **66**, 67
Young and the Restless 241
Youngblood, Herbert 154, 164, 167, 168
Youngblood Hawke 190
Younger, Cole 172
Young Love, First Love 171
Young Marrieds 18
Young Torless 192
You're Next! 7
Yulin, Harris 61, 156, **158**, 160, 161, 167, 185

Zacha, W.T. 160
Zacharek, Stephanie 166-167
Zaiman, Farihah 244
Zimbalist Jr., Efrem 198
Zinner, Peter 227-228
Zuckerman, Alex 102, 103

photo by Keith Richardson

Dr. Jeff Thompson lives in Nashville, Tennessee.

www.ingramcontent.com/pod-product-compliance
Lightning Source LLC
Chambersburg PA
CBHW081427070526
44586CB00020B/2513